1st SUPPLEMENT to DIRECTORY OF INTERNSHIPS, WORK EXPERIENCE PROGRAMS, AND ON-THE-JOB TRAINING OPPORTUNITIES

1st SUPPLEMENT to DIRECTORY OF INTERNSHIPS, WORK EXPERIENCE PROGRAMS, AND ON-THE-JOB TRAINING OPPORTUNITIES

Editor-in-Chief
ALVIN RENETZKY, Ph.D.

Editor
PHYLLIS ANN KAPLAN, M.S.L.S.

A Guide to Internship, Work Experience, and On-the-Job Training Opportunities Sponsored by Governmental Agencies, Business and Industry, Professional Associations, Foundations, and Various Social and Community Organizations

READY REFERENCE PRESS • THOUSAND OAKS, CA

Copyright © 1978 by

Specialized Indexes, Inc.

100 East Thousand Oaks Boulevard, Suite 224

Thousand Oaks, California 91360

Library of Congress Cataloging in Publication Data

Main entry under title:

1st Supplement to Directory of Internships, Work Experience Programs, and On-the-Job Training Opportunities.

   Includes Indexes.
   1. Occupational training — United States — Directories. 2. Occupational training — Canada — Directories. 3. Job vacancies — United States — Directories. 4. Job vacancies — Canada — Directories. 5. Interns — Directories.
I. Renetzky, Alvin. II. Kaplan, Phyllis Ann. III. Directory of Internships, Work Experience Programs, and On-the-Job Training Opportunities.

HD5715.2.D57 Suppl   374   77-4643
ISBN 0-916270-02-5

```
INDIANA
UNIVERSITY
LIBRARY
AUG 8 1978

SOUTHEAST
```

Printed in the United States of America
All Rights Reserved

In obtaining data contained herein, the editors have utilized information supplied to them from sources purporting to be current as of the date of publication. However, neither the editors nor the Publisher can be held responsible for inaccuracies and/or omissions which exist in this volume.

CONTENTS

INTRODUCTION 7

**INTERNSHIPS, WORK EXPERIENCE PROGRAMS,
ON-THE-JOB TRAINING OPPORTUNITIES:**
An Alphabetical Listing 17

APPENDICES 253
    A. Job Corps Centers 255
    B. Civil Service Commission Area Offices 269

INDEXES 275
    Program Title Index 277
    Geographic Index 293
    Subject Index 315
    Combined Sponsor Index 333

INTRODUCTION

BACKGROUND

The objective of the *1st Supplement* to the *Directory of Internships, Work Experience Programs and On-the-Job Training Opportunities* is to provide readers with a quick and convenient guide to the large number of training opportunities identified since the publication of the first edition of this volume.

The current volume describes program opportunities being offered by a wide variety of both public and private sources, including local, state and federal governmental agencies; business and industry; professional associations; foundations; and various social and community organizations. Also included are the details of appropriate programs from Canada and other foreign countries.

In a desire to make this *1st Supplement* as useful as possible to the widest range of readers, "training" has been defined in the same broad terms as it was in the first edition of the *Directory*. Accordingly, "training" opportunities covered in the *1st Supplement* range from internship programs suitable for high school and college youth through programs designed for doctoral and postdoctoral level researchers and faculty members. By setting the criteria for inclusion of training programs in this manner, the *1st Supplement* has (1) been able to include many important and valuable programs which otherwise would have had to be eliminated, and (2) significantly increased its importance as a resource in an area where detailed reference information is sorely needed.

TYPES OF TRAINING PROGRAMS

This *1st Supplement* provides detailed, up-to-date information on a wide variety of training programs currently being offered. For example, among the opportunities included in the *Supplement* are the following:

Journalist for the Albuquerque Journal through its Summer Internship Program.

Theatre production assistant with the Alliance for Arts Education as part of its Internship Program.

Legislative intern for the American Civil Liberties Union of the National Capital Area.

Participant on an applied research team at the American Institute of Architects Research Corporation.

Legal researcher for the American Judicature Society.

General reporter for the Augusta Chronicle as a Summer Intern on the newspaper.

Research assistant to the professional staff of the Business-Industry Political Action Committee.

Intern in the Office of the Lt. Governor of the State of California.

Clinical/Community psychology intern with the California Community Services Centers.

Participant in public service projects as an Intern with the Center for Public Affairs Service – Learning.

Administrative assistant in insurance through the College of Insurance Work Experience Program.

Clinical psychologist at the Community Mental Health Center of Scott County.

Magazine editor with the Council for Support of Education through its Editorial Internship Program.

Summer newsroom Intern for the Dallas Morning News.

Counselor for Eco Tour as part of its Bear Valley Winter Experience.

Museum education trainee at the Fine Arts Museum of San Francisco.

Agricultural worker as part of the Traineeships in Agriculture Program of the German Academic Exchange Service.

Potter at the Greenfield Village Pottery.

Graphic artist for the City of Honolulu as part of the College Student Summer Employment Program through the Mayor's Office.

Legislative researcher in the Illinois Private Sector Legislative Intern Program.

Staff member in the Indiana House of Representatives through the House Democratic Caucus Intern Program.

Draftsman for the Planning Department as part of the Intern Program in Jackson County, Oregon.

Broadcaster with the KIXY Station through the KIXY Internship Program.

Public administrator as an MPA Intern in Kansas City, Missouri.

Assistant to a buyer for Korvettes as part of its Merchandising Co-op Program.

Curatorial assistant in the Los Angeles County Museum of Art as part of its Museum Associate Internship Program.

Visiting researcher at the Lunar Science Institute.

Reporter for the Macon Chronicle-Herald through its On-The-Job Training Program.

Occupational therapist at the Marathon Health Center through its Field Training Program.

Summer law clerk for the Migrant Legal Action Program.

Radio announcer for the Mt. Susitna Broadcasting Corp. as part of its Trainee Program.

Environmental educator as part of the Naturalist Training Program of the National Audubon Society.

Counselor with the Youth Services Bureau at People for Community Action.

Economic researcher at the Public Interest Economics Foundation as a PIE-F intern.

Reporter for the Sentinal Star as part of its College Intern Program.

Museum trainee at the National Collection of Fine Arts.

Legal intern with the State Farm Insurance Companies.

Production assistant at WAVE-TV.

Community organizer with the Association for Community Organizations for Reform Now.

Administrative assistant in higher education through the Woodrow Wilson National Fellowship Foundation.

Researcher at the Worcester Foundation for Experimental Biology.

While every effort has been made to provide readers with the most comprehensive reference source possible, certain guidelines have been established regarding the inclusion of programs in a genuine effort to make the *Supplement* not merely comprehensive but a workable, useful and effective reference tool as well. Therefore, the following types of programs have not been included:

(a) Programs which are restricted to individuals attending a particular school or other educational institution and do not accept applications from individuals outside that institution.

(b) Programs associated with institutions which maintain their own internal recruitment procedures (e.g., medical internships in various hospitals) and therefore are not open to outside applicants.

(c) Programs which do not offer a genuine internship, work experience, or on-the-job training opportunity, but are merely efforts to recruit part-time help to assist with such activities as typing, stuffing envelopes, answering the telephone, etc.

(d) Programs which, for a variety of reasons, have specifically requested that they not be listed (e.g., when inquiries from applicants far exceed the number of openings that can possibly be considered).

SAMPLE ENTRY

As with the first edition of the *Directory,* each entry listed in the *Supplement* has been designed to provide readers with a clear, concise and up-to-date profile of the particular training program in question. While some variation will exist among entries, due to the individual nature or information available about the training opportunity in question, each entry is designed to include the following information: name of sponsoring organization, program title, purpose, nature of assignment, duration, eligibility, number of awards, financial data, stipulations (if applicable), special features (if applicable), application deadline, and source from which application may be obtained. The sample entry shown below illustrates the manner in which a training program is profiled in the *1st Supplement.* Following the sample entry is a brief description of each entry category.

[1] **FEDERAL NATIONAL MORTGAGE ASSOCIATION (FANNIE MAE)**

[2] **Program Title:**
Corporate Relations Intern Program

[3] **Purpose:**
To give prospective financial and business writers increased insight regarding American business and financial institutions, practical understanding of finance and mortgage banking, and exposure to the governmental process in Washington.

[4] **Nature of Assignment:**
Interns receive on-the-job training at Fannie Mae headquarters in Washington, D.C., where they work closely with corporate relations staff. Assignments include preparation of in-house newsletters, writing for corporate publications, and assistance in preparation of news releases. Interns also attend relevant Congressional hearings and are given work experience on the real estate and financial desks of a Washington daily newspaper.

[5] **Duration:**
6 months; January 1 - June 30 or July 1 - December 31.

[6] **Eligibility:**
Journalism students who have completed at least 3 years of college work and desire careers as business and/or financial reporters. Applicants must have the ability to initiate their own projects as well as complete assigned work.

[7] **Number of Awards:**
2 per year, 1 during each 6 month period.

[8] **Financial Data:**
Interns receive round-trip airfare to Washington and modest salaries; they are also eligible for employee benefits, such as medical insurance, life insurance, vacation, and sick leave.

[9] **Stipulations:**
Applicants must have some remaining degree work to complete, at either the undergraduate or graduate level.

[10] **Special Features:**
Some schools allow scholastic credit for Internship assignments.

[11] **Application Deadline:**
Third week of October each year.

[12] **Request Application from:**
Office of Corporate Relations
Federal National Mortgage Association
1133 Fifteenth Street, N.W.
Washington, D.C. 20005

DESCRIPTION OF ENTRY CATEGORIES

1 Sponsoring Organization:
Name of organization sponsoring the training program.

2 Program title:
Title of the training program.

3 Purpose:
Objective(s) of the training program.

4 Nature of Assignment:
Description of the type of training being offered, along with illustrations of the kinds of tasks performed.

5 Duration:
The length of the training program; any specified period during which training is available (e.g., Summer); amount of time required for participation in the program (e.g., full time, part time, etc.).

6 Eligibility:
Qualifications required of prospective applicants.

7 Number of Awards:
Number of awards offered each year (or other specified period).

8 Financial Data:
The financial details of the training program; whether program offers a stipend or is a volunteer opportunity; whether additional benefits are provided (e.g., room and board, travel expenses, etc.); whether there is a tuition charge for participation in the program and, if so, whether scholarship assistance is available.

9 Stipulations:
Any special conditions or requirements of the training program.

10 Special Features:
Any unusual highlights or benefits associated with the training program.

11 Application Deadline:
The closing date, if any, for acceptance of application.

12 Request Application from:
Source from which application may be obtained.

APPENDICES

In an effort to further enhance the usefulness of this *1st Supplement,* certain additional sources of training program information have been included in the form of appendices. While not necessarily sponsors of training programs themselves, these sources frequently offer counseling and referral services which can be of significant benefit to those in search of appropriate training opportunities. The following appendices are included in the *1st Supplement:*

Appendix A:
Job Corps Centers

Appendix B:
Civil Service Commission Area Offices

INDEXES

In order to aid users in their search for appropriate training programs, the following indexes have been included in the *1st Supplement:*

Program Title Index:
This index provides readers with an alphabetical listing of all programs, by title, contained in the *1st Supplement.*

Geographic Index:
This index enables readers to identify various training programs according to the individual city, county, state, or country in which they are principally located.

Subject Index:
This index allows readers to identify various training programs according to the subject field(s) in which they are offered. In order to accomplish this end, each entry in the *1st Supplement* has been carefully and thoroughly analyzed. In addition, particular attention has been placed upon "See" and "See also" references so that users may be able to benefit from multiple avenues of approach in their search for relevant training opportunities.

Combined Sponsor Index:

By combining in a single alphabet the names of sponsoring organizations covered in the first edition and the *1st Supplement,* this index provides readers with a quick and convenient avenue of approach to sponsors in both volumes.

References in all indexes refer to program entry number.

ONGOING RESEARCH PROGRAM

As with any effort of this kind, a certain number of programs will undoubtedly escape even the most systematic and rigorous of research procedures. Therefore Ready Reference Press, publisher of the *1st Supplement,* has established an ongoing research program which will strive to identify any additional training opportunities not covered in either the first edition of the *Directory* or this *1st Supplement.* These additional programs will be included in future supplements as well as new editions of the *Directory.*

To assist in this ongoing research effort, readers are urged to inform the editorial staff of the *Directory* of any appropriate training opportunities not covered to date as well as any corrections in the programs already listed.

Finally, any suggestions as to improvements for forthcoming supplements or future editions are warmly welcomed.

ABOUT THE EDITORS

Editor-in-Chief is Alvin Renetzky, Ph.D., formerly editor-in-chief of numerous American Library Association Outstanding Reference Book Selections including *Annual Register of Grant Support, Standard Education Almanac,* and *Yearbook of Higher Education.* Dr. Renetzky was editor-in-chief of the first edition of the *Directory of Internships, Work Experience Programs, and On-the-Job Training Opportunities* and is currently Editorial Director, Ready Reference Press.

Editor is Phyllis Ann Kaplan, M.S.L.S., formerly editor of *Annual Register of Grant Support* and *Standard Education Almanac.* Ms. Kaplan has been Director of Alumni Records at the University of Southern California (Los Angeles, California) and has also worked as a reference librarian for the Madison Public Library (Madison, Wisconsin). Currently residing in Boulder, Colorado, Ms. Kaplan is engaged in free-lance editorial and research assignments.

INTERNSHIPS, WORK EXPERIENCE PROGRAMS, AND ON-THE-JOB TRAINING OPPORTUNITIES:
An Alphabetical Listing

1st SUPPLEMENT

Directory of Internships, Work Experience Programs, and On-the-Job Training Opportunities

a

THE ADVERTISER-TRIBUNE [1]

Program Title:
Journalism Internships

Purpose:
To provide journalism majors with work experience in a newsroom for an 11,500 circulation daily.

Nature of Assignment:
Interns are given experience in writing, editing and reporting.

Duration:
10 weeks; full time.

Eligibility:
Upperclass (junior or senior) college students who are journalism majors. Applicants must be able to compete for Internships in the same manner as they would for full-time reporter positions.

Number of Awards:
4 per year.

Financial Data:
$90 per week, plus arrangements for low-cost housing at Heidelberg College in Tiffin.

Application Deadline:
Applications may be submitted at any time; however, Internships are awarded on a quarterly basis.

Request Application from:
Editor
The Advertiser-Tribune
320 Nelson St.
Tiffin, Ohio 44883

AFRICAN BIBLIOGRAPHIC CENTER [2]

Program Title:
ABC/Washington Task Force on African Affairs Volunteer and Internship Program

Purpose:
To train and/or give young professionals the opportunity to develop their skills in information collection and dissemination, specifically in international affairs.

Nature of Assignment:
Participants index and write for an international journal, report for a news service, observe and analyze Congressional activities, and conduct relevant research.

Duration:
Flexible.

Eligibility:
Individuals who are interested in international affairs with preference given to those having experience in international/African affairs. Typing skills would be helpful and some experience with French would be a plus.

Number of Awards:
Open.

1st SUPPLEMENT

Directory of Internships, Work Experience Programs, and On-the-Job Training Opportunities

Financial Data:
Volunteer only.

Special Features:
Participants are exposed to numerous international organizations and visitors.

Application Deadline:
Applications are accepted at any time.

Request Application from:
Administrative Editor
African Bibliographic Center
P.O. Box 13096
Washington, D.C. 20009

ALBUQUERQUE JOURNAL [3]

Program Title:
Summer Internship Program

Purpose:
To give advanced journalism students newspaper experience while at the same time helping the Journal during the Summer vacation period.

Nature of Assignment:
Interns are involved in various aspects of newspaper work. Duties might include covering the Federal beat, county departments, city hall and/or police activities as well as working on the copy desk and in the library.

Duration:
Full time during the Summer.

Eligibility:
Advanced journalism students who will be returning to school in the Fall. Preference is given to college and university students who will have completed their junior year before beginning an Internship.

Financial Data:
Interns are usually paid $3.00 per hour.

Application Deadline:
March 15 of each year.

Request Application from:
Managing Editor
Albuquerque Journal
P.O. Drawer J
Albuquerque, New Mexico 87103

ALBUQUERQUE, NEW MEXICO [4]

Program Title:
CETA Summer Youth Program

Purpose:
To provide meaningful employment for college students and other older youth out of high school.

Nature of Assignment:
Participants work in various City departments. Attempts are made to match the partial educational attainment of college students to the functions of the departments in which they are placed. Other older youth out of high school are offered valuable work experience through on-the-job training.

Duration:
Full time during the Summer.

Eligibility:
Residents of Bernalillo County who are 18 (or high school graduates) through 21 years old and economically disadvantaged.

Financial Data:
$2.50 - $2.95 per hour.

1st SUPPLEMENT

Directory of Internships, Work Experience Programs, and On-the-Job Training Opportunities

Special Features:
Participants receive supportive services through CETA.

Application Deadline:
May 15 of each year.

Request Application from:
City of Albuquerque - Personnel
P.O. Box 1293
Albuquerque, New Mexico 87103

ALBUQUERQUE, NEW MEXICO [5]

Program Title:
Urban Corps

Purpose:
To provide university students with meaningful work experience relating to their academic studies.

Nature of Assignment:
Work assignments vary with every attempt made to place students in departments relating to their academic training. For instance, business majors may be assigned as personnel department aides and sociology majors as probation officer aides.

Duration:
Ongoing program with students remaining in the Corps until their course work is completed.

Eligibility:
Students attending either the University of New Mexico or the University of Albuquerque who are eligible for work-study support.

Number of Awards:
12 per year.

Financial Data:
Corps members are paid $2.65 per hour during their first year of participation and $2.95 per hour thereafter.

Application Deadline:
Applications are accepted at any time.

Request Application from:
City of Albuquerque
P.O. Box 1293
Albuquerque, New Mexico 87103

ALLIANCE FOR ARTS EDUCATION [6]

Program Title:
Internship Program

Purpose:
To offer meaningful on-the-job experience in the area of arts education, and to provide students with firsthand knowledge of theatre production.

Nature of Assignment:
Interns work with the American Theatre Festival and other AAE festivals at different times during the year; they are also expected to complete a project under staff direction, working with arts education organizations of national importance. Interns are involved in all aspects of theatre production (from scheduling a performance season and booking the artists through all phases of production planning) for a season of children's programs offered as a part of the AAE's Children's Art Series.

1st SUPPLEMENT

Directory of Internships, Work Experience Programs, and On-the-Job Training Opportunities

Duration:
1 Semester or Summer.

Eligibility:
Applicants must be sponsored by a college or university willing to cooperate with the AAE Internship Program and by the State AAE Committee.

Number of Awards:
3 Interns for each of the 3 annual academic terms, or 9 per year.

Financial Data:
Interns receive travel expenses.

Application Deadline:
Applications must be submitted by April 15 for Summer Internships, July 31 for Internships during the Fall, and November 30 for Internships in the Spring.

Request Application from:
Coordinator, Intern Program
Alliance for Arts Education
Kennedy Center
Washington, D.C. 20566

AMERICAN ACADEMY IN ROME [7]

Program Title:
AAR/NEA Mid-Career Fellowships

Purpose:
To support a community of artists and scholars prepared to do independent work.

Nature of Assignment:
Participants pursue independent projects in architecture, planning or design. Fellows are able to utilize the Academy's facilities and vast library holdings for their work, as well as the many other resources available in Rome.

Duration:
6 months in residence at the Academy in Rome, Italy, beginning on September 1 or March 1.

Eligibility:
United States citizens who have earned the Bachelor's degree (or its equivalent) from an accredited institution, hold a license to practice if one is required, have had at least 5 years of professional experience, and are currently engaged in professional practice.

Number of Awards:
4 per year, resources permitting.

Financial Data:
Each Fellow receives a stipend of $5,000 and travel allowance of $1,300, plus living quarters (bedroom only) and a study or studio at the Academy. Double accomodations are available at the Academy for married Fellows, while those with children receive an additional $165 per month as a housing allowance. Fellows, but not their dependents, also receive daily (except Sunday) free lunches at the Academy.

Stipulations:
Fellowships are offered by the Academy in conjunction with the National Endowment for the Arts and are contingent on grant approval by the Endowment. Fellows are encouraged to learn Italian before going to Rome. Instruction is available there, of course, but previous preparation is recommended. There is a $10 nonrefundable application fee. Application to more than one Academy program and in more than one field is possible and requires no additional fee.

Special Features:
Although no formal courses of study are offered, each year several distinguished senior scholars and artists are in residence at the Academy and available to Fellows for consultation.

1st SUPPLEMENT

Directory of Internships, Work Experience Programs, and On-the-Job Training Opportunities

Application Deadline:
November 15 for Fellowships to be announced the following Spring. September or March starting dates are determined after selections through discussions between Fellows and the Academy.

Request Application from:
American Academy in Rome
41 East 65th Street
New York, New York 10021

AMERICAN ACADEMY IN ROME [8]

Program Title:
AAR/NEH Fellowships

Purpose:
To support a community of artists and scholars prepared to do independent work.

Nature of Assignment:
Participants pursue independent projects in classical, post-classical humanistic, or Italian studies, or in art history. Fellows are able to utilize the Academy's facilities and vast library holdings for their work, as well as the many other resources available in Rome.

Duration:
1 year in residence at the Academy in Rome, Italy, beginning September 1.

Eligibility:
United States citizens who hold a doctorate or will have received it before the Fellowship begins. Proposed projects must be in one of the areas listed above. The post-classical field (covering the period A.D. 300 to A.D. 1800) includes the history of literature; musicology; and political, economic, cultural and church history. Italian studies can embrace a wide variety of topics.

Number of Awards:
5 per year, resources permitting.

Financial Data:
Each Fellow receives a stipend of $4,600, travel allowance of $1,600 and $500 for working supplies, plus living quarters (bedroom only) and a study or studio at the Academy. Double accomodations are available at the Academy for married Fellows, while those with children receive an additional $165 per month as a housing allowance. Fellows, but not their dependents, also receive daily (except Sunday) free lunches at the Academy.

Stipulations:
Fellowships are offered by the Academy in conjunction with the National Endowment for the Humanities and are contingent on grant approval by the Endowment. Fellows are encouraged to learn Italian before going to Rome. Instruction is available there, of course, but previous preparation is recommended. There is a $10 nonrefundable application fee. Application to more than one Academy program and in more than one field is possible and requires no additional fee.

Special Features:
Although no formal courses of study are offered, each year several distinguished scholars and artists are in residence at the Academy and available to Fellows for consultation.

Application Deadline:
November 15 for Fellowships to be announced the following Spring.

Request Application from:
American Academy in Rome
41 East 65th Street
New York, New York 10021

1st SUPPLEMENT

Directory of Internships, Work Experience Programs, and On-the-Job Training Opportunities

AMERICAN ACADEMY IN ROME [9]

Program Title:
Mid-Career Fellowships in Architecture and Design

Purpose:
To support a community of artists and scholars prepared to do independent work.

Nature of Assignment:
Participants pursue independent projects in the broad areas of architecture and design. Fellows are able to utilize the Academy's facilities and vast library holdings for their work, as well as the many other resources available in Rome.

Duration:
6 months in residence at the Academy in Rome, Italy.

Eligibility:
United States citizens who are in mid-career of their professional practice and have appropriate projects in architecture or design.

Number of Awards:
At least 1 per year, more if resources permit.

Financial Data:
Each Fellow receives a stipend of $300 per month, $1,300 travel allowance, and $300 for working supplies, plus living quarters (bedroom only) and a study or studio at the Academy. Double accomodations are available at the Academy for married Fellows, while those with children receive an additional $165 per month as a housing allowance. Fellows, but not their dependents, also receive daily (except Sunday) free lunches at the Academy.

Stipulations:
Fellows are encouraged to learn Italian before going to Rome. Instruction is available there, of course, but previous preparation is recommended. There is a $10 nonrefundable application fee. Application to more than one Academy program and in more than one field is possible and requires no additional fee.

Special Features:
Although no formal courses of study are offered, each year several distinguished senior scholars and artists are in residence at the Academy and available to Fellows for consultation.

Application Deadline:
November 15 for Fellowships to be announced the following Spring.

Request Application from:
American Academy in Rome
41 East 65th Street
New York, New York 10021

AMERICAN ACADEMY IN ROME [10]

Program Title:
Rome Prize Fellowships

Purpose:
To support a community of artists and scholars prepared to do independent work.

Nature of Assignment:
Participants pursue independent projects in their particular fields of expertise. Fellows are able to utilize the Academy's facilities and vast library holdings for their work, as well as the many other resources available in Rome.

Duration:
1 year in residence at the Academy in Rome, Italy.

1st SUPPLEMENT

Directory of Internships, Work Experience Programs, and On-the-Job Training Opportunities

Eligibility:
Artists and scholars who are United States citizens and have proposed projects in a field covered by the School of Fine Arts or the School of Classical Studies at the Academy. The Schools include the following areas: architecture; landscape architecture; environmental, urban, interior or industrial planning and design; painting; sculpture; musical composition; creative writing; classical literature and history; classical archaeology; post-classical humanistic studies; Italian studies; and history of art.

Number of Awards:
A minimum of 1 Fellowship will be awarded in each of the above fields with as many additional awards as resources permit.

Financial Data:
Each Fellow receives a stipend of $300 per month, $1,300 travel allowance, and $300 - $800 for working supplies, plus living quarters (bedroom only) and a study or studio at the Academy. Double accomodations are available at the Academy for married Fellows, while those with children receive an additional $165 per month as a housing allowance. Fellows, but not their dependents, also receive daily (except Sunday) free lunches at the Academy.

Stipulations:
Fellows are encouraged to learn Italian before going to Rome. Instruction is available there, of course, but previous preparation is recommended. There is a $10 nonrefundable application fee. Application to more than one Academy program and in more than one field is possible and requires no additional fee.

Special Features:
Although no formal courses of study are offered, each year several distinguished senior scholars and artists are in residence at the Academy and available to Fellows for consultation.

Application Deadline:
November 15 for Fellowships to be announced the following Spring.

Request Application from:
American Academy in Rome
41 East 65th Street
New York, New York 10021

AMERICAN ASSOCIATION OF UNIVERSITY WOMEN. EDUCATIONAL CENTER [11]

Program Title:
Intern Program

Purpose:
To provide work experience for individuals interested in furthering their specific interests and developing career skills.

Nature of Assignment:
Interns may work in the Programs Office, Publications Office, Educational Foundation Programs Office or International Relations Office, depending on the interests and skills each Intern desires to develop.

Duration:
3 months to 1 year.

Eligibility:
Undergraduate or graduate students who have appropriate interests and abilities.

Number of Awards:
Varies, depending upon the quality of applications and/or needs of each Office.

Financial Data:
Volunteer only.

Stipulations:
Interviews are required of all prospective Interns.

Application Deadline:
Applications are accepted at any time.

Request Application from:
American Association of University Women
2401 Virginia Avenue, N.W.
Washington, D.C. 20037

AMERICAN CANCER SOCIETY. MINNESOTA DIVISION [12]

Program Title:
Internship Program

Purpose:
To promote the planning, organization and implementation of public education programs throughout the state.

Nature of Assignment:
Interns are assigned to develop an effective public education program on breast examination or smoking with the intended goal of reaching minority groups within the inner city of Minneapolis.

Duration:
Varies; determined in consultation with each Intern.

Eligibility:
Students who are currently enrolled in college or university programs.

Financial Data:
Usually volunteer only, although occasionally an Intern will be hired to conduct a special program.

Special Features:
In the past, Interns have received college/university credits for participation in the Program.

Application Deadline:
One month prior to the time that the desired Internship training would begin.

Request Application from:
Public Education Director
American Cancer Society
Minnesota Division
2750 Park Avenue
Minneapolis, Minnesota 55407

AMERICAN CIVIL LIBERTIES UNION OF THE NATIONAL CAPITAL AREA [13]

Program Title:
Legislative Internship

Purpose:
To protect civil liberties.

Nature of Assignment:
Interns monitor District of Columbia City Council legislation and Congressional legislation affecting the District, research and write position papers, and provide staff support to the Legislative Committee.

Duration:
Varies; Interns generally work 2 days a week.

Eligibility:
Interested individuals who have intelligence, writing ability and analytic skills.

Financial Data:
Volunteer only.

1st SUPPLEMENT

Directory of Internships, Work Experience Programs, and On-the-Job Training Opportunities

Application Deadline:
Applications are accepted at any time.

Request Application from:
Executive Director
ACLU of the National Capital Area
1345 E Street, N.W.
Suite 301
Washington, D.C. 20004

AMERICAN CIVIL LIBERTIES UNION OF THE NATIONAL CAPITAL AREA [14]

Program Title:
Newspaper Internship

Purpose:
To protect civil liberties.

Nature of Assignment:
Interns participate in all facets of producing a bimonthly newspaper sent to 5,500 Union members. Duties assigned include preparing copy, covering activities, editing, layout and graphics.

Duration:
Varies; Interns generally work 2 days a week.

Eligibility:
Interested individuals who have had at least one journalism course. Some experience would be helpful, but it is not essential.

Financial Data:
Volunteer only.

Application Deadline:
Applications are accepted at any time.

Request Application from:
Executive Director
ACLU of the National Capital Area
1345 E Street, N.W.
Suite 301
Washington, D.C. 20004

AMERICAN COMMITTEE ON AFRICA [15]

Program Title:
Volunteer/Internship/or Work-Study on Southern Africa

Purpose:
To assist the Committee in furthering its objectives of informing Americans about significant African issues, mobilizing public support for African freedom and working for policies which will strengthen this aim.

Nature of Assignment:
Depending upon the skills of the participants involved, work assignments can range from research and clerical tasks to organizing mass actions.

Duration:
Not limited.

Eligibility:
Individuals who have interests and backgrounds appropriate to the work of the Committee.

Number of Awards:
Not limited.

Financial Data:
Varies, depending upon skills of each participant and the financial status of the Committee.

Application Deadline:
Applications are accepted at any time.

Request Application from:
American Committee on Africa
305 East 46th Street
New York, New York 10017

AMERICAN COUNCIL OF THE BLIND [16]

Program Title:
Internship Program

Purpose:
To provide young people with educational and practical experience in government research and general office work.

Nature of Assignment:
Working under the supervision of an Administrative Coordinator, Interns keep records of pertinent current legislation and Federal regulations, compile records of past legislation and regulations affecting the handicapped in general and the visually handicapped in particular, and report on special areas of interest to the Council.

Duration:
Part-time academic year Internships or full-time Summer Internships.

Eligibility:
Undergraduate, graduate or law school students who are interested in doing governmental research.

Number of Awards:
1 or 2 each year.

Financial Data:
Varies; sometimes Internships are strictly volunteer, other times small stipends are provided.

Special Features:
Interns may arrange to receive academic credit for participation in the Program.

Application Deadline:
Applications are accepted at any time; initial inquiry for Summer Internships, however, should be made no later than May 1.

Request Application from:
American Council of the Blind
1211 Connecticut Avenue, N.W.
Suite 506
Washington, D.C. 20036

AMERICAN COUNCIL ON EDUCATION [17]

Program Title:
ACE Cooperative Personnel Exchange

Purpose:
To effect professional exchange of personnel between colleges/universities and the Federal government, corporations, educational associations and other institutions.

Nature of Assignment:
Participants receive professional, mid-career job experience at cooperating public and private agencies or organizations.

Duration:
1 - 2 years.

Eligibility:
Individuals who are on the faculty or staff of an ACE member college or university.

1st SUPPLEMENT

Directory of Internships, Work Experience Programs, and On-the-Job Training Opportunities

Number of Awards:
Unlimited.

Financial Data:
Salaries are paid by employing agencies.

Application Deadline:
February 1 of each year.

Request Application from:
American Council on Education
One Dupont Circle
Washington, D.C. 20036

AMERICAN DENTAL HYGIENISTS' ASSOCIATION [18]

Program Title:
Education Internship Program

Purpose:
To provide an opportunity for students to obtain knowledge and experience in varied areas of education, including the functioning of a professional association.

Nature of Assignment:
Interns are assigned tasks in keeping with their educational orientation and gain practical experience in association work.

Duration:
Varies; arranged according to mutual needs.

Eligibility:
Students who are completing Bachelor's or Master's degrees in education, preferably with emphasis on the health professions.

Number of Awards:
Varies, depending on the Association's activities.

Financial Data:
Volunteer only.

Application Deadline:
January 1 of each year.

Request Application from:
Administrative Assistant
American Dental Hygienists' Association
211 East Chicago Avenue - Suite 1616
Chicago, Illinois 60611

AMERICAN FRIENDS SERVICE COMMITTEE [19]

Program Title:
Newark Justice Program

Purpose:
To organize family and friends of inmates into groups which will foster better communication; and to work toward penal reform.

Nature of Assignment:
Participants put out newsletters, press releases and publications for the Program.

Eligibility:
Individuals interested in the Program who have some communications experience, particularly written.

Financial Data:
Volunteer only.

Application Deadline:
Applications are accepted at any time.

Request Application from:
American Friends Service Committee
Newark Justice Program
526 Central Avenue
Newark, New Jersey 07107

1st SUPPLEMENT
Directory of Internships, Work Experience Programs, and On-the-Job Training Opportunities

AMERICAN INSTITUTE FOR EXPLORATION [20]

Program Title:
Aleutian-Bering Sea Expedition Internships

Purpose:
To provide research training in various disciplines and expedition leadership experience.

Nature of Assignment:
Interns are assigned to various activities, such as working in field photography or expedition administration or as research or logistics assistants.

Duration:
May - September of each year.

Eligibility:
Individuals who have some background training in one of the field sciences; some skill in photography; and some experience in camping, boating, scuba, or expeditioning.

Number of Awards:
3 - 10 per year.

Financial Data:
Volunteer only.

Special Features:
The Institute will help place participants in salaried positions on other expeditions following Internship training.

Application Deadline:
March 1 of each year.

Request Application from:
Aleutian-Bering Sea Expedition
American Institute for Exploration
1809 Nichols Road
Kalamazoo, Michigan 49007

AMERICAN INSTITUTE OF ARCHITECTS RESEARCH CORPORATION [21]

Program Title:
AIA/RC Intern Program

Purpose:
To bring the complex problem-solving skills of architects into applied research activities relating to national problems and policies of the built environment.

Nature of Assignment:
Interns participate in a work-study program related to their skills and interests. The program involves the Intern as part of an applied research team working on a specific project and provides supplemental academic or learning activities related to the architectural research. Project research is interdisciplinary in scope and broad in subject matter, ranging from energy and sociological implications of architecture to environmental education and policy. Examples of recent AIA/RC projects are: Energy Conscious Design by Architects, The Architect's Role in Reducing Earthquake Damage to Buildings, Post Occupancy Evaluation, Building Regulation and Computer Technology, Constraints and Incentives to the Widespread Use of Solar Energy, and Performance Criteria for Planning Community Resource Centers.

Duration:
Interns must devote full time to the Program; this includes a school term (quarter, semester or Summer) in Washington, D.C., where Interns spend 25 hours per week working at AIA headquarters and an additional 15 hours per week in related learning activities.

Eligibility:
Architecture and environmental design undergraduate and graduate students who are interested in the applied research activities of the AIA/RC. Undergraduate

applicants must have completed at least 2 years of college level work.

Number of Awards:
Varies according to work flow with 12 - 20 Internships per year and an average of 4 or 5 Interns in residence at AIA headquarters at any given time.

Financial Data:
Interns are paid $5 per hour for 25 hours of work per week. The Program does not provide housing in Washington, although guidance in this area is available for those desiring it.

Stipulations:
Applicants must submit proposals indicative of their skills and interests in architectural research. A $5 application fee is required.

Special Features:
Interns may arrange to receive academic credit for participation in the Program.

Application Deadline:
April 15 for Summer and Fall Internships; October 15 for Winter and Spring Internships. Applications may be submitted for 2 time periods at once, but order of preference must be indicated.

Request Application from:
Association of Student Chapters/AIA
AIA/RC Intern Program
1735 New York Avenue, N.W.
Washington, D.C. 20006

AMERICAN JUDICATURE SOCIETY [22]

Program Title:
Research Assistantships

Purpose:
To encourage interdisciplinary research in judicial administration.

Nature of Assignment:
Assistants undertake legal and social science research in areas relating to the administration of justice.

Duration:
Full time during the Summer; part time during the academic year.

Eligibility:
Law students or graduate students in social science disciplines who have appropriate interests and abilities.

Number of Awards:
4 - 6 per year.

Financial Data:
Assistants are paid at the rate of $5.00 to $6.00 per hour; expenses are not paid.

Application Deadline:
Applications are accepted at any time, but those applicants interested in Summer positions should submit resumes by the preceding April 1.

Request Application from:
Director of Research
American Judicature Society
200 West Monroe - Suite 1606
Chicago, Illinois 60606

AMERICAN LABOR HISTORY SERIES, INC. [23]

Program Title:
Volunteer Program

1st SUPPLEMENT

Directory of Internships, Work Experience Programs, and On-the-Job Training Opportunities

Purpose:
To aid in the development of docu-dramas for Public Broadcasting based on incidents in the history of the American working people (1840-1940).

Nature of Assignment:
Volunteers are assigned to research tasks connected with gathering and organizing primary source material for each of the 10 90-minute episodes. They also aid in gathering information on and evaluating writers for the Series. Some typing and clerical work will be necessary.

Duration:
Indefinite.

Eligibility:
Applicants should have some background or interest in either film or history, preferably American; some office skills, including typing if possible; and knowledge of research procedures and library use.

Number of Awards:
5 per year.

Financial Data:
Volunteer only; expenses will be paid.

Application Deadline:
Applications are accepted at any time.

Request Application from:
Assistant to the Producer
American Labor History Series
333 Avenue of the Americas
New York, New York 10014

THE AMERICAN NUMISMATIC SOCIETY [24]

Program Title:
Grants for Summer Study in Numismatics

Purpose:
To provide selected students with a deeper understanding of the indispensable contribution numismatics makes to other fields of study.

Nature of Assignment:
Support is awarded for attendance at the Summer Seminar in Numismatics held at the Society's Museum in New York. The Seminar involves lectures and conferences, preparation and delivery of a paper on a topic of the attendee's choice, and actual contact with relevant coins. Seminar participants have the opportunity to attend formal and informal sessions conducted by the Museum's curators and other national or international specialists.

Duration:
2 months during the Summer, from mid-June through mid-August.

Eligibility:
Graduate students and junior faculty who are affiliated with colleges and universities in the United States or Canada. Student applicants must have completed, before the beginning of the Seminar, at least one year of graduate work in classics, archaeology, history, art history, economic history or other related disciplines. Faculty member applicants must have a degree in one of these fields. Areas of study within these fields may include the ancient Mediterranean or Near East, medieval Europe, Latin America, the Islamic world, and South or East Asia.

Number of Awards:
10 per year.

Financial Data:
$750 for the Seminar period.

Application Deadline:
March 1 of each year.

Request Application from:
The American Numismatic Society
Broadway Between 155th
and 156th Streets
New York, New York 10032

AMERICAN ORIENTAL SOCIETY [25]

Program Title:
Fellowship Award for the Study of Chinese Painting

Purpose:
To train future scholars in the history of Chinese painting.

Nature of Assignment:
Fellows conduct research projects which focus on some aspect of Chinese painting and its history.

Duration:
12 months, from July 1 through June 30.

Eligibility:
Students who have completed all requirements for a Ph.D. degree in the study of Chinese painting, except for research travel and the written dissertation. Applicants should have completed 3 years study of the Chinese language or the equivalent and should be able to demonstrate that they are committed to the serious study of this area of oriental art.

Number of Awards:
1 per year.

Financial Data:
Stipend of $5,000 for travel, sustenance, tuition and research expenses.

Application Deadline:
February 1 of the Award year.

Request Application from:
Secretary-Treasurer
American Oriental Society
329 Sterling Memorial Library
Yale Station
New Haven, Connecticut 06520

AMERICAN ORIENTAL SOCIETY [26]

Program Title:
Louise Wallace Hackney Fellowship for the Study of Chinese Art

Purpose:
To train future scholars in the field of Chinese art, especially painting and its reflection of Chinese culture, and to effect a better understanding of Chinese painting in the United States.

Nature of Assignment:
Fellows undertake research and study projects in the area of Chinese art, focusing on painting as a reflection of Chinese culture and possibly including the translation into English of works on the subject in order to promote an increased understanding of Chinese painting.

Duration:
12 months, from July 1 through June 30, with the possibility of renewal.

Eligibility:
Doctoral and postdoctoral students who are United States citizens, have completed 3 years study of the Chinese language or the equivalent, and can demonstrate a

commitment to the serious study of oriental art. In no case shall a Fellowship be awarded to scholars of well recognized standing, but shall be given to individuals who show aptitude or promise.

Number of Awards:
1 per year.

Financial Data:
Stipend of $5,000 for research, travel and other expenses.

Stipulations:
The aim of the Fellowship is to remind scholars that Chinese art, like all art, is not a disembodied creation but the outgrowth of the life and culture from which it has sprung, and Fellows must give special attention to this principle in their work.

Application Deadline:
February 1 of the Award year.

Request Application from:
Secretary-Treasurer
American Oriental Society
329 Sterling Memorial Library
Yale Station
New Haven, Connecticut 06520

AMERICAN PSYCHOLOGICAL ASSOCIATION [27]

Program Title:
APA-AAAS Congressional Science Fellow Program

Purpose:
To provide an understanding of public policy issues relevant to psychology and to assist Congress by having highly qualified scientists serve on Congressional staffs.

Nature of Assignment:
Fellows are placed on the staffs of Senators, Congresspersons, Congressional Committees, the Office of Technology Assessment, and other agencies on the Hill. In these positions, Fellows apply their knowledge of the psychological process to public policy issues.

Duration:
1 year, from September 1 through August 31.

Eligibility:
Individuals who have a Ph.D. in psychology or will have such a degree by the beginning of the Fellowship year. Mid-career psychologists and those on sabbatical are encouraged to apply as are individuals who have a strong interest in applying their knowledge toward the solution of social problems.

Number of Awards:
1 per year.

Financial Data:
Stipend of $15,000 plus a small amount for relocation purposes and travel.

Special Features:
Fellows participate in a 2 week orientation program which introduces them to many facets of Congress, portions of the Executive Branch, and people and organizations on the Washington scene.

Application Deadline:
April 30 of each year.

Request Application from:
Administrative Associate
Office of Programs and Planning
American Psychological Association
1200 17th Street, N.W.
Washington, D.C. 20036

1st SUPPLEMENT

Directory of Internships, Work Experience Programs, and On-the-Job Training Opportunities

AMERICAN RED CROSS. SOUTH EDDY COUNTY CHAPTER [28]

Program Title:
Training

Purpose:
To gain experience in a social, service and learning organization.

Nature of Assignment:
Assignments vary, but all involve participants in the community.

Duration:
Fitted to each individual's needs.

Eligibility:
Young people through elderly who are interested in the training experience.

Number of Awards:
30 per year.

Financial Data:
No remuneration.

Application Deadline:
Applications are accepted at any time.

Request Application from:
South Eddy Chapter
American Red Cross
208 West McKay Street
Carlsbad, New Mexico 88220

AMERICAN THEATRE ASSOCIATION [29]

Program Title:
Internship in Arts Management

Purpose:
To provide qualified individuals with experience in the field of arts management.

Nature of Assignment:
Interns are assigned independent projects in fund raising and public relations.

Duration:
Varies; arranged through agreement between Interns and Association.

Eligibility:
Individuals who have interests and abilities appropriate to the work. Preference is given to students who are degree candidates in arts management.

Number of Awards:
2 per year.

Financial Data:
Transportation allowance is provided plus a cost-of-living differential.

Application Deadline:
Applications are accepted at any time.

Request Application from:
American Theatre Association
1029 Vermont Avenue, N.W.
Washington, D.C. 20005

AMERICANS FOR DEMOCRATIC ACTION. YOUTH CAUCUS [30]

Program Title:
ADA Youth Caucus January Internship Program

1st SUPPLEMENT

Directory of Internships, Work Experience Programs, and On-the-Job Training Opportunities

Purpose:
To increase young Americans' understanding of and involvement in the workings of government.

Nature of Assignment:
Interns work for Congressional and interest group offices in Washington, D.C., and attend a series of workshops and seminars on the political process.

Duration:
3 or 4 weeks, beginning the first Tuesday in January; full time.

Eligibility:
College or university undergraduate and graduate students who evidence an interest in government. Applicants need not be political science majors. Recent college graduates interested in the workings of government are also eligible to apply for Internships.

Number of Awards:
40 per year.

Financial Data:
Volunteer only. Interns are responsible for their own transportation and living expenses. Assistance in locating free housing in Washington is available on a limited basis.

Application Deadline:
November 1 of each year.

Request Application from:
ADA Youth Caucus January Internship
  Program
1411 K Street, N.W.- Suite 850
Washington, D.C. 20005

ANCHOR, INC. [31]

Program Title:
Information and Referral Volunteer

Purpose:
To assist in providing a network for coordinating helping organizations and resources.

Nature of Assignment:
Volunteers take calls for help over the phone and then locate helping resources.

Duration:
Varies, depending upon individual volunteers; full-time work is possible.

Eligibility:
Individuals interested in providing help or information. The referral service is available to anyone in Etowah County, Alabama.

Financial Data:
Volunteer only

Application Deadline:
Applications are accepted at any time; however, training sessions are held in the Spring and the Fall.

Request Application from:
Director
Anchor, Inc.
224 North 5th St.
Gadsen, Alabama 35901

ANDROMEDA, INC. [32]

Program Title:
Internship Program

Purpose:
To provide on-the-job experience for students in the mental health fields.

1st SUPPLEMENT

Directory of Internships, Work Experience Programs, and On-the-Job Training Opportunities

Nature of Assignment:
Interns work with clinic staff in individual and group therapy, children's groups, and activity groups. There are also some research assignments as well as opportunities for supervised art and occupational therapy experience.

Duration:
No specific length.

Eligibility:
College and university students who are taking courses in social work, psychology, psychiatry or related mental health fields. Preference is given to individuals who are bilingual in Spanish and English.

Number of Awards:
No specific number.

Financial Data:
Volunteer only.

Application Deadline:
Applications are accepted at any time.

Request Application from:
Andromeda, Inc.
1823 18th Street, N.W.
Washington, D.C. 20009

ARCHITECTS' COMMUNITY TEAM [33]

Program Title:
Architectural Intern Program

Purpose:
To give recent graduates work experience while helping community groups improve their neighborhoods.

Nature of Assignment:
Interns participate in all work phases from client contact to designing, presentation and follow-up. Experience is gained in such areas as photography, drafting, bookkeeping and blueprinting.

Duration:
Usually 12 months.

Eligibility:
Recent college or university graduates who have C.E.T.A. eligibility and are familiar with urban design.

Financial Data:
Varies; designers/draftspeople in the past have been paid $640 per month as Public Service Employees.

Stipulations:
Interns are given a lot of responsibility and experience, but not much construction document drawing.

Application Deadline:
Applications are accepted at any time.

Request Application from:
Architects' Community Team
1026 Forest
Kansas City, Mo. 64106

ARIZONA. STATE LEGISLATURE [34]

Program Title:
Legislative Internship Program

Purpose:
To provide students with an actual learning experience in the legislative process and to acquaint them with the day-to-day operations of a legislative body.

Nature of Assignment:
Interns work in the state legislature attending committee meetings; engaging in research; and writing such items as bill fact sheets, bill summaries, detailed charts, responses to constituent letters, and speeches.

Duration:
Legislative session, usually from January through May.

Eligibility:
Applicants should be juniors or seniors who have completed most of their upper division major requirements, attend an Arizona university and show an interest in Arizona government.

Number of Awards:
Usually 30.

Financial Data:
$1,500 stipend for the duration of the session plus a relocation allowance of $100 where necessary.

Application Deadline:
The end of October of each year.

Request Application from:
Proper forms should be obtained from the academic vice president of each of Arizona's universities.

ARKANSAS. ARTS AND HUMANITIES OFFICE [35]

Program Title:
Volunteer Work/C.E.T.A. Jobs

Purpose:
To conduct arts and humanities programs for the State of Arkansas and to train interested people.

Nature of Assignment:
Participants help with public information and promotion and with grants administration.

Duration:
Full or part time for varying lengths of time.

Eligibility:
Interested individuals who have backgrounds in arts administration or experience in a particular field of the arts, such as crafts, drama, visual arts, or music. Applicants for C.E.T.A. jobs must qualify for program support.

Number of Awards:
Varies year to year.

Financial Data:
Participants in C.E.T.A. jobs are paid salaries; others are volunteer only.

Application Deadline:
Applications are accepted at any time.

Request Application from:
Arkansas Arts and Humanities Office
Continental Building - Suite 500
Little Rock, Arkansas 72201

ARKANSAS DEMOCRAT [36]

Program Title:
Internship Program

Purpose:
To give newspaper training to interested students who, in turn, fill in for vacationing staffers.

1st SUPPLEMENT — *Directory of Internships, Work Experience Programs, and On-the-Job Training Opportunities*

Nature of Assignment:
Interns participate in all phases of newspaper work, from general reporting to photography, sports coverage, writing for the feature section and editing copy on VDT's.

Duration:
Full time during the Summer.

Eligibility:
College juniors who are interested in newspaper experience and have appropriate skills. College sophomores of exceptional prospect will also be considered.

Number of Awards:
3 per year.

Financial Data:
Interns are paid the minimum wage and receive on-the-job expenses.

Application Deadline:
January 30 for an Internship the following Summer.

Request Application from:
Assistant Managing Editor
Arkansas Democrat
Capital Avenue and Scott Street
Little Rock, Arkansas 72203

ASSOCIATION FOR EDUCATION IN JOURNALISM [37]

Program Title:
Summer Journalism Internships for Minorities

Purpose:
To encourage more minority students to take courses in mass communications and thereby prepare themselves for entry into the field; to provide these young people with information on working conditions, job opportunities and graduate training in mass communications; and to give them experience in the industry.

Nature of Assignment:
Interns work in various aspects of the communications industry at participating newspapers, magazines, public relations firms, and other organizations. Participants are given job training which fosters the development of professional skills in the areas of broadcast journalism, print journalism, public relations, advertising and book publishing.

Duration:
10 weeks during the Summer; full time.

Eligibility:
College students who are members of minority groups, have completed at least 3 courses in mass communications, and are preferably juniors. Applicants must be able to show that they will receive college credit for the course work included in the Internship program.

Number of Awards:
Varies, depending on participating employers and sponsor support.

Financial Data:
$135 per week.

Stipulations:
Interns must attend a 2-credit evening seminar led by faculty members of the host university which, for the past 8 years, has been New York University (Washington Square Campus).

Special Features:
The program provides Interns with educational and job counseling as well as

the opportunity to discuss urban problems with top professionals in various areas of mass communications.

Application Deadline:
April 1 of each year.

Request Application from:
Institute of Afro-American Affairs
70 Washington Square South
New York, New York 10012

ASSOCIATION OF COMMUNITY ORGANIZATIONS FOR REFORM NOW (ACORN) [38]

Program Title:
Community Organizer Internship Program

Purpose:
To organize low-to-moderate income people into neighborhood groups better able to deal with areas of mutual concern, and to train community organizers for this purpose.

Nature of Assignment:
Interns participate in a 2 month in-house training program during which time they learn how to organize and maintain a neighborhood group, do research and develop strategies. Interns then work with neighborhood groups to increase participation and take action in such areas of concern as utility rates, neighborhood deterioration, taxes and health care.
Full-time Interns may assume responsibility for coordinating the organizing activities of existing neighborhood groups in one of ACORN's regional offices.

Duration:
Varies; up to 1 year of full-time work possible.

Eligibility:
Interested individuals who can demonstrate a concern for economic justice, a dedication to social change and an ability to work well with people of varied backgrounds. Applicants must have a willingness to move according to the needs of the Organization and possess a driver's license.

Number of Awards:
Approximately 15 per year.

Financial Data:
Internships for a year of full-time work provide living stipends of $220 per month, mileage subsidies, moving expenses, paid training and the option to be included in a group medical insurance plan. Internships for periods shorter than a year are non-paying.

Stipulations:
Interns might be required to attend project and statewide meetings and participate in ongoing training sessions.

Special Features:
Some colleges give credit for Internship work with ACORN.

Application Deadline:
Applications are accepted at any time.

Request Application from:
Recruitment Coordinator
ACORN
523 West 15th Street
Little Rock, Arkansas 72202

ATHENS COMMUNITY COUNCIL ON AGING, INC. [39]

Program Title:
Social Work Intern Program

1st SUPPLEMENT

Directory of Internships, Work Experience Programs, and On-the-Job Training Opportunities

Purpose:
To allow students to gain greater job skills in the area of geriatric social work.

Nature of Assignment:
Interns perform a full range of social work functions in dealing with the delivery of in-home services and in providing referrals.

Duration:
No specific length.

Eligibility:
Candidates for an M.S.W. degree who have an interest in working in geriatrics.

Number of Awards:
1 per year.

Financial Data:
Volunteer only; work-related expenses are paid.

Special Features:
Interns have the opportunity to attend training sessions sponsored by the State of Georgia.

Application Deadline:
March 1 of each year.

Request Application from:
Athens Community Council on Aging, Inc.
230 South Hull Street
Athens, Georgia 30605

THE AUGUSTA CHRONICLE [40]

Program Title:
Summer Internship Program

Purpose:
To introduce journalism students to the real world of newspapering and to help the Chronicle fill vacation spots.

Nature of Assignment:
Interns are assigned general reporting duties.

Duration:
10 weeks during the Summer; full time.

Eligibility:
Journalism majors who have completed their junior year of college.

Number of Awards:
2 per year.

Financial Data:
$110 per week.

Application Deadline:
March 1 of each year.

Request Application from:
Managing Editor
The Augusta Chronicle
News Building
Augusta, Georgia 30903

b

BARREN RIVER AREA DEVELOPMENT DISTRICT [41]

Program Title:
BRADD Internship Program

41

1st SUPPLEMENT

Directory of Internships, Work Experience Programs, and On-the-Job Training Opportunities

Purpose:
To offer practical experience for future planners and administrators.

Nature of Assignment:
Interns serve as research assistants to specific planners and technical assistants to local governments; solid experience in report writing is also provided.

Duration:
Varies with Interns involved; mainly part time.

Eligibility:
Graduate students who have a 3.5 grade point average, appropriate interests, and necessary skills.

Number of Awards:
3 - 10 per year.

Financial Data:
Mostly volunteer with expenses paid; some stipends are available, however, in the $300 a month range.

Application Deadline:
Although there is no deadline, it is preferred that applications be submitted prior to school registration.

Request Application from:
Administrative Assistant
Barren River Area Development District
P.O. Box 2120
Bowling Green, Kentucky 42101

BIG BROTHERS OF THE NATIONAL CAPITAL AREA [42]

Program Title:
Work Experience

Purpose:
To work in a program which matches male volunteers with fatherless boys ages 8 - 17 for guidance and counseling on a one-to-one basis.

Nature of Assignment:
Experience is provided in casework which involves interviewing those who want to participate in the program and the proper screening of volunteer men, mothers and sons to make a good match.

Duration:
Any length of time.

Eligibility:
High school graduates who have had at least a little counseling experience or background.

Financial Data:
Volunteer only.

Application Deadline:
Applications are accepted at any time.

Request Application from:
Big Brothers of the National Capital Area
1424 16th Street, N.W.
Washington, D.C. 20036

BOWIE, MARYLAND [43]

Program Title:
City of Bowie Internship Program

Purpose:
To give students and other individuals a working knowledge of various City government programs and activities, and to receive in return assistance and new ideas in carrying out these programs.

1st SUPPLEMENT

Directory of Internships, Work Experience Programs, and On-the-Job Training Opportunities

Nature of Assignment:
Interns work for different City departments in such capacities as research analysts for Administrative Services and Planning, counselors in the Youth Services Bureau or assistant director for the Recreation Department.

Duration:
The work experience usually coincides with the academic semester; other arrangements can be made, however.

Eligibility:
Individuals who have educational background, experience or interests in fields related to City government programs and activities.

Number of Awards:
16 per year.

Financial Data:
Volunteer only.

Application Deadline:
Applications are accepted any time.

Request Application from:
Personnel Department
City Hall
Bowie, Maryland 20715

THE BRONX COUNTY HISTORICAL SOCIETY [44]

Program Title:
Archives Program

Purpose:
To assist in cataloging the Bronx County archives.

Nature of Assignment:
Volunteers are involved in cataloging and indexing of the archives.

Duration:
6 months or longer.

Eligibility:
Individuals who are interested in the program and have experience and historical understanding appropriate to the work.

Financial Data:
Volunteer only.

Application Deadline:
Applications should be submitted by mid-October.

Request Application from:
The Bronx County Historical Society
3266 Bainbridge Avenue
Bronx, New York 10467

THE BROOKLYN MUSEUM [45]

Program Title:
Education Department Internship

Purpose:
To provide professional experience and on-the-job training for students with academic backgrounds but little or no practical experience.

Nature of Assignment:
Depending on academic training and individual abilities or skills, Interns are assigned to either teach or become involved in curatorial departments. Interns also work on special exhibitions.

1st SUPPLEMENT

Directory of Internships, Work Experience Programs, and On-the-Job Training Opportunities

Duration:
Minimum of 1 semester.

Eligibility:
College seniors or graduate students who are interested in the work and programs of the Museum. Exceptions are made in the case of outstanding undergraduate students or those possessing special skills.

Number of Awards:
Varies, depending on the quality of student applicants, with an average of 50 Interns per year.

Financial Data:
Volunteer only.

Special Features:
College credit can be arranged for participation in the Program. Interns receive discounts in Museum shops as well as free admittance to any other New York City museum.

Application Deadline:
December 1 for Internships during the Spring, April 1 for Summer Internships and June 1 for Internships in the Fall.

Request Application from:
Education Department Internships
The Brooklyn Museum
188 Eastern Parkway
Brooklyn, New York 11238

BUFFALO AND ERIE COUNTY HISTORICAL SOCIETY [46]

Program Title:
Independent Interns

Purpose:
To provide potential administrators of small museums or beginning professionals in larger institutions with some knowledge and experience in the field.

Nature of Assignment:
Interns assist a curator in general responsibilities and complete at least one study or project with an end product which can be adequately judged. Such independent work should be in historical research or historical administrative practices.

Duration:
Varies, depending upon Interns involved.

Eligibility:
Graduate and undergraduate students enrolled in degree programs at accredited area colleges or universities. Students in any field who have appropriate interests and abilities can apply.

Number of Awards:
Open.

Financial Data:
Volunteer only.

Stipulations:
Interns, their school advisors and the Society must agree upon the independent project to be pursued.

Application Deadline:
Applications are accepted at any time.

Request Application from:
Education Office
Buffalo and Erie County Historical Society
25 Nottingham Court
Buffalo, New York 14216

1st SUPPLEMENT
Directory of Internships, Work Experience Programs, and On-the-Job Training Opportunities

BUFFALO AND ERIE COUNTY HISTORICAL SOCIETY [47]

Program Title:
Library Interns

Purpose:
To provide potential administrators of small museums or beginning professionals in larger institutions with some knowledge and experience in the field.

Nature of Assignment:
Interns work as assistants in the Manuscript, Iconography or Reference Departments. Duties are varied, depending on the Department involved, with possible assignments including research, cataloging, indexing, patron service, and work on special projects.

Duration:
Varies with each Intern; full time.

Eligibility:
Bachelor's or Master's candidates who have good backgrounds, whether academic or work-related, in the procedures and functions of libraries or archival institutions. Master's degree candidates in Library Science are preferred.

Number of Awards:
4 per year.

Financial Data:
Volunteer only.

Application Deadline:
Applications are accepted at any time.

Request Application from:
Education Office
Buffalo and Erie County Historical Society
25 Nottingham Court
Buffalo, New York 14216

BUFFALO AND ERIE COUNTY HISTORICAL SOCIETY [48]

Program Title:
Senior or Graduate Interns

Purpose:
To provide potential administrators of small museums or beginning professionals in larger institutions with some knowledge and experience in the field.

Nature of Assignment:
Interns work in the Iconography Department assisting the curator in a variety of duties including research, working with the collection, and participating in the cataloging of a large collection of photographs relating to Buffalo and Western New York.

Duration:
Varies with each Intern; full time.

Eligibility:
Senior or graduate students who have the ability to do research and knowledge of sources. Students who have history or art history with printmaking backgrounds are preferred. Skill in local history research with a knowledge of local sources is required to assist in cataloging the photography collection.

Number of Awards:
2 per year.

Financial Data:
Volunteer only.

Application Deadline:
Applications are accepted at any time.

Request Application from:
Education Office
Buffalo and Erie County Historical Society
25 Nottingham Court
Buffalo, New York 14216

1st SUPPLEMENT

Directory of Internships, Work Experience Programs, and On-the-Job Training Opportunities

BUREAU OF REHABILITATION OF THE NATIONAL CAPITAL AREA [49]

Program Title:
Internship Program

Purpose:
To provide experience in rendering supportive services to those who have been/are arrested, detained or incarcerated and in offering supportive services to families of such individuals.

Nature of Assignment:
Interns work with the incarcerated as correctional institutional visitors and with families of the incarcerated as community specialists. Interns also act as counselor aides for those awaiting trial and as job counselors providing liaison between offenders and potential employers.

Duration:
Flexible; Interns can work part time, full time or only during the Summer, whatever fits their needs.

Eligibility:
Interested individuals who have relevant education and/or experience.

Number of Awards:
50 per year.

Financial Data:
Volunteer only; reimbursement is provided for travel to and from the office and field work; medical insurance is available.

Special Features:
Independent study programs can be arranged.

Application Deadline:
Applications are accepted at any time.

Request Application from:
Bureau of Rehabilitation of the National Capital Area
666 11th Street, N.W. - Suite 1100
Washington, D.C. 20001

BUSINESS-INDUSTRY POLITICAL ACTION COMMITTEE (BIPAC) [50]

Program Title:
BIPAC Intern Program

Purpose:
To provide professional staff with research assistance and to offer student exposure to practical politics as practiced by a private group.

Nature of Assignment:
Work assignments are open-ended with Interns usually involved in such areas as research on Federal campaign matters and analysis of candidate spending.

Duration:
1 semester at close to full-time hours.

Eligibility:
College or university students who have some knowledge of American government and of business.

Financial Data:
Volunteer only.

Special Features:
College credit can be arranged for participation in the Program. Interns also have access to mailing lists for purposes of circulating resumes.

Application Deadline:
Applications are accepted at any time.

1st SUPPLEMENT

Directory of Internships, Work Experience Programs, and On-the-Job Training Opportunities

Request Application from:
Business-Industry Political Action Committee
1747 Pennsylvania Avenue, N.W.
Washington, D.C. 20037

C

C. PAUL LUONGO COMPANY [51]

Program Title:
Press-Public Relations Program

Purpose:
To assist in business activities and thereby gain a knowledge of the field.

Nature of Assignment:
Participants are given specific public relations contact duties and writing assignments.

Duration:
Any time desired.

Eligibility:
College seniors and graduates who have interests and skills appropriate to the Company's work. A good telephone personality is required for certain aspects of public relations activities.

Financial Data:
Volunteer only; work-related expenses are paid.

Application Deadline:
Applications are accepted at any time.

Request Application from:
President
C. Paul Luongo Company
607 Boylston Street
Boston, Massachusetts 02116

CAGE TEEN CENTER [52]

Program Title:
Pre-Apprenticeship Training in Painting and Carpentry

Purpose:
To prepare young people with employment handicaps (e.g., school dropouts, probationers, drug and/or emotional problems, functional retardation) for the world of work.

Nature of Assignment:
Participants are given on-the-job training in painting and carpentry. Some classroom work is also involved in the program as well as weekly individual and group counseling sessions.

Duration:
6 months for 6 hours per day, 5 days a week.

Eligibility:
Economically disadvantaged individuals who are 17 - 24 years old, qualify under CETA requirements, and are residents of Westchester County (excluding Yonkers).

47

Financial Data:
Participants receive stipends of $62 per week plus $5 for transportation.

Application Deadline:
Applications are accepted at any time.

Request Application from:
Cage Teen Center
5 New Street
White Plains, New York 10601

CALIFORNIA. OFFICE OF THE LIEUTENANT GOVERNOR [53]

Program Title:
Internship Program

Purpose:
To acquaint students with the inner workings of California State government and politics and the role the Lt. Governor plays with respect to policy formation and implementation.

Nature of Assignment:
According to their backgrounds, Interns are assigned to the Press, Research, Legislation, Education or Special Projects Sections of the Lt. Governor's Office. Various duties are performed within each of these sections. Interns also attend seminars; informal luncheons with the Lt. Governor; informal meetings with political, governmental and media representatives in Sacramento; and informal Intern inter-personal activities.

Duration:
Interns work for 1 semester or 1 quarter during the academic year or for 10 weeks during the Summer.

Eligibility:
College or university undergraduates (preferably juniors and seniors) and graduate students who are self-motivated and have good writing ability. Journalistic skills are desired for Interns assigned to the Press Section and research skills are desirable for those assigned to the Research Section.

Number of Awards:
40 - 60 per year.

Financial Data:
Academic year Interns are non-paid volunteers; Interns serving during the Summer receive $500 - $600 per month.

Special Features:
Interns may arrange to receive academic credit for participation in the Program.

Application Deadline:
June 1 for Summer Internships; the beginning of each quarter or semester for academic year Internships.

Request Application from:
Special Assistant - Intern Coordinator
Office of the Lieutenant Governor
State Capitol - Room 1028
Sacramento, California 95814

CALIFORNIA COMMUNITY SERVICES CENTERS, INC. [54]

Program Title:
Postdoctoral Internship in Clinical/Community Psychology

Purpose:
To provide advanced training in community and clinical psychology, including administration of mental health care delivery systems; and to prepare Interns for the California License.

1st SUPPLEMENT

Directory of Internships, Work Experience Programs, and On-the-Job Training Opportunities

Nature of Assignment:
Intern assignments include: involvement in psychodiagnostic evaluations; participation in individual, group, couples and family psychotherapy; mental health consultation; some teaching possibilities; individual case supervision; case conferences; attending staff meetings; and training predoctoral students.

Duration:
12 months; half time.

Eligibility:
Applicants must have a Ph.D. degree in psychology with all predoctoral internship requirements for the California State License completed.

Number of Awards:
2 or 3 per year.

Financial Data:
Interns receive $3,000 plus benefits (such as health insurance) and extra remuneration for teaching.

Application Deadline:
April 15 of each year.

Request Application from:
CCSC, Inc.
3755 Beverly Boulevard - Room 214
Los Angeles, California 90004

CALIFORNIA COMMUNITY SERVICES CENTERS, INC. [55]

Program Title:
Predoctoral Internship in Community/Clinical Psychology

Purpose:
To prepare Interns for the predoctoral training requirements of the California License.

Nature of Assignment:
Intern assignments include: involvement in psychodiagnostic evaluations; participation in individual, group, couples and family psychotherapy, primarily with adolescents and adults; research; mental health consultation; and some administrative responsibilities.

Duration:
11 months, September - July.

Eligibility:
Applicants must have completed all Ph.D. course work and have a dissertation proposal accepted by a University offering an appropriate doctoral program.

Number of Awards:
2 - 4 per year.

Financial Data:
Uncertain at this time.

Application Deadline:
March 15 of each year.

Request Application from:
CCSC, Inc.
3755 Beverly Boulevard - Room 214
Los Angeles, California 90004

CALL FOR ACTION, INC. [56]

Program Title:
Intern Program

Purpose:
To form a bridge between people with problems and agencies, organizations or individuals with solutions; and to bring citizen complaints, agency inefficiency, program inadequacy, and new problems to public attention for redress.

Nature of Assignment:
Interns work in the National Office on special projects, such as research and communication.

Duration:
Part or full time for usually 8 weeks.

Eligibility:
Individuals who have interests and abilities appropriate to the Program. Interns usually are college students.

Number of Awards:
8 - 10 per year.

Financial Data:
$50 per week.

Special Features:
Volunteer positions are also available at the National Office and at the approximately 50 local affiliates.

Application Deadline:
Applications are accepted at any time.

Request Application from:
Call for Action, Inc.
1601 Connecticut Avenue, N.W.
Suite 780
Washington, D.C. 20036

CAMP FIRE GIRLS, INC. [57]

Program Title:
Traditional and New Special Projects

Purpose:
To extend community awareness of existing programs and to create new programs for children.

Nature of Assignment:
Assignments vary from working with pre-schoolers in a day care center to wilderness camping with teenagers, acting as medical volunteers in a free clinic, and doing group work in a residential shelter for youth.

Duration:
Anytime, year round; full time.

Eligibility:
Individuals who enjoy working with adolescents.

Financial Data:
Volunteer only; there is a possibility of working into full-time employment.

Application Deadline:
Applications are accepted at any time.

Request Application from:
Camp Fire Girls, Inc.
24 West Franklin Street
Baltimore, Maryland 21201

CAPITOL BROADCASTING COMPANY [58]

Program Title:
Work Experience Internship

Purpose:
To assist college seniors in learning broadcast operations by on-the-scene observations.

1st SUPPLEMENT

Directory of Internships, Work Experience Programs, and On-the-Job Training Opportunities

Nature of Assignment:
Interns are assigned as observers in various operating departments.

Duration:
1 - 10 weeks, depending on specific requests of schools.

Eligibility:
College seniors who are recommended by their Departments or Schools.

Number of Awards:
6 - 10 per year.

Financial Data:
Volunteer only.

Stipulations:
Heads of appropriate Schools or Departments should request Intern space.

Special Features:
Interns may arrange to receive college credit for their work experience.

Application Deadline:
Applications in the form of School or Department requests for space are accepted at any time.

Request Application from:
Capitol Broadcasting Company
Box 8887
Jackson, Mississippi 39204

CATHEDRAL CHURCH OF ST. JOHN THE DIVINE [59]

Program Title:
Summer Intern Program

Purpose:
To help children improve their existing skills and discover the delight of learning new things; and to help the elderly live in the city by making their living arrangements easier, helping them find solutions to their problems, and informing them of available services.

Nature of Assignment:
Interns participate in a day camp for children or in such programs for the elderly as daily picnics, health workshops, lessons in self-defense and general safety measures for city life, and assistance in obtaining needed services.

Duration:
10 weeks during the Summer, from the second week in June through the last week in August.

Eligibility:
Junior or senior high school students or college students who are interested in the Program. Group activity skills are helpful.

Financial Data:
Some stipends are available, but assistance is limited to approximately $350 for a Summer Internship.

Application Deadline:
May 15 for Internships beginning in June.

Request Application from:
Cathedral Church of St. John the Divine
1047 Amsterdam Avenue
New York, New York 10025

CENTER FOR GOVERNMENTAL SERVICES [60]

Program Title:
Legislative Internship Program

Purpose:
To provide both a learning experience for

students interested in the state legislative process and additional staff assistance for members of the Indiana General Assembly.

Nature of Assignment:
Interns are staff members of the individual legislative caucuses and as such attend staff committee meetings, compile and process bill data, conduct research on pending legislation, work in public relations, and handle constituent relations.

Duration:
Varies with the length of each legislative session.

Eligibility:
Undergraduate and graduate students who are in good standing academically with preference given to upperclass students and those with political science backgrounds.

Number of Awards:
8 - 15 per year.

Financial Data:
Expenses are paid with an upper limit of $75 - $80 per week.

Application Deadline:
Approximately October 15 of each year.

Request Application from:
Center for Governmental Services
201 Holmstedt Hall
Indiana State University
Terre Haute, Indiana 47809

CENTER FOR INQUIRY AND DISCOVERY [61]

Program Title:
Volunteer Program

Purpose:
To augment and enrich school experiences in large, metropolitan school systems by operating an innovative model learning environment that is a cross between a museum and a workshop.

Nature of Assignment:
Volunteers serve as floor staff working with visitors, do administrative and office work, present slide shows and talks, and work in the library cataloging or maintaining books and other printed material.

Duration:
Varies; ongoing, year-round program.

Eligibility:
Individuals who have an interest in the Center and a willingness to make a commitment. Some tasks assigned might require specific skills (e.g., graphics work).

Number of Awards:
Unlimited.

Financial Data:
Volunteer only.

Stipulations:
Participants working on floor staff must take part in a training program.

Application Deadline:
Applications are accepted at any time.

Request Application from:
Center for Inquiry and Discovery
1217 G Street, N.W.
Washington, D.C. 20005

CENTER FOR PUBLIC AFFAIRS SERVICE - LEARNING [62]

Program Title:
Public Service Internship Program/Resource Development Internship Project

1st SUPPLEMENT

Directory of Internships, Work Experience Programs, and On-the-Job Training Opportunities

Purpose:
To allow students to put classroom theory into practice via project-oriented internships of a public service nature.

Nature of Assignment:
Interns take part in short-term public service projects. In the past, Interns have undertaken projects in approximately 50 different subject areas including public financial management, environmental impact analysis, personnel management, survey research, community and economic development, and consumer affairs.

Duration:
12 weeks in the Fall, Spring or Summer; full time.

Eligibility:
Junior, senior or graduate students who either are enrolled in a midwestern college or university or have permanent residency in a midwestern state.

Number of Awards:
150 - 200 per year.

Financial Data:
Undergraduate Interns receive $1,200 and graduate Interns $1,400.

Application Deadline:
July 30 for Internships during the Fall, mid-November for those in the Spring, and March 30 for Summer Internships.

Request Application from:
Director
Center for Public Affairs Service - Learning
Indiana University
400 East 7th - Suite One
Bloomington, Indiana 47401

CENTER FOR THE STUDY OF AGING AND HUMAN DEVELOPMENT [63]

Program Title:
Research Training Programs in Aging and Adulthood

Purpose:
To encourage and support individuals who wish to pursue careers which include research in aging or in adult development.

Nature of Assignment:
Participants work closely with Center faculty on research projects of mutual interest in the area of aging or in the field of adult development with a focus on the middle years of life.

Duration:
1 - 2 years; full time.

Eligibility:
United States citizens who have appropriate research interests and hold doctoral degrees in biochemistry, immunology, neuroendocrinology, psychiatry, pharmacology, psychology, psychophysiology, sociology, political science, economics, and policy sciences.

Number of Awards:
Varies each year.

Financial Data:
Stipends range from $10,000 to $13,200 depending on experience. A small research budget is also provided.

Stipulations:
Attendance in a 2 year seminar series is required. The first year, the seminar covers multidisciplinary topics in order to provide all trainees with knowledge in the various disciplines relating to aging and adult development; smaller research seminars are held the second year.

1st SUPPLEMENT

Directory of Internships, Work Experience Programs, and On-the-Job Training Opportunities

Application Deadline:
March 1 of each year.

Request Application from:
Director, Research Training Programs
Center for the Study of Aging and Human Development
Duke University Medical Center
Durham, North Carolina 27710

CENTRAL DEKALB MENTAL HEALTH AND MENTAL RETARDATION CENTER [64]

Program Title:
Graduate and Undergraduate Placements

Purpose:
To provide experience in a balanced service system for the delivery of mental health services.

Nature of Assignment:
Participants may be assigned to work in any service area of the system (i.e., crisis stabilization, growth, sustenance, case management, prevention, general health, ancillary) or with administration, citizen participation, research and evaluation, or staff development elements of the system.

Duration:
Negotiable; commitment of 6 months is preferred.

Eligibility:
Graduate and undergraduate students in good standing who are enrolled in programs related to the work of the Center. Applicants can come from any discipline as long as it pertains to Center areas of involvement or service.

Financial Data:
Participants receive car expenses.

Application Deadline:
Applications are accepted at any time.

Request Application from:
Central DeKalb Mental Health and Mental Retardation Center
500 Winn Way
Decator, Georgia 30030

CENTRE COUNTY YOUTH SERVICE BUREAU [65]

Program Title:
Internship Program

Purpose:
To provide the opportunity for qualified students to utilize their training by working with youth in both primary and secondary delinquency prevention programs.

Nature of Assignment:
Interns work with rural youth on a one-to-one and/or group basis. Emphasis in the Program is on formal and informal counseling. Interns are given a lot of responsibility within their work assignments.

Duration:
Optional; a minimum of 4 months is preferred; full or part time.

Eligibility:
Students who are near graduation or in post graduate programs and have had training in human services with emphasis on communication skills and counseling techniques. Preference is given to those who have long-term goals of working with youth. Applicants must be mature, well-skilled, highly organized and flexible enough to meet the demands of outreach work.

Number of Awards:
As many as 20 per year, depending on duration of Internship commitment and availability of assignments.

Financial Data:
Volunteer only; travel reimbursement is provided at 12 cents per mile for local travel during Internship work.

Stipulations:
Interns must have transportation since it is important to the work of the Centre.

Special Features:
Interns are closely supervised by professional counselors and thus have the opportunity for additional training in communication skills and counseling techniques.

Application Deadline:
Applications are accepted at any time.

Request Application from:
Program Director
Centre County Youth Service Bureau
205 East Beaver Avenue
State College, Pennsylvania 16801

CERRELL ASSOCIATES, INC. [66]

Program Title:
Work Experience Program

Purpose:
To provide experience in working on political campaigns.

Nature of Assignment:
Participants conduct relevant research for and are involved in all phases of political campaign management.

Duration:
Varies; participants are expected to work through election day of the campaign involved.

Eligibility:
Interested individuals who are affiliated with the Democratic Party.

Number of Awards:
Varies.

Financial Data:
Volunteer only; on-the-job expenses are paid.

Application Deadline:
Applications are accepted at any time.

Request Application from:
Cerrell Associates, Inc.
5967 West 3rd Street - Suite 302
Los Angeles, California 90036

CHICAGO SYMPHONY ORCHESTRA [67]

Program Title:
Civic Orchestra of Chicago

Purpose:
To provide advanced training in ensemble techniques and broad experience in orchestral repertoire.

Nature of Assignment:
Participants play in the orchestra and attend full and chamber orchestra rehearsals, sectional rehearsals and chamber music coaching.

Duration:
Regular program, September - May, part time; 6 week Summer program in June - August, also part time.

Eligibility:
High proficiency in playing musical instruments should be demonstrated by all applicants.

Number of Awards:
Approximately 105 positions in both Regular and Summer programs.

Financial Data:
Scholarships are available in Regular program only.

Stipulations:
Members of orchestra must study regularly with an instrumental teacher or coach.

Application Deadline:
Auditions are held in mid-September for the Regular program and mid-May for the Summer program.

Request Application from:
Civic Orchestra of Chicago
220 South Michigan Avenue
Chicago, Illinois 60604

CHILDREN'S MUSEUM [68]

Program Title:
Museum Education Internship Program

Purpose:
To offer experience in teaching and working with many varieties of groups in a museum setting.

Nature of Assignment:
Duties performed by Interns include giving talks, answering questions, and running programs and activities for Museum visitors. Interns work with school groups, groups of children with special needs, and the general public. In addition, Interns participate in a 3 day orientation training session, one-half day per week of supervised planning and research time, weekly one hour support meetings following the special education visits, and a weekly discussion hour.

Duration:
3 months of full-time work from October through December, January to mid-March, mid-March through May, or June through August.

Eligibility:
Individuals who are energetic and enthusiastic about working with children. Some child development courses and/or experience with children would be helpful, but it is not essential.

Number of Awards:
14 every 3 month Internship period for a total of 56 per year.

Financial Data:
Interns receive stipends of approximately $30 per week and can visit other area museums free.

Application Deadline:
Applications are accepted at any time.

Request Application from:
Manager
Visitor Center
Children's Museum
Route 1, The Jamaicaway
Boston, Massachusetts 02130

CHILDREN'S MUSEUM, INC. [69]

Program Title:
Internship Program

1st SUPPLEMENT

Directory of Internships, Work Experience Programs, and On-the-Job Training Opportunities

Purpose:
To provide on-the-job training opportunities as a means of implementing educational skills, and to provide experience in and exposure to a nonprofit educational organization.

Nature of Assignment:
Interns perform various duties in the Museum with participation ranging from working on exhibits to staffing the floor, providing administrative services, designing and composing bimonthly newsletters, and taking part in fundraising activities.

Duration:
Varies; minimum commitment of 3 months requested.

Eligibility:
Individuals interested in the Museum who are at least 16 years old and have the desire to learn and share their skills.

Financial Data:
Volunteer only.

Application Deadline:
Applications should be received by January 10, June 1 or September 15.

Request Application from:
Administrative Coordinator
Children's Museum, Inc.
931 Bannock Street
Denver, Colorado 80204

CINCINNATI, OHIO. CITIZENS' COMMITTEE ON YOUTH [70]

Program Title:
Urban Corps Program

Purpose:
To provide work experience for college students.

Nature of Assignment:
Assignments vary, depending on where the student is placed.

Duration:
11 weeks of full-time work in the Summer; 10 weeks of full-time work in the Fall.

Eligibility:
Undergraduate or graduate students who are certified to work under the Urban Corps Program by their university financial aid offices.

Financial Data:
$2.60 per hour for undergraduate participants and $3.00 per hour for graduate students.

Application Deadline:
Applications are accepted at any time.

Request Application from:
Coordinator
Urban Corps Program
2147 Central Avenue
Cincinnati, Ohio 45214

CLEVELAND HEIGHTS, OHIO [71]

Program Title:
Urban Management Internships

Purpose:
To provide advanced students with an opportunity to apply academic training to the actual problems of urban management through a unique working/learning experience in a municipal government.

1st SUPPLEMENT

Directory of Internships, Work Experience Programs, and On-the-Job Training Opportunities

Nature of Assignment:
Interns participate in City programs in such areas as planning, community and public relations, housing, health care, public works, law, accounting and finance. Work assignments are made on the basis of the interests and academic preparation of Interns and the needs of City departments.

Duration:
Varies, depending upon each Intern's needs and scheduling.

Eligibility:
Students enrolled in institutions of higher education (e.g., colleges, universities, professional schools, trade schools, community colleges) in the disciplines of political science, business management, social service, law, engineering, economics, nursing, mathematics and urban studies. Applicants must demonstrate high interest in public affairs, thorough understanding of the urban government system and competence in their fields of study. Normally, only graduate students or senior undergraduates will possess the requisite levels of skill in communication and data analysis.

Number of Awards:
Varies; up to 20 Interns each school term.

Financial Data:
Volunteer only.

Stipulations:
Interns will be requested to write a personal performance evaluation and an analysis of the sponsoring department.

Special Features:
Academic credit is usually available for participation in the program.

Application Deadline:
Applications are accepted at any time.

Request Application from:
Assistant Director
Department of Planning and Development
City of Cleveland Heights
2953 Mayfield Road
Cleveland Heights, Ohio 44118

CLINTON COUNTY VOLUNTEER ACTION CENTER [72]

Program Title:
LEARN and VIPS

Purpose:
To participate in teaching adults to read and write English and to help students and teachers in the public schools.

Nature of Assignment:
Volunteers act as tutors and must complete a 10 hour course in the Laubach Literacy Method before receiving tutorial assignments.

Duration:
All year for LEARN volunteers; 9 months for VIPS.

Eligibility:
Individuals who have interests and skills appropriate to the program.

Number of Awards:
Unlimited.

Financial Data:
Volunteer only; tutors receive reimbursement for mileage.

Application Deadline:
Applications are accepted at any time.

1st SUPPLEMENT

Directory of Internships, Work Experience Programs, and On-the-Job Training Opportunities

Request Application from:
Volunteer Action Center
2698 Old State Route 73
Wilmington, Ohio 45177

COASTAL TELECOMMUNICATIONS CORPORATION [73]

Program Title:
Internship Program

Purpose:
To provide work experience in the field.

Nature of Assignment:
Interns work in traffic, public affairs, engineering and sales.

Duration:
Summer only; part time or full time.

Eligibility:
Students who are enrolled in programs reflecting an educational pursuit of broadcasting.

Number of Awards:
Varies, depending upon applicants.

Financial Data:
Open to discussion.

Application Deadline:
April 1 of each year.

Request Application from:
Coastal Telecommunications Corporation
334 North Charles Street
Baltimore, Maryland 21201

THE COLLEGE OF INSURANCE [74]

Program Title:
Work Experience Program

Purpose:
To give students an opportunity to receive professional experience during their college years.

Nature of Assignment:
Participants undertake various assignments in the administrative area at insurance or insurance-related companies. The responsibilities and challenges of the work experience increase as students develop in the Program.

Duration:
Alternating 4 months of work and 4 months of school for 5 years.

Eligibility:
Participants must be accepted as fully matriculated students in either Bachelor of Business Administration or Bachelor of Science in Actuarial Science degree programs.

Number of Awards:
No limit.

Financial Data:
Participants receive two-thirds tuition scholarships during the academic segment of the Program and salaries during the work period.

Special Features:
Participants graduate from college with 2½ years of work experience and a job offer.

Application Deadline:
July 15 for support to begin during the Fall semester.

1st SUPPLEMENT

Directory of Internships, Work Experience Programs, and On-the-Job Training Opportunities

Request Application from:
Director, Work-Study Adm.
The College of Insurance
123 Williams Street
New York, New York 10038

COLLEGE OF WILLIAM AND MARY/COLONIAL WILLIAMSBURG FOUNDATION [75]

Program Title:
Apprenticeship in Interpretation and Administration of Historical Sites.

Purpose:
To provide practical training in the administration of an historical museum.

Nature of Assignment:
Apprentices work and study in various departments of the Foundation where they are introduced to the history of architecture, the decorative arts, horticulture in America, and historical archaeology. They participate in such museum operations as the craft shops, interpretation, and tour planning, and also become familiar with other museum areas including archives, construction and maintenance, planning of exhibits, merchandising, personnel relations, publications, and public relations. This practical training is undertaken in conjunction with 9 months of academic study at the College leading to an M.A. degree in history.

Duration:
2 years, beginning July 1; work schedules are adjusted to apprentice needs and range from full time when not in school to a few hours each week during the academic session.

Eligibility:
Applicants must have a bachelor's degree from an accredited institution with at least 24 hours of history and a B average.

Number of Awards:
4 per year.

Financial Data:
Apprentices can apply to the College for financial aid with possible support ranging from partial tuition to $3,000 stipends plus tuition.

Stipulations:
Applicants must apply to and be accepted by the Department of History at the College for a program of study leading to a Masters of Arts degree.

Special Features:
Students who have completed an Apprenticeship can, at the advanced doctoral stage, apply for a 4 - 6 month Internship in historical administration.

Application Deadline:
February 15 of each year.

Request Application from:
Director of Graduate Studies
Department of History
College of William and Mary
Williamsburg, Virginia 23185

COLLEGE OF WILLIAM AND MARY/EARL GREGG SWEM LIBRARY AND THE COLONIAL WILLIAMSBURG FOUNDATION [76]

Program Title:
Apprenticeship in Archives and Manuscript Collections

60

1st SUPPLEMENT
Directory of Internships, Work Experience Programs, and On-the-Job Training Opportunities

Purpose:
To provide practical training in archival procedures.

Nature of Assignment:
Apprentices work under the supervision of the Archivist and the Curator of Manuscripts at the College and the Archivist, Research Archivist and Audio-Visual Librarian at the Foundation. This practical training is combined with 9 months of academic study at the College leading to an M.A. degree in history. Apprentices gain experience in working with papers, printed matter, photographs and microfilms. The focus of their technical training is on arrangement, description, cataloging, accessioning, inventorying, appraisal records management, preservation and reference service.

Duration:
12 months, July 1 - June 30; work schedules are adjusted to apprentice needs and range from full time when not in school to 8 - 10 hours per week during the academic term.

Eligibility:
Applicants must have a bachelor's degree from an accredited institution with at least 24 hours of history and a B average.

Number of Awards:
2 per year.

Financial Data:
Apprentices can apply to the College for financial aid with possible support ranging from partial tuition to $3,000 stipends plus tuition.

Stipulations:
Applicants must apply to and be accepted by the Department of History at the College for a program of study leading to a Masters of Arts degree.

Special Features:
Students who have completed an Apprenticeship can, at the advanced doctoral stage, apply for a 6 month Internship in the operations of archives and manuscript collections.

Application Deadline:
February 15 of each year.

Request Application from:
Director of Graduate Studies
Department of History
College of William and Mary
Williamsburg, Virginia 23185

COLLEGE OF WILLIAM AND MARY/INSTITUTE OF EARLY AMERICAN HISTORY AND CULTURE [77]

Program Title:
Apprenticeship in Editing of Historical Books and Magazines

Purpose:
To provide training in the editing of historical publications.

Nature of Assignment:
Practical training at the Institute is combined with 9 months of academic study at the College leading to an M.A. degree. Apprentices thus receive formal training in editorial method and acquire practical experience in copy editing, proofreading and other phases of historical publication under the supervision of the editorial staff of the Institute. Although the Institute's primary concern is in early American history to 1815, Apprentices may concentrate on United States history to the present, selected areas of British history, or the history of modern France, Germany or Russia.

Duration:
12 months, July 1 - June 30; work schedules are adjusted to Apprentice needs and range

from full time when not in school to an average of 10 hours per week during the academic term.

Eligibility:
Applicants must have a bachelor's degree from an accredited institution with at least 24 hours of history and a B average.

Number of Awards:
4 - 5 per year.

Financial Data:
Apprentices can apply to the College for financial aid with possible support ranging from partial tuition to $3,000 stipends plus tuition.

Stipulations:
Applicants must apply to and be accepted by the Department of History at the College for a program of study leading to a Masters of Arts degree.

Special Features:
Students who have completed an Apprenticeship can, at the advanced doctoral stage, apply for a 4 - 12 month editing Internship at the Institute.

Application Deadline:
February 15 of each year.

Request Application from:
Director of Graduate Studies
Department of History
College of William and Mary
Williamsburg, Virginia 23185

COMMUNITY HEALTH EDUCATION COUNCIL, INC. [78]

Program Title:
Internship Program

Purpose:
To whet the undergraduate student's taste for social service and to provide the graduate student with experience in counseling.

Nature of Assignment:
Interns work with adolescent offenders, heroin addicts, court referrals, mental health cases, and families. Interns are also involved in some administrative aspects of community mental health.

Duration:
Varies, depending upon each Intern's needs and scheduling.

Eligibility:
College juniors or seniors enrolled in a psychology or sociology curriculum or graduate students in counseling.

Financial Data:
Volunteer only.

Special Features:
College credit can be earned for participation in the Program.

Application Deadline:
Applications should be submitted before the beginning of an academic term.

Request Application from:
Community Health Education Council, Inc.
278 Elm Street
West Springfield, Massachusetts 01089

COMMUNITY MENTAL HEALTH CENTER OF SCOTT COUNTY [79]

Program Title:
Clinical Psychology Predoctoral Internships

Purpose:
To provide professional training for psychologists completing programs of doctoral studies.

Nature of Assignment:
Interns work under supervision in a variety of training settings. Assignments provide exposure and experience in community mental health services with Interns participating in such program areas as psychological assessments, psychotherapy, community consultation and intake interviews.

Duration:
1 year, beginning in early September; full time.

Eligibility:
Applicants must have completed at least 2 years of doctoral level coursework in Clinical or Counseling Psychology including courses in the areas of tests and measurements, personality theory, psychopathology, psychotherapy and/or counseling, learning theory, and social or community psychology. In addition, applicants must have completed a year of supervised practicum in clinical work.

Number of Awards:
2 per year.

Financial Data:
Stipends of $6,000.

Special Features:
Vacation and administrative leave is offered.

Application Deadline:
January preceding the expected September starting date.

Request Application from:
Supervisor of Psychology Intern Training
Community Mental Health Center of Scott County
1441 West Central Park Avenue
Davenport, Iowa 52804

COMMUNITY SERVICES, INC. [80]

Program Title:
Family Life Education Program Trainee

Purpose:
To educate interested persons in the dynamics of family interaction and to teach family therapy skills.

Nature of Assignment:
Trainees are expected to see families in in short-term sessions to aid in re-negotiating family rules and improving family communications.

Duration:
Variable.

Eligibility:
Interested individuals who have the ability to work with groups, deal with hostile persons and make clinical decisions.

Number of Awards:
1 per year.

Financial Data:
Volunteer only.

Application Deadline:
April 1 of each year.

Request Application from:
Clinical Director
Community Services, Inc.
Box 2390
Grand Junction, Colorado 81501

COMPREHENSIVE MENTAL HEALTH CENTER OF TACOMA-PIERCE COUNTY [81]

Program Title:
Internships in Social Work, Psychology and Occupational Therapy

1st SUPPLEMENT

Directory of Internships, Work Experience Programs, and On-the-Job Training Opportunities

Purpose:
To provide quality mental health care for the city of Tacoma and part of Pierce County.

Nature of Assignment:
Interns are involved in 2 - 4 therapy groups and are responsible for approximately 6 - 8 clients on a case manager basis, seeing 2 or 3 of these clients for individual ongoing therapy. In addition, Interns do intake interviews; attend psychiatric consultations, student training sessions and staff meetings; and maintain records.

Duration:
Year-round program.

Eligibility:
College seniors or master's and doctoral degree candidates who are enrolled in appropriate programs and have good emotional health.

Financial Data:
Some expenses are paid; a limited number of stipends are also available on a work-study basis.

Application Deadline:
Applications are accepted at any time.

Request Application from:
Comprehensive Mental Health Center of
    Tacoma-Pierce County
P.O. Box 5007
Tacoma, Washington 98405

CONCERT ARTISTS GUILD [82]

Program Title:
Internship Program

Purpose:
To provide firsthand experience in publicity and arts management in the nonprofit sector.

Nature of Assignment:
Interns prepare news releases, concert listings and ads; coordinate distribution of flyers; maintain membership lists; and develop memberships and audiences, especially for community concerts in the burroughs. Interns may also become involved in audition activities, assist with box office and audience at actual concerts, and assist in preparation of newsletters.

Duration:
Full or part time during the Summer or the concert season.

Eligibility:
High school graduates with appropriate interests who have organizational ability and can type accurately.

Number of Awards:
2 per year.

Financial Data:
Volunteer; some expenses may be paid.

Application Deadline:
Applications may be submitted at any time but should be received by May for Summer Internships and August for Internships during the concert season.

Request Application from:
Internship Program
Concert Artists Guild
154 West 57th Street - Suite 136
New York, New York 10019

CONSUMER FEDERATION OF AMERICA [83]

Program Title:
CFA Internship Program

Purpose:
To provide experience in substantive areas of consumer legislation and exposure to lobbying, the legislative process, and Federal agencies.

Nature of Assignment:
Interns perform a variety of tasks including research, writing, office work, assisting in preparation of newsletters and assisting at conferences. Interns also do legislative work in such areas as health and safety, regulatory reform, product liability and safety, financial institutions and credit, food and marketing, and insurance.

Duration:
Flexible; at least 15 hours per week during a school term, Summer, or intersession period.

Eligibility:
Individuals who have interests and skills appropriate to the Program. A background in economics, law, journalism or political science is helpful but not required.

Number of Awards:
Varies; up to 4 Interns in the Program at any one time.

Financial Data:
Volunteer only.

Application Deadline:
Applications are accepted at any time.

Request Application from:
Consumer Federation of America
1012 14th Street, N.W.
Washington, D.C. 20003

COOK COUNTY LEGAL ASSISTANCE FOUNDATION, INC. [84]

Program Title:
Training Program

Purpose:
To provide legal assistance (in civil matters only) to low income residents of suburban Cook County, Illinois.

Nature of Assignment:
Assignments are available from time to time in paralegal training, law clerk training and secretarial training.

Eligibility:
People who have an interest in the legal field; some previous experience would be helpful.

Financial Data:
Basically volunteer, although participants would be considered for possible job openings.

Application Deadline:
Applications are accepted at any time.

Request Application from:
Cook County Legal Assistance Foundation
19 South LaSalle Street - Room 1419
Chicago, Illinois 60603

COOPER-HEWITT MUSEUM [85]

Program Title:
Internship Program

Purpose:
To develop an interest in and an understanding of museum curatorial and administrative tasks.

Nature of Assignment:
Interns serve as assistants to department directors in such areas as education, membership, drawing and the library.

Duration:
Varies with interests of Interns and needs of Museum.

Eligibility:
Individuals who have had prior experience in art history and design and have writing ability.

Financial Data:
Volunteer only.

Special Features:
Interns have the opportunity to attend exhibition galas and audit decorative arts and design classes.

Application Deadline:
2 months in advance of requested Internship starting date.

Request Application from:
Membership Office
Cooper-Hewitt Museum
2 East 91st Street
New York, New York 10028

COUNCIL FOR ADVANCEMENT AND SUPPORT OF EDUCATION (CASE) [86]

Program Title:
Editorial Internship Program

Purpose:
To give students an opportunity to learn all phases of magazine editorial and production work.

Nature of Assignment:
Interns edit articles, write occasional items, correspond with authors, edit letters to the editor, proofread and propose article ideas.

Duration:
Winter program, September - May, or Summer program, June - August; full time.

Eligibility:
Students with at least one year of college who have an aptitude for writing and either have prior experience on high school or college newspapers or have taken courses in journalism.

Number of Awards:
2 per year, 1 during the Winter program and 1 during the Summer.

Financial Data:
$125 per week plus full benefits (except paid vacation) for the September-May Intern; volunteer only for the Summer Intern.

Application Deadline:
April 1 of each year.

Request Application from:
Vice President
Council for Advancement and Support of Education
One Dupont Circle
Washington, D.C. 20036

CREATIVE ARTS THERAPY INSTITUTE [87]

Program Title:
Internship Program

Purpose:
To assist in the Institute's efforts of providing arts experiences for all types of handicapped persons.

Nature of Assignment:
Interns are involved in activities to publicize the Institute's program of arts for the handicapped, raise funds for program development, encourage local and national interest in and/or commitment to the program, work with government agencies on the Institute's behalf, and help administer a school for therapist training.

Duration:
8 months or 1 year, depending on each Intern's needs.

Eligibility:
Individuals who are interested in the Institute's program and have the ability to work with arts groups as well as with the handicapped. Applicants should have management, human services or public relations backgrounds.

Number of Awards:
2 per year.

Financial Data:
Volunteer only; future salary could possibly be developed.

Application Deadline:
Applications are accepted at any time.

Request Application from:
Director
Creative Arts Therapy Institute
1370 Forest Street
Denver, Colorado 80220

CREATIVE LIFE SERVICES [88]

Program Title:
Resocialization Program

Purpose:
To assist in providing information and referral services, support and assistance as needed, and community activity programs for the elderly.

Nature of Assignment:
Tasks performed by participants include outreach, recreation, information and referral services, and office work.

Duration:
Varies with individual needs, but long enough to make the training effort worthwhile.

Eligibility:
Individuals interested in helping others by doing things with them, not to them.

Financial Data:
Volunteer only; there is a possibility of some remuneration in the future.

Stipulations:
Participation in training is necessary as attitude is the most important part of the Program.

Application Deadline:
Applications are accepted at any time.

Request Application from:
Executive Director
Creative Life Services
P.O. Box 68
Scottsdale, Arizona 85252

d

DC PUBLIC INTEREST RESEARCH GROUP [89]

Program Title:
Internship Program

1st SUPPLEMENT

Directory of Internships, Work Experience Programs, and On-the-Job Training Opportunities

Purpose:
To provide experience in a student-run research and advocacy group dealing with consumer-related problems.

Nature of Assignment:
Interns work with volunteer students and paid professional staff on a variety of projects including research, testimony, publication, and community education. All projects are goal oriented and deal with consumer problems in such areas as utilities, health care, housing, energy and discrimination.

Duration:
Nothing specific established.

Eligibility:
Individuals with appropriate interests who live in the District of Columbia area.

Financial Data:
Volunteer only.

Special Features:
Interns gain an affiliation with many other consumer groups in the District of Columbia.

Application Deadline:
Applications are accepted at any time.

Request Application from:
Internship Program
DC Public Interest Research Group
P.O. Box 19542
Washington, D.C. 20036

THE DAILY NEWS [90]

Program Title:
Summer Internship Program

Purpose:
To provide college students with a chance to work under professional conditions and the guidance of a professional newspaper staff.

Nature of Assignment:
Interns work under the close supervision of regular staff members and are involved primarily in reporting with both beat and feature writing assignments. Some photography is also assigned. Interns participate in a team project of organizing, writing and editing (including copy editing, head writing and design) a tabloid section on a county fair.

Duration:
13 weeks during the Summer; full time.

Eligibility:
College students who will have completed their junior year before beginning an Internship and plan on returning to school in the Fall. Applicants must have demonstrated ability to report. Preference is given to Washington state residents and those with camera ability.

Number of Awards:
1 each year.

Financial Data:
$130 per week.

Application Deadline:
December 31 for an Internship the following Summer.

Request Application from:
Managing Editor
The Daily News
P.O. Box 2126
Port Angeles, Washington 98362

1st SUPPLEMENT
Directory of Internships, Work Experience Programs, and On-the-Job Training Opportunities

DAILY STATESMAN [91]

Program Title:
News/Advertising Internship

Purpose:
To train young students in news writing and editing and to teach them advertising sales and promotion.

Nature of Assignment:
Interns participate in general news and editorial work as well as advertising preparation.

Duration:
Varies with interests of the Intern and needs of the newspaper.

Eligibility:
Journalism school undergraduates with appropriate interests and skills.

Financial Data:
Salary to be negotiated.

Application Deadline:
Applications can be submitted at any time.

Request Application from:
Daily Statesman
Dexter, Missouri 63841

THE DALLAS MORNING NEWS [92]

Program Title:
Summer Newsroom Intern Program

Purpose:
To give students, while still in school, an opportunity to work on a newspaper which will then consider them for future employment after they graduate.

Nature of Assignment:
Interns are involved in news reporting for various newsroom departments and are also assigned some copy editing. Generally, Interns are treated the same as new employees, except with more personal supervision.

Duration:
10 - 13 weeks during the Summer; full time.

Eligibility:
College and university students who have interests and skills appropriate to the work. Applicants must be completing their junior year.

Number of Awards:
Varies, with around 6 Internships awarded per year.

Financial Data:
Interns are paid a weekly wage of approximately $125.

Stipulations:
Applicants should have clips for submission.

Application Deadline:
February 1 of each year.

Request Application from:
Summer Newsroom Intern Program
The Dallas News
Communications Center
Dallas, Texas 75222

DAYTON, OHIO [93]

Program Title:
Urban Corps Internship and College Work-Study Program

Purpose:
To place students in work assignments that offer them on-the-job experience particular to their academic training.

Nature of Assignment:
Interns perform various tasks and duties, depending on the agency in which they are placed. The intent is to relate work assignments to each Intern's academic background and interests.

Duration:
Year round work is possible; part and full time.

Eligibility:
College and university students who qualify for work-study support.

Financial Data:
$2.50 to $3.00 an hour.

Stipulations:
Students must be certified by and apply through the schools in which they are enrolled.

Application Deadline:
Applications must be made through an appropriate college or university.

Request Application from:
Dayton Urban Corps
40 South Main Street - Suite 201
Dayton, Ohio 45402

DISTRICT OF COLUMBIA. SUPERIOR COURT. SOCIAL SERVICE DIVISION [94]

Program Title:
Intern/Volunteer Program

Purpose:
To provide a learning experience for students interested in correctional services who need practicum placements to meet course requirements, and to provide opportunities for individuals who want to assist court staff in working with probationers.

Nature of Assignment:
Working under the supervision of probation offices, participants serve as probation aides, educational and vocational aides, counselors in a one-to-one program, research assistants and clerical aides.

Duration:
Indeterminate, depending on needs of the Division and interests of individuals involved. Interns must be available for assignment a minimum of 8 hours per week and Volunteers at least 4 hours a week.

Eligibility:
Undergraduate and graduate students who have interests and skills appropriate to the work. Applicants for Intern positions must be recommended by their local schools. Preference is given to residents of and students in the Metropolitan Washington, D.C., area.

Number of Awards:
Indeterminate; an effort is made to place all interested and qualified candidates.

Financial Data:
No remuneration is offered; travel expenses connected with assignments are reimbursed.

Application Deadline:
Intern applications should be submitted well in advance of the practicum period desired. Volunteer applications are accepted at any time.

Request Application from:
Social Service Division
Superior Court of D.C.
613 G Street, N.W.
Washington, D.C. 20001

1st SUPPLEMENT

Directory of Internships, Work Experience Programs, and On-the-Job Training Opportunities

DISTRICT OF COLUMBIA LUNG ASSOCIATION [95]

Program Title:
Internship

Purpose:
To assist in protecting and securing accomodation for the rights of non-smokers through legislation, community education and citizen action.

Nature of Assignment:
Interns are assigned as program researchers to work on one of the following projects: studying area hospital smoking policies and conducting a hospital-focused test program, canvasing local restaurants to encourage non-smoking policies, lobbying District of Columbia Council representatives, or staffing and organizing a small citizen's group with responsibilities including writing and publishing newsletters.

Duration:
20 - 30 hours per week.

Eligibility:
Individuals who have interests and abilities appropriate to the work.

Financial Data:
Volunteer only.

Application Deadline:
Applications are accepted at any time.

Request Application from:
Director
Metropolitian Washington Coalition for Clean Air
1714 Massachusetts Avenue, N.W.
Washington, D.C. 20036

DR. SOLOMON CARTER FULLER MENTAL HEALTH CENTER [96]

Program Title:
Inpatient/Outpatient Services

Purpose:
To help people with problems to better understand themselves and be productive citizens.

Nature of Assignment:
Participants are assigned work in various areas of the Center, depending on individual needs. Duties might be involved with psychiatry, psychology, social work, nursing, or recreation, or the clerical and business element of the Center's work.

Duration:
Varies; full time or part time; Summer possible.

Eligibility:
Individuals with appropriate interests and abilities. Applicants must have a sincere desire to work with people. Certain tasks or assignments might require special skills.

Financial Data:
Volunteer only.

Special Features:
If student credit is desired, the Center can set up the required relationship with the school involved.

Application Deadline:
Applications are accepted at any time.

Request Application from:
Director, Clinical Social Work
Dr. Solomon Carter Fuller Mental Health Center
85 East Newton Street
Boston, Massachusetts 02118

DUMBARTON OAKS CENTER FOR STUDIES IN THE HISTORY OF LANDSCAPE ARCHITECTURE [97]

Program Title:
Fellowship Program

Purpose:
To promote research in the history of landscape architecture and the related fields of garden design and garden ornament, and in the history of horticulture.

Nature of Assignment:
Fellows utilize the library at the Center in Washington, as well as complimentary materials in other nearby collections, to conduct independent research. Appropriate projects would include those dealing with any aspect of garden and landscape architecture (including decorations such as sculpture and fountains) and buildings, the history of horticulture and related topics, the development of landscape designs, or the restoration of historic gardens.

Duration:
It is normally expected that Fellows will spend the academic year in residence at Dumbarton Oaks in Washington, D.C.

Eligibility:
Qualified individuals who have appropriate research projects. Applications may be submitted by graduate students who have completed all requirements for the doctorate except the dissertation or final project; young scholars with graduate degrees; and distinguished scholars in the fields of landscape architecture, history of art, and history of horticulture.

Number of Awards:
3 per year.

Financial Data:
Fellowships carry stipends of $5,000 for Junior Fellows, $6,500 for Visiting Fellows, and an amount related to the awardee's current salary for Senior Fellows. In addition, housing is provided at the Center as well as daily lunches. Travel funds are available for Fellows coming from outside of the United States.

Application Deadline:
December 1 for awards to be announced the following March.

Request Application from:
Director
Center for Studies in Landscape Architecture
Dumbarton Oaks
1703 32nd Street, N.W.
Washington, D.C. 20007

EAST TENNESSEE COMMUNITY DESIGN CENTER [98]

Program Title:
Internship and Work-Experience Program

1st SUPPLEMENT

Directory of Internships, Work Experience Programs, and On-the-Job Training Opportunities

Purpose:
To offer on-the-job experience in providing architectural, planning and related design and programming assistance to community groups unable to pay normal professional fees.

Nature of Assignment:
Participants are assigned duties in a variety of areas, such as design programming, community participation, architectural design, neighborhood and town planning, interior design and housing rehabilitation.

Duration:
Flexible, ranging from 10 week architecture student Internships to several year VISTA teams.

Eligibility:
Architecture students and other interested individuals who have appropriate degrees or have relevant work experience, community participant experience in design or planning, or construction experience.

Number of Awards:
Average of 12 per year.

Financial Data:
Volunteer only.

Application Deadline:
Applications are accepted at any time.

Request Application from:
East Tennessee Community Design Center
1522 Highland Avenue
Knoxville, Tennessee 37916

EAST-WEST CENTER [99]

Program Title:
Fellow Awards

Purpose:
To attract outstanding postdoctoral and mid-career scholars and authorities to the Center for involvement in Center projects and interaction with Center staff and other participants.

Nature of Assignment:
Fellows join in Center projects of education, research and training in a wide variety of subject disciplines; accept research and development responsibilities in specific Center projects related to their backgrounds and interests; and participate in seminars, training activities and program development planning.

Duration:
4 - 12 months.

Eligibility:
Citizens or legal permanent residents of an Asian or Pacific country or of the United States who have professional qualifications and interests relevant to active participation in projects of Center Institutes or in Open Grants Team Projects. Applicants can be educators, researchers, business leaders, political figures or professionals who are affiliated with institutions of higher learning, government organizations or private agencies, or are engaged in independent pursuits.

Number of Awards:
45 - 70 per year.

Financial Data:
Fellows receive round-trip travel to Honolulu and stipends comparable to salaries received from employment at time of Award or salaries of Center staff with equivalent rank. No additional housing allowances are provided, but the Center assists in location of suitable housing.

Stipulations:
Fellows are expected to spend the full period of their Award at the Center, except

for any short fieldwork requirements of Center projects.

Special Features:
Fellows are normally provided with office space, including usual furnishings and equipment, and the total program resources of the Center are available to them.

Application Deadline:
Preferably 12 - 18 months before desired starting date of Award.

Request Application from:
Awards Coordinator
Academic Program Services
East-West Center
1777 East West Road
Honolulu, Hawaii 96848

EAST-WEST CENTER [100]

Program Title:
Joint Doctoral Research Intern Awards

Purpose:
To provide outstanding doctoral candidates of institutions other than the University of Hawaii with an opportunity to work in Center projects relevant to their dissertations.

Nature of Assignment:
Interns are given supervised practical experience in problem-oriented research by participating in projects at Center Institutes, which represent a wide variety of subject disciplines. Interns are also able to conduct dissertation fieldwork and have the opportunity to develop proficiency in an Asian or Pacific language or in English as a foreign language.

Duration:
1 -2 years.

Eligibility:
Citizens or legal permanent residents of an Asian or Pacific country or of the United States who, by the time of Award activity, will have completed all doctoral degree requirements except the dissertation and possibly language. Applicants must specify how their professional qualifications and interests are relevant to active participation in Center projects.

Number of Awards:
20 - 25 per year.

Financial Data:
Interns receive round-trip travel to Honolulu, housing or $200 per month housing allowance, health and accident insurance, tuition and fees for any required language study, monthly stipends of $250 and possibly fieldwork costs.

Stipulations:
At least one-half of the Award time must be spent at the Center, including the last month of support. An agreement must be arranged between the institution where the Intern will receive the doctorate and the Center with a Center staff member appointed to the Intern's dissertation committee.

Application Deadline:
Preferably 12 - 18 months before desired starting date of Award.

Request Application from:
Awards Coordinator
Academic Program Services
East-West Center
1777 East West Road
Honolulu, Hawaii 96848

EAST-WEST CENTER [101]

Program Title:
Professional Associate Awards.

1st SUPPLEMENT

Directory of Internships, Work Experience Programs, and On-the-Job Training Opportunities

Purpose:
To attract leaders and mid- or upper-echelon managers of government, business and education to the Center to work with each other across national and cultural lines.

Nature of Assignment:
Associates participate in seminars, workshops, conferences and planning sessions dealing with the application of research to practice, development of educational programs and materials, demonstration of these materials, and sharing of experiences.

Duration:
1 week - 12 months.

Eligibility:
Citizens or legal permanent residents of an Asian or Pacific country or of the United States who have professional interests, backgrounds or employment status in project areas of Center Institutes. Applicants can come from various fields of endeavor, but must demonstrate interest in intercultural communication.

Number of Awards:
1,000 - 1,500 per year.

Financial Data:
Associates receive round-trip travel to Honolulu, housing or $200 per month housing allowance, health and accident insurance, stipends of $13 per day or $380 per month, program costs, and funds for project relevant materials.

Stipulations:
Associates may or may not have graduate degrees; in any case, Awards are for non-degree participation in Center projects.

Application Deadline:
Applications for Cultural Learning Institute Associateships should be submitted by August 1 for Awards the following year; applications for all other Institutes should be submitted preferably 6 - 10 months before desired starting date of Award.

Request Application from:
Awards Coordinator
Academic Program Services
East-West Center
1777 East West Road
Honolulu, Hawaii 96848

EAST-WEST CENTER [102]

Program Title:
Professional Intern Awards

Purpose:
To attract highly promising potential leaders to the Center for managerial experience through project participation.

Nature of Assignment:
Interns are placed on international research and managerial teams at one of the Center's Institutes where they have the opportunity to develop managerial experience in educational research or development activities.

Duration:
1 - 12 months.

Eligibility:
Citizens or legal permanent residents of an Asian or Pacific country or of the United States who have research and/or professional interests and experience in project areas of Center Institutes.

Number of Awards:
30 - 50 per year.

Financial Data:
Interns receive round-trip travel to Honolulu, housing or $200 per month housing

allowance, health and accident insurance, monthly stipends of $380, program costs, and funds for project relevant research support services and materials.

Stipulations:
Interns may or may not have graduate degrees; in any case, Awards are for non-degree participation in Center projects.

Application Deadline:
Preferably 6 - 10 months before desired starting date of Award.

Request Application from:
Awards Coordinator
Academic Program Services
East-West Center
1777 East West Road
Honolulu, Hawaii 96848

EAST-WEST CENTER [103]

Program Title:
Research Intern Awards

Purpose:
To attract highly promising research workers to the Center for problem-oriented, interdisciplinary research training in specific Center projects.

Nature of Assignment:
Interns receive supervised practical experience by participating on problem-focused team research projects at Center Institutes, which represent a wide variety of subject disciplines. Through such participation, Interns have the opportunity to develop proficiency in specific interdisciplinary research procedures.

Duration:
1 - 12 months.

Eligibility:
Citizens or legal permanent residents of an Asian or Pacific country or of the United States who have research and/or professional interests and experience in project areas of Center Institutes.

Number of Awards:
10 - 20 per year.

Financial Data:
Interns receive round-trip travel to Honolulu, housing or $200 per month housing allowance, health and accident insurance, monthly stipends of $380, program costs, and funds for project relevant research support services and materials.

Stipulations:
Interns may or may not have graduate degrees; in any case, Awards are for non-degree participation in Center projects.

Application Deadline:
Preferably 6 - 10 months before desired starting date of Award.

Request Application from:
Awards Coordinator
Academic Program Services
East-West Center
1777 East West Road
Honolulu, Hawaii 96848

EAST-WEST CENTER [104]

Program Title:
Visiting Research Associate Awards

Purpose:
To attract outstanding international senior scholars and authorities to the Center for involvement in Center projects and activities.

1st SUPPLEMENT

Directory of Internships, Work Experience Programs, and On-the-Job Training Opportunities

Nature of Assignment:
Associates are assigned to Center Institutes in visiting staff member roles which include teaching in professional study and training projects, working with student seminars and activities, and participating in research on Center projects, which represent a wide variety of subject disciplines.

Duration:
2 - 3 years.

Eligibility:
Citizens or legal permanent residents of an Asian or Pacific country or of the United States who have professional qualifications and interests relevant to active participation in Center projects.

Number of Awards:
5 - 10 per year.

Financial Data:
Associates receive round-trip travel to Honolulu and stipends comparable to salaries of Center staff with equivalent rank and experience.

Stipulations:
Associates are expected to spend full time at the Center, except for short fieldwork requirements of Center projects.

Special Features:
Associates are provided with office space, including usual furnishings and equipment, and the total program resources of the Center are available to them.

Application Deadline:
Preferably 12 - 18 months before desired starting date of Award.

Request Application from:
Awards Coordinator
Academic Program Services
East-West Center
1777 East West Road
Honolulu, Hawaii 96848

ECO TOUR [105]

Program Title:
Bear Valley Winter Experience

Purpose:
To teach elementary through high school students about winter survival concepts and give them a general respect for the harsh winter environment.

Nature of Assignment:
Participants act as counselors to small groups for 2 different 3 day sessions per week, instructing and helping in such areas as cross country skiing, snow shoeing and nature study.

Duration:
January - February; full time.

Eligibility:
Fourth and fifth year college students who have appropriate interests and skills with preference given to those in recreation or environmental education. Applicants must have a driver's license, possess good survival skills, and be able to ski, snow shoe and drive a snowmobile.

Number of Awards:
6 - 8 per year.

Financial Data:
Participants receive lodging, expenses and small stipends.

Stipulations:
Participants must have sleeping bags which go to 0 degrees.

Special Features:
Students can earn 8 - 10 units in education or recreation from a California State College for participation in the program.

Application Deadline:
November 1 of each year.

1st SUPPLEMENT

Directory of Internships, Work Experience Programs, and On-the-Job Training Opportunities

Request Application from:
General Manager
Eco Tour
41811 Blacow Road
Fremont, California 94538

THE EDMUND NILES HUYCK PRESERVE, INC. [106]

Program Title:
Fellowships and Grants for Research

Purpose:
To support graduate and post-graduate research on the flora and fauna of the Huyck Preserve and vicinity.

Nature of Assignment:
Participants design and conduct high quality research in which the natural resources of the Huyck Preserve are utilized. The Preserve, located on the Helderberg Plateau in New York, includes natural and reforested woodlands, oil fields, Lake Myosotis (100 acres), Lincoln Pond (10 acres) and approximately 3 miles of intermittent streams.

Duration:
Research is typically conducted for 3 months during the Summer, though facilities are available all year round.

Eligibility:
Candidates for graduate degrees and post-graduates in the natural sciences who have appropriate research proposals.

Number of Awards:
Varies; usually 5 per year.

Financial Data:
Participants receive free lodging for themselves and their families, laboratory space, travel allowance of up to $300, a stipend of up to $2,000, and the possibility of support for undergraduate or graduate research associates.

Stipulations:
Research projects must be conducted on the Huyck Preserve.

Application Deadline:
Applications for Fellowship support should be submitted by January 15 with selections announced by March 15; applications for Grants are accepted at any time.

Request Application from:
Executive Director
The Edmund Niles Huyck Preserve and
  Biological Station
P.O. Box 77
Rensselaerville, New York 12147

ELYRIA CHRONICLE - TELEGRAM [107]

Program Title:
Newsroom Internship Program

Purpose:
To help train prospective journalists.

Nature of Assignment:
Interns are assigned general newsroom duties including reporting, editing and photography.

Duration:
12 weeks; full time.

Eligibility:
Preference is generally given to college or university journalism majors interested in Internship training between their junior and senior years.

Number of Awards:
3 per year.

Financial Data:
$120 per week.

Application Deadline:
April 1 of each year.

Request Application from:
Managing Editor
Elyria Chronicle-Telegram
225 East Avenue
Elyria, Ohio 44035

THE EXPERIMENT IN INTERNATIONAL LIVING [108]

Program Title:
Internship Program

Purpose:
To introduce high school and college students to the field of international educational exchange by exposing them to national and local organizations concerned with international education and to the logistics and organization of a regional office.

Nature of Assignment:
Interns are assigned projects in such general areas as public relations, communications, foreign student placement, host family preparation, foreign student orientation and cross-cultural study.

Duration:
1 - 6 months at any time during the year.

Eligibility:
Individuals who are interested in promoting international education and experimental learning, are enthusiastic and self-directed, and have some administrative skills. Foreign language ability is desirable but not required.

Number of Awards:
Several each year.

Financial Data:
Subsistence allowances are sometimes offered, depending on budget limitations.

Application Deadline:
Applications are accepted at any time.

Request Application from:
Director
The Experiment in International Living
1346 Connecticut Avenue, N.W. - Suite 802
Washington, D.C. 20036

f

FARNHAM YOUTH DEVELOPMENT CENTER [109]

Program Title:
Volunteer Program

1st SUPPLEMENT

Directory of Internships, Work Experience Programs, and On-the-Job Training Opportunities

Purpose:
To assist in providing information, referral and counseling services within a completely confidential, non-threatening atmosphere which serves as an alternative to more traditional agencies.

Nature of Assignment:
After completing Farnham's training course, Volunteers are assigned to such areas as hotline work, inter-agency communications, outreach work, newsletter coordination, fundraising and/or grantseeking, and public relations.

Duration:
Varies, depending on each Volunteer.

Eligibility:
Individuals who have interests and abilities appropriate to the Center's work.

Number of Awards:
Unlimited.

Financial Data:
Volunteer only.

Stipulations:
Volunteers must complete an 8 week training course before they will be given assignments by the Center.

Application Deadline:
Applications may be submitted at any time; however, the mandatory training sessions are only offered in September, January and June.

Request Application from:
Farnham Youth Development Center
145 East Bridge Street
Oswego, New York 13126

FEDERAL HOME LOAN BANK BOARD [110]

Program Title:
Summer Employment Program

Purpose:
To provide professional and administrative Summer job opportunities with the Board.

Nature of Assignment:
Students are assigned work involving accounting, economics, business administration, finance or legal knowledge.

Duration:
Summer.

Eligibility:
Graduate students who are currently enrolled in school and plan to return in the Fall, or undergraduate students who have applied to graduate school for entrance in the Fall. Applicants for positions requiring legal ability must have completed 2 years of law school and be in the top 10 percent rating.

Number of Awards:
Limited number.

Financial Data:
Students are paid salaries based on an annual rate of approximately $10,000 - $15,000; specific compensation depends on the level of schooling completed.

Application Deadline:
Applications should be submitted as soon as possible but no later than approximately March 31.

Request Application from:
Summer Employment Coordinator
Personnel Management Division
Federal Home Loan Bank Board
320 First Street, N.W. - Room 1034
Washington, D.C. 20552

1st SUPPLEMENT
Directory of Internships, Work Experience Programs, and On-the-Job Training Opportunities

FEDERAL NATIONAL MORTGAGE ASSOCIATION (FANNIE MAE) [111]

Program Title:
Corporate Relations Intern Program

Purpose:
To give prospective financial and business writers increased insight regarding American business and financial institutions, practical understanding of finance and mortgage banking, and exposure to the governmental process in Washington.

Nature of Assignment:
Interns receive on-the-job training at Fannie Mae headquarters in Washington, D.C., where they work closely with the corporate relations staff. Assignments include preparation of in-house newsletters, writing for corporate publications, and assistance in preparation of news releases. Interns also attend relevant Congressional hearings and are given work experience on the real estate and financial desks of a Washington daily newspaper.

Duration:
6 months; January 1 - June 30 or July 1 - December 31.

Eligibility:
Journalism students who have completed at least 3 years of college work and desire careers as business and/or financial reporters. Applicants must have the ability to initiate their own projects as well as complete assigned work.

Number of Awards:
2 per year, 1 during each 6 month period.

Financial Data:
Interns receive round-trip airfare to Washington and modest salaries; they are also eligible for employee benefits, such as medical insurance, life insurance, vacation, and sick leave.

Stipulations:
Applicants must have some remaining degree work to complete, at either the undergraduate or graduate level.

Special Features:
Some schools allow scholastic credit for Internship assignments.

Application Deadline:
Third week of October each year.

Request Application from:
Office of Corporate Relations
Federal National Mortgage Association
1133 Fifteenth Street, N.W.
Washington, D.C. 20005

FINE ARTS MUSEUM OF SAN FRANCISCO [112]

Program Title:
Internship Program

Purpose:
To train museum education specialists.

Nature of Assignment:
Interns participate in a training curriculum and receive work experience in exhibits and programs at the Fine Arts Museum.

Duration:
1 year.

Eligibility:
Individuals who have a Master's degree in Humanities, Art or Education and experience beyond the degree in community arts or museum work.

Number of Awards:
8 - 10 per year.

Financial Data:
$7,000 stipend.

Application Deadline:
July of each year.

Request Application from:
deYoung Museum Art School
Golden Gate Park
San Francisco, California 94118

FLORIDA PUBLISHING COMPANY [113]

Program Title:
Summer News Intern Program

Purpose:
To provide practical experience for college undergraduates whose career plans include the editorial aspects of newspaper production.

Nature of Assignment:
Interns are given on-the-job experience through assignment to city, sports and women's news desks. It is expected that Interns will carry out their assignments in the same manner as full-time staff members.

Duration:
June through August; full time.

Eligibility:
Students who have had at least one year of college with those already into their major fields preferred and returning seniors given highest priority. A journalism major is not an absolute requirement, but commitment to entering print journalism is.

Number of Awards:
8, with the possibility of more.

Financial Data:
$100 per week salary for first-year Interns; $10 per week added for succeeding Summers.

Special Features:
Some copy desk experience is available to particularly well qualified Interns.

Application Deadline:
March 15 of each year.

Request Application from:
Assistant Executive Editor
Florida Publishing Company
P.O. Box 1949
Jacksonville, Florida 32201

FORT WORTH STAR-TELEGRAM [114]

Program Title:
Editorial Internships

Purpose:
To give college students some professional experience.

Nature of Assignment:
Interns are assigned regular work as reporters and copy desk editors.

Duration:
13 weeks during the Summer; full time.

Eligibility:
Journalism students who will be between their junior and senior years during the Internship. Preference is given to students from Texas colleges and universities.

Number of Awards:
2 - 4 per year.

Financial Data:
Salary of $125 per week.

Stipulations:
Applicants must be prepared to travel to Fort Worth, Texas, to be interviewed.

Application Deadline:
December for Internships the following Summer.

Request Application from:
Fort Worth Star-Telegram
P.O. Box 1870
Fort Worth, Texas 76101

FORUM FOR THE ADVANCEMENT OF STUDENTS IN SCIENCE AND TECHNOLOGY (FASST) [115]

Program Title:
Business Management Internships

Purpose:
To give students direct experience with the technical and policy aspects of science issues.

Nature of Assignment:
Interns gain experience in the management of a nonprofit organization which operates much the same as a small profitmaking business. The work involved includes long and short range planning, accounting, tax matters, personnel, fiscal responsibility, fund raising and proposal writing, and marketing.

Duration:
Tailored to meet each student's needs.

Eligibility:
Graduate or undergraduate students who have appropriate skills and expressed interest in the better understanding of science issues and in communicating this understanding to the lay public.

Number of Awards:
No limit.

Financial Data:
Volunteer only; FASST will support requests to be sponsored under work-study programs.

Special Features:
Past Interns have received up to 15 hours academic credit for their work with FASST.

Application Deadline:
Applications are accepted at any time.

Request Application from:
President
FASST
2030 M Street, N.W. - Suite 402
Washington, D.C. 20036

FORUM FOR THE ADVANCEMENT OF STUDENTS IN SCIENCE AND TECHNOLOGY (FASST) [116]

Program Title:
FASST Internship Program

Purpose:
To give students direct experience with the technical and policy aspects of science issues.

Nature of Assignment:
Interns design programs to fit into their own specific areas of academic interests and abilities. This allows students to pursue ideas for internships which do not fall into other delineated FASST internship programs.

Duration:
Tailored to meet each student's needs.

Eligibility:
Graduate or undergraduate students who have appropriate skills and expressed interest in the better understanding of science issues and in communicating this understanding to the lay public.

Number of Awards:
No limit.

Financial Data:
Volunteer only; FASST will support Intern requests to be sponsored under work-study programs.

Stipulations:
An outline of the proposed Internship program must be submitted to FASST.

Special Features:
Past Interns have received up to 15 hours of academic credit for their work with FASST.

Application Deadline:
Applications are accepted at any time.

Request Application from:
President
FASST
2030 M Street, N.W. - Suite 402
Washington, D.C. 20036

FORUM FOR THE ADVANCEMENT OF STUDENTS IN SCIENCE AND TECHNOLOGY (FASST) [117]

Program Title:
Journalism Internships

Purpose:
To give students direct experience with the technical and policy aspects of science issues.

Nature of Assignment:
Interns write articles for FASST NEWS (quarterly tabloid) and FASST TRACKS (membership newsletter) and press releases for the FASST News Service.

Duration:
Tailored to meet each student's needs.

Eligibility:
Graduate or undergraduate students who have appropriate skills and expressed interest in the better understanding of science issues and in communicating this understanding to the lay public.

Number of Awards:
No limit.

Financial Data:
Volunteer only; FASST will support requests to be sponsored under work-study programs.

Special Features:
Past Interns have received up to 15 hours of academic credit for their work with FASST.

Application Deadline:
Applications are accepted at any time.

Request Application from:
President
FASST
2030 M Street, N.W. - Suite 402
Washington, D.C. 20036

FORUM FOR THE ADVANCEMENT OF STUDENTS IN SCIENCE AND TECHNOLOGY (FASST) [118]

Program Title:
Marketing Internships

Purpose:
To give students direct experience with the technical and policy aspects of science issues.

Nature of Assignment:
Interns will be asked to design a marketing plan for membership promotion/development for FASST.

Duration:
Tailored to meet each student's needs.

Eligibility:
Graduate or undergraduate students who have appropriate skills and expressed interest in the better understanding of science issues and in communicating this understanding to the lay public.

Number of Awards:
No limit.

Financial Data:
Volunteer only; FASST will support requests to be sponsored under work-study programs.

Special Features:
Past Interns have received up to 15 hours of academic credit for their work with FASST.

Application Deadline:
Applications are accepted at any time.

Request Application from:
President
FASST
2030 M Street, N.W. - Suite 402
Washington, D.C. 20036

FORUM FOR THE ADVANCEMENT OF STUDENTS IN SCIENCE AND TECHNOLOGY (FASST) [119]

Program Title:
Research Internships

Purpose:
To give students direct experience with the technical and policy aspects of science issues.

Nature of Assignment:
Interns select a specific science issue and prepare a paper on its policy implications to include relevant legislation, regulations, and who (agency, association, etc.) should be involved in discussion of the issue.

Duration:
Tailored to meet each student's needs.

Eligibility:
Graduate or undergraduate students who have appropriate skills and expressed interest in the better understanding of science issues and in communicating this understanding to the lay public.

Number of Awards:
No limit.

Financial Data:
Volunteer only; FASST will support requests to be sponsored under work-study programs.

Special Features:
Past Interns have received up to 15 hours of academic credit for their work with FASST.

Application Deadline:
Applications are accepted at any time.

Request Application from:
President
FASST
2030 M Street, N.W. - Suite 402
Washington, D.C. 20036

g

GERMAN ACADEMIC EXCHANGE SERVICE (DAAD) [120]

Program Title:
German Studies (MAT) Summer Program

Purpose:
To promote international relations between universities, especially in the area of academic and scientific exchange, and to provide the opportunity for Americans to spend some time in Germany.

Nature of Assignment:
Participants attend a special course offered by the University of California at the Universitat Tubingen in West Germany. The course emphasizes the social and economic structure of West Germany through lectures and field study programs.

Duration:
6 weeks during the Summer.

Eligibility:
United States citizens who are graduate students in German, and teachers of German at high schools or colleges.

Number of Awards:
Varies from year to year, depending on available funds.

Financial Data:
Participants receive stipends for course fees and living expenses, but no travel allowances.

Special Features:
Participants may obtain University of California credit, but applicants do not have to be enrolled in the University.

Application Deadline:
January 31 of each year.

Request Application from:
German Academic Exchange Service (DAAD)
New York Office
One Fifth Avenue
New York, New York 10003

GERMAN ACADEMIC EXCHANGE SERVICE (DAAD) [121]

Program Title:
Hochschulferienkurs

Purpose:
To promote international relations between universities, especially in the area of academic and scientific exchange, and to provide the opportunity for Americans to spend some time in Germany.

Nature of Assignment:
Participants attend the West German University of their choice where they take courses in German studies and/or German language.

Duration:
3 weeks during the Summer.

Eligibility:
Students enrolled in American universities who have a good reading and speaking knowledge of German, have had at least 3 years of college level German, are between 19 and 32 years of age, and are United States citizens.

Number of Awards:
Varies from year to year, depending on available funds.

Financial Data:
Participants receive stipends to cover course fees and partial living expenses.

Application Deadline:
January 31 of each year.

Request Application from:
German Academic Exchange Service (DAAD)
New York Office
One Fifth Avenue
New York, New York 10003

GERMAN ACADEMIC EXCHANGE SERVICE (DAAD) [122]

Program Title:
Information Visits

Purpose:
To promote international relations between universities, especially in the area of academic and scientific exchange, and to provide the opportunity for Americans to spend some time in Germany.

Nature of Assignment:
Participants increase their knowledge of specific German subjects and/or institutions within the framework of an academic study tour in West Germany.

Duration:
7 - 21 days.

Eligibility:
Professors and students who are affiliated with accredited American institutions of higher learning and are United States citizens. Applications are accepted only from groups of eligible people and each group must have at least 10 but no more than 30 members.

Number of Awards:
Varies from year to year, depending on available funds.

Financial Data:
Program arrangements are provided as well as financial assistance on a per person, per diem basis.

Stipulations:
No Visits can be organized for July and August.

Application Deadline:
Applications must be received at least 6 months prior to desired departure date and no later than February 15, October 1 or December 1.

Request Application from:
German Academic Exchange Service (DAAD)
New York Office
One Fifth Avenue
New York, New York 10003

GERMAN ACADEMIC EXCHANGE SERVICE (DAAD) [123]

Program Title:
Short Term Study and Research

Purpose:
To promote international relations between universities, especially in the area of academic and scientific exchange, and to provide the opportunity for Americans to spend some time in Germany.

Nature of Assignment:
Participants conduct dissertation or postdoctoral research in West Germany.

Duration:
2 - 6 months.

Eligibility:
Advanced graduate students who are pursuing dissertation research and recent Ph.D.'s. Applicants must be United States citizens between 18 and 32 years of age.

Number of Awards:
Varies from year to year, depending on available funds.

Financial Data:
Participants receive monthly allowances for maintenance, but no funds for international travel.

Application Deadline:
January 31 and October 31 of each year.

Request Application from:
German Academic Exchange Service
(DAAD)
New York Office
One Fifth Avenue
New York, New York 10003

GERMAN ACADEMIC EXCHANGE SERVICE (DAAD) [124]

Program Title:
Study and Research Program

Purpose:
To promote international relations between universities, especially in the area of academic and scientific exchange, and to provide the opportunity for Americans to spend some time in Germany.

Nature of Assignment:
Participants travel to West Germany where they undertake graduate studies, conduct doctoral dissertation research, or pursue postdoctoral work.

Duration:
7 - 10 months.

Eligibility:
Individuals who have interests and abilities appropriate to the Program. Applicants must be United States citizens between 18 and 32 years of age and must hold a Bachelor's degree or its equivalent.

Number of Awards:
Varies from year to year, depending on available funds.

Financial Data:
Participants receive stipends for maintenance, international travel, tuition and fees, and other relevant expenses.

Application Deadline:
November 1 for support the following academic year.

Request Application from:
German Academic Exchange Service
(DAAD)
New York Office
One Fifth Avenue
New York, New York 10003

1st SUPPLEMENT

Directory of Internships, Work Experience Programs, and On-the-Job Training Opportunities

GERMAN ACADEMIC EXCHANGE SERVICE (DAAD) [125]

Program Title:
Study Visits

Purpose:
To promote international relations between universities, especially in the area of academic and scientific exchange, and to provide the opportunity for Americans to spend some time in Germany.

Nature of Assignment:
Participants conduct research projects in West Germany.

Duration:
Varies, up to maximum support of 3 months.

Eligibility:
United States citizens who have Ph.D. degrees and at least 2 years of teaching or research experience beyond the doctorate.

Number of Awards:
Varies from year to year, depending on available funds.

Financial Data:
Monthly maintenance allowance and funds for travel inside West Germany but not international travel.

Application Deadline:
January 31 and October 31 of each year.

Request Application from:
German Academic Exchange Service
 (DAAD)
New York Office
One Fifth Avenue
New York, New York 10003

GERMAN ACADEMIC EXCHANGE SERVICE (DAAD) [126]

Program Title:
Summer Language Courses at Goethe Institutes

Purpose:
To promote international relations between universities, especially in the area of academic and scientific exchange, and to provide the opportunity for Americans to spend some time in Germany.

Nature of Assignment:
Participants attend an intensive language program at one of the Goethe Institutes in West Germany.

Duration:
2 months during the Summer.

Eligibility:
United States citizens who are enrolled in American universities; have completed at least 2 years of college, including a year of college level German; and are between 19 and 32 years of age. German majors are not eligible for support through this program.

Number of Awards:
Varies from year to year, depending on available funds.

Financial Data:
Participants receive stipends to cover tuition and fees, room, and partial board.

Application Deadline:
January 31 of each year.

Request Application from:
German Academic Exchange Service
 (DAAD)
New York Office
One Fifth Avenue
New York, New York 10003

1st SUPPLEMENT

Directory of Internships, Work Experience Programs, and On-the-Job Training Opportunities

GERMAN ACADEMIC EXCHANGE SERVICE (DAAD) [127]

Program Title:
Traineeships in Agriculture

Purpose:
To promote international relations between universities, especially in the area of academic and scientific exchange, and to provide the opportunity for Americans to spend some time in Germany.

Nature of Assignment:
Trainees participate in work experience programs on farms or in agricultural research institutes in West Germany.

Duration:
3 months during the Summer with the possibility of extending the stay.

Eligibility:
Students in agriculture or related disciplines who have had previous practical training in agriculture, possess a driver's license and have a working knowledge of German. Applicants must be United States citizens.

Number of Awards:
Varies from year to year, depending on available funds.

Financial Data:
Trainees receive free room and board plus an extra allowance; no funds for travel costs are provided.

Application Deadline:
November 30 for a Traineeship the following Summer.

Request Application from:
German Academic Exchange Service (DAAD)
New York Office
One Fifth Avenue
New York, New York 10003

GIRLS CLUB OF ALBANY, GEORGIA, INC. [128]

Program Title:
Volunteer, Internship and Work Study Programs

Purpose:
To help girls make use of their leisure time through involvement in program activities at an education and guidance center.

Nature of Assignment:
Participants assist various class instructors; work directly with girls in numerous areas, such as recreation, homework, rap sessions and individual instruction; and take part in weekly staff meetings.

Duration:
Open.

Eligibility:
Individuals who have interests and skills appropriate to the Club's program. Applicants must enjoy and be able to work with a group or girls and genuinely care about girls' problems, growth and self-improvement.

Number of Awards:
Open.

Financial Data:
Varies; participants can volunteer without pay receive Intern remuneration through CETA or be paid by a college work-study program.

Special Features:
Participants can arrange to receive college credit for working with the Club.

Application Deadline:
Applications are accepted at any time.

1st SUPPLEMENT

Directory of Internships, Work Experience Programs, and On-the-Job Training Opportunities

Request Application from:
Girls Club of Albany
P.O. Box 1366
Albany, Georgia 31702

GRAND RAPIDS, MICHIGAN [129]

Program Title:
Urban Corps

Purpose:
To employ college students in positions that correlate with their major courses of study.

Nature of Assignment:
Participants are assigned various duties with City departments and agencies. The assignments are intended to give Corps members on-the-job work experience relating to their academic studies.

Duration:
Varies, depending upon available funding.

Eligibility:
College students who meet HEW work-study criteria as interpreted by their school's financial aid office.

Number of Awards:
Approximately 350 per year.

Financial Data:
$3.00 per hour for undergraduates and $3.25 per hour for graduate students.

Application Deadline:
Varies, depending on applicant's college schedule.

Request Application from:
Coordinator
Grand Rapids Urban Corps
Sheldon Complex - Lower Level
121 Franklin SE
Grand Rapids, Michigan 49507

GREATER PHILADELPHIA GROUP NEWSPAPERS [130]

Program Title:
College Internship Program

Purpose:
To offer journalism background to those interested in a writing career.

Nature of Assignment:
Interns gain experience in various aspects of newspaper work including reporting, photography, editing and layout.

Duration:
Flexible.

Eligibility:
College juniors or seniors who have interests and abilities appropriate to the work.

Number of Awards:
Varies from year to year.

Financial Data:
Volunteer only.

Application Deadline:
Applications are accepted at any time.

Request Application from:
Greater Philadelphia Group Newspapers
250 West Girard Avenue
Philadelphia, Pennsylvania 19123

GREENFIELD VILLAGE AND HENRY FORD MUSEUM [131]

Program Title:
Special Internships

1st SUPPLEMENT

Directory of Internships, Work Experience Programs, and On-the-Job Training Opportunities

Purpose:
To provide college students with an opportunity to become familiar with various aspects of museum operations and collections.

Nature of Assignment:
Interns work on a one-to-one basis with a Museum staff Sponsor who can come from any department of the Village or Museum, such as curatorial, education, crafts, public relations, display and conservation. Interns are assigned all types of duties by their Sponsors.

Duration:
Varies, with arrangements mutually agreed upon by Intern and Sponsor; full or part time.

Eligibility:
College and university students (undergraduate and graduate) who have interests and abilities appropriate to working in a museum setting. Applicants must obtain and submit a letter stating that, if accepted, the Special Internship would be considered an official part of their college program, with or without credit.

Number of Awards:
Varies, Internships are available only on a limited basis.

Financial Data:
Volunteer only.

Stipulations:
During the selection process, applicants must be prepared to travel to Dearborn, Michigan, and appear before the Intern Committee.

Special Features:
Interns may arrange to receive academic credit for participation in the program.

Application Deadline:
At least 3 months before the desired beginning date of an Internship.

Request Application from:
Educational Resources Division
Education Department
Greenfield Village
Dearborn, Michigan 48121

GREENFIELD VILLAGE AND HENRY FORD MUSEUM [132]

Program Title:
Work-Study Internship for Undergraduate Potters

Purpose:
To provide an opportunity for a pottery student to gain experience in studio operation and to specialize in a certain period and style of ceramics.

Nature of Assignment:
The Internship provides for full-time work in the Greenfield Village Pottery where experience will be gained in pottery shop operation including production, record keeping, and marketing. By working in an environment which illustrates late 19th Century operations, Interns gain unique experience in clay and glaze preparation, kiln work, wheel throwing, hand building, and decorating-finishing.

Duration:
8 - 12 weeks, depending on the Intern's schedule, during the Summer; full time (5 8-hour days per week).

Eligibility:
Undergraduate students presently enrolled in degree programs who have been making pottery for at least 2 years, including wheel work.

Number of Awards:
1 per year.

Financial Data:
Honorarium of $100 per week.

1st SUPPLEMENT

Directory of Internships, Work Experience Programs, and On-the-Job Training Opportunities

Stipulations:
Interns must keep regular hours and thus learn the regimen necessary for economically practical studio production. The Intern's schedule will include both week-ends and holidays. Applicants must be prepared to travel to Dearborn, Michigan, for personal interview.

Special Features:
Interns may arrange to receive college credit for work at the Village.

Application Deadline:
Approximately May 10 preceding the desired Internship Summer.

Request Application from:
Educational Resources Division
Education Department
Greenfield Village
Dearborn, Michigan 48121

h

HARRISBURG AREA RAPE CRISIS CENTER [133]

Program Title:
Internship Program

Purpose:
To train people in support of the Center's program.

Nature of Assignment:
Interns are assigned a variety of tasks including crisis counseling for victims of sexual assault; accompaniment of victims through medical, police and legal systems; public and professional education; research; and statistical compilation. Participants also act as legislative liaisons and assist in layout and writing for Center newsletters.

Duration:
Varies, with a minimum 3 month commitment preferred.

Eligibility:
Undergraduate or graduate college students who have appropriate interests and abilities, are at least 18 years of age, and have a commitment to assist victims of sexual assault.

Number of Awards:
No limitation.

Financial Data:
No financial reimbursement available.

Stipulations:
Participants must attend an 8 week initial training program for one evening per week.

Application Deadline:
Applications are accepted at any time.

Request Application from:
Harrisburg Area Rape Crisis Center
P.O. Box 38
Harrisburg, Pennsylvania 17018

HAWTHORNE GIRL SCOUT COUNCIL, INC. [134]

Program Title:
Executive Staff Internship Program

Purpose:
To give college students the opportunity to experience firsthand the job of an executive staff member in girl scouting.

Nature of Assignment:
Interns work with incumbent staff in bringing service to geographic units of jurisdiction, complete a relevant independent project, and participate in supervised on-the-job training.

Duration:
Minimum of 8 weeks and maximum of 1 semester during the school year; preferably full time.

Eligibility:
College students who are at least in their junior year with preference given to seniors. Applicants must have their own car.

Number of Awards:
3 per year.

Financial Data:
Volunteer only; on-the-job travel expenses are paid.

Special Features:
Council will also consider requests for Public Relations or Program Interns.

Application Deadline:
Applications are accepted at any time.

Request Application from:
Executive Director
Hawthorne Girl Scout Council, Inc.
42 Locust Street
Danvers, Massachusetts 01923

HEBREW UNIVERSITY OF JERUSALEM [135]

Program Title:
Tobias Landau Fellowships in Marine Biology

Purpose:
To support research in marine biology and promote the exchange of researchers between the United States and Israel.

Nature of Assignment:
American participants conduct research at the Heinz Steinitz Marine Biology Laboratory in Elat, Israel, while Israeli participants conduct research at an appropriate marine station in the United States.

Duration:
1 year or less.

Eligibility:
Postdoctoral researchers in marine biology who are American or Israeli citizens.

Number of Awards:
1 with the possibility of more.

Financial Data:
Fellowships are limited to a total of $5,000 per year.

Application Deadline:
December 31 of each year.

Request Application from:
Tobias Landau Fellowships
918 16th Street, N.W.
Suite 503
Washington, D.C. 20006

HIGH POINT MUSEUM [136]

Program Title:
Internship Program

Purpose:
To provide practical training experience for students of museumology.

Nature of Assignment:
Interns are assigned tasks in all phases of museum work from exhibit design to management.

Duration:
4 months.

Eligibility:
Bachelor's or Master's degree candidates or graduates who have appropriate interests and academic backgrounds.

Number of Awards:
6 per year.

Financial Data:
Interns pay a fee of $400 for the training program.

Application Deadline:
Applications are accepted at any time.

Request Application from:
Director
High Point Museum
1805 East Lexington Avenue
High Point, North Carolina 27262

HIGH POINT YOUTH FOR CHRIST, INC. [137]

Program Title:
Youth Guidance and Campus Life Internship Program

Purpose:
To train college graduates for a full-time ministry with delinquent youth or high school age young people.

Nature of Assignment:
Interns perform various work and counseling duties and are involved with young people on a daily basis through several types of programs. Interns spend 4 hours per week in the classroom and are assigned 30 hours a week field experience with a full-time staff member as supervisor.

Duration:
1 - 2 years; full time.

Eligibility:
College graduates who are interested in young people and want a full-time Christian ministry.

Financial Data:
Participants must support themselves during the Internship.

Stipulations:
Interns must participate in a training program which includes 3 - 4 weeks of indepth classroom work at Rockford College in Illinois.

Application Deadline:
April 30 and October 30 of each year.

Request Application from:
Y.F.C.I. - Training Division
P.O. Box 419
Wheaton, Illinois 60187
  or
High Point Youth For Christ
P.O. Box 1135
High Point, North Carolina 27261

HINTON RURAL LIFE CENTER [138]

Program Title:
Volunteer Action Service Teams (VAST)

Purpose:
To train young persons in ministry to people and to provide needed Summer staff for church-related programs.

Nature of Assignment:
Participants work in a church-related ministry under the supervision of a field director and usually fit into an ongoing ministry by helping to develop a new phase of work which the regular staff has not had time to develop. Work assignments are varied from lake front activities to teaching Vatican Church School, leading day camps, working with children of underprivileged families, or developing a Summer recreation program.

Duration:
9 weeks during the Summer: 1 week of training and 8 weeks of work.

Eligibility:
Individuals who have had one year of college and are interested in working in church-related positions for the Summer.

Financial Data:
Participants are guaranteed room, board, and travel expenses connected with their work after arrival at Hinton Center. A small stipend, ranging from $100 to $200 for the Summer, is usually also provided.

Stipulations:
Attendance is required at a training program held at the Center in early June. At the end of the training period, participants leave the Center for assigned ministries.

Application Deadline:
April 1 preceding the desired Summer work.

Request Application from:
Hinton Rural Life Center
P.O. Box 27
Hayesville, North Carolina 28904

THE HISTORICAL SOCIETY OF DELAWARE [139]

Program Title:
Summer Intern Program

Purpose:
To give senior students of American history an opportunity to work in the field of library administration.

Nature of Assignment:
Interns work at facilities of The American Philosophical Society, The Library Company of Philadelphia or The Historical Society of Delaware. Duties assigned Interns expose them to all types of library work including the cataloging and preservation of various kinds of resource materials, such as manuscripts and rare books.

Duration:
Summer; full time.

Eligibility:
College students who have completed junior year studies majoring in American history and who will be returning to school as seniors after participation in the Program. Applicants must be residents of the Wilmington-Philadelphia area.

Number of Awards:
1 - 4 per Summer.

Financial Data:
Stipends of $75 per week and transportation costs between Philadelphia and Wilmington.

Stipulations:
Applicants must complete a 3 hour examination which tests their reading and writing abilities and general accumulated knowledge.

Application Deadline:
April 1 of each year.

Request Application from:
The Historical Society of Delaware
505 Market Street
Wilmington, Delaware 19801

HOLY TRINITY COMMUNITY CENTER [140]

Program Title:
Youth and Community Development Program

Purpose:
To offer experience in the area of youth work, delinquency prevention and neighborhood improvement.

Nature of Assignment:
Participants are involved in coordinating year-round youth programs, developing new programs for youth and adults, and conducting community organizational work.

Duration:
Full-time or part-time work during the Summer.

Eligibility:
Individuals who have had experience working in a city and have the ability to work with youth.

Financial Data:
Volunteer with the possibility of maintenance and a stipend being offered.

Application Deadline:
Applications are accepted at any time.

Request Application from:
Director
Holy Trinity Community Center
643 West 17th Street
Erie, Pennsylvania 16502

HONOLULU, HAWAII. MAYOR'S OFFICE OF INFORMATION AND COMPLAINT [141]

Program Title:
College Student Summer Employment: Artist Position

Purpose:
To provide work experience for graphic arts students and to provide them with an income to help defray college expenses.

Nature of Assignment:
The artist is assigned to do artwork for City publications, posters, and layout work. Supervision and instruction in these tasks will be provided.

Duration:
Full time during the Summer.

Eligibility:
Students who have completed at least the freshman year of college and have had some graphic arts experience.

Number of Awards:
1 each year.

Financial Data:
Hourly wage is paid, based on years of college completed; student earns approximately $1,500 for the Summer.

Application Deadline:
April 1 of each year.

Request Application from:
Department of Civil Service
Recruitment Branch
City Hall Annex
Honolulu, Hawaii 96813

1st SUPPLEMENT

Directory of Internships, Work Experience Programs, and On-the-Job Training Opportunities

HONOLULU, HAWAII. MAYOR'S OFFICE OF INFORMATION AND COMPLAINT [142]

Program Title:
College Student Summer Employment: Information Position

Purpose:
To provide work experience for journalism students and to provide them with an income to help defray college expenses.

Nature of Assignment:
The student writes press releases, answers inquiries about the City and County of Honolulu, and performs other duties as assigned.

Duration:
Full time during the Summer.

Eligibility:
Students who have completed at least the freshman year of college and have had some journalism or other writing experience.

Number of Awards:
1 each year.

Financial Data:
Hourly wage is paid, based on years of college completed; student earns approximately $1,500 for the Summer.

Stipulations:
Applicants must have some knowledge of Honolulu.

Application Deadline:
April 1 of each year.

Request Application from:
Department of Civil Service
Recruitment Branch
City Hall Annex
Honolulu, Hawaii 96813

HUNGARIAN CULTURAL FOUNDATION [143]

Program Title:
Internship Program

Purpose:
To acquaint interested parties, especially students, with the editorial and corporate functions of the Foundation and to prepare students for Hungarian studies or travel in Hungary.

Nature of Assignment:
Interns are assigned various duties, such as preparing manuscripts for publication, contacting publishers and maintaining the library.

Duration:
Full or part time during the Summer.

Eligibility:
High school graduates who plan to continue their education and are interested in Hungarian studies or culture. Some knowledge of the Hungarian language would be helpful.

Number of Awards:
2 per year.

Financial Data:
Volunteer only; room and board is available.

Special Features:
Interns are provided an opportunity to practice the Hungarian language.

Application Deadline:
Applications are accepted at any time.

Request Application from:
Hungarian Cultural Foundation
P.O. Box 364
Stone Mountain, Georgia 30086

i

ILLINOIS LEGISLATIVE STUDIES CENTER [144]

Program Title:
Illinois Private Sector Legislative Internship Program

Purpose:
To afford graduate students of promise the opportunity to observe the operations of the Illinois General Assembly from the perspective of a private association while at the same time pursuing studies related to the influence of the private sector on public policy.

Nature of Assignment:
Interns are assigned to legislative research positions with private associations, such as the Illinois Manufacturers Association and the Illinois Realtors Association.

Duration:
9½ months, October 1 - July 15; full time.

Eligibility:
Students who will have completed the Bachelor's degree prior to starting an Internship and have demonstrated capability for graduate study. Applicants must have a minimum grade point average of 2.75 (A = 4.0) in the last 2 years of undergraduate study or previous graduate work.

Number of Awards:
Approximately 5 per year.

Financial Data:
Stipend of $650 per month.

Stipulations:
Interns are required to participate in an academic seminar carrying 8 semester hours credit at Sangamon State University. A major research paper will also be required.

Application Deadline:
March 1 of each year.

Request Application from:
Director
Illinois Legislative Studies Center
Sangamon State University
Brookens 310 F
Springfield, Illinois 62708

IMMIGRATION HISTORY RESEARCH CENTER [145]

Program Title:
Work Experience and On-the-Job Training

Purpose:
To train qualified individuals in the basic archival and library techniques useful in non-English language collections.

Nature of Assignment:
Participants are assigned to preliminary processing of manuscript collections and preliminary cataloging of monographs and periodicals.

Duration:
Varies; terms negotiated with the Curator of the Center.

Eligibility:
Individuals who have an interest in library and/or archival work and reading ability in one or more of the languages represented in the Center's library. The Center includes source material on American ethnic groups originating in Eastern and Southern Europe and the Middle East.

Number of Awards:
Varies.

Financial Data:
Volunteer only.

Application Deadline:
Applications are accepted at any time.

Request Application from:
Curator
Immigration History Research Center
University of Minnesota
826 Berry Street
St. Paul, Minnesota 55114

IN RECORDS AUDIO PRESENTATIONS [146]

Program Title:
Program Development Internships

Purpose:
To train program production personnel in writing, researching and announcing for radio.

Nature of Assignment:
Interns are assigned to writing, researching and announcing for weekly, biweekly and monthly radio series and general syndication specials.

Duration:
Varies, depending on Intern.

Eligibility:
Individuals who have interests and skills appropriate to production of radio shows with musical formats. Preference is given to applicants under 30.

Number of Awards:
10 - 20 per year.

Financial Data:
Volunteer with some expenses paid and the possibility of leading to a salaried position.

Stipulations:
Some travel will be required, mainly to interview artists.

Application Deadline:
Applications are accepted at any time.

Request Application from:
In Records Audio Presentations
P.O. Box 7293
Riverside, California 92513

INDEPENDENT COMMUNITY CONSULTANTS, INC. [147]

Program Title:
Community Development Internship Program

Purpose:
To train students, as well as employed social change and community development workers, in special community development skill areas.

Nature of Assignment:
Interns are assigned to ICC offices where they work on structured learning programs that are self-directed.

Duration:
4 - 12 weeks during the Summer, or the entire Summer.

Eligibility:
Students who are enrolled in accredited B.A./B.S. degree programs or individuals who are employed in community development programs. Applicants must be able to identify specific learning goals to be achieved through Internships participation.

Number of Awards:
Maximum of 5 per year.

Financial Data:
There is a $300 per month fee to join the Internship Program.

Application Deadline:
Applications are accepted at any time.

Request Application from:
Director
Independent Community Consultants, Inc.
P.O. Box 141
Hampton, Arkansas 71744

INDIANA. HOUSE OF REPRESENTATIVES [148]

Program Title:
House Democratic Caucus Intern Program

Purpose:
To give students a firsthand look at the legislative process and an opportunity to develop basic skills necessary to properly filling a staff position.

Nature of Assignment:
The Intern is considered a regular member of the staff and performs duties in a variety of areas, such as constituent relations, legislative analysis, press relations and research.

Duration:
Length of a session: 4 months in odd numbered years and 3 months in even numbered years.

Eligibility:
College students in any subject area who are interested in the legislative process.

Number of Awards:
1 each year.

Financial Data:
$75 per week.

Application Deadline:
December 5 of each year.

Request Application from:
House Democratic Caucus Intern Program
State House
Indianapolis, Indiana 46205

INDIANAPOLIS, INDIANA [149]

Program Title:
Mayor's Summer Intern Program

Purpose:
To utilize the abilities and talents of college students while at the same time introducing them to the mechanics of local government.

Nature of Assignment:
Interns research projects on matters relating to the City of Indianapolis. Weekly seminars are held for the purpose of instructing Interns in the operations of city government.

Duration:
12 weeks during the Summer; full time.

Eligibility:
Students who are registered in accredited colleges or universities and are residents of Marion County, Indiana.

Number of Awards:
  4 per year.

Financial Data:
  $100 per week.

Application Deadline:
  April 1 of each year.

Request Application from:
  Mayor's Summer Intern Program
  Room 2501
  City-County Building
  Indianapolis, Indiana 46204

INLAND DIVISION, GENERAL MOTORS CORPORATION [150]

Program Title:
  Coop and Internship Program

Purpose:
  To acquaint students with the Corporation in order to recruit for permanent positions.

Nature of Assignment:
  Interns are given a variety of assignments in all staff areas including manufacturing, engineering, comptroller's office, quality control, and production material control.

Duration:
  Summer or other agreed upon Coop periods.

Eligibility:
  College and university students who are candidates for technical or engineering degrees and have the required grade point average.

Financial Data:
  Varies, depending on students and assignments involved.

Application Deadline:
  Applications are accepted from September to April.

Request Application from:
  Manager, Salaried Employment
  Inland Division
  General Motors Corporation
  P.O. Box 1224
  Dayton, Ohio 45401

INNER CITY CULTURAL CENTER [151]

Program Title:
  Internship Program

Purpose:
  To provide opportunities for interested persons to acquire knowledge of the operations of a multi-purpose cultural facility.

Nature of Assignment:
  Interns are assigned duties in administrative, technical, publicity, publications and concessions aspects of the Center.

Duration:
  Undetermined; full or part time.

Eligibility:
  Individuals who have strong interests in the arts and abilities appropriate to working with a major cultural institution serving a varied ethnic and economic constituency.

Number of Awards:
  Unlimited.

Financial Data:
  Volunteer only.

Application Deadline:
  Applications are accepted at any time.

Request Application from:
Inner City Cultural Center
1308 South New Hampshire Avenue
Los Angeles, California 90006

INROADS/MILWAUKEE, INC. [152]

Program Title:
Summer Internships

Purpose:
To stimulate and assist minority students in obtaining degrees in Business Administration or Engineering.

Nature of Assignment:
Interns are exposed to work related to their academic careers in business or engineering.

Duration:
4 consecutive Summers of work.

Eligibility:
Minority students who are high school seniors planning to attend 4 year colleges or universities and interested in business or engineering. Applicants must reside in the Milwaukee area.

Number of Awards:
6 - 8 per year.

Financial Data:
Summer earnings vary, depending on each Intern's abilities and job assignment.

Application Deadline:
April 30 of each year.

Request Application from:
INROADS/Milwaukee, Inc.
P.O. Box 1241
Milwaukee, Wisconsin 53201

INROADS/ST. LOUIS, INC. [153]

Program Title:
General Program Assistance

Purpose:
To assist in providing minority (black and latin) college and pre-college students with educational support services and direct on-the-job career opportunities.

Nature of Assignment:
Participants offer counseling and guidance services to small groups of high school or college students, conduct training sessions (i.e. Assertive Training, Time Management, Motivational Training) and perform other remedial tasks.

Duration:
Negotiable.

Eligibility:
Individuals who have interests and skills appropriate to working with INROADS. Applicants must be able to relate to gifted minority students, members of the corporate-business sector and educational administrators in a variety of settings.

Number of Awards:
Open.

Financial Data:
Negotiable, depending upon such factors as participant's experience and amount of time available for commitment to the program.

Application Deadline:
Applications are accepted at any time.

Request Application from:
Assistant Director
Student Training and Development
INROADS/St. Louis, Inc.
P.O. Box 8766
St. Louis, Missouri 63102

1st SUPPLEMENT

Directory of Internships, Work Experience Programs, and On-the-Job Training Opportunities

INSTITUTE OF CONTEMPORARY ART [154]

Program Title:
Volunteer Program

Purpose:
To offer the opportunity to participate in the non-curatorial aspects of museum administration.

Nature of Assignment:
Participants are assigned tasks in library cataloging, archive organization and updating, and catalog exchange.

Duration:
Ongoing; part time.

Eligibility:
Interested individuals who have a college degree in art history or library science.

Financial Data:
Volunteer only.

Application Deadline:
Applications are accepted at any time.

Request Application from:
Coordinator of Volunteer Activities
Institute of Contemporary Art
955 Boylston Street
Boston, Massachusetts 02115

INSTITUTE OF GOVERNMENT [155]

Program Title:
Summer Intern Program in State Government

Purpose:
To provide students with a meaningful research or administrative experience in state government.

Nature of Assignment:
Interns work in state agencies helping with research or administrative assignments. Duties vary widely, depending on each agency's needs and Intern's interests and abilities. Interns also participate in an orientation program, attend frequent self-determined seminars, plan and take field trips, and are involved in other activities designed to provide a learning experience tailored to Intern needs and interests.

Duration:
11 weeks during the Summer; full time.

Eligibility:
North Carolina residents who are currently enrolled in college or university programs and will have completed at least 3 years of study before becoming Summer Interns. Students may be attending school within or outside of North Carolina and may be headed for definite public service careers or interested in business, engineering, forestry, teaching, medicine, government administration, politics or law.

Number of Awards:
25 per year.

Financial Data:
$125 a week.

Stipulations:
Unmarried Interns must live in group housing on the North Carolina State University Campus, the cost for which is approximately $130 for the Summer.

Special Features:
Interns may arrange with their own schools to receive academic credit for participation in the Program. As an alternative, 3 hours of political science credit may be received from North Carolina State University by

satisfactorily completing all assignments and paying a registration fee.

Application Deadline:
February 1 of each year.

Request Application from:
Institute of Government
University of North Carolina
P.O. Box 990
Chapel Hill, North Carolina 27514

INSTITUTE OF SOCIETY, ETHICS AND THE LIFE SCIENCES [156]

Program Title:
Student Intern Program

Purpose:
To promote research into the social, ethical and legal problems posed by contemporary work in the life sciences.

Nature of Assignment:
Interns are assigned independent research projects, and usually the production of a paper. Work is done under supervision of a staff member.

Duration:
1 - 3 months; full time.

Eligibility:
College and university students on any level who are working in degree programs. Preference is given to students preparing for careers in law and medicine.

Number of Awards:
10 - 15 per year.

Financial Data:
Small stipends are sometimes available.

Application Deadline:
April 1 for Internships during the Summer; 2 months in advance of desired starting date for Internships at any other time of the year.

Request Application from:
The Hastings Center
360 Broadway
Hastings-on-Hudson, New York 10706

INTER-AMERICAN FOUNDATION [157]

Program Title:
Graduate Student Intern Program

Purpose:
To provide opportunities to apply learning experience to practical problems, and to provide a linkage between the Foundation and social science thinking centered at universities.

Nature of Assignment:
Interns are assigned various tasks, such as project analysis of both future and past work, research on project-related topics, drafting of amendments, and writing letters.

Duration:
Maximum of 1 year or 1040 hours.

Eligibility:
Students enrolled in graduate schools who have analytical abilities; good language skills in Spanish, Portuguese or French; and background courses of living experience in Latin America or the Caribbean.

Number of Awards:
5 - 7 each year.

Financial Data:
Interns are paid by the hour with amounts varying, depending on each Intern's background and training.

Application Deadline:
September 1 of each year.

Request Application from:
Intern Coordinator
Inter-American Foundation
1515 Wilson Boulevard
Rosslyn, Virginia 22209

INTERNATIONAL ASSOCIATION FOR THE EXCHANGE OF STUDENTS FOR TECHNICAL EXPERIENCE/UNITED STATES (IAESTE/US) [158]

Program Title:
IAESTE Trainee Program

Purpose:
To provide career experience and training in a country other than their own for college and university students of engineering, architecture, agriculture, mathematics and the sciences.

Nature of Assignment:
Trainees travel to assigned foreign countries where they receive on-the-job practical training related to their fields and levels of study. Placement may be in a research laboratory, design office, production department or field location, depending on the nature of each trainee's field, background and interests. Offers of training opportunities are requested from other IAESTE member countries on the basis of American student applications. Available offers are then matched with student applicants.

Duration:
Most placements are for 8 - 12 weeks during the Summer, although training programs may be available at other times and for periods of up to 1 year.

Eligibility:
Students currently enrolled in 4 year colleges or universities who will be at least sophomores by the start of the training period but not yet finished with the doctorate if in a Ph.D. program. Applicants must be majoring in one of the fields covered by the sciences, engineering, mathematics, architecture or agriculture.

Number of Awards:
No set amount; varies according to number of applications received from American students and number of offers provided by American employers for use by foreign trainees.

Financial Data:
Trainees receive a maintenance allowance to cover living expenses while in training but are responsible for travel costs and expenses incurred other than during the training period. Trainees can expect $600 - $800 of such extra expenses for a typical 8 - 12 week Summer assignment in Europe.

Stipulations:
Applicants must pay a $50 membership/application fee, $25 of which is refundable if a traineeship is not received. Some of the participating IAESTE countries require Trainees to speak their language, others accept English. A list of participating countries and language requirements is available from IAESTE/US.

Application Deadline:
December 15 for training during the Summer; minimum of 4 months in advance of anticipated starting date for training at any other time of the year.

1st SUPPLEMENT

Directory of Internships, Work Experience Programs, and On-the-Job Training Opportunities

Request Application from:
IAESTE/US, Inc.
217 American City Building
Columbia, Maryland 21044

INTERNATIONAL INSTITUTE OF BUFFALO [159]

Program Title:
Volunteer Work

Purpose:
To help the foreign born and their children become a part of American life and institutions.

Nature of Assignment:
Volunteers act as community aides, teach English, engage in cultural and inter-cultural work with different nationality groups and do clerical tasks.

Duration:
Any length.

Eligibility:
Individuals with interests and skills appropriate to working with the Institute and the ability to relate to people of different backgrounds.

Number of Awards:
Varies, depending on Volunteers' areas of interest and Institute's needs.

Financial Data:
Volunteer only.

Application Deadline:
Applications are accepted at any time.

Request Application from:
International Institute of Buffalo
864 Delaware Avenue
Buffalo, New York 14209

INTERNATIONAL PROGRAM FOR HUMAN RESOURCE DEVELOPMENT, INC. [160]

Program Title:
Intern Positions

Purpose:
To promote educational and employment opportunities in less-developed countries and to help in the marketing of crafts from such areas.

Nature of Assignment:
Assignments vary with Program needs. Interns in the past have done administrative and organizational work, clerical and office tasks, writing and editing, bookkeeping and publicity, marketing and retail selling.

Duration:
6 months or longer.

Eligibility:
Individuals who are interested in working with the Program. The primary requirements are flexibility and willingness to work hard.

Number of Awards:
Varies with needs of the Program.

Financial Data:
$70 per week.

Special Features:
Many Interns fit their academic requirements into their work.

Application Deadline:
Applications are accepted at any time.

Request Application from:
Administrative Assistant
International Program for Human Resource Development, Inc.
7720 Wisconsin Avenue
Bethesda, Maryland 20014

1st SUPPLEMENT

Directory of Internships, Work Experience Programs, and On-the-Job Training Opportunities

IOWA. GENERAL ASSEMBLY [161]

Program Title:
Joint Legislative Internship Program

Purpose:
To offer interested students the opportunity to become better familiar with and partake in the legislative process.

Nature of Assignment:
Interns' duties include writing speeches, drafting and researching legislation, and resolving and responding to constituent inquiries.

Duration:
Legislative session only, January through May.

Eligibility:
Undergraduate and graduate students who are attending Iowa colleges or universities.

Financial Data:
Volunteer only.

Stipulations:
Interns cannot be registered lobbyists.

Special Features:
Participating schools offer credit hours for Internship work.

Application Deadline:
December 1 of each year.

Request Application from:
Office of the Secretary of the Senate
State House
Des Moines, Iowa 50319

IOWA. HOUSE OF REPRESENTATIVES [162]

Program Title:
Internship Program

Purpose:
To acquaint college students with the legislative process and to develop a reservoir of partially trained people for future years.

Nature of Assignment:
Interns assist legislators in a variety of legislative matters, except lobbying other legislators.

Duration:
Legislative session only, January through May.

Eligibility:
College juniors, seniors or graduate students who are interested in the Program and qualify under regulations of sponsoring schools.

Number of Awards:
30 - 40 per year.

Financial Data:
Volunteer only with the possibility of some financial support in the future.

Application Deadline:
November 15 of each year.

Request Application from:
Iowa House of Representatives
Capitol Building
Des Moines, Iowa 50319

j

JACKSON COUNTY, OREGON [163]

Program Title:
Intern Program

Purpose:
To provide on-the-job experience for college students.

Nature of Assignment:
Interns work in the County Planning or Parks Department where they gain experience in drafting, surveying (limited), and elementary landuse planning.

Duration:
1 college term (quarter or semester).

Eligibility:
College or university students majoring in appropriate fields. Applicants can be enrolled in architecture, urban planning, and public administration programs or studying in other relevant areas.

Number of Awards:
1 in each Department per term, or 6 per year.

Financial Data:
Interns receive a limited salary.

Application Deadline:
Applications are accepted at any time.

Request Application from:
Personnel Office
Courthouse
Main and Oakdale
Medford, Oregon 97501

JACKSON COUNTY, OREGON [164]

Program Title:
Work-Study Program

Purpose:
To provide work experience for eligible college students.

Nature of Assignment:
Participants work for the Jackson County Library where they assist in performing routine library duties.

Duration:
Students can participate in the Program for up to their entire college careers.

Eligibility:
College students who are eligible for work-study support.

Number of Awards:
6 - 8 per year.

1st SUPPLEMENT

Directory of Internships, Work Experience Programs, and On-the-Job Training Opportunities

Financial Data:
Participants are paid the minimum wage.

Application Deadline:
Applications are accepted at any time.

Request Application from:
Personnel Office
Courthouse
Main and Oakdale
Medford, Oregon 97501

JOHN WOODMAN HIGGINS ARMORY MUSEUM [165]

Program Title:
On-the-Job Training

Purpose:
To provide training opportunities for those interested in museum or arts administration and curatorial skills, while receiving the benefit of extra manpower in return.

Nature of Assignment:
Assignments are varied. Administrative duties might include handling admissions and reservations, dealing with the public (both adults and children, singly and in groups), using audio-visual equipment, providing educational services and doing office work. Curatorial duties involve the care, repair and storage of metal art objects as well as tapestries and carvings.

Duration:
Varies.

Eligibility:
Individuals who have interests and skills appropriate to the Museum's work.

Financial Data:
Volunteer with the possibility of later support. Work-study arrangements with local colleges are also possible.

Special Features:
The Museum is one of the few in the country where the staff is qualified to care for arms and armour.

Application Deadline:
Applications are accepted at any time.

Request Application from:
Higgins Armory
100 Barber Avenue
Worcester, Massachusetts 01606

JOINT CENTER FOR POLITICAL STUDIES [166]

Program Title:
Institutional Development Interns

Purpose:
To assist the Center in providing research, public policy analysis, technical assistance and information for black and other minority elected and appointed officials.

Nature of Assignment:
Interns work with the Director of Development. Duties assigned include research of source data on the philanthropic world, identification of Center markets, and assisting in the formulation of development plans.

Duration:
Interns are accepted on a quarterly or semester basis and are expected to work a minimum of 15 hours per week.

Eligibility:
Upper division undergraduate and graduate students who have appropriate interests and abilities. Preference is given to students with backgrounds in marketing, journalism or business.

Financial Data:
Volunteer only. Arrangements for work-study support may be negotiated in some cases.

Application Deadline:
Applications are accepted at any time.

Request Application from:
Intern Coordinator
Joint Center for Political Studies
1426 H Street, N.W. - Suite 926
Washington, D.C. 20005

JOINT CENTER FOR POLITICAL STUDIES [167]

Program Title:
Public Affairs Interns

Purpose:
To assist the Center in providing research, public policy analysis, technical assistance, and information programs for blacks and other minority elected and appointed officials.

Nature of Assignment:
Interns work with staff specialists in print and broadcast journalism. Duties assigned include editing, media relations, and public relations. Interns also write articles on public policy issues and minority political participation.

Duration:
Interns are accepted on a quarterly or semester basis and are expected to work a minimum of 15 hours per week.

Eligibility:
Upper division undergraduate and graduate students who have long-term interests in journalistic careers. Students with journalism, advertising and public relations majors are preferred, although students in other disciplines may also apply.

Financial Data:
Volunteer only. Arrangements for work-study support may be negotiated in some cases.

Application Deadline:
Applications are accepted at any time.

Request Application from:
Intern Coordinator
Joint Center for Political Studies
1426 H Street, N.W. - Suite 926
Washington, D.C. 20005

JOINT CENTER FOR POLITICAL STUDIES [168]

Program Title:
Research Interns

Purpose:
To assist the Center in providing research, public policy analysis, technical assistance, and information programs for blacks and other minority elected and appointed officials.

Nature of Assignment:
Interns participate in continuing research on public policy issues which affect minority and poor Americans. Such research might deal with small town planning, urban development, drug abuse, housing needs of the black elderly, and various aspects of black political participation.

1st SUPPLEMENT

Directory of Internships, Work Experience Programs, and On-the-Job Training Opportunities

Duration:
Interns are accepted on a quarterly or semester basis and are expected to work a minimum of 15 hours per week.

Eligibility:
Upper division undergraduate and graduate students who have appropriate interests and abilities. Students with the following majors are encouraged to apply: Political Science, Black Studies, Urban Affairs/Planning, Economics, Public Affairs/Administration, Sociology, Geography, History, Education, Statistics and Law.

Financial Data:
Volunteer only. Arrangements for work-study support may be negotiated in some cases.

Stipulations:
Interns must be prepared to contribute substantially to major research efforts and to participate in Center seminars and conferences.

Application Deadline:
Applications are accepted at any time.

Request Application from:
Intern Coordinator
Joint Center for Political Studies
1426 H Street, N.W. - Suite 926
Washington, D.C. 20005

THE JUNCTION, YOUTH RESOURCE CENTER [169]

Program Title:
Internship Program

Purpose:
To provide people with exposure to and experience in a comprehensive youth program which deals with problem prevention, intervention and treatment.

Nature of Assignment:
Interns perform various duties in the areas of clinical, administrative and youth development work. Clinical assignments involve handling small caseloads under close supervision and doing intake work-ups. Administrative duties include assisting in research and report writing. Interns working in youth development help in special programming, such as outdoor experience.

Duration:
Flexible.

Eligibility:
Applicants must be able to work in a progressive environment and function as a youth advocate. Advanced undergraduate students are preferred. Special consideration is given to capable adolescents.

Number of Awards:
5 per year.

Financial Data:
Usually volunteer only; on-the-job travel expenses are reimbursed.

Application Deadline:
Applications are accepted at any time.

Request Application from:
The Junction
Youth Resource Center
65 Daniel Street
Portsmouth, New Hampshire 03801

k

KCSJ/KDJQ RADIO [170]

Program Title:
Internship Program

Purpose:
To provide basic training opportunities for minority students interested in news and air work.

Nature of Assignment:
Participants are given broad responsibilities with specific assignments based on Intern ability and including news gathering as well as some on-air work.

Duration:
Highly flexible.

Eligibility:
Students who are presently enrolled in college or plan to be, are able to read and write well above the average, and have a desire to learn about radio.

Number of Awards:
Varies from year to year.

Financial Data:
Volunteer.

Special Features:
There is the possibility of Internships leading into employment at the station.

Application Deadline:
Applications are accepted at any time.

Request Application from:
KCSJ/KDJQ Radio
315 West 8th
Pueblo, Colorado 81002

KEED [171]

Program Title:
News Internship Program

Purpose:
To facilitate the learning of broadcast news techniques.

Nature of Assignment:
Interns are involved in gathering, writing and reporting radio news and are trained in certain of the technical skills required for such work.

Duration:
Internships of various lengths are available.

Eligibility:
Students who are enrolled in college degree programs, possess appropriate knowledge and skills, and have trainable voices.

Financial Data:
Remuneration is possible.

1st SUPPLEMENT

Directory of Internships, Work Experience Programs, and On-the-Job Training Opportunities

Special Features:
Interns have the opportunity of working with professional staff at a *Billboard* "Country Station of the Year."

Application Deadline:
Applications are accepted at any time.

Request Application from:
KEED
1245 Charnelton
Eugene, Oregon 97401

KFRC RADIO [172]

Program Title:
News/Community Affairs Internship Program

Purpose:
To give students, especially women and minorities, the chance to experience the broadcast industry firsthand.

Nature of Assignment:
Interns are assigned to write public service announcements from the mail; schedule, record and produce free speech messages (done by listeners); interview and edit (including writing cut sheets) for newscasts; write and record a complete newscast (not aired); conduct interviews for, edit, write (script plus appropriate music) and produce a half-hour documentary; and complete other tasks as requested.

Duration:
At least 6 hours a day, Monday through Friday, for a minimum of 6 weeks.

Eligibility:
Applicants must be college students who have arranged to receive academic credit for their Internship work. Preference is given to juniors, seniors and graduate students.

Number of Awards:
Varies; usually 2 Interns at a time.

Financial Data:
Volunteer only.

Application Deadline:
Applications are accepted at any time.

Request Application from:
Community Affairs Director
KFRC Radio
415 Bush Street
San Francisco, California 94108

KIVA-TV [173]

Program Title:
KIVA-TV Internship Program

Purpose:
To train students for possible future employment, or to offer training experience for future job-seeking endeavors.

Nature of Assignment:
Interns are given a variety of assignments in news reporting and photography, production photography, editing, and commercial script writing.

Duration:
Flexible.

Eligibility:
College students who are working toward degrees in areas associated with broadcasting.

Financial Data:
Volunteer only.

Application Deadline:
Applications are accepted at any time.

Request Application from:
KIVA-TV
P.O. Box 1620
Farmington, New Mexico 87401

Request Application from:
The KIXY Stations
City Hall Plaza
San Angelo, Texas 76903

THE KIXY STATIONS [174]

Program Title:
KIXY Internship Program

Purpose:
To develop careers for young men and women in all phases of the broadcast industry.

Nature of Assignment:
Interns are given experience in all aspects of broadcasting from working as air personalities to assignments in news, investigative reporting, traffic, sales and bookkeeping.

Duration:
Flexible; full or part time acceptable.

Eligibility:
Interested people who have skills appropriate to the work and at least a high school education.

Number of Awards:
Varies year to year.

Financial Data:
Amount of remuneration is dependent on job classification; Interns also receive expenses.

Application Deadline:
Applications are accepted at any time.

KWKI - FM [175]

Program Title:
KWKI Internship Program

Purpose:
To provide students with a broadbased knowledge of radio station operations in a major market.

Nature of Assignment:
Interns perform various duties as they are rotated through the sales, operations and programming departments.

Duration:
3 months for 12 hours per week.

Eligibility:
College and university students who are enrolled in programs with a broadcast based curriculum.

Number of Awards:
Maximum of 8 per year.

Financial Data:
Volunteer only.

Application Deadline:
Applications are reviewed on a quarterly basis and should be submitted by March 15, May 15, August 15 or December 15.

Request Application from:
Internship Program
KWKI - FM
1722 Main Street
Kansas City, Missouri 64108

1st SUPPLEMENT

Directory of Internships, Work Experience Programs, and On-the-Job Training Opportunities

KANSAS. DEPARTMENT OF HEALTH AND ENVIRONMENT [176]

Program Title:
Work Experience Program

Purpose:
To promote good health among seasonal and migrant farmworkers and to teach them to become independent.

Nature of Assignment:
Participants are assigned to assist the health educator, assist public health nurses, or perform secretarial work.

Duration:
Summer only.

Eligibility:
Individuals who have appropriate interests and skills with Spanish speaking applicants preferred.

Number of Awards:
3 each Summer.

Financial Data:
Volunteer only.

Stipulations:
Participants should be able to travel.

Application Deadline:
May 5 of each year.

Request Application from:
Migrant Health Service
1516 North Taylor
Garden City, Kansas 67846

KANSAS CITY, MISSOURI [177]

Program Title:
MPA Internship

Purpose:
To provide opportunities for training and practical experience in public administration.

Nature of Assignment:
Interns rotate among various staff and line departments.

Duration:
1 year, beginning in May.

Eligibility:
Applicants must be recent MPA graduates or have completed all course work with an internship required for graduation.

Number of Awards:
3 per year.

Financial Data:
$1,000 per month on contract.

Application Deadline:
March 1 of each year.

Request Application from:
Director of Administration
City Manager's Office
City Hall - 29th Floor
Kansas City, Missouri 64106

KENTUCKY. DEPARTMENT FOR LOCAL GOVERNMENT [178]

Program Title:
HUD Work Study Program

Purpose:
To attract qualified applicants into careers in state and local government.

Nature of Assignment:
Participants work with professional staff at the Department or with those of local governments and area development districts.

Duration:
Varies; usually Summer or semester in length.

Eligibility:
Interested and qualified students who have backgrounds in public administration, planning, economics or political science. Preference is given to Kentucky residents or students attending school in Kentucky.

Number of Awards:
Varies, depending upon budget considerations.

Financial Data:
Students are paid varying amounts, depending on their backgrounds and assignments.

Application Deadline:
Applications are accepted at any time.

Request Application from:
Chief Executive Assistant
Department for Local Government
318 Capitol Annex
Frankfurt, Kentucky 40601

KENTUCKY. DEPARTMENT FOR LOCAL GOVERNMENT [179]

Program Title:
Internship Program

Purpose:
To attract qualified applicants into careers in state and local government.

Nature of Assignment:
Interns are assigned various research tasks.

Duration:
Varies; usually Summer or semester in length.

Eligibility:
Individuals who have interests and skills appropriate to the work. Preference is generally given to senior undergraduate or graduate students who are Kentucky residents or attending schools in Kentucky.

Number of Awards:
Varies, depending upon budget.

Financial Data:
Interns have been both unpaid and paid in the past.

Application Deadline:
Applications are accepted at any time.

Request Application from:
Chief Executive Assistant
Department for Local Government
318 Capitol Annex
Frankfurt, Kentucky 40601

KING COUNTY ASSOCIATION FOR RETARDED CITIZENS [180]

Program Title:
Social Work with the Handicapped

Purpose:
To give students experience in assisting developmentally disabled persons and their families cope with problems and receive appropriate services.

Nature of Assignment:
Participants conduct interviews and provide supportive casework services.

Duration:
Varies; can be arranged to meet needs of student volunteers.

Eligibility:
Graduate or undergraduate students who are enrolled in social work, social welfare or counseling programs.

Number of Awards:
2 per year.

Financial Data:
Volunteer only; reimbursement for mileage incurred on the job.

Application Deadline:
Applications are accepted at any time.

Request Application from:
King County Association for Retarded Citizens
2230 Eighth Avenue
Seattle, Washington 98121

KING COUNTY ASSOCIATION FOR RETARDED CITIZENS   [181]

Program Title:
Specialized Recreation Program

Purpose:
To give students experience in providing specialized recreation for mildly retarded young adults.

Nature of Assignment:
Participants teach or assist with classes in recreation skills.

Duration:
Varies; can be arranged to meet needs of student volunteers.

Eligibility:
College and university students who are enrolled in programs of therapeutic recreation.

Number of Awards:
2 per year.

Financial Data:
Volunteer only; reimbursement for mileage incurred on the job.

Application Deadline:
Applications are accepted at any time.

Request Application from:
King County Association for Retarded Citizens
2230 Eighth Avenue
Seattle, Washington 98121

KORVETTES   [182]

Program Title:
Merchandising Co-Op

Purpose:
To acquaint trainees with the operations and functions of a chain store buying office.

Nature of Assignment:
Student participants are engaged in para-professional activities. Each serves as an assistant to a buyer and has the opportunity to observe vendor negotiations, attend advertising meetings, and have extensive store and vendor contact. Weekly seminars are held during the Fall session.

Duration:
6 weeks - 6 months, depending on university work release period; full time.

Eligibility:
College students who have completed at least 2 years of course work, are committed to careers in retail merchandising, and have had some retail selling experience.

Number of Awards:
Approximately 25 per year.

Financial Data:
Participants receive highly competitive salaries plus merchandise discounts.

Application Deadline:
Applications should be submitted by August 1 for Merchandising Co-Op positions during the Fall.

Request Application from:
College Relations Manager
Korvettes/Personnel
450 West 33rd Street
New York, New York 10001

LARIMER COUNTY, COLORADO [183]

Program Title:
CETA Programs

Purpose:
To train and employ disadvantaged people to enhance their possibilities for continued unsubsidized employment and extend avenues for their upward mobility.

Nature of Assignment:
Participants receive on-the-job training and work-experience assignments in a variety of county placements.

Duration:
On-the-job training is full time; work-experience assignments are part time.

Eligibility:
County residents who are economically disadvantaged, unemployed, underemployed, or specially targeted segments of the County population.

Financial Data:
Varied, depending on nature of job assignments; includes regular County benefits, such as sick and normal leave.

Application Deadline:
Applications are accepted at any time.

Request Application from:
Director
Larimer County CETA
P.O. Box 1190
Fort Collins, Colorado 80522

LAS VEGAS MENTAL HEALTH CENTER [184]

Program Title:
Internship in Community Mental Health

Purpose:
To provide a supervised training experience within a comprehensive community mental health center setting.

Nature of Assignment:
Interns receive assignments on a rotating basis with experience provided in assessment and individual, family and group psychotherapy. Interns work with adolescents and adults, as both outpatients and inpatients. Placement with a staff member from advocacy, active involvement in community consultation and program evaluation, and the opportunity to learn about administration from a director's point of view can be arranged.

Duration:
1 year, beginning July 1.

Eligibility:
Applicants must have completed all course work for the Ph.D. degree in clinical or counseling psychology, including supervised practica, and the dissertation should be close to completion.

Number of Awards:
1 per year.

Financial Data:
Stipend of approximately $10,500 plus vacation and sick leave.

Stipulations:
Interviews may be required of applicants.

Application Deadline:
January 30 for an Internship to begin in July.

Request Application from:
Director of Training
Las Vegas Mental Health Center
6161 West Charleston
Las Vegas, Nevada 89102

LEADERSHIP TRAINING INSTITUTE. HOPE COMMUNITY CENTER [185]

Program Title:
Volunteer Program

Purpose:
To stress community leadership and increase resident awareness in the areas of community services, education and increased educational motivation.

Nature of Assignment:
Volunteers are responsible for implementing and evaluating the tutorial program. Volunteers also work in the community to involve residents in the Center and its programs.

Duration:
Volunteers can work anytime during the year, full or part time.

Eligibility:
Individuals interested in the Center's work who have college degrees in some social science area and/or experience in community outreach and youth programs.

Financial Data:
Volunteer only.

Application Deadline:
Applications are accepted at any time.

Request Application from:
Director
LTI Hope Community Center
4411 Meadow Street
Dallas, Texas 75215

1st SUPPLEMENT

Directory of Internships, Work Experience Programs, and On-the-Job Training Opportunities

LEXINGTON PLANNED PARENTHOOD CENTER, INC. [186]

Program Title:
On-the-Job Training

Purpose:
To provide work experience for students.

Nature of Assignment:
Participants receive on-the-job training as pregnancy counselors, doctor's assistants, and patient educators and are given general clerical experience for work in counseling situations or medical offices.

Duration:
Prefer commitment of at least 1 semester, not shorter than 4 months.

Eligibility:
Individuals who have interests and skills appropriate to the Center. Preference is given to college students in community health, education, psychology or counseling. Applicants must believe in the philosophy of the agency.

Number of Awards:
2 - 3 per year.

Financial Data:
Volunteer only.

Application Deadline:
Applications are accepted at any time.

Request Application from:
Executive Director
Lexington Planned Parenthood Center, Inc.
508 West Second Street
Lexington, Kentucky 40508

THE LISLE FELLOWSHIP, INC. [187]

Program Title:
Institute in Intercultural Human Relations

Purpose:
To offer educational programs, here and abroad, which allow for personal development, intercultural group living and experiential learning.

Nature of Assignment:
Participants receive practical experience through field assignments as part of small international teams with human service programs. Assignments involve participants in daily activities of the staff. Arrangements are informal and stress the goal of sharing cross-cultural perspectives.

Duration:
6 weeks during the Summer; part time.

Eligibility:
Upper division students and non-students between the ages of 18 and 35 who have the openness to share in intercultural group settings.

Financial Data:
Participants pay varying fees, specific amounts depending on the field work area involved; for instance, programs in Washington, D.C. have a $650 fee while those abroad are higher. Some scholarship assistance is available.

Application Deadline:
April 15 of each year.

Request Application from:
The Lisle Fellowship, Inc.
511 Meadow Hill Drive
Rockville, Maryland 20851

1st SUPPLEMENT — *Directory of Internships, Work Experience Programs, and On-the-Job Training Opportunities*

LOCUST GROVE HISTORIC HOME [188]

Program Title:
Internship Program

Purpose:
To introduce college students to museum/historic home work.

Nature of Assignment:
Intern helps in the development of educational programs.

Duration:
6 weeks during the Summer; 6 hours per day.

Eligibility:
Current undergraduate college students who are interested in history, art or American studies.

Number of Awards:
1 per year.

Financial Data:
$300 for the Summer session.

Application Deadline:
May 1 of each year.

Request Application from:
Locust Grove Historic Home
561 Blankenbaker Lane
Louisville, Kentucky 40207

LOS ANGELES COUNTY MUSEUM OF ART [189]

Program Title:
Museum Associate Internship

Purpose:
To assist in raising the level of museum professionalism by training well-qualified potential curators, and to provide opportunity for well-qualified graduate students to enter the museum profession through an organized program of development in a museum setting. A related goal is to possibly introduce minority graduate students in Art History to a museum training experience and professional development opportunity which might not otherwise be available.

Nature of Assignment:
The Intern works under the general guidance and supervision of a senior member of the professional staff and participates in the activities of various Museum departments. Training and work assignments include cataloging; planning; designing and installing exhibitions; museum registration methods; packing, handling, shipping and insurance of art objects; conservation; curatorial research; and art museum education. The Intern is also assigned to assist a curator in the Intern's art specialty.

Duration:
1 year; full time.

Eligibility:
Students who have completed at least a Master's degree in Art History at a recognized graduate school. Advanced post-graduate study in the field (i.e., doctoral candidate or postdoctoral status) will receive additional consideration. Academic achievement and distinction is important, while reading and writing fluency in at least one foreign language is desirable.

Number of Awards:
1 per year.

Financial Data:
Stipend of $9,600.

Stipulations:
Applicants must be willing to travel to Los Angeles at their own expense for interviews during the final selection process.

Special Features:
The Museum may not be in a position to offer permanent placement to the Intern after completion of the Program; however, the Internship Committee will be available to counsel and advise the Intern regarding placement in other institutions.

Application Deadline:
Some time in May or June of each year.

Request Application from:
Intern Program
Los Angeles County Museum of Art
5905 Wilshire Boulevard
Los Angeles, California 90036

LUNAR SCIENCE INSTITUTE [190]

Program Title:
Educational Visiting Scientist

Purpose:
To support educational program development in the lunar and lunar-related sciences and in comparative planetology.

Nature of Assignment:
Participants are involved in educational program development activities at the Institute with the intent of gaining information to be used in developing new courses or course supplements.

Duration:
Appointments vary in length, from 1 week to as long as 1 year, with the possibility of renewal.

Eligibility:
Educators in the earth sciences, astronomy, planetary sciences or other related areas who have appropriate institutional affiliations.

Number of Awards:
Varies, depending on applicants and funding.

Financial Data:
Financial assistance is available in several forms with arrangements made individually for each appointment according to need.

Application Deadline:
Applications are accepted at any time.

Request Application from:
The Director
Lunar Science Institute
3303 NASA Road #1
Houston, Texas 77058

LUNAR SCIENCE INSTITUTE [191]

Program Title:
Post-Doctoral Fellow

Purpose:
To support experimental and theoretical research in the lunar and lunar-related sciences and in comparative planetology.

Nature of Assignment:
Fellows engage in independent or cooperative research projects at the Institute or the Johnson Space Center.

Duration:
Appointments vary in length, from 1 week to as long as 1 year, with the possibility of renewal.

Eligibility:
Recent postdoctoral graduates who have appropriate research interests and abilities.

Number of Awards:
Varies, depending on applicants and funding.

Financial Data:
Financial assistance is available in several forms with arrangements made individually for each appointment according to need.

Stipulations:
Applicants who wish to propose experimental research programs should first contact the Institute concerning the availability of necessary laboratory facilities at the Johnson Space Center.

Application Deadline:
Applications are accepted at any time.

Request Application from:
The Director
Lunar Science Institute
3303 NASA Road #1
Houston, Texas 77058

LUNAR SCIENCE INSTITUTE [192]

Program Title:
Research Scientist

Purpose:
To support experimental and theoretical research in the lunar and lunar-related sciences and in comparative planetology.

Nature of Assignment:
Participants conduct independent research in relevant project areas utilizing facilities at the Institute or the Johnson Space Center.

Duration:
Appointments vary in length, from 1 week to as long as 1 year, with the possibility of renewal.

Eligibility:
Scientists who have appropriate research interests; at least 2 - 3 years of postdoctoral, independent research experience; and no other institutional affiliation.

Number of Awards:
Varies, depending on applicants and funding.

Financial Data:
Financial assistance is available in several forms with arrangements made individually for each appointment according to need.

Stipulations:
Applicants who wish to propose experimental research programs should first contact the Institute concerning availability of necessary laboratory facilities at the Johnson Space Center.

Application Deadline:
Applications are accepted at any time.

Request Application from:
The Director
Lunar Science Institute
3303 NASA Road #1
Houston, Texas 77058

LUNAR SCIENCE INSTITUTE [193]

Program Title:
Visiting Graduate Fellow

1st SUPPLEMENT

Directory of Internships, Work Experience Programs, and On-the-Job Training Opportunities

Purpose:
To support experimental and theoretical research in the lunar and lunar-related sciences and in comparative planetology.

Nature of Assignment:
Fellows participate in supervised research projects under the guidance of advisors from the Institute or the Johnson Space Center.

Duration:
Appointments vary in length, from 1 week to as long as 1 year, with the possibility of renewal.

Eligibility:
Graduate students with appropriate interests who are actively engaged in supervised research and for whom cooperative arrangements can be made with their home institutions and with qualified temporary research advisors at the Institute or the Center.

Number of Awards:
Varies, depending on applicants and funding.

Financial Data:
Financial assistance is available in several forms with arrangements made individually for each appointment according to need.

Stipulations:
Applicants who wish to propose experimental research programs should first contact the Institute concerning the availability of necessary laboratory facilities at the Johnson Space Center.

Application Deadline:
Applications are accepted at any time.

Request Application from:
The Director
Lunar Science Institute
3303 NASA Road #1
Houston, Texas 77058

LUNAR SCIENCE INSTITUTE [194]

Program Title:
Visiting Scientist Program

Purpose:
To support experimental and theoretical research in the lunar and lunar-related sciences and in comparative planetology.

Nature of Assignment:
Participants conduct independent research in relevant project areas utilizing facilities at the Institute or the Johnson Space Center.

Duration:
Appointments vary in length, from 1 week to as long as 1 year, with the possibility of renewal.

Eligibility:
Scientists who have appropriate research interests and abilities and hold academic or other institutional affiliations elsewhere.

Number of Awards:
Varies, depending on applicants and funding.

Financial Data:
Financial assistance is available in several forms with arrangements made individually for each appointment according to need.

Stipulations:
Applicants who wish to propose experimental research programs should first contact the Institute concerning availability of necessary laboratory facilities at the Johnson Space Center.

Application Deadline:
Applications are accepted at any time.

Request Application from:
The Director
Lunar Science Institute
3303 NASA Road #1
Houston, Texas 77058

1st SUPPLEMENT

Directory of Internships, Work Experience Programs, and On-the-Job Training Opportunities

LUNAR SCIENCE INSTITUTE [195]

Program Title:
Visiting Undergraduate Intern

Purpose:
To support experimental and theoretical research in the lunar and lunar-related sciences and in comparative planetology.

Nature of Assignment:
Interns conduct projects under the supervision of scientists, educators or administrators at the Institute or the Johnson Space Center.

Duration:
Internships are usually for a Summer of supervised work.

Eligibility:
Undergraduate students who have research interests in fields which can be accomodated at facilities of the Institute or the Center.

Number of Awards:
Varies, depending on applicants and funding.

Financial Data:
Financial assistance is available in several forms. Arrangements are made individually for each Intern with amounts varying according to need.

Application Deadline:
Deadlines vary; prospective applicants should notify the Institute of their interest in the program.

Request Application from:
The Director
Lunar Science Institute
3303 NASA Road #1
Houston, Texas 77058

LYNN HISTORICAL SOCIETY [196]

Program Title:
Internship Program

Purpose:
To support students who wish to assume responsibility for projects and educational programs necessary for a small museum; and to extend the resources of the Society to the general public of Lynn.

Nature of Assignment:
Interns perform varied tasks with assignments falling in the areas of art (working in design, graphics, models and crafts), history (involving displays, research for special projects, urban studies and geography) and education (conducting relevant school programs).

Duration:
1 semester.

Eligibility:
Undergraduate students who are attending accredited institutions with preference given to juniors and seniors at neighboring colleges and highest consideration accorded Lynn residents.

Financial Data:
Volunteer only.

Special Features:
Interns may arrange to receive academic credit for participation in the Program.

Application Deadline:
Applications are accepted at any time.

Request Application from:
Director
Lynn Historical Society
125 Green Street
Lynn, Massachusetts 01902

m

MCKINLEY AREA SERVICES FOR THE HANDICAPPED, INC. (MASH) [197]

Program Title:
Work Experience/On-the-Job Training

Purpose:
To assist in providing full life services to handicapped persons.

Nature of Assignment:
Participants are involved in adult vocational rehabilitation activities which include a residential component and deal with developmentally disabled people. Participants also work with the Early Childhood program which provides preschool and homebound services to the severely handicapped.

Duration:
Minimum of 2 months; full or part time.

Eligibility:
Individuals who have appropriate interests and skills as well as the ability to work in a cross cultural situation (i.e., with Native American, Spanish Speaking and Anglo people).

Financial Data:
Volunteer only.

Special Features:
The Program provides an introduction to opportunities for rehabilitation in rural, multi-cultural communities.

Application Deadline:
Applications are accepted at any time.

Request Application from:
Executive Director
MASH
P.O. Box 1332
Gallup, New Mexico 87301

MACON CHRONICLE-HERALD [198]

Program Title:
On-the-Job Training

Purpose:
To develop news and advertising people.

Nature of Assignment:
News trainees are assigned feature stories, local coverage, general news stories and news layouts. Advertising trainees work on layout and local selling.

Duration:
Summer only, during vacation months; full time.

Eligibility:
Students who have interests and abilities appropriate to the job. Preference is given to Journalism school students and those from the local area.

Financial Data:
Trainees are paid the minimum wage.

1st SUPPLEMENT

Directory of Internships, Work Experience Programs, and On-the-Job Training Opportunities

Application Deadline:
Interested students should apply as early as possible in the calendar year for which Summer work is sought.

Request Application from:
Publisher
Macon Chronicle-Herald
Box 7
Macon, Missouri 63552

MAINE. OFFICE OF THE GOVERNOR [199]

Program Title:
Governor's Summer Internship Program

Purpose:
To give students the opportunity to participate in the state government of Maine.

Nature of Assignment:
Interns are assigned to work in various departments and agencies within the state government.

Duration:
Summer only; full time.

Eligibility:
College and university students who are interested in gaining experience in some aspect of state government. Applicants must be residents of Maine. Specific assignments might require special qualifications.

Number of Awards:
Approximately 50 per year.

Financial Data:
Approximately $125 per week.

Application Deadline:
Applications are accepted at any time.

Request Application from:
Appointments Coordinator
Office of the Governor
State House
Augusta, Maine 04333

MANCHESTER HISTORIC ASSOCIATION [200]

Program Title:
Work Study, CEP and Volunteer Programs

Purpose:
To give interested people an opportunity to aid in the work of the Association's museum and library.

Nature of Assignment:
If at all possible, participants are assigned jobs tailored to fit their interests and abilities. Possible work assignments include such things as library sorting and cataloging, museum accessioning and cataloging, setting up exhibits, typing, tape recording local history, and conducting tours.

Duration:
Varies, depending upon participant and program involved.

Eligibility:
Individuals who are interested in the programs of the Association, are reliable, have the ability to think independently, and can work on their own as well as under supervision. Typing ability is usually necessary. Any requirements determined by CEP or Work Study Programs must be met.

Number of Awards:
Varies.

Financial Data:
Work Study and CEP Programs pay participant expenses; volunteers work without pay.

1st SUPPLEMENT

Directory of Internships, Work Experience Programs, and On-the-Job Training Opportunities

Application Deadline:
Applications from volunteers are accepted at any time; application deadlines for other programs vary.

Request Application from:
Director
Manchester Historic Association
129 Amherst Street
Manchester, New Hampshire 03104

MARATHON HEALTH CARE CENTER [201]

Program Title:
Field Training Program for Occupational Therapy Students

Purpose:
To provide students with the opportunity to interact with clients and to acquire the skills necessary to perform and teach the processes involved in specific life tasks and activities.

Nature of Assignment:
Trainees take part in a sequential learning experience, moving from the role of observer to entry level therapist. Participants are involved in comprehensive mental health training which includes working in the areas of behavior modification, geriatrics, alcohol/drug abuse and developmentally disabled.

Duration:
5 - 10 weeks; full time.

Eligibility:
Applicants must be enrolled in accredited Occupational Therapy programs at either 4 year colleges or 2 year technical schools.

Number of Awards:
Maximum of 7 per year.

Financial Data:
Trainees receive complimentary meal tickets.

Application Deadline:
Application must be made through colleges/schools with which occupational therapy students are affiliated.

Request Application from:
Director of Occupational Therapy
Marathon Health Care Center
1100 Lake View Drive
Wausau, Wisconsin 54401

MARYLAND. LEGISLATIVE STUDY GROUP [202]

Program Title:
Intern Program

Purpose:
To provide students with a highly responsible, practical and educational experience in a state legislature.

Nature of Assignment:
Interns perform a variety of legislative tasks including monitoring and summarizing meetings, writing bill summaries and analyses, maintaining a library, developing surveys, authoring press releases, and conducting both indepth and spot or quick research. Interns are also involved in intensive research and writing in many policy areas.

Duration:
Flexible; Interns usually work approximately 4 months, but Internships of up to a year have occurred; minimum commitment of 15 hours per week is required.

Eligibility:
College and university students who have interests and abilities appropriate to the work. Students in junior standing are preferred.

Number of Awards:
Maximum of 15 per year.

Financial Data:
Interns have expenses paid and receive additional remuneration depending upon circumstances.

Special Features:
Interns establish valuable contacts in the governmental job market.

Application Deadline:
Application deadline is flexible; applications should be received by approximately May 1, August 15 and December 5.

Request Application from:
Executive Director
State of Maryland
Legislative Study Group
88 State Circle
Annapolis, Maryland 21401

MASSACHUSETTS. INTERNSHIP OFFICE [203]

Program Title:
General Internship Program

Purpose:
To arrange internship placements for high school and college students.

Nature of Assignment:
Interns work in both public and private agencies, mainly in the metropolitan Boston area. Intern assignments fall into the following general categories: arts, commerce/business, education, human services, law, media/communications, planning and environment, politics and public interest, recreation, and technical support/research.

Duration:
10 - 15 hours per week during Fall and Spring semesters; full-time positions available in January and in the Summer.

Eligibility:
High school and college students who are interested in an internship work experience. Certain jobs might require special skills.

Financial Data:
Varies with individual job placements. Most Internships are offered on an unpaid basis, although sometimes with the opportunity for reimbursement of job-related expenses. Some work-study arrangements are possible, and a few small stipends are available. The Internship Office offers on-the-job accident and medical insurance coverage at no charge to all Interns.

Stipulations:
Applicants must be willing to commit themselves for at least 10 - 15 hours per week and to work in the Boston area.

Special Features:
Students may arrange to receive academic credit for participation in the Program.

Application Deadline:
Flexible; applications should be received sometime during the first part of each semester.

Request Application from:
Massachusetts Internship Office
One Ashburton Place - Room 611
Boston, Massachusetts 02108

MASSACHUSETTS ARTS AND HUMANITIES FOUNDATION [204]

Program Title:
Informal Program

Purpose:
To provide the opportunity for interested individuals to gain experience by helping the Foundation meet its staffing needs.

Nature of Assignment:
Participants assist in programming, operating, clerical and administrative activities.

Duration:
Varies.

Eligibility:
Individuals who have interests and skills appropriate to working with the Foundation.

Financial Data:
Participants are most often volunteers, occasionally salaried.

Application Deadline:
Applications are accepted at any time.

Request Application from:
Massachusetts Arts and Humanities Foundation
14 Beacon Street
Boston, Massachusetts 02108

MECOSTA COUNTY, MICHIGAN. COMMISSION ON AGING [205]

Program Title:
Training in Human Services

Purpose:
To provide a training ground for students interested in helping to serve seniors, those 60 years old and over.

Nature of Assignment:
On-the-job training is provided in all areas of service for seniors, such as health screening, information and referral, para-legal, outreach, transportation and home services. Duties also involve management, coordination and clerical work.

Duration:
9 months during the school year or 3 months during the Summer; 20 hours per week.

Eligibility:
College students majoring in some field of human services or related area who are interested in working with older citizens.

Number of Awards:
2 per year.

Financial Data:
Volunteer with mileage reimbursement for outreach work.

Special Features:
Participants can also take advantage of training sessions arranged by the Region VIII Area Agency on Aging in Grand Rapids, Michigan.

Application Deadline:
Applications should be received by June 1 or September 1.

Request Application from:
Mecosta County Commission on Aging
223 South Stewart Street
Big Rapids, Michigan 49307

1st SUPPLEMENT

Directory of Internships, Work Experience Programs, and On-the-Job Training Opportunities

MIDLAND BROADCASTING [206]

Program Title:
Radio Internship

Purpose:
To offer students experience beyond college radio.

Nature of Assignment:
Interns are assigned a variety of duties including news reporting, copywriting, traffic, research, sales, and programming management. Interns are provided with on-the-job experience in a high-power radio station.

Duration:
Year round.

Eligibility:
High school seniors and college students who have interests and abilities appropriate to the work.

Number of Awards:
Numerous.

Financial Data:
Volunteer.

Application Deadline:
Applications are accepted at any time.

Request Application from:
Midland Broadcasting
P.O. Box 4407
Topeka, Kansas 66604

MIGRANT LEGAL ACTION PROGRAM, INC. [207]

Program Title:
Summer Law Clerk Program

Purpose:
To provide experience for qualified law students and assistance for MLAP.

Nature of Assignment:
Participants assist staff attorneys in research of issues that arise out of litigation in which MLAP is involved.

Duration:
Summer, full time; occasionally extending into Winter for 12 - 20 hours per week.

Eligibility:
Second or third year law school students who have good academic records.

Number of Awards:
Varies year to year.

Financial Data:
Participants receive $4.25 - $4.75 an hour. Law school students are also accepted in the Program as volunteers.

Application Deadline:
Applications are accepted at any time.

Request Application from:
Executive Director
Migrant Legal Action Program, Inc.
806 15th Street, N.W.
Washington, D.C. 20019

MINNEAPOLIS TRIBUNE [208]

Program Title:
College Internships

Purpose:
To provide newsroom experience for liberal arts students.

Nature of Assignment:
Interns are assigned general newsroom work, including both reporting and copy editing.

Duration:
1 school term.

Eligibility:
Liberal arts students attending Minnesota colleges and universities other than the University of Minnesota who have interests and abilities appropriate to the work. Applicants must be recommended by their schools.

Number of Awards:
1 or 2 each year.

Financial Data:
Interns receive $500 stipends.

Application Deadline:
Applications are accepted at any time, but applicants must have their school's recommendation.

Request Application from:
Administrative Assistant
Minneapolis Tribune
425 Portland Avenue
Minneapolis, Minnesota 55488

MINNEAPOLIS TRIBUNE [209]

Program Title:
Minority Program

Purpose:
To provide newsroom experience for minority students.

Nature of Assignment:
Interns are assigned general newsroom work, including both reporting and copy editing.

Duration:
Up to 1 year.

Eligibility:
Minority students who are interested in reporting with preference usually given to those who have degrees and demonstrated writing ability.

Number of Awards:
2 per year.

Financial Data:
Interns receive first-year reporter's regular pay.

Application Deadline:
Applications are accepted at any time.

Request Application from:
Administrative Assistant
Minneapolis Tribune
425 Portland Avenue
Minneapolis, Minnesota 55488

MINNESOTA. HOUSE OF REPRESENTATIVES [210]

Program Title:
House Internship Program

Purpose:
To provide students with an opportunity to observe and participate in the legislature firsthand and to provide some needed staff assistance for individual legislators.

Nature of Assignment:
Duties vary depending on with which

member the Intern works. Assignments usually involve some research, monitoring of committee meetings, handling of constituent correspondence and office organization.

Duration:
Usually session only: January - May in odd numbered years, January - March in even numbered years.

Eligibility:
College and university students who are interested in the Program. Other specific ability requirements vary according to representatives' needs and desires.

Number of Awards:
Usually 75 - 120 per session.

Financial Data:
Volunteer only.

Application Deadline:
Although there is no application deadline, it is recommended that students apply by December 1 of the year preceding the desired Internship.

Request Application from:
House Internship Program
House of Representatives
State Capitol
St. Paul, Minnesota 55155

MISSOURI. HOUSE OF REPRESENTATIVES [211]

Program Title:
College-Level Internship Program

Purpose:
To increase the awareness and interest of students in the legislative process and to provide members of the House with staff assistance.

Nature of Assignment:
Duties of Interns vary with the needs of the House members to whom they are assigned. In general, Interns perform research necessary for drafting and amending legislation and for answering constituent inquiries. Interns also do some general office work.

Duration:
Academic term.

Eligibility:
Students in Missouri who have completed high school and are interested in the Program. Interns are usually enrolled in college or university courses.

Number of Awards:
100 - 125 per year.

Financial Data:
No remuneration currently offered.

Special Features:
Interns can arrange to receive college credit for work performed through the Program.

Application Deadline:
October prior to the desired Internship.

Request Application from:
College-Level Internship Program
Missouri House of Representatives
State Capitol Building
Jefferson City, Missouri 65101

MISSOURI VOLUNTEER OFFICE [212]

Program Title:
Internship Program

1st SUPPLEMENT

Directory of Internships, Work Experience Programs, and On-the-Job Training Opportunities

Purpose:
To provide interested individuals with training in volunteerism and offer them an opportunity to work with Missouri's Lt. Governor.

Nature of Assignment:
Interns research and design projects on volunteerism with the intent of expanding and stimulating volunteer program development.

Duration:
Interns may work during the Fall, Spring and/or Summer.

Eligibility:
College and university students who are working toward a degree in Social Work or are interested in some aspect of the social services.

Financial Data:
Volunteer only.

Application Deadline:
Applications are accepted at any time.

Request Application from:
Missouri Volunteer Office
Box 563
Jefferson City, Missouri 65101

MOBILE COMMUNITY ORGANIZATION [213]

Program Title:
Training in Community Organizing

Purpose:
To provide experience working with a community organization which deals with neighborhood and city-wide issues.

Nature of Assignment:
Training is offered in the principles, methods and skills of organizing neighborhood residents around issues of their own self-interest. Experience is also available in working with city-wide coalitions of organizations.

Duration:
Generally, a minimum of 1 year.

Eligibility:
Individuals who are at least 18 years old and have had some college experience with preference given to those having degrees.

Number of Awards:
Varies; approximately 12 at any one time.

Financial Data:
Participants receive stipends of approximately $300 per month provided through the VISTA program.

Application Deadline:
Applications are accepted at any time.

Request Application from:
Director
Mobile Community Organization
926½ Conti Street
Mobile, Alabama 36604

MONMOUTH COUNTY, NEW JERSEY. BOARD OF FREEHOLDERS [214]

Program Title:
High School Internship Program

Purpose:
To provide high school students with practical and professional work experience, exposure to County Government and public administration, and an awareness of how County Government affects them daily.

Nature of Assignment:
Interns are assigned Administrative Assistant level positions in 19 different County offices. Interns assist administrators in their daily duties with specific experiences and activities varying widely between departments.

Duration:
15 weeks during the Fall or Spring; scheduling is flexible, arranged between Interns and County departments involved.

Eligibility:
Junior and senior high school students who attend any public, private or parochial school in the County. Applicants must have their school administration's approval and be able to provide their own transportation.

Number of Awards:
30 per year.

Financial Data:
Volunteer only; personal expenses other than transportation are paid.

Application Deadline:
Third week of September for Internships during the Fall and the third week in January for Spring Internships.

Request Application from:
Monmouth County High School Internship Program
Superintendent of Schools Office
Highway 9
Freehold, New Jersey 07728

MORGAN - SCOTT PROJECT FOR COOPERATIVE CHRISTIAN CONCERNS [215]

Program Title:
Graduate Internships

Purpose:
To provide concerned individuals with a training ground for studying community development in an interdisciplinary manner.

Nature of Assignment:
Interns work with professionals in the areas of social work, pastoral care, church and community, and education. Specific assignments are determined in an attempt to fit the interests and abilities of individual Interns with the needs of the community. Preceptors work weekly with Interns in individual and group situations as well as on the job.

Duration:
1 - 2 year Internships are preferred, but 3 - 6 month Internships can be offered in certain situations.

Eligibility:
Individuals who have interests and skills appropriate to the work. Preference is given to college graduates, but high priority is also placed on experience, maturity and readiness of applicants for the type of experience offered by the program.

Financial Data:
In most cases, only expenses are paid.

Application Deadline:
Application deadlines vary; inquiries can be submitted at any time.

Request Application from:
Morgan-Scott Project
Box 8
Deer Lodge, Tennessee 37726

1st SUPPLEMENT
Directory of Internships, Work Experience Programs, and On-the-Job Training Opportunities

MT. SUSITNA BROADCASTING CORPORATION [216]

Program Title:
Announcer Trainee

Purpose:
To train members of minority groups and/or women who want to work in radio.

Nature of Assignment:
Participants receive formal instruction and on-the-job training in production techniques, announcing techniques, formatting, and FCC rules and regulations. Promising licensed trainees are assigned part-time shifts where they perform actual on-air duties while both licensed and unlicensed trainees participate in station promotional programs.

Duration:
1 - 6 months for unlicensed trainees and 2 - 6 months for licensed trainees, depending on individuals involved.

Eligibility:
Members of minority groups and women who have had some exposure to announcing techniques (at any radio station, through speech courses, or at broadcasting school). Applicants must have good enunciation and diction, excellent ability to read orally and manual dexterity.

Number of Awards:
1 - 2 per year.

Financial Data:
$3.50 per hour.

Stipulations:
Trainees should have either an FCC 3rd Class Radiotelephone License with Broadcast Endorsement or an FCC Provisional License application with enrollment in a broadcast course leading to licensing.

Special Features:
Completion of training can lead into employment at the station.

Application Deadline:
Applications are accepted at any time.

Request Application from:
KANC Radio
8819 Jewel Lake Road
Anchorage, Alaska 99502

MT. SUSITNA BROADCASTING CORPORATION [217]

Program Title:
Radio Sales Trainee

Purpose:
To train members of minority groups and/or women who want to work in radio.

Nature of Assignment:
Trainees first study an RKO Sales Course; RAB materials; and in-house production, traffic, copy, and accounting procedures and techniques. Then trainees sell and service advertisers. Initially, they are accompanied and supervised by management personnel; but ultimately, trainees work on their own.

Duration:
Maximum of 3 months.

Eligibility:
Members of minority groups and women who are interested in the training program. Applicants should be neat appearing, have extroverted personalities, have command of basic English and mathematics, and demonstrate some natural empathy.

Number of Awards:
Average of 2 per year.

1st SUPPLEMENT

Directory of Internships, Work Experience Programs, and On-the-Job Training Opportunities

Financial Data:
$4.90 per hour for 3 months; commission thereafter.

Stipulations:
Participants must spend 2 weeks in formal training before they are given any on-the-job assignments.

Special Features:
Completion of training can lead into employment at the station.

Application Deadline:
Applications are accepted at any time.

Request Application from:
KANC Radio
8819 Jewel Lake Road
Anchorage, Alaska 99502

MT. TOP YOUTH FOR CHRIST [218]

Program Title:
Internship Program/Associate-Volunteer Staff

Purpose:
To provide experience in a non-denominational but evangelical youth ministry.

Nature of Assignment:
Participants work with teens, primarily in a counseling capacity.

Duration:
Varies, adjustable to each participants needs.

Eligibility:
Individuals who have Christian commitment and dedication. Applicants for the Associate-Volunteer staff should be high school graduates while applicants for Internships should be college graduates.

Number of Awards:
Unlimited.

Financial Data:
Volunteer.

Application Deadline:
60 days in advance of desired starting date.

Request Application from:
Mt. Top Youth for Christ
P.O. Box 286
Oakland, Maryland 21550

MUSEUM OF CARTOON ART [219]

Program Title:
Work Experience

Purpose:
To provide museum work experience for students and to aid in the Museum's organization and operation.

Nature of Assignment:
Participants receive work experience in various aspects of the Museum's operations. Training is available in such areas as archive cataloging, publicity mailing, exhibit mounting, and fund raising.

Duration:
Flexible; full or part time.

Eligibility:
Individuals of high school age and up who have interests and skills appropriate to the work.

Financial Data:
Volunteer only.

Special Features:
References are provided upon completion of the work experience.

1st SUPPLEMENT

Directory of Internships, Work Experience Programs, and On-the-Job Training Opportunities

Application Deadline:
Applications are accepted at any time.

Request Application from:
Museum of Cartoon Art
384 Field Point Road
Greenwich, Connecticut 06830

n

NATIONAL ASSOCIATION FOR RETARDED CITIZENS [220]

Program Title:
Governmental Affairs Office Internship Program

Purpose:
To provide students with knowledge of the legislative process as well as knowledge of Federal programs and how they impact on the disabled population, especially mentally retarded citizens.

Nature of Assignment:
Interns are assigned various tasks and responsibilities, such as monitoring Congressional hearings and Federal agency meetings; analyzing questionnaires; answering basic inquiries on Federal programs; writing reports; and summarizing meetings, hearings and legislation.

Duration:
Varies; Internships are arranged at times convenient to the Intern, his/her university or college, and the Association.

Eligibility:
College or university students who have interests and abilities appropriate to the Program. Preference is given to students with backgrounds in fields of or relating to mental retardation or the government.

Financial Data:
Volunteer only.

Special Features:
Interns may arrange to receive academic credit for participation in the Program.

Application Deadline:
Applications are accepted at any time.

Request Application from:
National Association for Retarded Citizens
1522 K Street, N.W. - Suite 516
Washington, D.C. 20005

NATIONAL ASSOCIATION OF ACCOUNTANTS FOR THE PUBLIC INTEREST [221]

Program Title:
Internship and Work/Study Programs

Purpose:
To assist the Association in providing volunteer accounting services for the objective examination and consideration of public policy issues.

Nature of Assignment:
Participants work with local affiliates of the Association in projects aimed at providing information on selected public issues.

Specific assignments vary from affiliate to affiliate. Organizations in approximately 15 states are currently affiliated with the Association.

Duration:
Various and flexible; up to local affiliates.

Eligibility:
Upper division or graduate college and university students who are majoring in accounting.

Number of Awards:
Varies from area to area.

Financial Data:
Funds are provided by local affiliates with support of varying degrees available.

Application Deadline:
Applications are accepted at any time.

Request Application from:
National Association of Accountants for the Public Interest
233 Sansome Street - Room 400
San Francisco, California 94104

NATIONAL AUDUBON SOCIETY. AUDUBON CENTER IN GREENWICH [222]

Program Title:
Naturalist Training Program: Environmental Education Internships

Purpose:
To provide experiences that would help an individual become a confident and competent teacher-naturalist.

Nature of Assignment:
Participants receive on-the-job training experience with emphasis on the teaching elements of the field. In addition to the educational activities, Trainees are involved in such programs and services as trail interpretation, exhibitry, writing educational and promotional materials, and sanctuary and habitat management.

Duration:
13 weeks; approximately the third week in September to the third week in December or the second week in March through the first week in June of each year.

Eligibility:
Applicants must be interested in interpretive work, be able to interact with people, and have a desire to enter the naturalist field. College training in natural sciences or education and some teaching experience is helpful but not necessary. Practical experience may substitute for formal course work. Personal interviews are recommended.

Number of Awards:
2 per session per year.

Financial Data:
No salary is available; however, housing is provided.

Stipulations:
Trainees first participate in 2 weeks of orientation after which they design their own particular programs in cooperation with Center staff. A $25 registration fee is required upon acceptance into the Program; the fee will be returned after satisfactory completion of training.

Special Features:
At termination of the training period, Trainee evaluations are available for prospective employers.

1st SUPPLEMENT

Directory of Internships, Work Experience Programs, and On-the-Job Training Opportunities

Application Deadline:
Applications should be received by March 1 for the Fall session and September 1 for the Spring session; early application (4 - 6 months ahead of deadline) is recommended.

Request Application from:
Audubon Center in Greenwich
613 Riversville Road
Greenwich, Connecticut 06830

NATIONAL AUDUBON SOCIETY. AULLWOOD AUDUBON CENTER [223]

Program Title:
Naturalist Training Program: Environmental Education Internships

Purpose:
To provide the opportunity for college students, graduates and other adults to learn about and help with the management of the sanctuary, the mechanics of operating a bookstore, and the care and treatment of the Center's live animal collection.

Nature of Assignment:
Trainees are assigned many of the same responsibilities as are regular employees including planning for and conducting classes for school children, conducting adult education classes, leading short-term field trips for both children and adults, working with the Center's teenage group, and participating in educational programs held away from the Center. Trainees are expected to become somewhat familiar with the native plants, animals and ecology of the Center.

Duration:
13 weeks; approximately the third week in September to the third week in December or the second week in March through the first week in June of each year.

Eligibility:
Individuals who have interests and abilities appropriate to working in the naturalist field. Possession of a car is useful but not essential. Personal interviews are recommended.

Number of Awards:
2 per session per year.

Financial Data:
No salary is available; however, housing is provided.

Stipulations:
A $25 registration fee is required upon acceptance into the Program; the fee will be returned after satisfactory completion of training.

Special Features:
At termination of the training period, Trainee evaluations will be available for prospective employers.

Application Deadline:
Early application is essential; approximately 4 - 6 months before the desired starting date of training is recommended.

Request Application from:
Aullwood Audubon Center
1000 Aullwood Road
Dayton, Ohio 45414

NATIONAL AUDUBON SOCIETY. AULLWOOD AUDUBON FARM [224]

Program Title:
Naturalist Training Program: Environmental Education Internships

141

1st SUPPLEMENT

Directory of Internships, Work Experience Programs, and On-the-Job Training Opportunities

Purpose:
To provide the opportunity for on-the-job experience in all aspects of the Farm's educational programs and farming operations.

Nature of Assignment:
Among other duties, Trainees observe and lead school tours; work with teachers and parents in planning and guiding extended class visits; plan and participate in workshops and special public programs; attend staff meetings; prepare exhibits, displays and trail signs; and generally help with routine maintenance chores as well as with the farming operation. Trainees will be encouraged to utilize the Farm's educational resources to develop their teaching abilities.

Duration:
13 weeks; approximately the third week in September to the third week in December or the second week in March through the first week in June of each year.

Eligibility:
Individuals who have interests and abilities appropriate to the training experience on the Farm. Personal interviews are recommended.

Number of Awards:
2 per session per year.

Financial Data:
No salary is available; however, housing is provided.

Stipulations:
A $25 registration fee is required upon acceptance into the Program; the fee will be returned after satisfactory completion of training.

Special Features:
Trainees have the opportunity to interact with staff at the Aullwood Audubon Center. At termination of the training period, Trainee evaluations will be available for prospective employers.

Application Deadline:
Early application is essential; approximately 4 - 6 months before the desired starting date of training is recommended.

Request Application from:
Aullwood Audubon Farm
9101 Frederick Road
Dayton, Ohio 45414

NATIONAL AUDUBON SOCIETY. RICHARDSON BAY WILDLIFE SANCTUARY [225]

Program Title:
Naturalist Training Program: Environmental Education Internships

Purpose:
To provide interested students with the opportunity to participate in all phases of Wildlife Sanctuary and Education Center operations.

Nature of Assignment:
Participants serve as Administrative Assistant to the Manager and receive on-the-job experience in program management, sanctuary operations, field research, and teaching and interpretive programs.

Duration:
At least 2 quarters or 1 semester; full-time work for 5 days a week.

Eligibility:
College or university students who have interests and abilities appropriate to the Programs. Personal interviews are recommended.

Financial Data:
No salary is available; however, housing is provided.

Stipulations:
A $25 registration fee is required upon acceptance into the Program; the fee will be returned after satisfactory completion of training. It is hoped that participating students will pursue training activity for credit under an Independent Study or Work-Learn Program.

Special Features:
At termination of the training period, Trainee evaluations will be available for prospective employers.

Application Deadline:
Applications are accepted at any time, but submission well in advance of anticipated starting date is recommended.

Request Application from:
Richardson Bay Wildlife Sanctuary and
  Whittell Education Center
376 Greenwood Beach Road
Tiburon, California 94920

NATIONAL AUDUBON SOCIETY. SHARON AUDUBON CENTER [226]

Program Title:
Naturalist Training Program: Environmental Education Internships

Purpose:
To provide on-the-job experience in a sanctuary which attempts to change individual attitudes and behavior for the betterment of the people and the Earth.

Nature of Assignment:
Trainees take part in the Center's flexible programming and participate with staff members as they interact with visitors, deal with natural history, and help with the management and caretaking aspects of the Center's operation.

Duration:
13 weeks; approximately the third week in September to the third week in December or the second week in March through the first week in June of each year.

Eligibility:
Individuals who have interests and abilities appropriate to the training and the ability to engage in really flexible programming. Personal interviews are recommended.

Number of Awards:
2 per session per year.

Financial Data:
No salary is available; however, housing is provided.

Stipulations:
Trainees receive 1 week of orientation to the Center, staff and community after which they design their own programs in cooperation with Center staff. A $25 registration fee is required upon acceptance into the Program; the fee will be returned after satisfactory completion of training.

Special Features:
At termination of the training period, Trainee evaluations will be available for prospective employers.

Application Deadline:
Applications are accepted at any time, but submission well in advance of anticipated starting date is recommended.

Request Application from:
Sharon Audubon Center
Route 4
Sharon, Connecticut 06069

1st SUPPLEMENT

Directory of Internships, Work Experience Programs, and On-the-Job Training Opportunities

THE NATIONAL CENTER FOR URBAN ETHNIC AFFAIRS [227]

Program Title:
National Neighborhood Institute (NNI)

Purpose:
To train persons interested in community organizing; to help people develop the necessary skills for organizing on a neighborhood level; and to help build a sense of justice and personal dignity among neighborhood people.

Nature of Assignment:
NNI offers a variety of training programs, all geared toward helping people become better qualified for community organizing. The Institute combines academic and experiential learning techniques in its curriculum.

Duration:
Varies; in the past, NNI has sponsored 6 month on-site training programs, smaller 1 day and week-long programs, and 2 week training sessions.

Eligibility:
Individuals who are interested in community organizing. Applicants must be willing to become fully involved with people as they live in their neighborhoods and must want to help bring a sense of justice, worth and dignity to the neighborhood agenda.

Financial Data:
6 month trainees receive stipends from their sponsoring groups; smaller sessions require varying tuitions.

Special Features:
Depending on the program, NNI offers certificates to its trainees.

Application Deadline:
Application deadlines vary, depending upon the program involved.

Request Application from:
National Neighborhood Institute
1521 16th Street, N.W.
Washington, D.C. 20036

NATIONAL CONSUMER AFFAIRS INTERNSHIP PROGRAM [228]

Program Title:
National Consumer Affairs Internship Program

Purpose:
To provide college students interested in consumer affairs with a meaningful and rewarding work experience and a greater understanding of the expanding role of consumerism.

Nature of Assignment:
Interns are assigned to companies, Federal government agencies, associations and nonprofit organizations where they work on specific projects formulated by their sponsors. Such projects provide Interns with the opportunity for active participation in the sponsoring group. Projects relate to consumer affairs and usually involve research or acting as a staff assistant.

Duration:
3 annual classes of 15 weeks each: January - April, May - August, and September - December; full time.

Eligibility:
Students who have completed all requirements for undergraduate degrees at accredited colleges or universities or who are candidates for graduate degrees. Internships are available to interested students from all major fields of study.

Number of Awards:
20 - 30 Interns per class or 60 - 90 Interns per year.

Financial Data:
Interns receive $1,500 for the 15 week period plus reimbursement for travel expenses to and from work assignments.

Application Deadline:
November 30 for January - April sessions, February 28 for Internships beginning in May, and June 30 for those beginning in September.

Request Application from:
National Consumer Affairs Internship Program
Box 4277
Tucson, Arizona 85717

NATIONAL COUNCIL FOR A WORLD PEACE TAX FUND [229]

Program Title:
Internship Program

Purpose:
To provide an opportunity to learn from experienced lobbyists and movement workers by working in the office of a grassroots organization.

Nature of Assignment:
Interns are assigned numerous duties apropos of working in any small office. Assignments vary from visiting Congressional offices at lobbyists' directions to answering correspondence, writing for a small quarterly newsletter, contacting other Washington area groups and conducting necessary research.

Duration:
Open to any placement.

Eligibility:
Individuals who are interested in the work of the Council. Applicants should like to relate to people, enjoy the public relations aspect of the work, be willing to help with office paperwork and be able to type accurately.

Financial Data:
Volunteer; for placements of 2 months or more, the Council would pay transportation and attempt to arrange low-cost housing.

Application Deadline:
Applications are accepted at any time.

Request Application from:
National Council for a World Peace Tax Fund
2111 Florida Avenue, N.W.
Washington, D.C. 20008

NATIONAL HISTORICAL PUBLICATIONS AND RECORDS COMMISSION [230]

Program Title:
Volunteer Intern Program

Purpose:
To give students job experience in a government cultural institution specializing in historical and archival work.

Nature of Assignment:
Interns work with the Commission's guide project, which is producing a computer-based guide to historical records in the United States, or with the Commission's research staff, which provides document searches and other services to Commission-sponsored documentary editing projects.

Duration:
To be arranged; year round, but within a 24 - 32 hour per week time frame.

Eligibility:
Undergraduate and graduate college or university students who have strong backgrounds in American history and are interested in archival work.

Number of Awards:
Varies each year.

Financial Data:
No remuneration nor paid expenses.

Special Features:
Small staff size permits specialized individual training and personal contact with professional archivists.

Application Deadline:
Applications are accepted at any time but generally should be submitted 2 months before desired beginning date of Internship.

Request Application from:
National Historical Publications and Records Commission
National Archives
Washington, D.C. 20408

NATIONAL MORATORIUM ON PRISON CONSTRUCTION [231]

Program Title:
General Internship

Purpose:
To monitor prison and jail expansion plans nationwide; to assist organizations working to halt additional prison construction; and to provide information and rationale for a moratorium on further construction.

Nature of Assignment:
Interns monitor prison, jail, and juvenile detention construction plans; analyze such plans according to alternatives and other factors; review literature and research in the field; and write or edit for a bimonthly national newsletter.

Duration:
Varies; minimum of 3 months; full-time work preferred.

Eligibility:
Interested individuals who have a basic familiarity with the operation of the existing criminal administration process, basic opposition to further prison proliferation, and basic desire to work toward an implicit social justice goal.

Number of Awards:
2 per year.

Financial Data:
$200 per month maximum for exceptionally qualified individuals.

Special Features:
Possible placement in Atlanta, Georgia, or San Francisco, California, offices.

Application Deadline:
Applications are accepted at any time.

Request Application from:
Coordinator
National Moratorium on Prison Construction
3106 Mt. Pleasant Street, N.W.
Washington, D.C. 20010

NATIONAL RESEARCH COUNCIL OF CANADA [232]

Program Title:
Industrial Postdoctoral Fellowship Program

1st SUPPLEMENT

Directory of Internships, Work Experience Programs, and On-the-Job Training Opportunities

Purpose:
To encourage highly qualified students to seek careers with Canadian industrial organizations.

Nature of Assignment:
Participants work for cooperating industrial organizations in Canada where they may be assigned to duties in research laboratories or jobs in any other department of the employing company.

Duration:
12 months, full time, with the possibility of renewal for an additional 12 months.

Eligibility:
Applicants must have recently received, or expect to complete before undertaking the Fellowship, a doctorate degree in a scientific or engineering field normally supported by the Council. Candidates with psychology degrees who are qualified to work as industrial psychologists may be nominated by participating companies. Applicants must also be unemployed Canadian citizens or landed residents and if the latter have the doctorate from a Canadian university. Qualified candidates remain eligible for this Program until they become permanently employed. Awards are made on the basis of scholastic achievement and demonstrated interest in a career in industry.

Number of Awards:
Limited number.

Financial Data:
Fellows negotiate salaries with participating companies; the Council reimburses such companies a maximum of $12,000 per year for each Fellow employed. Fellows also receive normal company benefits, such as holidays and sick leave.

Stipulations:
Qualified candidates must submit applications to participating companies which forward applications and supporting documents to the Council. A list of participating organizations is available upon request to the Council at the address below.

Application Deadline:
Applications are accepted at any time.

Request Application from:
The Scholarships Officer
Office of Grants and Scholarships
National Research Council of Canada
Building M 58, Montreal Road
Ottawa, Canada K1A OR6

NATIONAL SUGGESTION BOX [233]

Program Title:
National Suggestion Box Internship Program

Purpose:
To act as a conduit between the American people and national policymakers, to encourage Americans to write to the National Suggestion Box with inventive ideas for the country, and to screen and research these ideas for publication in the national media and for potential implementation.

Nature of Assignment:
Interns investigate submitted suggestions by conducting research in conjunction with government, public interest and commercial policymakers. Resulting research is then compiled into reports for release to media sources.

Duration:
Varies, depending on each Intern; 16 - 40 hours per week, preferably a full-time commitment.

Eligibility:
Individuals who are interested in the Program, have journalism skills, and have research and writing abilities.

Number of Awards:
Unlimited.

Financial Data:
Currently Internships are volunteer with expenses paid; however, stipends may be available in the future.

Special Features:
Interns write reports for release to such national media sources as the Suggestion Box's syndicated column, ABC's Good Morning America, the Mutual Broadcasting Network, and columnist Jack Anderson.

Application Deadline:
Applications should be submitted at least 6 weeks before desired starting date for an Internship.

Request Application from:
National Suggestion Box
1418 15th Street, N.W.
Washington, D.C. 20005

NATIONAL TRUST FOR HISTORIC PRESERVATION [234]

Program Title:
Summer Intern Program

Purpose:
To provide work-training experience for students interested in the protection and preservation of the American cultural heritage.

Nature of Assignment:
Interns are assigned special projects at the National Trust headquarters in Washington, D.C., its historic museum properties or selected member preservation agencies throughout the United States. Project assignments are made in accordance with each Intern's academic and employment background. Field trips and research assignments may also be included in the Program.

Duration:
12 weeks during the Summer.

Eligibility:
Undergraduate and graduate college students who are majoring in architectural history, architecture, art history, economics, history, horticulture, the humanities, journalism, landscape architecture, law, library science and planning.

Number of Awards:
50 per year.

Financial Data:
Interns receive stipends of $135 per week but are responsible for their own room and board.

Special Features:
Interns participate in a special 3 day seminar on historic preservation, held in Washington, D. C. The seminar serves as an introduction to preservation at the public and private levels.

Application Deadline:
Approximately February 15 each year.

Request Application from:
Youth Programs Assistant
Office of Preservation Services
National Trust for Historic Preservation
740-748 Jackson Place, N.W.
Washington, D.C. 20006

NATIONAL TRUST FOR HISTORIC PRESERVATION [235]

Program Title:
Williamsburg Seminar on Historical Administration

1st SUPPLEMENT

Directory of Internships, Work Experience Programs, and On-the-Job Training Opportunities

Purpose:
To provide a training course in the principles and practices of historical administration.

Nature of Assignment:
Participants explore the various aspects of historical administration: philosophy, finances, sources of income, internal organization, conservation of collections, legal aspects, and community education. Training sessions are led by authorities in the field who emphasize practical approaches and solutions to the problems of historical agencies.

Duration:
4 weeks during the Summer.

Eligibility:
Professionals and graduate students who are interested in the field of historical administration.

Number of Awards:
18 per year.

Financial Data:
Tuition scholarships are awarded to Seminar participants.

Special Features:
Participants also have an opportunity to study the historical administration of Colonial Williamsburg and other historical agencies in the region.

Application Deadline:
Approximately February 15 of each year.

Request Application from:
Williamsburg Seminar Administrator
Office of Preservation Services
National Trust for Historic Preservation
740-748 Jackson Place, N.W.
Washington, D.C. 20006

NATIONAL TRUST FOR HISTORIC PRESERVATION [236]

Program Title:
Woodlawn Conference on Historic Site Administration

Purpose:
To provide a training opportunity for individuals interested in the preservation and protection of the American cultural heritage.

Nature of Assignment:
Participants examine pertinent aspects of the function, administration and operation of historic sites during training sessions led by professionals in the field.

Duration:
1 week.

Eligibility:
Staff members and volunteer workers at historic sites, museums and restoration projects who would like to participate in the training opportunity offered.

Number of Awards:
14 per year.

Financial Data:
Expenses for tuition, room and board, tours and educational materials are provided.

Special Features:
Participants live at Woodlawn Plantation, a historic property owned and administered by the National Trust.

Application Deadline:
Applications should be submitted approximately one month in advance of the Conference, which is usually held in February.

149

Request Application from:
Community Education Coordinator
Office of Preservation Services
National Trust for Historic Preservation
740-748 Jackson Place, N.W.
Washington, D.C. 20006

NATIONAL URBAN COALITION [237]

Program Title:
Internship Program

Purpose:
To provide a worthwhile learning experience for students while at the same time obtaining needed services for the organization.

Nature of Assignment:
Interns are involved primarily with research, although some writing and typing duties are also assigned.

Duration:
Varies, depending on Intern's scheduling.

Eligibility:
College students in good standing who are interested in working with the Coalition.

Number of Awards:
4 - 5 each year.

Financial Data:
Volunteer only; local travel expenses of up to $10 per week are paid.

Application Deadline:
Applications are accepted at any time.

Request Application from:
National Urban Coalition
1201 Connecticut Avenue, N.W. - Suite 400
Washington, D.C. 20036

NATIONAL URBAN FELLOWS, INC. [238]

Program Title:
Fellowship Program

Purpose:
To recruit and train people in their mid-20's and 30's, primarily members of minority groups, for careers in urban administration.

Nature of Assignment:
The Program consists of 3 basic components: a short, but intensive, Summer session at Yale University; an internship with a mayor, city manager or other prominent city, state or Federal administrator; and a residential semester at Occidental College. The Summer session, conducted by NUF staff, Yale faculty and visiting practitioners, focuses on public management, urban finance, legislation, and the preparation of relevant case studies. Internship assignments involve Fellows in the real work of urban administration. The residential semester at Occidental, which is optional, leads to a Master of Arts Degree in Urban Studies.

Duration:
6 week Summer session, followed by 9 month Internship (September - June) and optional 10 week residential semester.

Eligibility:
United States citizens 25 - 40 years old who have a B.A., B.S. or equivalent degree (or, in exceptional cases, equivalent experience), have had 2 years work (preferably administrative) experience, have leadership potential and commitment to the solutions of urban problems, and are willing to relocate.

Number of Awards:
10 - 20 per year.

Financial Data:
Fellows receive stipends commensurate with their previous annual salaries but not to exceed $15,000, limited travel expenses, comprehensive medical and dental insurance, and relocation allowances.

Stipulations:
An interview is required of all applicants selected as semi-finalists.

Special Features:
Participants attend an intensive one week leadership development program at the Center for Creative Leadership in Greensboro, North Carolina, during the Fellowship assignment.

Application Deadline:
March of each year.

Request Application from:
National Urban Fellows, Inc.
246 Church Street - Room 207
New Haven, Connecticut 06510

NEIGHBORHOODS UNITING PROJECT, INC. [239]

Program Title:
Neighborhood Studies Internship Program

Purpose:
To help citizens in a 12-town area of Prince George's County, Maryland, help themselves work on community issues that they feel are important.

Nature of Assignment:
Intern duties are varied, from researching and writing to organizing meetings, making phone calls, typing and undertaking other tasks as they arise.

Duration:
Full-time commitment is preferable, part-time work is acceptable.

Eligibility:
Individuals who are interested in the Program with preference given to graduate students who have some background in social work, urban studies or related fields.

Number of Awards:
An average of 10 per year.

Financial Data:
No remuneration is available.

Application Deadline:
Applications are accepted at any time.

Request Application from:
Neighborhoods Uniting Project
4300 Rhode Island Avenue
Brentwood, Maryland 20722

NEVADA. MENTAL HYGIENE AND MENTAL RETARDATION DIVISION [240]

Program Title:
Public Service Intern Program

Purpose:
To secure and apply to work situations a broad knowledge of occupational principles and practices, major laws, and the purposes and operations of State agencies.

Nature of Assignment:
Interns are placed in various Division offices where, under supervision of professional staff members, they receive training and complete a variety of assignments and activities.

Duration:
Varies; full or part time possible.

Eligibility:
Applicants must meet a 6 month residency requirement and must be enrolled in an accredited college or university with major work in a field related to State governmental operations and with successful completion of at least 30 credit hours.

Financial Data:
Interns receive salaries at an annual rate of approximately $6,400 to $15,200 depending on the level of schooling completed.

Application Deadline:
Applications are accepted at any time.

Request Application from:
Personnel Division
State of Nevada
Blasdel Building
Carson City, Nevada 89701

NEW CASTLE COUNTY, DELAWARE. DEPARTMENT OF PARKS AND RECREATION [241]

Program Title:
Student Field Work Program

Purpose:
To offer outstanding college and university students exposure to the functions and operations of the Department and to provide an opportunity for the exchange of ideas and insights.

Nature of Assignment:
Students work in a variety of capacities to gain the broadest experience possible as it relates to their professional goals. First students participate in a comprehensive orientation which introduces them to the Department's operations in the areas of park maintenance, recreation programming, parkland acquisition and development, operation of special facilities, and general administration. Each student then selects one of these function areas for concentrated experience, including specific project assignments.

Duration:
10 - 14 weeks during the Summer; full time.

Eligibility:
Students who are degree-seeking candidates in colleges and universities offering Parks and Recreation related curricula. Applicants must have their own transportation.

Financial Data:
Volunteer only.

Application Deadline:
March 1 of each year.

Request Application from:
Field Work Program Coordinator
Department of Parks and Recreation
102 Middleboro Road
Wilmington, Delaware 19804

NEW ENGLAND GERONTOLOGY CENTER [242]

Program Title:
College Work-Study/Graduate Assistantships/Internships

Purpose:
To provide students with an opportunity to work in a highly active organization dealing with adult learners and practitioners in the field of aging.

Nature of Assignment:
Participants are involved in a wide range of activities with specific assignments based on student interests and organizational needs.

Duration:
Part-time work for part or all of the year.

Eligibility:
College and university students who are eligible for work-study support or enrolled in graduate school programs. Applicants must be interested in the work of the Center and can come from a variety of disciplines including gerontology, sociology, management, accounting, computer programming, and library science.

Number of Awards:
5 - 15 per year, depending on funding.

Financial Data:
Work-Study students are paid an hourly wage; Graduate Assistants receive $2,000 - $5,000 plus tuition; and Interns have some expenses reimbursed.

Application Deadline:
Applications are accepted at any time.

Request Application from:
New England Gerontology Center
15 Garrison Avenue
Durham, New Hampshire 03824

NEW MEXICO. STATE PERSONNEL OFFICE [243]

Program Title:
State Government Intern Program

Purpose:
To provide an opportunity for students to gain professional maturity, practical experience and educational benefit while at the same time having the regular staff of sponsoring agencies supplemented by Interns with usable skills.

Nature of Assignment:
Interns are placed with State agencies; duties assigned are varied, depending on each agency's needs and objectives.

Duration:
Part or full time during the Summer; part time during the academic year.

Eligibility:
Students who are currently enrolled in accredited colleges or universities, have completed 2 years (60 semester hours) of college credit, and have a 2.5 grade point average on a 4.0 scale. Applicants must be New Mexico residents (and have been for at least one year) but may be attending school either within or outside of the state.

Financial Data:
Varies; funding sources are derived from each agency's budget so that an individual Intern's remuneration depends on the agency with which he/she is placed.

Stipulations:
Applicants attending out-of-state schools apply to the State Personnel Office; applicants attending schools inside of New Mexico must contact their school's Placement Office.

Application Deadline:
April 1 of each year.

Request Application from:
State Personnel Office
130 South Capitol
Santa Fe, New Mexico 87501

NEW YORK. ASSEMBLY [244]

Program Title:
Assembly Faculty Fellow

Purpose:
To provide a learning experience in State government.

Nature of Assignment:
The Assembly Faculty Fellow holds training sessions and seminars and serves as an on-site advisor for Assembly undergraduate and graduate interns.

Duration:
January - August or September - June.

Eligibility:
College faculty members who hold Ph.D. degrees in appropriate fields.

Number of Awards:
1 each year.

Financial Data:
A competitive stipend is paid.

Application Deadline:
October 1 of each year.

Request Application from:
New York State Assembly Intern Program
The Capitol - Room 518
Albany, New York 12248

THE NEWBERRY LIBRARY [245]

Program Title:
Short-Term Resident Fellowships for Individual Research

Purpose:
To foster the productive use of Newberry resources.

Nature of Assignment:
Fellows conduct independent research in any field appropriate to the Library's collection.

Duration:
Not to exceed 3 months.

Eligibility:
Applicants must have the Ph.D. degree or have completed all doctoral requirements except the dissertation. Preference is given to individuals who particularly need to use Newberry resources and to those from outside the Chicago area.

Financial Data:
$500 per month.

Application Deadline:
March 15 or November 1 of each year.

Request Application from:
Committee on Awards
The Newberry Library
60 West Walton Street
Chicago, Illinois 60610

THE NEWS JOURNAL [246]

Program Title:
Summer Internship

Purpose:
To give journalism students on-the-job experience.

Nature of Assignment:
Interns are assigned general news reporting duties.

Duration:
Summer only; full time.

Eligibility:
College and university juniors and seniors who have appropriate interests and skills. Preference is given to students planning on entering the newspaper field upon graduation.

Number of Awards:
2 per year.

Financial Data:
$135 a week.

Application Deadline:
April 15 of each year.

Request Application from:
The News Journal
70 West Fourth Street
Mansfield, Ohio 44901

THE NEWSPAPER FUND [247]

Program Title:
Editing Internship Program

Purpose:
To provide on-the-job experience for students interested in careers as editors and to provide an opportunity for such students to improve their reporting and writing talents by approaching news journalism from the editor's standpoint.

Nature of Assignment:
Interns work on copydesks of cooperating daily newspapers and wire services.

Duration:
At least 10 weeks during the Summer (from the end of an intensive training course until school begins in the Fall); full time.

Eligibility:
College and university students who will have finished their junior year by the Internship Summer and are interested in careers as editors. Applicants who have declared journalism as a major or minor or those who have received a previous news Internship will be considered for the Editing Internship Program even though they have applied to the Fund's Reporting Program.

Number of Awards:
40 per year.

Financial Data:
Interns are paid salaries by the newspapers or wire services with which they affiliate with specific amounts decided directly by the employing news organization. A $700 scholarship check, made payable to the Intern's school, will be sent by the Fund upon completion of an Internship.

Stipulations:
Interns are responsible for making their own Internship arrangements. Interns may be asked to contact particular newspapers to arrange employment with such newspapers making the final decision on Intern selection.

Special Features:
Prior to beginning their on-the-job assignments, Interns attend an intensive copyediting training course, paid for by the Fund, at a designated university.

Application Deadline:
December 1 for an Internship the following Summer.

Request Application from:
The Newspaper Fund
P.O. Box 300
Princeton, New Jersey 08540

THE NEWSPAPER FUND [248]

Program Title:
Reporting Internship Program

Purpose:
To provide on-the-job experience for students with news writing and reporting ambitions but no newspaper training.

Nature of Assignment:
Interns are assigned as reporters on cooperating newspapers where they perform general news gathering and writing duties.

Duration:
At least 12 weeks during the Summer (from as soon as possible after classes end in the Spring until resumption of classes in the Fall); full time.

Eligibility:
College and university students who will have finished their junior year by the Internship Summer, have had little or no previous journalism preparation at college, and have not held a journalism internship before. Applicants who have declared journalism as a major or minor or those who have received a previous news internship will be considered for the Fund's Editing Internship Program rather than the Reporting Program.

Number of Awards:
20 per year.

Financial Data:
Interns are paid salaries by the newspapers with which they affiliate with specific amounts decided directly by the employing news organization. A $500 scholarship check, made payable to the Intern's school, will be sent by the Fund at completion of an Internship.

Stipulations:
Interns are responsible for making their own Internship arrangements. Those selected as Interns are given the names of newspapers which have hired Interns in the past and biographical sketches of Interns are sent to the newspapers. Interns make application directly to the newspapers of their choice with the final decision on a job offer made by the newspapers involved. Interns are required to clear their job choice with the Fund before accepting an offer.

Application Deadline:
December 1 for an Internship the following Summer.

Request Application from:
The Newspaper Fund
P.O. Box 300
Princeton, New Jersey 08540

NORTH CENTRAL FEDERATION, INC. [249]

Program Title:
North Central Youth Service Bureau Training Program

Purpose:
To assist the Bureau in providing counseling, educational and vocational services to youth; functioning as an alternative to the police and courts for youthful offenders; and involving youth in constructive community endeavors.

Nature of Assignment:
Participants serve as youth and family counselors and tutors and are given on-the-job training in working directly with young people, both on the streets and in their homes.

Duration:
All year or Summer only; full or part time.

1st SUPPLEMENT

Directory of Internships, Work Experience Programs, and On-the-Job Training Opportunities

Eligibility:
High school graduates or those with equivalency diplomas who have interests and skills appropriate to the work. Preference is given to residents of the North Central area. College applicants must be eligible for work-study funds.

Financial Data:
Expenses are paid; work-study support is arranged in cooperation with each student's school.

Special Features:
Participants may also attend training courses offered through the Juvenile Services Administration.

Application Deadline:
Applications are accepted at any time.

Request Application from:
North Central Youth Service Bureau
4000 York Road
Baltimore, Maryland 21218

NORTH PENN VALLEY BOYS' CLUB [250]

Program Title:
Recreational Program Trainee

Purpose:
To give trainees a better understanding of how a Boys' Club is operated and to provide them with valuable job experience.

Nature of Assignment:
Trainees organize and conduct vocational, educational, social and recreational programs for boys ages 8 - 18. Participants are trained by professional staffers and work under the guidance of the Program Director.

Duration:
All year; part or full time.

Eligibility:
College and university students who are majoring in recreation, physical education or sociology/social work.

Financial Data:
Volunteer only.

Application Deadline:
Applications are accepted at any time.

Request Application from:
North Penn Valley Boys' Club
P.O. Box 103
Landsdale, Pennsylvania 19446

O

OAKLAWN COMMUNITY MENTAL HEALTH CENTER [251]

Program Title:
Internship Program

Purpose:
To provide training in mental health services and programs.

Nature of Assignment:
Interns are assigned a variety of duties in the following mental health program areas: inpatient, partial hospital, outpatient, emergency, consultation, education, alcohol, drugs, and aging services.

Duration:
Minimum of 3 months.

Eligibility:
Individuals interested in the Program who have appropriate academic status for specific experience desired.

Number of Awards:
Varying, usually 1 or 2 in each discipline involved.

Financial Data:
Interns receive stipends commensurate with the work assigned, except that there is no pay for undergraduate placements.

Application Deadline:
3 - 4 months prior to the desired beginning date for an Internship.

Request Application from:
Professional Education Committee
Oaklawn Community Mental Health Center
2600 Oakland Avenue
Elkhart, Indiana 46514

OFFENDER AID AND RESTORATION OF NORTH CAROLINA [252]

Program Title:
Training Program

Purpose:
To help in reducing recidivism through the use of trained community volunteers who are assigned on a one-to-one basis to persons incarcerated in local county jails.

Nature of Assignment:
Participants receive training in the criminal justice system, management, administration and related areas. Duties and tasks assigned involve program development, volunteer coordination, staff training, program audits and technical assistance.

Duration:
Open to discussion.

Eligibility:
Individuals who are interested in the work and have the ability to communicate well with others. Applicants with some knowledge of the justice system are preferred.

Financial Data:
Volunteer only.

Application Deadline:
Applications are accepted at any time.

Request Application from:
Offender Aid and Restoration of North Carolina
133½ South Salisbury Street
Raleigh, North Carolina 27601

OFFENDER AID AND RESTORATION OF THE U.S., INC. [253]

Program Title:
Intern Program

Purpose:
To help jailed inmates, and to upgrade the criminal justice system.

Nature of Assignment:
Interns work in the Program Department of OAR/USA. Duties assigned include such tasks as community organizing, public relations, troubleshooting and providing technical assistance to OAR sites. Some travel may be required. Interns receive initial orientation and ongoing training with the educational goals of each Intern kept in mind.

Duration:
Minimum of 6 months.

Eligibility:
Persons who have interests and abilities appropriate to working in the Program.

Number of Awards:
2 per year.

Financial Data:
No financial remuneration; travel expenses will be paid.

Application Deadline:
1 month prior to desired beginning date.

Request Application from:
Offender Aid and Restoration of the U.S.
414 4th Street, N.E.
Charlottesville, Virginia 22901

OKLAHOMA. LEGISLATIVE COUNCIL [254]

Program Title:
Legislative Council Internship Program

Purpose:
To provide an educational experience for interested students by involving them in all substantive phases of the legislative process, especially decisionmaking.

Nature of Assignment:
The Intern works closely with an Intern Supervisor who is a senior level researcher. The Intern is exempted from busywork assignments and instead is introduced to and involved in the diverse work performed by staff support offices. In addition, the Intern is encouraged to select an area(s) of particular interest and develop a degree of expertise in it.

Duration:
1 semester coincident with the regular annual legislative session, approximately January - June; half time.

Eligibility:
College or university students majoring in political science who have junior level standing, outstanding academic records, and demonstrated initiative. Applicants must be attending Oklahoma schools or be Oklahomans attending out-of-state schools.

Number of Awards:
1 each year.

Financial Data:
Volunteer only.

Application Deadline:
November 15 of each year.

Request Application from:
Director of Research and Reference Services
State Legislative Council
305 State Capitol
Oklahoma City, Oklahoma 73105

1st SUPPLEMENT

Directory of Internships, Work Experience Programs, and On-the-Job Training Opportunities

OLDSMOBILE DIVISION, GENERAL MOTORS CORPORATION [255]

Program Title:
Summer Hiring Program

Purpose:
To provide training and experience for engineering students, and to identify potential future employees for Oldsmobile.

Nature of Assignment:
Students are assigned engineering positions in manufacturing, plant engineering, production engineering, chemical and experimental laboratories, and product engineering.

Duration:
Summer only; full time.

Eligibility:
College and university students who have completed at least 2 years of an engineering program, majoring in mechanical, electrical, chemical or industrial engineering.

Number of Awards:
30 plus each Summer.

Financial Data:
Students are paid an hourly wage, the specific amount determined by curriculum followed in school and years of study completed.

Application Deadline:
April 15 of each year.

Request Application from:
Summer Hiring Program
Salaried Personnel
Oldsmobile Division, General Motors
Lansing, Michigan 48921

OPERATION CROSSROADS AFRICA [256]

Program Title:
West Indies Workcamp Program

Purpose:
To provide an opportunity for students to learn about the culture of other people, and to learn more about their own culture in the process.

Nature of Assignment:
Students become part of the life of a West Indian community by working alongside local counterparts on a wanted project, such as the construction of a vitally needed facility (e.g., daycare center, medical clinic or school). In addition, there are several individual programs where students with experience in such fields as sports, handicrafts, tutoring, dance or music are assigned to work with local people in the development of special projects.

Duration:
6 weeks during the Summer, from approximately the beginning of July through mid-August.

Eligibility:
High school and college students who have an enthusiasm for learning about the life style of people representing another culture and are open to learning new things about themselves.

Financial Data:
Participants pay $1,100 which includes all expenses except personal spending money and round-trip transportation to New York City; limited financial aid is available.

Stipulations:
There is a nonrefundable $10 application fee.

Special Features:
Students participate in a 2 day orientation in New York prior to departure for the West Indies.

Application Deadline:
May 15 of each year.

Request Application from:
Director
West Indies Program
Operation Crossroads Africa
150 Fifth Avenue
New York, New York 10011

OREGON. LEGISLATIVE ASSEMBLY [257]

Program Title:
Internship Program

Purpose:
To provide college and university students with an opportunity to see a state legislature in action and to provide assistance to legislators.

Nature of Assignment:
Interns are assigned a variety of duties, such as conducting research, providing constituent assistance, performing office work, handling correspondence, writing speeches, and testifying when members are unable to.

Duration:
Length of legislative session, approximately 2 academic quarters; full or part time.

Eligibility:
Students attending Oregon colleges and universities who are interested in the Program, have been accepted for participation by their school departments, and have been accepted by a legislator. Students in any field of study may apply.

Number of Awards:
Approximately 50 - 100 each year.

Financial Data:
Volunteer only.

Special Features:
Students may arrange to receive academic credit for participation in the Program.

Application Deadline:
Autumn of each even numbered year.

Request Application from:
Legislative Administration Committee
State Capitol - Room 5401
Salem, Oregon 97310

ORGANIZATION OF AMERICAN STATES [258]

Program Title:
OAS Student Intern Program

Purpose:
To provide students with an opportunity to gain a better understanding of the Inter-American system and to prepare them for public service careers in such fields as economics, social development, science, education and management.

Nature of Assignment:
Interns gain direct work experience in some aspect of OAS activities with every effort made in work placement to match Intern interests and skills with those of the professional staff. Interns are assigned to Programs, Departments or Offices of the General Secretariat where they are integrated with the staff and perform a wide variety of functions including research, analysis, writing, project design, and administration.

Duration:
Usually for an academic term, quarter or semester (i.e., Winter, Spring, Summer or Fall session).

Eligibility:
College and university students in the last 2 years of undergraduate study or at the graduate level who have at least a 3.0 grade point average, possess a thorough knowledge of at least 2 of the official OAS languages (English, Spanish, French and Portuguese), and have the recommendation of a professor in their major field of study. Applicants can come from any academic field. Nationals of OAS member states are given preference.

Financial Data:
No remuneration provided; this does not preclude Interns from receiving support from other sources.

Stipulations:
At the conclusion of their assignments, and on a monthly basis during the assignment, Interns are to submit written evaluations of their experiences.

Special Features:
Interns may arrange to receive academic credit for participation in the Program. Interns take part in an Orientation Program and attend weekly seminars conducted by different areas of the General Secretariat.

Application Deadline:
At least 2 months prior to the desired beginning of an Internship.

Request Application from:
Chief, Recruitment and Placement Unit
Office of Personnel
Organization of American States
1735 Eye Street, N.W. - Room 1025
Washington, D.C. 20006

OWENSBORO BROADCASTING COMPANY, INC. [259]

Program Title:
O.B.C. Air Personality Internship

Purpose:
To train minorities for employment in the broadcast industries.

Nature of Assignment:
Interns receive training in the operation of all pertinent control room equipment, instruction in the writing and production of radio commercials, and experience with actual on-air shifts.

Duration:
Minimum of 13 weeks, beginning January 1, April 1, July 1, or October 1.

Eligibility:
Individuals who are interested in radio careers and have an understandable command of the English language, both written and verbal.

Number of Awards:
4 per year.

Financial Data:
Interns receive the minimum wage.

Special Features:
Interns have the possibility of joining the O.B.C. staff as permanent members or receive assistance in joining other broadcast operations.

Application Deadline:
30 days prior to the desired beginning of an Internship.

Request Application from:
WOMI/WBKR
P.O. Box 1330
Owensboro, Kentucky 42301

1st SUPPLEMENT

Directory of Internships, Work Experience Programs, and On-the-Job Training Opportunities

OWENSBORO BROADCASTING COMPANY, INC. [260]

Program Title:
O.B.C. News Internship

Purpose:
To train minorities for employment in the broadcast industries.

Nature of Assignment:
Interns receive on-line training in the operation of a small market radio station, including experience in news reporting and writing.

Duration:
Minimum of 13 weeks, beginning January 1, April 1, July 1 or October 1.

Eligibility:
Individuals who are interested in radio careers and have an understandable command of the English language, both written and verbal.

Number of Awards:
4 per year.

Financial Data:
Interns receive the minimum wage.

Special Features:
Interns have the possibility of joining the O.B.C. staff as permanent members or receive assistance in joining other broadcast operations.

Application Deadline:
30 days prior to the desired beginning of an Internship.

Request Application from:
WOMI/WBKR
P.O. Box 1330
Owensboro, Kentucky 42301

p

PALM BEACH COUNTY MENTAL HEALTH CENTER [261]

Program Title:
Psychology Internship Program

Purpose:
To provide clinical experience for predoctoral students.

Nature of Assignment:
Interns are involved in psychotherapy and crisis intervention training programs.

Duration:
11 months, September - August.

Eligibility:
Predoctoral psychology students who are enrolled in clinical/counseling degree programs.

Number of Awards:
2 per year.

Financial Data:
Interns receive stipends of $6,000 plus benefits.

Application Deadline:
January 15 of each year.

Request Application from:
Psychology Internship Program
Palm Beach County CMHC
1041 45th Street
West Palm Beach, Florida 33407

PENNSYLVANIA. HOUSE OF REPRESENTATIVES [262]

Program Title:
Student Volunteers

Purpose:
To provide experience in the legislative setting.

Nature of Assignment:
Assignments vary according to each student's background and field of academic concentration. Students are placed in leadership offices or with the various standing committees.

Duration:
Part-time commitment is required.

Eligibility:
Students who have interests and abilities appropriate to working in the legislature. Specific assignments might require special skills.

Financial Data:
Volunteer only at this time with the possibility of support in the future.

Application Deadline:
Applications are accepted at any time.

Request Application from:
Speaker's Office
Pennsylvania House of Representatives
Capitol Building - Room 139
Harrisburg, Pennsylvania 17120

PEOPLE FOR COMMUNITY ACTION. YOUTH SERVICES BUREAU [263]

Program Title:
Community Organization Outreach Internship

Purpose:
To assist in providing direct service, referral and advocacy, to youth and families in their own environment.

Nature of Assignment:
Interns identify and serve groups of teens at their natural gathering spots and respond to community crises involving young people. Interns receive in-service training focusing on the prevention of drug abuse, delinquency and ungovernability.

Duration:
1 semester or Summer; minimum of 10 hours per week.

Eligibility:
Students who have had 2 years of college study including courses in psychology, counseling, social work or related areas.

Number of Awards:
3 per semester.

Financial Data:
Volunteer; travel expenses occurring in course of duties are paid.

Application Deadline:
Applications are accepted at any time.

1st SUPPLEMENT

Directory of Internships, Work Experience Programs, and On-the-Job Training Opportunities

Request Application from:
People for Community Action
Youth Services Bureau
1707 Taylor Avenue
Baltimore, Maryland 21234

PEOPLE FOR COMMUNITY ACTION. YOUTH SERVICES BUREAU [264]

Program Title:
Graduate Intern in Counseling

Purpose:
To assist in providing direct services, referral and advocacy, to youth and families in their own environments.

Nature of Assignment:
Intern is assigned counseling duties within the programs of the Bureau. Clinical supervision is provided.

Duration:
1 semester or Summer; minimum of 10 hours per week.

Eligibility:
Graduate students in counseling who have interests and skills appropriate to the work and are near completion of the Master's degree.

Number of Awards:
1 per semester.

Financial Data:
Volunteer; travel expenses occurring in course of duty are paid.

Application Deadline:
Applications are accepted at any time.

Request Application from:
People for Community Action
Youth Services Bureau
1707 Taylor Avenue
Baltimore, Maryland 21234

PEOPLE'S MEDIA COLLECTIVE [265]

Program Title:
PMC Radio Training Program

Purpose:
To provide training and practical experience in radio production, especially for women and minority persons.

Nature of Assignment:
Trainees participate in production of documentary news and other programming for use by Bay area radio stations and syndication. Trainees also perform some organizational work, such as publicity, maintenance, live recording, office work and fund raising.

Duration:
6 months; 10 hours per week minimum.

Eligibility:
Interested people who have the ability to work with a group on a team project, are reliable, and are consistent in doing assigned tasks. Preference is given to women, gay and third world people.

Number of Awards:
Flexible.

Financial Data:
Volunteer only.

Special Features:
Trainees prepare for an FCC 3rd class broadcast license.

Application Deadline:
Applications are accepted July 15 - January 15.

Request Application from:
Haight-Ashbury Community Radio
618 Shrader Street
San Francisco, California 94117

PICO-UNION NEIGHBORHOOD COUNCIL [266]

Program Title:
In-School Work Experience/Adult Work Experience/On-the-Job Training

Purpose:
To provide training and jobs for low-income residents of the city of Los Angeles.

Nature of Assignment:
Participants are placed at jobs in both the public and private sectors. Training covers a wide range of activities, from work in the health services to clerical duties, landscape training and housing restoration or rehabilitation.

Duration:
1 - 3 years for In-School Work Experience; 12 - 26 weeks for Adult Work Experience; and up to 1 year for On-the-Job Training.

Eligibility:
High School students who are 14 - 18 years old and residents of Los Angeles are eligible for the In-School Work Experience program. Applicants for other work experience must be City residents 16 - 29 years old who have been unemployed for 26 weeks or meet other special criteria (e.g., handicapped, high school drop-outs, ex-offenders, veterans, women with no prior job experience).

Financial Data:
In-School Work Experience enrollees are paid $2.50 per hour, adults receive $3.00 an hour; amounts paid On-the-Job Trainees vary, depending on actual private sector wages.

Special Features:
Participants receive medical, dental, optical, counseling, academic and emergency supportive services.

Application Deadline:
Applications are accepted at any time.

Request Application from:
Pico-Union Neighborhood Council
1625 South Toberman Street
Los Angeles, California 90015

PINE BLUFF COMMERCIAL [267]

Program Title:
Summer Internships

Purpose:
To develop news gathering, news writing and editing skills in college bound or college students.

Nature of Assignment:
Interns are first assigned to the copy desk where they learn the newspaper's style and the VDT system; then they are moved to general assignment, social or sports reporting positions.

Duration:
Summer only, 3 months; full time.

Eligibility:
Students who are or will be attending college and have acceptable language skills. Applicants must demonstrate language skills by taking separate spelling, copyediting and writing tests.

Number of Awards:
Approximately 2 per year.

Financial Data:
$110 per week plus on-the-job expenses.

Application Deadline:
May 15 of each year.

Request Application from:
Managing Editor
Pine Bluff Commercial
P.O. Box 6469
300 Beach Street
Pine Bluff, Arkansas 71611

THE POPULATION INSTITUTE. EDUCATION DIVISION [268]

Program Title:
Intern Program

Purpose:
To assist in the Division's program to expand and improve the coverage of population education in American schools.

Nature of Assignment:
Interns are involved in the development and coordination of an extensive textbook evaluation process; they also assist in identifying and contacting educational leadership organizations to stimulate their own program development in population education. In general, Interns are provided a varied work experience with as much responsibility assigned as possible.

Duration:
Varies, depending on Interns; full time during the Summer.

Eligibility:
Applicants should be college juniors, seniors or graduate students with a willingness to take initiative, personal creativity, oral and written facility, and moderate typing skills. Interest, academic background or experience in population and related fields is desirable.

Number of Awards:
1 or 2 each year.

Financial Data:
Volunteer; daily travel expenses are provided.

Stipulations:
Continuation of the Program is dependent upon funding of the Division.

Special Features:
Interns may arrange to receive academic credit for participation in the Program.

Application Deadline:
Applications are accepted at any time but must be received by April 1 for Summer Internships.

Request Application from:
Education Division
The Population Institute
110 Maryland Avenue, N.E.
Washington, D.C. 20002

PORTLAND COMMUNITY DESIGN CENTER [269]

Program Title:
C.D.C. Student Practicum Internship

Purpose:
To offer students valuable work experience where they can apply the skills and knowledge learned in school.

Nature of Assignment:
Interns are given one or more projects for which they are responsible, following each through from start to finish. For instance, Interns meet with clients requesting C.D.C. help and then make any measured, working or remodeling drawings necessary to complete the resulting project.

Duration:
Varies; the Center is open to arranging Internships according to students' needs.

Eligibility:
Students who are dependable, responsible and capable of making measured/working drawings. Applicants could be advanced architectural draftspeople or perhaps fifth year architecture students.

Financial Data:
Volunteer; all direct costs involved in Intern projects are paid by the Center.

Application Deadline:
Applications are accepted at any time.

Request Application from:
Portland Community Design Center
723 Southeast Grand Avenue
Portland, Oregon 97214

PROJECT ON THE STATUS AND EDUCATION OF WOMEN [270]

Program Title:
Project Interns

Purpose:
To provide a clearinghouse of information about women in higher education, focusing on the status of women as employees and as students as well as the education of women in general.

Nature of Assignment:
Interns perform a variety of tasks. At times they work on substantive assignments germane to the Project's focus, at other times Interns assist Project staff members in carrying out their daily work.

Eligibility:
Individuals who have an interest in and/or commitment to educational equity and equal rights.

Number of Awards:
Maximum of 2 or 3 Interns at any one time.

Financial Data:
No remuneration is provided.

Application Deadline:
Applications are accepted at any time.

Request Application from:
Project on the Status and Education of Women
Association of American Colleges
1818 R Street, N.W.
Washington, D.C. 20009

PUBLIC INTEREST ECONOMICS FOUNDATION [271]

Program Title:
PIE-F Internship

Purpose:
To involve young economists in public policy formation.

Nature of Assignment:
Interns work with the Director of Education or the Director of the Clearinghouse, or they are involved in pursuing individual economic research on current public issues.

1st SUPPLEMENT

Directory of Internships, Work Experience Programs, and On-the-Job Training Opportunities

Duration:
Semester, part time; or Summer, full time.

Eligibility:
Students who have interests and abilities appropriate to the work and whose course of study reflects an economic concentration.

Number of Awards:
4 - 6 per year.

Financial Data:
Interns receive $800 during the Summer; expenses only are paid during the academic year.

Application Deadline:
Applications are accepted at any time.

Request Application from:
Public Interest Economics Foundation
1714 Massachusetts Avenue, N.W.
Washington, D.C. 20036

q

QUAKER UNITED NATIONS OFFICE [272]

Program Title:
Quaker U.N. Interns Program

Purpose:
To provide the opportunity for young graduate students from all different parts of the world to share in the work of the Quaker U.N. Office (QUNO) and to involve themselves directly in issues of special interest that are before the United Nations.

Nature of Assignment:
Interns work as program assistants to QUNO staffers and, as such, are fuly involved members of the Quaker U.N. Team. Interns may be assigned to follow reports and attend committee meetings and U.N. sessions devoted to one of the program priorities of QUNO, interpret specific issues and/or the U.N. generally to the Quaker constituency around the world, develop programs for Quaker action in QUNO priority areas, assist in research and information gathering, participate in meetings with U.N. delegates and officials to help convey the Quaker view on specific issues, and travel with the Friends World Committee to interpret international concerns.

Duration:
2 - 3 months; full time.

Eligibility:
Graduate students from any country in the world who are fluent in written and spoken English, between 20 and 30 years old, able to work well with others, and able to adapt to New York climate and customs. Members of the Society of Friends are preferred.

Number of Awards:
Varies year to year.

Financial Data:
Interns receive accomodations (including housing, breakfast and dinner), $5 per day living allowance, and round-trip travel costs to New York when necessary.

Application Deadline:
Applications are accepted at any time. QUNO appoints Interns to specific program

assignments for various periods throughout the year; both specific projects and application deadlines therefor vary from year to year.

Request Application from:
Quaker United Nations Office
345 East 46th Street
New York, New York 10017

r

R.O.O.C. WORKSHOP [273]

Program Title:
Internship in Vocational Evaluation

Purpose:
To provide a practical and real experience in vocational evaluation.

Nature of Assignment:
Interns perform vocational evaluations on clients in a rehabilitation facility.

Duration:
Varies.

Eligibility:
Individuals who are interested in the program and have at least a B.S. degree in a relevant field.

Number of Awards:
Open.

Financial Data:
Amount of financial remuneration is arranged individually.

Application Deadline:
Applications are accepted at any time.

Request Application from:
R.O.O.C. Workshop
2809 North St. Helen Road
St. Helen, Michigan 48656

RADIO FREE GEORGIA BROADCASTING FOUNDATION, INC. [274]

Program Title:
Volunteer Program

Purpose:
To serve community broadcasting needs and to learn broadcast skills.

Nature of Assignment:
Assignments vary and may include on-the-air announcing, broadcast engineering, publicity, production duties and/or office work.

Duration:
Determined individually. Applicants should have a high degree of interest in learning about and participating in broadcasting.

1st SUPPLEMENT

Directory of Internships, Work Experience Programs, and On-the-Job Training Opportunities

Financial Data:
Volunteer only.

Application Deadline:
Applications are accepted at any time.

Request Application from:
WRFG
1091 Euclid Avenue
Atlanta, Georgia 30307

RAVENSWOOD HOSPITAL COMMUNITY MENTAL HEALTH CENTER [275]

Program Title:
Clinical Internship for Master's Level Psychologists and Social Workers.

Purpose:
To provide a training experience in psychodiagnosis and treatment with severely disturbed adults.

Nature of Assignment:
Interns are assigned to work in psychodiagnosis, individual and group therapy with clients served by an Adult Day Treatment Partial Hospitalization Program.

Duration:
Minimum 20 hours per week for at least 3 months; longer training periods can be arranged.

Eligibility:
Applicants must be enrolled in M.A. or M.S.W. degree programs in clinical and counseling psychology.

Financial Data:
Although there is no regular stipend provided, it may be possible to offer some financial assistance depending on student needs and availability of funds.

Application Deadline:
April 15 for Internships during the Summer, July 15 for Fall Internships, and November 15 for Internships in the Winter or Spring.

Request Application from:
Training and Research Department
Ravenswood Hospital Community Mental Health Center
4550 North Winchester Avenue
Chicago, Illinois 60640

RENSSELAER COUNTY HISTORICAL SOCIETY AND MUSEUM [276]

Program Title:
Internship Program

Purpose:
To provide training in museum curatorial work.

Nature of Assignment:
The Intern is given various assignments in the curatorial department including accessioning, cataloging, exhibit work, and conservation tasks.

Duration:
2 months; full time for 5 days a week.

Eligibility:
Interested individuals who have had some prior training or experience in museum work. Preference is given to applicants with undergraduate or graduate degrees in history or art history.

Number of Awards:
1 per year.

Financial Data:
Stipend of $1,000.

Special Features:
Selected volunteers are also welcome for curatorial work on a regular basis.

Application Deadline:
February 1 of each year.

Request Application from:
Director
Rensselaer County Historial Society
59 Second Street
Troy, New York 12180

RENSSELAER COUNTY, NEW YORK. MENTAL HEALTH DEPARTMENT [277]

Program Title:
United Services Volunteer Program

Purpose:
To assist in providing outpatient counseling to mental hygiene clients of all ages.

Nature of Assignment:
Duties assigned vary, from involvement in case aid to outreach work. Participants receive informal training specific to the particular tasks to be performed.

Eligibility:
Interested individuals who have a bachelor's degree in psychology, social work or a related field.

Number of Awards:
1 per year, possibly more.

Financial Data:
Volunteer only.

Application Deadline:
Applications are accepted at any time.

Request Application from:
United Services - Volunteer Work
Rensselaer County Mental Health Department
33 Second Street
Troy, New York 12180

RESOURCE CENTER FOR NONVIOLENCE [278]

Program Title:
Internship Program

Purpose:
To offer a unique opportunity to learn about and experience nonviolence as a force for personal and social change, and to give people firsthand experience in the programs and work of an educational center in a local community.

Nature of Assignment:
Interns undertake specific projects or tasks of particular interest to them; participate in events; plan and direct such activities as study-groups, speakers, workshops and other educational programs; join in the day-to-day operations of the Center, including office work; and help put out a newspaper.

Duration:
Negotiable according to interest and need; usually from 1 - 6 months.

Eligibility:
Individuals who have an active interest in nonviolence and are willing to share in a cooperative work situation both in the office and in programming.

Number of Awards:
Up to 12 per year, usually no more than 3 at any one time.

Financial Data:
No remuneration is offered, although there is the possibility of limited support for housing.

Application Deadline:
Applications are accepted at any time.

Request Application from:
Resource Center for Nonviolence
P.O. Box 2324
Santa Cruz, California 95063

RHODE ISLAND HISTORICAL SOCIETY [279]

Program Title:
Student Internship Program

Purpose:
To familiarize students interested in historical society/museum/library work with the nature of the business in order that they can better decide if they wish to pursue the field as a career and select courses for future educational advantage.

Nature of Assignment:
Interns are assigned to assist Society staff in the general areas of history museum work, historical research libraries, or publications. Interns learn to catalog collections of manuscript documents, books and newspapers, films, or museum objects. They also gain experience in documentary editing, interpretation of historic sites and houses, historic preservation and restoration of buildings, public programs and museum education.

Duration:
At present, Summer only.

Eligibility:
College and university students with demonstrated interest in the history/museum field who have course concentration in American Studies and History of Art.

Number of Awards:
10 per year.

Financial Data:
No stipends are provided.

Application Deadline:
March 15 of each year.

Request Application from:
Rhode Island Historical Society
52 Power Street
Providence, Rhode Island 02906

RICHMOND TIMES-DISPATCH [280]

Program Title:
Summer News Department Interns

Purpose:
To encourage talented college writers and editors to enter the newspaper field as a career.

Nature of Assignment:
Interns serve as Summer replacements for staff members with duties ranging from working as news clerks to functioning as reporters/editors.

Duration:
Summer only; full time.

Eligibility:
College and university students who have a strong commitment to professional print journalism and demonstrated writing or editing ability. Preference is given to students completing their third year of study.

Financial Data:
Interns are paid competitive salaries.

Application Deadline:
February 1 of each year.

Request Application from:
Assistant Managing Editor
Richmond Times-Dispatch
333 East Grace Street
Richmond, Virginia 23219

ROBERT F. KENNEDY CHILDREN'S CENTER [281]

Program Title:
Internships in Residential Treatment

Purpose:
To assist in providing long-term treatment, mileau therapy and special education to emotionally disturbed boys with the aim of reintegrating them back into their families, communities, and public schools.

Nature of Assignment:
Interns are assigned supervised child care work and special education teaching duties. They are involved in the total care, education and treatment of Center residents.

Duration:
January - June, Summer, September - January, or longer periods if desired.

Eligibility:
Individuals who have interests and abilities appropriate to the work with preference given to applicants of maturity and serious commitment.

Number of Awards:
4 per year, 2 in child care and 2 in teaching.

Financial Data:
Volunteer only.

Application Deadline:
Applications should be submitted 2 months in advance of the desired Internship period.

Request Application from:
RFK Children's Center
Box 7 Old Common Road
Lancaster, Massachusetts 01523

S

SABRE FOUNDATION [282]

Program Title:
Journalism Fund

Purpose:
To assure young journalists a chance for experience with small periodicals, and to assist small (circulation of less than 100,000) politically-oriented journals improve their coverage of governmental problems.

Nature of Assignment:
Participants investigate and write about problems created by existing governmental activities in the areas of civil liberties, economic freedom and efficiency, or foreign affairs. Resulting articles are descriptive rather than argumentative or philosophical. Recipients of Fund awards have the option of interning with participating periodicals (such as *New Republic*, *Progressive*, *Alternative* and *Reason*) while researching the article for which they received their awards.

Duration:
Varies; arranged by each grant recipient.

Eligibility:
Individuals who have interests and skills appropriate to the work, are less than 30 years old, and have had some previous writing experience.

Number of Awards:
12 per year.

Financial Data:
Awardees receive grants of $1,000 and up to $500 in research expenses for articles written. Internships provided by participating periodicals are unpaid in most cases, but Journalism Fund grants can be applied toward living expenses during the internship period.

Stipulations:
Articles underwritten by Fund awards are to be donated to journals participating in the Sabre program.

Application Deadline:
February 1 and July 1 of each year.

Request Application from:
Sabre Foundation Journalism Fund
221 West Carrillo Street
Santa Barbara, California 93101

SACRAMENTO COUNTY, CALIFORNIA [283]

Program Title:
College Work Study Program

Purpose:
To enable financially disadvantaged students to complete their junior and senior years of college when financial problems would otherwise have forced them to drop out of school.

Nature of Assignment:
Students are assigned to various County departments and agencies where they work at jobs which provide the opportunity for them to qualify for permanent professional level positions within the County.

Duration:
2 academic years; part time.

Eligibility:
Students in the Sacramento area who have completed 2 years of college, are enrolled in degree programs at accredited 4 year institutions, and are economically disadvantaged, unemployed or underemployed.

Number of Awards:
21 per year.

Financial Data:
Students are paid for their work.

1st SUPPLEMENT

Directory of Internships, Work Experience Programs, and On-the-Job Training Opportunities

Special Features:
Students who complete the program and obtain the bachelor's degree are normally transitioned into permanent County positions.

Application Deadline:
Applications are accepted at any time.

Request Application from:
Special Employment Unit
Department of Personnel Management
901 G Street - Room 227
Sacramento, California 95814

SACRAMENTO COUNTY, CALIFORNIA [284]

Program Title:
Special Student Trainee Program

Purpose:
To assist in the development of handicapped high school students to the point where they can qualify for advancement to regular permanent positions.

Nature of Assignment:
Trainees are assigned to various County departments or agencies where they gain work experience in nonprofessional jobs.

Eligibility:
Handicapped high school students in the Sacramento area who are enrolled in approved Work Experience school programs and have the recommendation of the program coordinator.

Number of Awards:
6 per year.

Financial Data:
Students are paid for their work.

Application Deadline:
Applications are accepted at any time.

Request Application from:
Special Employment Unit
Department of Personnel Management
901 G Street - Room 227
Sacramento, California 95814

SACRAMENTO COUNTY, CALIFORNIA [285]

Program Title:
Student Trainee Program

Purpose:
To provide students with an opportunity to become familiar with the practical application of the courses they are studying.

Nature of Assignment:
Trainees are assigned to various County departments and agencies where they gain work experience in different academic-related areas.

Duration:
Part time during the academic year.

Eligibility:
College and university students in the Sacramento area who have completed 3 years of a curriculum leading to a bachelor's or an advanced degree.

Number of Awards:
22 per year.

1st SUPPLEMENT

Directory of Internships, Work Experience Programs, and On-the-Job Training Opportunities

Financial Data:
Students are paid for their work.

Stipulations:
The program does not provide for permanent employment following graduation.

Application Deadline:
Applications are accepted at any time.

Request Application from:
Special Employment Unit
Department of Personnel Management
901 G Street - Room 227
Sacramento, California 95814

SACRAMENTO COUNTY, CALIFORNIA [286]

Program Title:
Summer Work Program

Purpose:
To provide disadvantaged youth with a better opportunity for obtaining permanent employment in the future.

Nature of Assignment:
Participants are assigned to various County departments and agencies where they gain work experience in nonprofessional jobs.

Duration:
June - August.

Eligibility:
Young people between the ages of 16 and 21 who are economically disadvantaged and reside in the unincorporated areas of the County.

Number of Awards:
Approximately 300 each year.

Financial Data:
Participants are paid for their work.

Application Deadline:
Applications are accepted at any time.

Request Application from:
Special Employment Unit
Department of Personnel Management
901 G Street - Room 227
Sacramento, California 95814

ST. CLOUD DAILY TIMES [287]

Program Title:
Internship Program

Purpose:
To provide on-the-job training for college journalism majors who have established a sound base of skills through college classes or working with college publications.

Nature of Assignment:
Interns work as reporters, photographers or copy editors and receive the same type of assignments as do full-time staff members. Guidance and critiques are provided by key editors.

Duration:
Summer, full time; academic year, full or part time.

Eligibility:
College or university journalism majors who are juniors or seniors and are prepared to handle training on the professional level, as attested to by faculty member recommendations.

Number of Awards:
1 - 2 during the Summer; maximum of 3 per college term.

Financial Data:
Summer Interns receive 80 percent of a beginning reporter's salary, plus expenses; academic year Interns are only paid for on-the-job expenses.

Stipulations:
Preference is given to St. Cloud State University students for Internships during the academic year; Summer Internships are open equally to all qualified applicants.

Application Deadline:
Applications should be received at least 4 weeks before the start of a desired Internship period.

Request Application from:
Editor
St. Cloud Times
P.O. Box 768
St. Cloud, Minnesota 56301

ST. VINCENT'S HOUSE [288]

Program Title:
Neighborhood Community Center

Purpose:
To explore residents' ideas and feelings about their community and offer ways of helping solve particular problems affecting families' ability to mobilize.

Nature of Assignment:
Participants make home visits, travel to and from social service agencies, act as advocates to achieve rights and benefits, and work with Summer and after-school recreation programs.

Eligibility:
Individuals who have interests and skills appropriate to working at the Center.

Financial Data:
Volunteer only.

Application Deadline:
Applications are accepted at any time.

Request Application from:
St. Vincent's House
P.O. Box 576
2817 Postoffice Street
Galveston, Texas 77550

SAN ANTONIO, TEXAS [289]

Program Title:
Summer Work-Study Program

Purpose:
To provide job opportunities so that students may earn tuition money and to benefit City departments.

Nature of Assignment:
Students are assigned to City departments and agencies where they perform a variety of tasks from such paraprofessional duties as research, counseling and management to clerical work.

Duration:
June - August.

Eligibility:
Students who are interested in the work experience and qualify under their school's work-study program.

Number of Awards:
Approximately 6 per year; depending on available funding, more may be awarded.

Financial Data:
Students receive hourly wages with the City paying part of the salary and each student's school also contributing.

Application Deadline:
April 30 of each year.

Request Application from:
City of San Antonio
Public Service Careers
P.O. Box 9066
San Antonio, Texas 78285

SAN FRANCISCO VOLUNTEER BUREAU/VOLUNTARY ACTION CENTER [290]

Program Title:
Volunteer Management Training

Purpose:
To teach interested individuals the necessary skills for volunteer management.

Nature of Assignment:
Trainees are involved in interviewing, assisting with statistics, making agency visits, and various other administrative tasks.

Duration:
3 - 9 months; part or full time.

Eligibility:
Individuals who are personable and interested in community work with preference given to college students.

Financial Data:
Volunteer only.

Application Deadline:
Applications are accepted at any time.

Request Application from:
Voluntary Action Center
San Francisco Volunteer Bureau
33 Gough Street
San Francisco, California 94103

SAN JUAN, PUERTO RICO. WASHINGTON OFFICE [291]

Program Title:
Internship Program

Purpose:
To enable students to apply theory learned in academia to the broad Washington experience, cutting across the Federal government, the legislative process and the various public interest organizations in the Capital.

Nature of Assignment:
Interns may be assigned to attend Congressional hearings, report on meetings at Federal agencies, research various Federal aid programs applicable to the City of San Juan, and provide routine support services to the staff and office.

Duration:
3 months.

Eligibility:
Interested students from any field are eligible to apply; preference is given to those with government, political science or urban affairs academic backgrounds.

Financial Data:
Volunteer only.

Application Deadline:
Applications are accepted at any time.

Request Application from:
Washington Representative
City of San Juan
1620 Eye Street, N.W.
Washington, D.C. 20006

SCIENTISTS INSTITUTE FOR PUBLIC INFORMATION [292]

Program Title:
Margaret Mead Internship in Policy Related Science

Purpose:
To involve undergraduate science students academically and publicly in the socially relevant problems facing science today.

Nature of Assignment:
Interns propose, develop and complete their own research projects aimed at solving socially relevant problems in the fields of energy options, recombinant DNA research, use of technology (mostly computers) in the criminal justice system, and scientific aid to Indochina. The research project will be presented publicly as well as in the form of a written report.

Duration:
Spring and Fall semesters; full time.

Eligibility:
Undergraduate science students who have the ability to do independent research which involves interviewing as well as writing and library skills.

Number of Awards:
20 plus each year.

Financial Data:
Interns receive stipends of up to $100 per week, depending on need.

Stipulations:
Applicants must be available for interview.

Special Features:
The Institute helps Interns earn college credit for their work.

Application Deadline:
Applications are accepted until all Internship positions are filled.

Request Application from:
Educational Director
Margaret Mead Internship in Policy Related Science
Scientists Institute for Public Information
49 East 53rd Street
New York, New York 10022

SEA EDUCATION ASSOCIATION (SEA) [293]

Program Title:
Sea Semester

Purpose:
To teach college students about the oceans through active participation in research and ship operations at sea and to provide them with a rigorous academic, scientific and practical learning experience.

Nature of Assignment:
After a period of instruction and training ashore, students serve aboard a research vessel (125 foot staysail schooner) where they are assigned responsibilities in oceanographic and maritime activities, maintenance and operation of equipment, and standing watches at sea.

Duration:
6 week basic shore component at Woods Hole, Maine, followed by 6 weeks at sea; optionally, the sea component may be followed by an additional 7 week advanced shore component at Woods Hole.

Eligibility:
Students who have the motivation and emotional maturity necessary for rigorous courses, long hours of work and, while at sea, difficult living conditions. The academic work involved assumes sophomore-level competence.

Number of Awards:
6 courses of 22 students each are offered per year.

Financial Data:
Tuition is charged to students, who are also responsible for living expenses and travel. Scholarship assistance is possible.

Special Features:
Students can arrange to receive a full semester of academic credit through Boston University and other institutions.

Application Deadline:
Applications are accepted at any time.

Request Application from:
Sea Education Association
P.O. Box 6
Woods Hole, Maine 02543

SEASIDE POST NEWS-SENTINEL [294]

Program Title:
Summer Internships

Purpose:
To provide practical and educational experience in working on a newspaper.

Nature of Assignment:
Participants are given general news writing and feature writing assignments.

Duration:
Summer; full or part time.

Eligibility:
Interested individuals who have basic writing skills and high motivation.

Financial Data:
Non-paid work.

Application Deadline:
May 15 of each year.

Request Application from:
Editor
Seaside Post News-Sentinel
P.O. Box 670
Seaside, California 93950

SENTINEL STAR COMPANY [295]

Program Title:
College Intern Program

Purpose:
To provide journalism students with actual work experience.

Nature of Assignment:
Interns are given assignments in basic reporting, feature writing and copy editing.

Duration:
Minimum of 10 weeks during the Summer; full time.

Eligibility:
College or university students majoring in journalism who will have completed their junior year before beginning an Internship.

Number of Awards:
8 per year.

Financial Data:
Interns receive salaries comparable to that of beginning reporters.

Application Deadline:
December 31 of each year.

Request Application from:
Sentinel Star Company
P.O. Box 2833
Orlando, Florida 32802

SILVER STREET DAY CARE CENTER, INC. [296]

Program Title:
Internship in Child Care Administration

Purpose:
To provide the opportunity for on-the-job skills training and exposure in a community-based day care center.

Nature of Assignment:
Duties assigned the Intern will include: acting as liaison between the Center and other community groups; assisting in the preparation of a resource booklet detailing child care services available in Racine County (Wisconsin); assisting in the implementation of a comprehensive community-based program in early childhood education, involving issues and advocacy; preparing and submitting regular reports and other documents; and attending regular staff meetings.

Duration:
Summer only; full time.

Eligibility:
Undergraduate college students and others who are contemplating careers in child care administration or are interested in the early childhood/day care field.

Number of Awards:
1.

Financial Data:
Volunteer only.

Special Features:
The Intern will have the opportunity to undertake a specialized individual research project.

Application Deadline:
May 15.

Request Application from:
Internship Program
Silver Street Day Care Center, Inc.
815 Silver Street
Racine, Wisconsin 53404

SMITHSONIAN INSTITUTION [297]

Program Title:
Graduate Fellowship

1st SUPPLEMENT

Directory of Internships, Work Experience Programs, and On-the-Job Training Opportunities

Purpose:
To provide graduate students with an opportunity for research training supplementary to university instruction.

Nature of Assignment:
Fellows engage in supervised research at facilities of the Smithsonian. Appropriate projects can be proposed by Fellows or suggested by Smithsonian staff members.

Duration:
10 - 12 weeks.

Eligibility:
Students who are enrolled in formal university programs at the graduate level and have research interests in areas covered by the Institution.

Number of Awards:
Varies from year to year.

Financial Data:
Fellows receive from $800 to $1,000. Some students may be awarded research appointments but not given any financial assistance.

Stipulations:
Individuals who have had fellowships from the Smithsonian will not be eligible for a second award.

Application Deadline:
Generally there is no deadline; however, if a student wishes support during the Summer, an application should be submitted by March 1 of the year in which an appointment is sought.

Request Application from:
Office of Academic Studies
Room 356, SI Building
Smithsonian Institution
Washington, D.C. 20560

SMITHSONIAN INSTITUTION [298]

Program Title:
Museum Study Program

Purpose:
To provide an opportunity for students to learn about specific subjects while participating in the ongoing work of an Institution staff member.

Nature of Assignment:
Participants are assigned supervised tasks in all areas of the Smithsonian with work conducted in various Institution facilities.

Duration:
Varies, from a few weeks or more to a year; a minimum tenure of 12 weeks is usually required.

Eligibility:
College and university students who have interests and backgrounds in areas covered by the Smithsonian.

Number of Awards:
Varies from year to year.

Financial Data:
As a rule, no financial assistance is provided; however, support may be periodically available for certain classes of students or in certain fields of study.

Special Features:
The Smithsonian will cooperate with schools wishing to grant academic credit for Museum Study assignments.

Application Deadline:
Applications are accepted at any time.

Request Application from:
Office of Academic Studies
Room 356, SI Building
Smithsonian Institution
Washington, D.C. 20560

1st SUPPLEMENT

Directory of Internships, Work Experience Programs, and On-the-Job Training Opportunities

SMITHSONIAN INSTITUTION [299]

Program Title:
Short-Term Visits

Purpose:
To encourage the fullest practical use of Smithsonian facilities and staff specialists.

Nature of Assignment:
Participants work on specific projects requiring short-term access to Smithsonian facilities and staff.

Duration:
Short periods of time, but not less than 1 week.

Eligibility:
Students and scholars who have interests and backgrounds in areas covered by the Institution.

Number of Awards:
Varies from year to year.

Financial Data:
Financial support in small amounts is available.

Application Deadline:
Applications are accepted at any time.

Request Application from:
Office of Academic Studies
Room 356, SI Building
Smithsonian Institution
Washington, D.C. 20560

SMITHSONIAN INSTITUTION [300]

Program Title:
Study and Research Appointments

Purpose:
To offer a flexible program of research training and study at Smithsonian facilities.

Nature of Assignment:
Participants engage in supervised projects which they propose or which are suggested by Smithsonian staff members.

Duration:
Varies, depending on each project.

Eligibility:
Individuals with interests and abilities appropriate to working at the Smithsonian. Each applicant's capacity to pursue independent research will depend on his/her previous background and training. This program is intended for other than predoctoral and postdoctoral people.

Number of Awards:
Varies from year to year.

Financial Data:
Financial support may be available, but it is not necessarily provided.

Stipulations:
Individuals who have had previous fellowships from the Smithsonian are not eligible for a second award.

Application Deadline:
Applications are accepted at any time.

Request Application from:
Office of Academic Studies
Room 356, SI Building
Smithsonian Institution
Washington, D.C. 20560

1st SUPPLEMENT

Directory of Internships, Work Experience Programs, and On-the-Job Training Opportunities

SMITHSONIAN INSTITUTION. NATIONAL COLLECTION OF FINE ARTS [301]

Program Title:
Museum (Art) Internship

Purpose:
To train art historians for a career in the museum field.

Nature of Assignment:
Interns are given assignments at National Collection facilities where they perform varied duties related to museum work.

Duration:
Summer, or 2 semesters (Winter and Spring).

Eligibility:
Students who are enrolled in university art history programs. Applicants for Internships during the Summer must be seniors in accredited universities while those applying for Winter-Spring Internships must be M.A. or Ph.D. degree candidates.

Number of Awards:
Varies from year to year.

Financial Data:
Financial support in varying amounts is provided.

Application Deadline:
February 15 of each year.

Request Application from:
Office of Professional Training Programs
National Collection of Fine Arts
Smithsonian Institution
Washington, D.C. 20560

THE SOLOMON R. GUGGENHEIM MUSEUM [302]

Program Title:
Work/Experience Internship Program

Purpose:
To provide students with work experience in a museum setting.

Nature of Assignment:
Interns are placed in various Museum departments where they assist professional staff. Intern assignments are made on the basis of interviews, skills, abilities and recommendations. Duties performed vary, from working on special project research, exhibitions, art preparation and cataloging to assisting in curatorial work, conservation projects, public affairs tasks, compilation of statistical reports and management of the bookstore or restaurant.

Duration:
Semester or Summer; full or part time. Each Intern is assigned to a department for at least 1 month, possibly 3.

Eligibility:
Students from a variety of relevant disciplines who have had at least 2 years of college. Applicants must be good typists (50 wpm) or have special skills in such areas as printing, business and finance, matting, and framing. Foreign language knowledge is desirable and recommendations from 2 professors are necessary.

Number of Awards:
Approximately 10 a semester and 20 - 25 during the Summer.

Financial Data:
Internships are primarily volunteer; a limited number of scholarships are available, however, for students who are considered needy and are eligible for college work/study programs.

1st SUPPLEMENT

Directory of Internships, Work Experience Programs, and On-the-Job Training Opportunities

Stipulations:
Applicants must be available for interview with the Program Coordinator.

Application Deadline:
Applications are accepted at any time but must be received by February for Internships during the Summer.

Request Application from:
The Solomon R. Guggenheim Museum
1071 Fifth Avenue
New York City, New York 10028

SOUTH CAROLINA. ARTS COMMISSION [303]

Program Title:
Governor's Internship Program

Purpose:
To allow college students to have an introductory vocational experience in arts administration.

Nature of Assignment:
Interns are assigned varied tasks in arts administration and assist in program coordination.

Duration:
Interns can work part time throughout the year.

Eligibility:
Students with interests and skills appropriate to the work who are enrolled in South Carolina colleges and have a certification of economic eligibility.

Financial Data:
Interns are paid varying amounts, depending upon their backgrounds and assignments.

Application Deadline:
Applications should be received before the beginning of each academic semester or the Summer.

Request Application from:
Governor's Intern Program
South Carolina Arts Commission
829 Richland Street
Columbia, South Carolina 29201

SOUTH CAROLINA. DIVISION OF ADMINISTRATION [304]

Program Title:
Governor's Intern Program

Purpose:
To provide college students with professional off-campus learning experiences while offering agencies additional manpower services.

Nature of Assignment:
Interns work in State agencies and departments at jobs which offer them training related to their major fields of study.

Duration:
12 week part-time programs in the Fall and Spring; 10 week Summer program.

Eligibility:
College and university juniors, seniors or graduate students who are South Carolina residents or out-of-state students attending South Carolina schools.

Financial Data:
Undergraduate Interns receive at least the minimum wage, graduate students slightly more.

Application Deadline:
Applications should be received by approximately the end of January for Internships during the Spring, end of April for Summer Internships and end of September for the Fall program.

Request Application from:
Governor's Intern Program
Sumter Street Building - Room 114
1026 Sumter Street
Columbia, South Carolina 29201

SOUTH CAROLINA. STATE SENATE AND OFFICE OF THE LIEUTENANT GOVERNOR [305]

Program Title:
Intern and Page Program

Purpose:
To give college students an opportunity to engage in legislative research, and to generally assist legislators and the Lt. Governor's Office in constituent affairs.

Nature of Assignment:
Interns conduct research on legislative issues, service constituent requests and inquiries, and assist in office and clerical tasks. Pages perform basically routine services, carrying messages, obtaining reports, and checking with agencies.

Duration:
Most participants work during legislative sessions only, January - June; part time. There are a small number of year-round Internships.

Eligibility:
South Carolina citizens who are attending colleges or universities and are available for 15 - 20 hours of work per week.

Number of Awards:
Approximately 50 per year.

Financial Data:
Participants receive $3.50 to $4.00 an hour.

Application Deadline:
Applications should be received before the legislature convenes in January.

Request Application from:
Intern and Page Program
P.O. Box 142
The State House
Columbia, South Carolina 29202

SOUTH COUNTY COMMUNITY MENTAL HEALTH CENTER [306]

Program Title:
Internship Program

Purpose:
To provide work experience and on-the-job training in a mental health center as well as formal training in basic psychotherapeutic skills.

Nature of Assignment:
Duties assigned Interns involve them in individual, couples, family and group psychotherapy; provision of supervised crisis intervention; counseling for adults, children and adolescents; and work with substance abusers. Both formal and informal training is provided.

Duration:
Negotiable.

Eligibility:
The Program is open to psychologists, social workers, mental health workers, and counselors. Specific academic training and skills are required by certain assignments. Applicants must have a California driver's license.

Financial Data:
No remuneration is available.

Application Deadline:
Applications are accepted at any time.

Request Application from:
South County Community Mental Health Center
P.O. Box 1744
Gilroy, California 95020

SOUTHWEST YOUTH DEVELOPMENT [307]

Program Title:
Arts and Crafts Training Program

Purpose:
To provide on-the-job training opportunities which, if satisfactorily completed, can lead to regular job placement.

Nature of Assignment:
Participants learn how to use raw materials to produce marketable items. Training provided depends on individual trainees, while duties assigned are determined by the Gallery supervisor.

Duration:
Year-round program.

Eligibility:
Young people living in southwest Toledo, Ohio, who are interested in the Program and qualify for Youth Development support.

Financial Data:
Volunteer with the possibility for future job placement.

Application Deadline:
Applications are accepted at any time.

Request Application from:
Southwest Youth Development
669 Indiana Avenue
Toledo, Ohio 43602

SPOKANE LEGAL SERVICES CENTER [308]

Program Title:
Legal Clerkships

Purpose:
To provide experience for those interested in the legal field.

Nature of Assignment:
Clerkship assignments include research, legal drafting and client interviewing.

Eligibility:
Interested individuals who have completed at least one year of law school.

Number of Awards:
Varies from year to year.

1st SUPPLEMENT

Directory of Internships, Work Experience Programs, and On-the-Job Training Opportunities

Financial Data:
Volunteer only.

Application Deadline:
Application inquiries are accepted at any time; deadlines are sporadic.

Request Application from:
Spokane Legal Services Center
West 246 Riverside
Spokane, Washington 99201

SPOKANE LEGAL SERVICES CENTER [309]

Program Title:
Legal Internships

Purpose:
To provide experience for those interested in the legal field.

Nature of Assignment:
Intern assignments include limited practice in state courts.

Eligibility:
Interested individuals who have completed two-thirds of their legal education.

Number of Awards:
Varies from year to year.

Financial Data:
No salaries are provided although Interns can arrange to receive work-study support.

Application Deadline:
Application inquiries are accepted at any time; deadlines are sporadic.

Request Application from:
Spokane Legal Services Center
West 246 Riverside
Spokane, Washington 99201

SPOKANE, WASHINGTON. PARKS AND RECREATION DEPARTMENT [310]

Program Title:
Parks and Recreation Internship Program

Purpose:
To make available to area college and university students a comprehensive training program in the parks and recreation profession.

Nature of Assignment:
Interns are given an indepth look into all facets of the field. Assignments include responsibility for program development and supervision.

Duration:
9 - 12 weeks maximum; no Internships during Summers.

Eligibility:
College and university students who attend area schools, have at least junior standing, and are majoring in the field of Parks and Recreation.

Number of Awards:
9 per year.

Financial Data:
No remuneration; mileage is paid for use of personal car.

Stipulations:
Applicants must be available for interview by the Internship Coordinator.

Application Deadline:
Applications should be submitted an academic term before the term during which an Internship is desired.

Request Application from:
Intern Coordinator
Parks and Recreation Department
504 City Hall
Spokane, Washington 99201

THE SPOKESMAN REVIEW [311]

Program Title:
Reporting and Editing Internships

Purpose:
To discover and give experience to qualified journalism students who can function as vacation replacements for reporters and editors.

Nature of Assignment:
Interns are given general reporting and editing assignments.

Duration:
Summer only; full time.

Eligibility:
College and university students who will have finished 3 years of school in a journalism program before beginning an Internship.

Number of Awards:
3 per year.

Financial Data:
Interns receive $140 per week.

Application Deadline:
Selections are made in May of each year; interested applicants should submit letters of inquiry between February and May.

Request Application from:
Managing Editor
The Spokesman Review
Spokane, Washington 99210

STAR-NEWS [312]

Program Title:
Journalism Internships

Purpose:
To train qualified potential newspersons to the point where they can handle entry-level jobs on newspapers.

Nature of Assignment:
Intern duties vary according to individual abilities. Interns are first given basic rewrites and then, as they progress, regular assignments in general news, lifestyle, sports and photo departments.

Duration:
Varies; specific commitments worked out with Interns and cooperating schools.

Eligibility:
Students who have completed at least one year of college and have had some journalism courses. Applicants must be recommended by their department chairmen and pass the newspaper's basic spelling, typing and writing tests.

1st SUPPLEMENT
Directory of Internships, Work Experience Programs, and On-the-Job Training Opportunities

Number of Awards:
Varies; preference is for no more than 3 Interns at any one time, although 5 would be possible in instances with exceptionally well-qualified applicants.

Financial Data:
No financial remuneration is provided.

Stipulations:
Interns must arrange to receive college credit for their work.

Application Deadline:
Applications are accepted at any time.

Request Application from:
Managing Editor
Star-News
Pasadena, California 91109

STARKVILLE, MISSISSIPPI. REGIONAL MENTAL HEALTH COMPLEX [313]

Program Title:
Psychology Internship

Purpose:
To provide a complete experience in clinical psychology in a rural community mental health setting with the emphasis on direct participation.

Nature of Assignment:
Interns are involved in the full range of psychological services found in a community mental health center setting including therapy, diagnostics, inpatient and outpatient, consultation/education and administration. Emphasis is placed on rural mental health/mental retardation services.

Duration:
1 year.

Eligibility:
Doctoral candidates in psychology from accredited universities who are interested in clinical experience.

Number of Awards:
2 per year.

Financial Data:
Interns receive $5,000 plus health insurance.

Application Deadline:
January 1 of each year.

Request Application from:
Regional Mental Health Complex
P.O. Box 1567
Starkville, Mississippi 39759

STATE FARM INSURANCE COMPANIES [314]

Program Title:
Legal Internship

Purpose:
To provide law students with an opportunity to work in a corporate law department and to evaluate such Interns for possible future departmental openings.

Nature of Assignment:
Interns are assigned a variety of research and other special project activities.

Duration:
Interns work for 10 - 12 weeks during the Summer at Corporate Headquarters in Indiana; full time.

Eligibility:
Students who will have completed their second year of law school before the Internship Summer.

Number of Awards:
1 - 2 per year.

Financial Data:
Approximately $800 per month.

Application Deadline:
Although there is no official deadline, it is better to submit applications in the Fall for maximum consideration.

Request Application from:
Employment Manager
State Farm Insurance Companies
One State Farm Plaza
Bloomington, Illinois 61701

STATE FARM INSURANCE COMPANIES [315]

Program Title:
Minority Summer Internship Program

Purpose:
To provide minority college students with an opportunity to work and gain business exposure in the insurance industry, to give meaningful Summer employment to students plus an opportunity for them to save money for their Fall schooling, and to give both management and students a chance to examine mutual interests in future career employment at State Farm.

Nature of Assignment:
Interns first receive an orientation to State Farm and the insurance industry. They are then assigned to various departments of the Company. On the job, Interns become familiar with their department's role within the Company and they gain insights into duties of departmental functions. Where possible, Interns are assigned sole responsibility for special projects to be completed during the Internship period.

Duration:
Interns work for 10 weeks during the Summer at Corporate Headquarters in Indiana; full time.

Eligibility:
Minority college students completing their junior year who have interests and abilities appropriate to the work. Candidates can be selected for the Program in cooperation with various college placement directors and faculty members. In addition, qualified people can set up interviews during the Company's campus recruiting visits.

Financial Data:
Interns receive biweekly salaries of $300 or gross pay of $1,500 for the Summer, housing in dormitories at Illinois State University, and round trip travel expenses to Bloomington.

Special Features:
At the conclusion of the Program, each Intern receives a performance evaluation and is awarded a certificate of completion.

Application Deadline:
Applications are accepted at any time and can be made through college placement offices, Company Fall/Spring recruiters, or Corporate Headquarters.

Request Application from:
Employment Manager
State Farm Insurance Companies
One State Farm Plaza
Bloomington, Illinois 61701

STONER BROADCASTING [316]

Program Title:
KSO/KGGO News Internship

Purpose:
To train entry-level students of broadcasting and to provide actual experience in a working newsroom.

Nature of Assignment:
Interns are assigned the full duties of a newsperson including writing, editing, interviewing, and preparing actualities within specific formats for newscasts.

Duration:
1 semester (Fall or Spring) or Summer.

Eligibility:
Students in broadcasting attending Iowa State University, University of Iowa, Drake University or Grandview College (Des Moines) who have had a minimum of actual training.

Financial Data:
No remuneration.

Application Deadline:
Applications should be submitted one month prior to the beginning of the semester or Summer when an Internship is desired.

Request Application from:
KSO/KGGO News Internship
3900 Northeast Broadway
Des Moines, Iowa 50317

SUPPORT CENTER [317]

Program Title:
Volunteer Program

Purpose:
To provide management assistance to nonprofit organizations including assistance in bookkeeping, accounting, fund raising planning, evaluation, organizational development, public relations, office management, administrative duties and information systems.

Nature of Assignment:
Assignments could be with client organizations providing management assistance as outlined above, or volunteers could work on internal office projects, such as the national conference or Center publications.

Duration:
At least a 3 month commitment is required.

Eligibility:
Individuals who have a general aptitude for, interest in and concern about the Center's management-related work with nonprofit organizations.

Financial Data:
Volunteer only.

Application Deadline:
Applications are accepted at any time.

Request Application from:
Executive Director
Support Center
1424 16th Street, N.W. - Room 201
Washington, D.C. 20036

TENNESSEE. GENERAL ASSEMBLY [318]

Program Title:
Legislative Internship Program

Purpose:
To provide well-qualified college students with an educational experience in the practical operation of the legislative process.

Nature of Assignment:
Interns are assigned to legislative leadership and committees where they are given research duties as well as a variety of other job assignments in connection with the work of the General Assembly.

Duration:
1 Legislative session; full time.

Eligibility:
College or university juniors, seniors and graduate students who are residents of Tennessee and enrolled in cooperating public or private schools in the state. Applicants can be majoring in political science, law, history, administration, social work, economics, sociology, journalism or related fields.

Number of Awards:
Approximately 20 per year.

Financial Data:
Interns are paid stipends of $390 a month; out-of-county Interns also receive transportation allowances for one round trip a week to Nashville.

Stipulations:
Interns cannot be enrolled in college course work during the Internship period. Participants are expected to attend seminars on state government with emphasis on the legislature and the legislative process.

Special Features:
Academic credit will be given for participation in the Program with an average of 9 - 12 semester hours or its equivalent.

Application Deadline:
Applications must be submitted by early October for Internships during the Legislative Session beginning the following January.

Request Application from:
Application must be made through official faculty representatives at cooperating institutions.

TEXAS. UNIVERSITY. MEDICAL BRANCH. DIVISION OF CHILD AND ADOLESCENT PSYCHIATRY [319]

Program Title:
Postdoctoral Fellowship in Child Clinical Psychology

Purpose:
To train child clinical psychologists in all aspects of care for the emotionally disturbed child and his/her family.

1st SUPPLEMENT
Directory of Internships, Work Experience Programs, and On-the-Job Training Opportunities

Nature of Assignment:
Participants receive training in inpatient/outpatient evaluation and treatment involving individual, family and parental counseling, filial therapy, multiple impact therapy and other relevant areas. Training is also provided in consultations within the hospital setting and with the community as well as in the supervision of others and in diagnosis and treatment.

Duration:
2 years; full time.

Eligibility:
Participants must have received a Ph.D. degree from an APA approved university and an APA approved internship in clinical psychology.

Number of Awards:
4 per year.

Financial Data:
$9,500 for the first year and $10,100 for the second year plus participation in a retirement plan.

Application Deadline:
January 15 of each year.

Request Application from:
Division of Child and Adolescent Psychiatry
Department of Psychiatry and Behavioral Sciences
University of Texas Medical Branch
Galveston, Texas 77550

THEATER WORKSHOP BOSTON [320]

Program Title:
Work-Experience Opportunity

Purpose:
To train volunteers in behind the scenes theater work.

Nature of Assignment:
Participants are given the opportunity to gain skills in theater production and supportive office tasks. Duties range from working with lighting, sound equipment, sets and costumes to handling mailing lists, assisting in the office, answering phone inquiries and working on advertising.

Duration:
Full or part time throughout the year, including Summer.

Eligibility:
Individuals who have interests and skills appropriate to the work; some previous office experience is desirable.

Financial Data:
Volunteer only.

Application Deadline:
Applications are accepted at any time.

Request Application from:
Theater Workshop Boston
551 Tremont
Boston, Massachusetts 02116

3M COMPANY [321]

Program Title:
Summer Technical Program

Purpose:
To give students on-the-job technical training and the opportunity of assaying the possibilities of a career at 3M, and to give the Company a good look at potential technical employees.

Nature of Assignment:
Participants are assigned to projects typical of industrial laboratories and manufacturing situations, and they gain experience in the practical application of fundamentals learned in school. Working under the guidance of 3M scientists and engineers, students design and carry out particular projects, are involved in the everyday use of laboratory instruments and have widespread contact with people within the Company.

Duration:
3 months during the Summer; full time.

Eligibility:
Students must have completed a minimum of 3 years of technical training in order to participate in the Program. Although applicants can come from other fields, curricula of principal interest are chemistry; physics; and chemical, mechanical, electrical, metallurgical and ceramic engineering.

Financial Data:
Students receive salaries commensurate with their educational backgrounds.

Stipulations:
Upon completion of summer employment, students must submit progress reports summarizing the status of their projects and recommending further action.

Special Features:
Students tour 3M facilities and attend seminars presented by 3M technical personnel.

Application Deadline:
February 1 of each year.

Request Application from:
Summer Technical Coordinator
Staffing Department 224-1W
3M Company
St. Paul, Minnesota 55101

THURSTON YOUTH SERVICES SOCIETY. THE UNION STREET CENTER [322]

Program Title:
Juvenile Division Internship/Paraprofessional Program

Purpose:
To assist the Center in its work of receiving clients from the police/courts/other agencies in lieu of their proceeding through the juvenile justice system.

Nature of Assignment:
Interns/paraprofessionals are trained in counseling skills and then meet with clients on a one-to-one basis or in groups. Other tasks assigned could include interviewing clients and parents for an assessment of their needs, public relations work, office duties, and research.

Duration:
Negotiable.

Eligibility:
Individuals with interests and skills appropriate to the Program who are at least 18 years old and willing to work.

Financial Data:
Most interns/paraprofessionals volunteer, although some paid positions are available throughout the year.

Application Deadline:
Applications are accepted at any time.

Request Application from:
Volunteer Coordinator
The Union Street Center
417 East Union
Olympia, Washington 98501

1st SUPPLEMENT

Directory of Internships, Work Experience Programs, and On-the-Job Training Opportunities

TUSCALOOSA, ALABAMA. REGIONAL ALCOHOLISM COUNCIL [323]

Program Title:
CETA Training and Volunteer Programs

Purpose:
To train interested individuals in the many areas of the alcohol field, such as public information and referral, education and prevention.

Nature of Assignment:
Participants are assigned varied duties, from involvement in DWI Counterattack Program and instructor certification to employee assistance programs and industry, crisis intervention counseling, grant writing, research, and some administrative work.

Duration:
Varies according to individual programs, from semester to year long.

Eligibility:
Individuals who have interests, skills and educational training appropriate to the work. Applicants for CETA Training must meet necessary CETA requirements.

Financial Data:
CETA Trainees receive monthly wages, volunteers receive no pay.

Special Features:
Periodically, the Council funds Internships which carry stipend support. The Council also currently offers internships to University of Alabama students who receive academic credit for their work.

Application Deadline:
Varies according to specific program; application inquiries are accepted at any time.

Request Application from:
Regional Alcoholism Council
P.O. Box 2341
Tuscaloosa, Alabama 35401

u

UNITED NATIONS. INTERNATIONAL LEAGUE FOR HUMAN RIGHTS [324]

Program Title:
Internship Program

Purpose:
To help people around the world in accordance with international legal standards.

Nature of Assignment:
Interns participate in research and writing activities relating to the field of international human rights. They also perform some office work.

Duration:
Internships of all lengths are possible.

197

Eligibility:
Interested persons who have bachelor's, master's or law degrees with emphasis on international relations or international law. Foreign language knowledge would be helpful.

Number of Awards:
1 or 2 per year.

Financial Data:
Volunteer only.

Application Deadline:
Applications are accepted at any time.

Request Application from:
International League for Human Rights
777 United Nations Plaza, 6F
New York, New York 10017

UNITED NATIONS ASSOCIATION, USA [325]

Program Title:
Internship Program

Purpose:
To give students a chance to conduct meaningful research and observe Congress firsthand, and to provide assistance for the Association's office in its daily functioning.

Nature of Assignment:
The majority of Intern time is spent in substantive research, the main purpose of which is to help the Association keep Congress informed about UN activities and world events and to keep Association headquarters informed about Congressional events. Interns also spend some time in office support, performing such tasks as procuring documents, clipping newspapers and clipping the Congressional Record.

Duration:
2 - 3 months minimum; full or part time.

Eligibility:
Students who are completing at least the freshman year of college with preference given to those of junior standing or above.

Number of Awards:
1 full-time or 2 half-time Interns per year.

Financial Data:
Volunteer only.

Application Deadline:
June 1 for Internships in the Summer; September 1 for Fall Internships; and December 1 for Internships during the Spring.

Request Application from:
United Nations Association, USA
413 East Capitol Street, S.E.
Washington, D.C. 20003

U.S. BUREAU OF THE CENSUS [326]

Program Title:
Summer Employment Program

Purpose:
To give students professional and administrative experience at the Bureau.

Nature of Assignment:
Students are assigned work involving statistics (economic, mathematical and demographic), geography, sociology,

operations research, mathematics and/or computer science.

Duration:
Summer.

Eligibility:
Students who are planning to undertake graduate programs related to data collection, processing and analysis.

Number of Awards:
Limited number.

Financial Data:
Students are paid salaries based on an annual rate of approximately $10,000 or more; specific amount depends on the level of schooling completed.

Application Deadline:
Applications should be submitted as soon as possible but no later than approximately April 15.

Request Application from:
Summer Employment Coordinator
Bureau of the Census
Department of Commerce
Washington, D.C. 20233

U.S. CIVIL SERVICE COMMISSION [327]

Program Title:
Federal Summer Employment Program for Youth: Summer Aids

Purpose:
To provide an opportunity for substantive numbers of needy people to obtain Summer work experience with the Federal government.

Nature of Assignment:
Participants are given meaningful work assignments in Federal agencies with every effort made to place Aids in jobs commensurate with their interests and abilities.

Duration:
May 13 - September 30; full time.

Eligibility:
Young people 16 through 21 who need work experience with preference given to youths whose family income is at or near the poverty level.

Number of Awards:
Approximately 42,000 per year.

Financial Data:
Participants are paid the Federal minimum wage or the equivalent applicable state or municipal minimum wage, whichever is higher.

Special Features:
Employing agencies sponsor special activities, such as orientation programs, job-related training, and cultural enrichment opportunities, with the goal of providing a well-balanced Summer employment experience.

Application Deadline:
Referrals of Summer Aids are made by local offices of the State Employment Service in the Spring of each year.

Request Application from:
Students interested in participating in the Program should register with the local office of their State employment service or contact appropriate school officials.

1st SUPPLEMENT

Directory of Internships, Work Experience Programs, and On-the-Job Training Opportunities

U.S. CIVIL SERVICE COMMISSION [328]

Program Title:
Federal Summer Intern Program

Purpose:
To involve talented student leaders in operations of the Federal government and to provide such students with practical experience in some phase of Federal activity related to their anticipated career fields.

Nature of Assignment:
Interns are assigned to meaningful career-related jobs at Federal agencies in Washington, D.C., or located at other areas throughout the country. Assignments include such positions as personnel staffing specialist, aerospace technician, program analyst, writer-editor, computer programmer, park ranger, biological assistant, research psychologist, statistician and legal aid.

Duration:
Full time during the Summer.

Eligibility:
Most 4 year colleges and universities are invited by Federal agencies to nominate student candidates. Nominees must have completed at least 2 years (60 semester hours) of school by June of the Internship Summer, be United States citizens, and have demonstrated leadership qualities through in-school and extracurricular activities. Undergraduates must be in the upper one-third of their class and graduate students in the upper one-half.

Number of Awards:
Approximately 1,000 per year.

Financial Data:
Salaries are based on annual rates determined by each Intern's level of education (e.g., approximately $9,000 for 2 years of college or $15,000 for 2 years of graduate work).

Stipulations:
The Program is designed for students who will be returning to school in the Fall.

Special Features:
As part of their training, Interns spend at least 4 hours per week in specially designed, agency-sponsored developmental activities, such as seminars, discussion groups, field trips, research projects or lectures.

Application Deadline:
Colleges select nominees and submit candidates in March of each year.

Request Application from:
Students interested in the Program should contact their college placement offices in February.

U.S. CIVIL SERVICE COMMISSION [329]

Program Title:
Presidential Management Intern Program

Purpose:
To provide internships in Federal government agencies for persons having recently completed graduate education programs in public management.

Nature of Assignment:
Interns are placed in general managerial and administrative positions in Federal agencies with assignments made at main headquarters, field installations, and regional offices. Typical tasks assigned would involve Interns as budget analysts, personnel specialists and management analysts, or in related work.

1st SUPPLEMENT

Directory of Internships, Work Experience Programs, and On-the-Job Training Opportunities

Duration:
2 years; full time.

Eligibility:
Individuals who, during the academic year of nomination, will receive an advanced degree in public management. The degree program must involve public administration, public policy analysis, public affairs and general management.

Number of Awards:
250 per year.

Financial Data:
Interns are paid at the GS-9 level, approximately $15,000 a year.

Stipulations:
Qualified individuals must be nominated by their schools.

Special Features:
Interns have the possibility of conversion to the career service at the completion of their assignments.

Application Deadline:
Nominations should be received by approximately January 1 of each year.

Request Application from:
U.S. Civil Service Commission
Bureau of Intergovernmental Personnel Programs
1900 E Street, N.W. - Room 2510
Washington, D.C. 20415

U.S. CIVIL SERVICE COMMISSION [330]

Program Title:
The President's Stay-in-School Program

Purpose:
To assist young people in gaining work experience and insight into what will be required of them when they seek full-time employment, and to allow needy youth to continue their education without interruptions caused by financial pressures.

Nature of Assignment:
Students work at varied assignments in Federal agencies.

Duration:
Up to 16 hours per week during school terms and 40 hours a week during extended vacation periods.

Eligibility:
Students 16 through 21 years of age enrolled in accredited secondary schools or institutions of higher learning who meet the financial need criterion of the Program.

Number of Awards:
Approximately 22,000 per year.

Financial Data:
Students are paid at least the Federal minimum wage or the local State or municipal wage if that is higher.

Application Deadline:
Appointments can be made at any time during the year, except May 1 through August 31 when Summer jobs are filled.

Request Application from:
Students interested in the Program should register with the local office of their State employment service or contact appropriate school officials.

1st SUPPLEMENT

Directory of Internships, Work Experience Programs, and On-the-Job Training Opportunities

U.S. CONGRESS. HOUSE. OFFICE OF DAVID E. BONIOR [331]

Program Title:
Bonior Internship Program

Purpose:
To have Interns experience the actual workings of a Congressional office as well as to provide new ideas that will benefit the Office.

Nature of Assignment:
Interns are expected to be able to do everything in the Office, from acting as a receptionist to answering legislative correspondence.

Duration:
Full-time work for flexible lengths of time.

Eligibility:
Individuals interested in the work experience with preference given to those who come from the 12th Congressional District of Michigan and so have prior knowledge of that area. Computer background is helpful but not necessary, while the ability to type at least 40 wpm is required.

Number of Awards:
2 each year.

Financial Data:
Interns receive scholarships of $500.

Special Features:
Internships are also available for qualified volunteers.

Application Deadline:
March 1 for Internships during the Summer, August 1 for those in the Fall, and December 1 for work in the Winter.

Request Application from:
Rep. David E. Bonior
1123 Longworth House Office Building
Washington, D.C. 20515

U.S. CONGRESS. HOUSE. OFFICE OF JOHN CONYERS, JR. [332]

Program Title:
High School or College Internship Program

Purpose:
To expose students to the workings of government from the legislative viewpoint.

Nature of Assignment:
Interns provide research assistance and are also assigned writing and clerical tasks.

Duration:
Flexible; year round possibilities.

Eligibility:
Applicants must be high school or college (either undergraduate or graduate) students with good writing and typing skills. Constituents of the Congressman are usually preferred for paid Internship positions.

Financial Data:
LBJ Internship Fund provides payment for 2 Interns per year; others are volunteer.

Application Deadline:
Applications should be received at least 6 weeks or 2 months prior to the desired date for starting an Internship.

Request Application from:
Rep. John Conyers, Jr.
2444 Rayburn House Office Building
Washington, D.C. 20515

1st SUPPLEMENT

Directory of Internships, Work Experience Programs, and On-the-Job Training Opportunities

U.S. CONGRESS. HOUSE. OFFICE OF PHILIP M. CRANE [333]

Program Title:
Congressional Internship

Purpose:
To give students firsthand experience with the workings of a Congressional office.

Nature of Assignment:
Interns are given a variety of assignments from doing research for legislation, speeches and articles to helping out with general office duties.

Duration:
Approximately 5 weeks.

Eligibility:
Students who have an interest in politics.

Financial Data:
Volunteer only.

Application Deadline:
Approximately 1 month before the desired starting date.

Request Application from:
Rep. Philip M. Crane
1406 Longworth House Office Building
Washington, D.C. 20515

U.S. CONGRESS. HOUSE. OFFICE OF BOB ECKHARDT [334]

Program Title:
Bi-Partisan Intern Program

Purpose:
To provide Interns with an opportunity to gain firsthand knowledge of current issues and activities of the Congress.

Nature of Assignment:
Interns open and answer mail and are involved in general office work.

Duration:
Flexible; year round, part or full time.

Eligibility:
Applicants should have interest and background in environmental, energy, and labor issues and/or casework. Filing experience would be helpful and some typing ability is preferred but not necessary.

Number of Awards:
Approximately 12 per year.

Financial Data:
Volunteer only.

Application Deadline:
Those who wish Summer Internships should apply by April 1.

Request Application from:
Rep. Bob Eckhardt
1741 Longworth House Office Building
Washington, D.C. 20515

U.S. CONGRESS. HOUSE. OFFICE OF MICKEY EDWARDS [335]

Program Title:
Volunteer

Purpose:
To provide an opportunity to work in a Congressional office.

Nature of Assignment:
Participants assist in both legislative research and daily office routines.

Eligibility:
Bright, hardworking people who have the ability to follow instructions and work with others.

Financial Data:
Volunteer only.

Application Deadline:
Applications are accepted at any time.

Request Application from:
Rep. Mickey Edwards
1223 Longworth House Office Building
Washington, D.C. 20515

U.S. CONGRESS. HOUSE. OFFICE OF HAROLD FORD [336]

Program Title:
Congressional Internship Program

Purpose:
To extend the opportunity for college and vocational students to learn more about Congress and the legislative process by direct involvement.

Nature of Assignment:
Most Intern time is devoted to substantive work, such as drafting responses to constituent inquiries, conducting basic research on various legislative projects, and preparing remarks for insertion in the Congressional Record and other speeches. The rest of the time, Interns are involved in routine office tasks.

Duration:
Fall, Spring and Summer programs; full time.

Eligibility:
Students enrolled in post-secondary college or vocational institutions. Summer program is open only to residents of Tennessee's 8th Congressional District.

Number of Awards:
Varies.

Financial Data:
Volunteer only during Fall and Spring programs; some small stipends may be available for Summer Interns.

Application Deadline:
September for Internships in the Fall, February for Spring Internships, and April for Internships in the Summer.

Request Application from:
Rep. Harold Ford
1230 Longworth House Office Building
Washington, D.C. 20515

U.S. CONGRESS. HOUSE. OFFICE OF LAMAR GUDGER [337]

Program Title:
LBJ and 11th District Academic/Merit Internships

Purpose:
To foster an understanding of the duties of a Congressional office and to show the interaction between Federal agencies and Congressional offices.

Nature of Assignment:
Interns are given varied duties with specific assignments individualized to each student's needs and interests. LBJ Interns perform general office tasks.

Duration:
LBJ Interns: 1 month; Academic/Merit Interns: 8 weeks.

Eligibility:
Applicants for LBJ Internships must be residents of North Carolina, while applicants for Academic/Merit Internships must be enrolled at Western Carolina College, UNC - Asheville, Warren Wilson College, or Mars Hill College.

Number of Awards:
2 LBJ and 4 Academic/Merit Internships per year.

Financial Data:
Interns receive $590 per month.

Application Deadline:
Applications are accepted at any time.

Request Application from:
Rep. Lamar Gudger
428 Cannon House Office Building
Washington, D.C. 20515

U.S. CONGRESS. HOUSE. OFFICE OF RICHARD KELLY [338]

Program Title:
Special Projects Intern

Purpose:
To research and work on special projects related to the Congressman's assignments on the Banking and Currency and Agriculture Committees.

Nature of Assignment:
Interns attend certain Committee meetings, conduct research and attend seminars. They receive on-the-job training for their work. Interns must produce written papers resulting from their assignments.

Duration:
Tailored to meet the schedule of each Intern.

Eligibility:
College and university undergraduate and graduate students who are interested in the work experience.

Number of Awards:
6 per year.

Financial Data:
Volunteer only.

Stipulations:
Applicants must interview with the Congressman.

Application Deadline:
Applications are accepted at any time.

Request Application from:
Rep. Richard Kelly
307 Cannon House Office Building
Washington, D.C. 20515

U.S. CONGRESS. HOUSE. OFFICE OF EDWARD I. KOCH [339]

Program Title:
Internships/Lyndon B. Johnson Congressional Intern Program

Purpose:
To acquaint students wtih the legislative process in all facets of a Congressional office.

Nature of Assignment:
Interns are given a variety of assignments depending on their ability and resourcefulness. Duties may include drafting testimony and statements for the Congressional Record, researching background preparatory to authoring legislation, composing responses to constituent mail, and performing clerical tasks.

Duration:
Varies; Semester (not under LBJ Program) and Summer Programs.

Eligibility:
College or university students interested in the work experience who have good writing and typing skills. Summer Internships are given only to residents of the 18th Congressional District of New York. When possible, interviews are desired.

Number of Awards:
4 Summer Internships and 3 in the Semester Program.

Financial Data:
Summer Interns receive $60 per week; Semester Program Interns are usually unpaid.

Special Features:
Interns may arrange to receive academic credit for their work.

Application Deadline:
March 30 for Summer Internships, August 1 for Internships during the Fall, and December 1 for Internships in the Spring.

Request Application from:
Rep. Edward I. Koch
1126 Longworth House Office Building
Washington, D.C. 20515

U.S. CONGRESS. HOUSE. OFFICE OF JIM LEACH [340]

Program Title:
Lyndon Baines Johnson Intern Program and Senior Citizens Volunteers.

Purpose:
To become acquainted wtih the legislative branch of our government.

Nature of Assignment:
Participants assist with the many duties in a Congressional office from conducting research, attending committee meetings, and working on special projects to opening and answering the mail, typing, and answering the phone.

Duration:
Indefinite; 1 month, the Summer or any other time period.

Eligibility:
Applicants must live in or be a resident of the Representative's Congressional District.

Financial Data:
LBJ Interns are paid; other participants are volunteer only.

Application Deadline:
Applications are accepted at any time, but inquiries should be submitted as soon as possible because of the many Internship requests received.

Request Application from:
Rep. Jim Leach
1724 Longworth House Office Building
Washington, D.C. 20515

1st SUPPLEMENT

Directory of Internships, Work Experience Programs, and On-the-Job Training Opportunities

U.S. CONGRESS. HOUSE. OFFICE OF MATTHEW F. MCHUGH [341]

Program Title:
Internship Program

Purpose:
To expose Interns to the work of a Congressional office, give them a sense of how Congress operates, and have them perform necessary support functions for the Congressman and his staff.

Nature of Assignment:
Interns are assigned research, correspondence and clerical duties with approximately half of the work falling in the first two categories.

Duration:
Summer: June - August; Fall: September - December; Winter: January - April.

Eligibility:
College and university students who are at least juniors, have good academic standing and writing skills, and have had some previous work experience.

Financial Data:
Presently volunteer only.

Stipulations:
Applicants must be available for personal interview.

Application Deadline:
Applications are accepted at any time but should be submitted well in advance of the period for which an Internship is desired.

Request Application from:
Rep. Matthew F. McHugh
1204 Longworth House Office Building
Washington, D.C. 20515

U.S. CONGRESS. HOUSE. OFFICE OF RON MARLENEE [342]

Program Title:
Office Internship

Purpose:
To provide firsthand experience in a Congressional office.

Nature of Assignment:
Interns perform various duties in the Office including mailing preparation, front desk work, letter writing, research, computer assignments, and constituent contact. Much leeway is given for Interns to participate in special programs as learning tools.

Duration:
Open.

Eligibility:
Individuals of at least college age who are able to do research, can handle themselves with limited supervision, and are able to type.

Financial Data:
Limited financial assistance is provided.

Application Deadline:
Applications are accepted at any time.

Request Application from:
Rep. Ron Marlenee
128 Cannon House Office Building
Washington, D.C. 20515

U.S. CONGRESS. HOUSE. OFFICE OF NED PATTISON [343]

Program Title:
Congressional Internship Program

1st SUPPLEMENT

Directory of Internships, Work Experience Programs, and On-the-Job Training Opportunities

Purpose:
To provide an opportunity for college students to gain experience in a Congressional office.

Nature of Assignment:
Interns are assigned tasks similar to those of the regular staff.

Duration:
Minimum of 10 weeks; full time.

Eligibility:
College students on any level and in any major who are interested in the work experience. Applicants should have good writing and typing skills.

Number of Awards:
Maximum of 4 at any one time, usually 4 per semester.

Financial Data:
2 Summer Interns are paid, the rest are volunteers.

Application Deadline:
Applications are accepted at any time.

Request Application from:
Rep. Ned Pattison
1127 Longworth House Office Building
Washington, D.C. 20515

U.S. CONGRESS. HOUSE. OFFICE OF RICHARDSON PREYER [344]

Program Title:
Internship Program

Purpose:
To both provide office input of young talent and give that talent some Washington experience.

Nature of Assignment:
Assignments are varied with some challenging work and some routine. Intern duties range from writing, research, casework and special assignments to clerical or office jobs.

Duration:
6 weeks during the Summer.

Eligibility:
People who are interested in the work experience. Special assignments might require special skills.

Number of Awards:
5 - 6 per year.

Financial Data:
Interns receive salaries of approximately $130 a week.

Application Deadline:
Approximately February 1 of each year.

Request Application from:
Rep. Richardson Preyer
2344 Rayburn House Office Building
Washington, D.C. 20515

U.S. CONGRESS. HOUSE. OFFICE OF FORTNEY H. STARK, JR. [345]

Program Title:
Internship in Congressional Office

Purpose:
To provide opportunities to observe Congress in action and to watch the process of lawmaking.

Nature of Assignment:
Interns are assigned to both special projects and routine office work.

Duration:
2 - 3 months.

Eligibility:
Students who have interests and skills appropriate to the work.

Number of Awards:
Approximately 15 per year.

Financial Data:
Remuneration is almost never available.

Application Deadline:
Applications are accepted at any time.

Request Application from:
Rep. Fortney H. Stark, Jr.
1034 Longworth House Office Building
Washington, D.C. 20515

U.S. CONGRESS. HOUSE. OFFICE OF DON YOUNG [346]

Program Title:
Summer Intern Program

Purpose:
To provide students wtih experience in working at the Capitol and with the Government.

Nature of Assignment:
Interns are assigned a variety of duties including work on special projects, research, handling correspondence, filing and typing.

Duration:
Summer, for no specified length of time.

Eligibility:
Applicants should be high school graduates who are interested in the Program.

Financial Data:
Interns are both paid and volunteer.

Application Deadline:
Applications are accepted at any time.

Request Application from:
Rep. Don Young
1210 Longworth House Office Building
Washington, D.C. 20515

U.S. CONGRESS. SENATE. OFFICE OF MIKE GRAVEL [347]

Program Title:
Internship

Purpose:
To provide a firsthand understanding of the workings of the government with an emphasis on the legislative process.

Nature of Assignment:
Interns are assigned assorted tasks in the Office including case work, filing, research, correspondence and other duties which may involve working with Federal agencies as well as state and local offices.

Duration:
Flexible.

Eligibility:
College students who are not turned off by the kind of work associated with a large office. Internships are recommended for those with an interest in political science and government.

Number of Awards:
Variable.

Financial Data:
Volunteer only.

Application Deadline:
Applications are accepted at any time.

Request Application from:
Sen. Mike Gravel
3121 Dirksen Senate Office Building
Washington, D.C. 20510

U.S. CONGRESS. SENATE. OFFICE OF ORRIN G. HATCH [348]

Program Title:
Summer and Winter Senate Interns

Purpose:
To offer background and training in Senate office procedures.

Nature of Assignment:
Interns undertake limited legislative research, do case work in constituent affairs, handle mail, file, and assist in general office duties.

Duration:
Varies; full or part time.

Eligibility:
Individuals who are interested in the work experience with preference given to college students.

Number of Awards:
Varies, depending upon applications.

Financial Data:
One Intern is paid $500 a month; all others are volunteer.

Application Deadline:
Applications are accepted at any time.

Request Application from:
Sen. Orrin G. Hatch
6317 Dirksen Senate Office Building
Washington, D.C. 20510

U.S. CONGRESS. SENATE. OFFICE OF GEORGE MCGOVERN [349]

Program Title:
Summer Intern Program

Purpose:
To provide qualified young people with an opportunity to work in a Senator's Office.

Nature of Assignment:
Interns are assigned primarily research tasks with some routine office duties also required.

Duration:
Summer only.

Eligibility:
Applicants must have completed at least 2 years of college level work. South Dakota residents have preference.

Number of Awards:
5 per year.

Financial Data:
Interns are given monthly stipends to cover living expenses.

Application Deadline:
March 1 of each year.

Request Application from:
Sen. George McGovern
4239 Dirksen Senate Office Building
Washington, D.C. 20510

U.S. CONGRESS. SENATE. OFFICE OF WILLIAM PROXMIRE [350]

Program Title:
Work Experience

Purpose:
To provide juniors and seniors with an opportunity to work in a Congressional office and learn the legislative process from the inside.

Nature of Assignment:
Participants are given a mix of substantive legislative research and writing with some routine clerical work. The latter never exceeds the former.

Duration:
1 academic semester.

Eligibility:
College students of at least junior standing who have demonstrated writing, organizational and analytic skills.

Number of Awards:
No specific number set.

Financial Data:
Participants receive $100 per week in the Summer; the same rate of pay is provided during the rest of the year if funds are available.

Application Deadline:
February 28 for work in the Summer, June 30 for the Fall, and November 15 for participation during the Winter-Spring semester.

Request Application from:
Sen. William Proxmire
5241 Dirksen Senate Office Building
Washington, D.C. 20510

U.S. DEPARTMENT OF COMMERCE. OFFICE OF MINORITY BUSINESS ENTERPRISE (OMBE) [351]

Program Title:
Business Management Fellowship Program

Purpose:
To assist the OMBE and private industry to develop a new generation of business managers and owners, and to provide talented high school seniors with meaningful jobs and income throughout their college years as well as promising career opportunities after graduation.

Nature of Assignment:
Students work for participating business firms throughout the country. Specific job assignments vary, depending on each student's course of study and the needs of the participating company with which the student is placed.

1st SUPPLEMENT

Directory of Internships, Work Experience Programs, and On-the-Job Training Opportunities

Duration:
Students work full time in the Summer and possibly part time during the school year until their college education programs are completed (maximum of 4 years).

Eligibility:
Graduating high school seniors who are in the upper 10% of their class, are socially or economically disadvantaged, have applied to or been accepted by an accredited college or university, and intend to major in a field which is of interest to a participating organization.

Number of Awards:
Varies year to year; during the first 4 years of the Program, approximately 3,200 students were placed with participating firms.

Financial Data:
Students are paid by the companies with which they are placed.

Application Deadline:
Applications are not solicited. Qualified students are identified by and must work through their high school counselors.

Request Application from:
Graduating seniors should discuss the Program with their counselors.

U.S. DEPARTMENT OF COMMERCE. OFFICE OF THE SECRETARY [352]

Program Title:
Summer Employment Program

Purpose:
To provide advanced college students and graduates with Summer job opportunities at the Department.

Nature of Assignment:
Participants are given professional and administrative level work assignments.

Duration:
Summer.

Eligibility:
College graduates or graduate students (or individuals with equivalent experience) who have backgrounds in business administration, economics, finance, marketing, statistics, computer programming, travel and tourism, electronic engineering, fire administration or law.

Number of Awards:
Limited number.

Financial Data:
Participants are paid salaries based on an annual rate of approximately $10,000 - $18,000; specific amount depends on the level of schooling completed.

Application Deadline:
Applications should be submitted as soon as possible but no later than approximately April 15.

Request Application from:
Office of the Secretary
Department of Commerce
Operations Division
Room 5114
Washington, D.C. 20230

1st SUPPLEMENT

Directory of Internships, Work Experience Programs, and On-the-Job Training Opportunities

U.S. DEPARTMENT OF STATE. BUREAU OF EDUCATIONAL AND CULTURAL AFFAIRS [353]

Program Title:
Summer Intern Program

Purpose:
To expose students to Government foreign affairs and to provide them with an opportunity to assist the Department in strengthening educational and cultural programs while contributing their own ideas and viewpoints to the process.

Nature of Assignment:
Interns work on a variety of research and action projects involving international communications programs, particularly those relating to exchanges of students, professors, artists, athletes, government leaders, journalists, managers and other professionals. Assignments take into account students' interests with Interns able to use a great deal of initiative in carrying out their projects. Interns work under the guidance of designated mentors.

Duration:
Internships generally begin near the end of June; termination is flexible; Interns are expected to remain through August but not longer than September 30.

Eligibility:
United States citizens who will have completed at least 3 years of undergraduate work before entering the Program. Preference is given to students with demonstrated interest in foreign affairs and cross-cultural human relations. Writing and research abilities are essential while prior foreign travel, language ability and career plans are important factors.

Number of Awards:
5 per year.

Financial Data:
Interns have the rank of Foreign Service Staff-nine (FSS-9) and are paid salaries based on an annual rate of approximately $9,250 - $10,000; specific amount depends on level of education completed.

Application Deadline:
Approximately January 1 of each year.

Request Application from:
Chief
Administrative Division
Bureau of Educational and Cultural Affairs
Room 4809
Department of State
Washington, D.C. 20520

U.S. FISH AND WILDLIFE SERVICE [354]

Program Title:
Summer Employment Program

Purpose:
To provide professional and administrative Summer job opportunities with the Service.

Nature of Assignment:
Majority of positions assigned are as biological technicians working with fish and wildlife.

Duration:
Summer.

Eligibility:
College graduates or graduate students who have academic backgrounds in fish and/or wildlife biology or closely related fields, or individuals with equivalent experience.

Number of Awards:
Limited number.

Financial Data:
Participants are paid salaries based on an annual rate of approximately $10,000 or more; specific amount depends on the level of schooling completed.

Application Deadline:
Applications should be submitted as soon as possible but no later than approximately April 15.

Request Application from:
Applications should be addressed to the Regional Director, Bureau of Sports Fisheries and Wildlife, U.S. Department of Interior at one of the following locations (depending on the area where employment is desired):
P.O. Box 3737; Portland, OR 97208
Federal Bldg.; Minneapolis, MN 55111
U.S. Post Office & Court House; Boston, MA 02109
500 Gold Ave., SW; Albuquerque, NM 87103
17 Executive Park Dr., NE; Atlanta, GA 30329
18th & C Sts., NW; Washington, D.C. 20240

U.S. FOREST SERVICE [355]

Program Title:
Summer Aids and Technicians

Purpose:
To provide Summer job opportunities in Forest Service Regions or Areas or at Experiment Stations.

Nature of Assignment:
Participants work as aids and technicians in forestry (including timber, fire, range, recreation, wildlife and conservation work), engineering, surveying and relevant areas of the physical and biological sciences.

Duration:
Summer.

Eligibility:
Students who are majoring in forestry, engineering or related sciences or individuals with appropriate experience. Applicants must be at least 18 years old at the time they report for duty and must be capable of performing arduous work.

Number of Awards:
Limited number.

Financial Data:
Participants are paid salaries based on an annual rate of approximately $6,200 - $8,900; specific amount depends on the level of schooling completed.

Stipulations:
New Summer jobs are primarily in Regions; very few are in the Areas or at Experiment Research Stations.

Application Deadline:
Application should be made to only one Region, Experiment Station or Area Office of the Service. Applications should be submitted as soon after January 1 as possible but no later than approximately February 15.

Request Application from:
Requests should be sent to the Region, Experiment Station or Area Office where employment is desired at one of the following addresses:
Northern Region:
    Federal Building
    Missoula, MT 59808
Rocky Mountain Region:
    11177 W. 8th Ave.
    Lakewood, CO 80225

1st SUPPLEMENT

Directory of Internships, Work Experience Programs, and On-the-Job Training Opportunities

Southwestern Region:
  517 Gold Ave., SW
  Albuquerque, NM 87101
Intermountain Region:
  324 25th St.
  Ogden, UT 84401
California Region:
  630 Sansome St.
  San Francisco, CA 94111
Pacific Northwest Region:
  319 SW Pine St.
  Portland, OR 97208
Southern Region:
  1720 Peachtree Rd., NW
  Atlanta, GA 30309
Eastern Region:
  633 W. Wisconsin
  Milwaukee, WI 53203
Alaska Region:
  Federal Office Building
  Juneau, AK 99502
Northeastern Forest Experiment Station:
  6816 Market St.
  Upper Darby, PA 19082
North Central Forest Experiment Station:
  Folwell Ave.
  St. Paul, MN 55108
Southeastern Forest Experiment Station:
  P.O. Box 2750
  Asheville, NC 28802
Southern Forest Experiment Station:
  701 Loyola Ave.
  New Orleans, LA 70113
Rocky Mountain Forest & Range Experiment Station:
  240 W. Prospect St.
  Fort Collins, CO 80521
Intermountain Forest & Range Experiment Station:
  507 25th St.
  Ogden, UT 84401
Pacific Northwest Forest & Range Experiment Station:
  809 NE 6th Ave.
  Portland, OR 97208
Pacific Southwest Forest & Range Experiment Station:
  1960 Addison St.
  San Francisco, CA 94701

U.S. GEOLOGICAL SURVEY [356]

Program Title:
Summer Employment Program

Purpose:
To provide professional and administrative Summer job opportunities with the Survey.

Nature of Assignment:
Participants are assigned to positions involving geological and/or geophysical field work throughout the United States.

Duration:
Summer.

Eligibility:
College graduates or graduate students who have academic training in geology, geophysics or petroleum/mining engineering, or individuals with equivalent experience.

Number of Awards:
Limited number.

Financial Data:
Participants are paid salaries based on an annual rate of approximately $10,000 - $18,000; specific amount depends on the level of schooling completed.

Stipulations:
Individuals interested in engineering positions should apply to the Geological Survey Regional Office covering the part of the country where work is desired.

Application Deadline:
Applications should be submitted as soon as possible but no later than approximately April 15.

Request Application from:
Professional Staffing Committee, MS-911
U.S. Geological Survey
12201 Sunrise Valley Drive
Reston, Virginia 22092

1st SUPPLEMENT

Directory of Internships, Work Experience Programs, and On-the-Job Training Opportunities

U.S. INFORMATION AGENCY (USIA) [357]

Program Title:
Summer College Intern Program

Purpose:
To offer students an opportunity to apply their academic learning.

Nature of Assignment:
Interns work in various areas of responsibility and routine at USIA offices in Washington, D.C.

Duration:
Summer only; full time.

Eligibility:
College students of at least junior standing who are actively pursuing a degree.

Financial Data:
Interns receive salaries based on annual rates of approximately $9,500.

Application Deadline:
Approximately January 1 of each year.

Request Application from:
Special Programs Office
United States Information Agency
Washington, D.C. 20547

U.S. NATIONAL INSTITUTES OF HEALTH [358]

Program Title:
Minority Access to Research Careers (MARC)

Purpose:
To increase the number of minority scientists.

Nature of Assignment:
Participants are involved in predoctoral or postdoctoral scientific research training.

Duration:
1 - 3 years; full time.

Eligibility:
Applicants must be full-time faculty of minority institutions or students attending such institutions.

Number of Awards:
14 - 20 per year.

Financial Data:
Trainees receive stipends of varying amounts and expenses.

Application Deadline:
Applications should be submitted by February 1, June 1 or October 1.

Request Application from:
Division of Research Grants
National Institutes of Health
Bethesda, Maryland 20014

U.S. NATIONAL INSTITUTES OF HEALTH [359]

Program Title:
National Research Service Awards (NRSA)

Purpose:
To offer health specialists and clinicians an opportunity for training experience to broaden their scientific background and extend their potential for research in health-related areas.

Nature of Assignment:
Fellows undertake biomedical or behavioral research training with an opportunity to carry out supervised research in specified areas.

Duration:
1 year with the possibility of continued support for up to 3 years; full time.

Eligibility:
United States citizens, nationals or permanent residents who will have by the beginning date of the training experience, a Ph.D., M.D., D.D.S., D.O., D.V.M., O.D., Sc.D., D.Eng., D.N.S., or equivalent degree. Applicants must propose research training in one of the discipline areas covered by NIH and must arrange for appointment to an appropriate institution and acceptance by a sponsor who will supervise the training.

Financial Data:
Participants receive stipends of $10,000 - $13,200 depending on relevant postdoctoral experience.

Stipulations:
Awards are not made for study leading to a professional degree or for non-research clinical training. Fellows must sign a payback agreement indicating they agree to engage in biomedical or behavioral research, teaching, or special service for a period equal to the period of NIH support.

Special Features:
NRSA recipients have 12 months from the date of notification in which to activate the Award.

Application Deadline:
October 1 for Awards announced by the following June, February 1 for notifications sent by November, and June 1 for announcements made by March.

Request Application from:
Office of Grants Inquiries
Division of Research Grants
National Institutes of Health
Bethesda, Maryland 20014

U.S. NATIONAL INSTITUTES OF HEALTH [360]

Program Title:
Research Career Development Awards (RCDA)

Purpose:
To provide an opportunity for individuals in early stages of research career development to acquire the necessary skills and experience for independent research.

Nature of Assignment:
Awardees undertake research projects in the biomedical or behavioral sciences and research-related activities which may include research training as well as participating in workshops and scientific or professional meetings.

Duration:
5 years; full time.

Eligibility:
United States citizens, nationals or permanent residents with high potential for biomedical or behavioral research careers who will have had 3 years of relevant postdoctoral experience prior to receiving an Award. Candidates must be nominated by non-Federal public or private nonprofit institutions engaged in health-related research. Awards are not intended for established investigators.

Financial Data:
Awards are made to eligible institutions on behalf of qualified individuals. RCDA recipients are paid by their institutions, which are given salary grants of up to $30,000 per year for an Awardee.

Stipulations:
Fees resulting from clinical practice, professional consultation or other comparable work required by the research or research-related activities of an Award may not be retained by the RCDA recipient.

Application Deadline:
February 1 for Awards starting no earlier than December 1, June 1 for Awards beginning no earlier than the following April 1, and October 1 for Awards starting no sooner than July 1.

Request Application from:
Office of Grants Inquiries
Division of Research Grants
National Institutes of Health
Bethesda, Maryland 20014

U.S. NATIONAL PARK SERVICE [361]

Program Title:
Summer Employment: Park Rangers/Technicians/Aids

Purpose:
To provide Summer job opportunities in the National Park Service.

Nature of Assignment:
Participants are assigned to various duties at different parks within the National Park system.

Duration:
Summer.

Eligibility:
Applicants must be at least 18 years old, except for those applying for positions requiring predominantly law enforcement or public safety duties who must be a minimum of 21 years of age. Other requirements are: 2½ years of college or 2 years of park conservation experience for Park Ranger positions; 2 years of related college level study or 2 years of experience in a park or similar situation for Park Technicians; and high school education or 6 months of experience in a park or similar situation for Park Aids.

Number of Awards:
Limited number.

Financial Data:
Participants are paid salaries based on an annual rate of approximately $6,200 - $8,900; specific amount depends on the level of schooling completed.

Stipulations:
A few specialized positions require special skills and/or academic training. Further information on such jobs is available from the Service.

Application Deadline:
Applications should be sent to the NPS Regional Office covering the area where employment is desired and should be submitted as soon after January 1 as possible but no later than approximately February 15.

Request Application from:
Requests should be addressed to one of the following NPS Regional Offices:
North Atlantic Region:
  150 Causeway St.
  Boston, MA 02114
Mid-Atlantic Region:
  143 So. 3rd St.
  Philadelphia, PA 19106

1st SUPPLEMENT

Directory of Internships, Work Experience Programs, and On-the-Job Training Opportunities

Southeast Region:
   3401 Whipple St.
   Atlanta, GA 30344
Midwest Region:
   1709 Jackson St.
   Omaha, NB 68102
Rocky Mountain Region:
   P.O. Box 25287
   Denver, CO 80225
Southwest Region:
   Old Santa Fe Trail
   Santa Fe, NM 87501
Western Region:
   450 Golden Gate Ave.
   San Francisco, CA 94102
Pacific Northwest Region:
   1424 4th Ave.
   Seattle, WA 98101
National Capitol Parks:
   1100 Ohio Dr., SW
   Washington, DC 20242

U.S. NATIONAL SCIENCE FOUNDATION [362]

Program Title:
Scientists and Engineers in Economic Development (SEED) Program

Purpose:
To enable United States scientists and engineers to share experiences with their counterparts in developing nations through the conduct of research and education projects.

Nature of Assignment:
Individuals who receive Research/Teaching Grants collaborate with their counterparts in developing countries on joint research or teaching projects requiring at least a semester of work. Travel awards are given for participation in projects requiring only short periods of time or merely consultative visits.

Duration:
Research/Teaching Awards vary, from 5 - 12 months; International Travel Awards are for shorter periods.

Eligibility:
Scientists or engineers from American academic institutions who have at least 5 years of postdoctoral or equivalent experience in teaching or research. Project proposals will be considered in the fields of engineering, physical sciences, earth sciences, biological sciences, social sciences and science education. Applicants must plan on returning to their institutions upon completion of their projects.

Financial Data:
Research/Teaching Awards for 5 - 8 months include only travel expenses and stipends to cover lost salary and fringe benefits, while those for 9 - 12 months also include dependent travel allowances, education allowances for up to 2 children and $500 for materials to be left at the host institution. In no case will total support exceed $1,500 a month. Travel awards consist only of round-trip airfare.

Stipulations:
Recipients must travel to one of the countries designated by the Agency for International Development (AID). A list of eligible AID countries is available from the Foundation.

Application Deadline:
Research/Training proposals should be submitted by June 1 or December 1; applications for travel awards are accepted at any time. Approximately 5 months are required to process applications.

Request Application from:
Scientists and Engineers in Economic Development
Division of International Programs
National Science Foundation
Washington, D.C. 20550

U.S. POSTAL SERVICE [363]

Program Title:
Management Associate Program

Purpose:
To promote mid-level operations management development.

Nature of Assignment:
Participants are given management experience in the postal system including assignment as supervisor of mail processing and responsibilities in the areas of customer service and finance.

Duration:
Maximum of 32 months; full time.

Eligibility:
Individuals with interests and abilities appropriate to the Program who hold Master of Business Administration degrees.

Financial Data:
Participants receive salaries in the $16,000 to $25,000 range.

Application Deadline:
Applications are accepted at any time.

Request Application from:
Special Management Programs
U.S. Postal Service
Washington, D.C. 20260

U.S. VETERANS ADMINISTRATION [364]

Program Title:
Graduate Student Summer Employment Program

Purpose:
To provide professional and administrative Summer job opportunities with the Administration.

Nature of Assignment:
Students work at VA hospitals in positions related to their academic studies.

Duration:
Summer.

Eligibility:
Graduate students who are in psychology, nursing, social work, biology, dietetics, blind rehabilitation, library science, dentistry, medicine, engineering, pharmacy, occupational or physical therapy, and other health-related fields.

Number of Awards:
Limited number.

Financial Data:
Students are paid salaries based on an annual rate of approximately $10,000 - $15,000; specific amount depends on the level of schooling completed.

Application Deadline:
Applications should be submitted as soon as possible but no later than approximately April 15.

Request Application from:
Applicants should contact the VA hospital in the area where they desire employment; hospitals are listed in local telephone directories under United States Government - Veterans Administration.

1st SUPPLEMENT

Directory of Internships, Work Experience Programs, and On-the-Job Training Opportunities

U.S. VETERANS ADMINISTRATION [365]

Program Title:
On-job Training/Apprenticeship

Purpose:
To offer training programs to veterans and eligible spouses/surviving spouses chosing to use their VA education benefits to become skilled in a trade.

Nature of Assignment:
Participants are given on-job or apprenticeship training in actual job situations under the supervision of qualified persons already working in the field.

Duration:
On-job Training: 2 years or less; Apprenticeships: 3 - 4 years.

Eligibility:
Applicants must have active duty service for more than 180 continuous days between January 31, 1955, and January 1, 1977, with an other than dishonorable discharge, or must have contracted with the Armed Forces prior to January 1, 1977, under the Delayed Entry Program or a similar program.

Financial Data:
Participants with no dependents receive $212 per month for the first 6 months of support, $159 per month for the second 6 months, $106 per month for the third 6 months, and $53 per month for the fourth and any succeeding 6 month periods.

Application Deadline:
Applicants have 10 years from date or discharge to complete a training program.

Request Application from:
Interested applicants should contact the VA Regional Office nearest to their home. Additional information can also be obtained from:
Education and Rehabilitation Service
Department of Veterans Benefits
Veterans Administration
Washington, D.C. 20420

U.S. VETERANS ADMINISTRATION [366]

Program Title:
Social Work Graduate Student Trainees

Purpose:
To train social workers interested in careers in health care.

Nature of Assignment:
Trainees are given field placments in the VA hospital system where they work with individuals, families and groups.

Duration:
4 month block placements or 9 months (September - June) of 2½ days per week.

Eligibility:
Interested individuals who are officially enrolled in accredited Graduate Schools of Social Work.

Financial Data:
Trainees receive stipends ranging from $2,990 to $6,000 depending on level of course work completed.

Application Deadline:
Candidates must be nominated at the beginning of the school year.

Request Application from:
Nominations are made by Graduate Schools of Social Work affiliated with VA facilities.

U.S. VETERANS ADMINISTRATION [367]

Program Title:
Summer Employment Program

Purpose:
To provide Summer job opportunities for superior students sincerely interested in health careers.

Nature of Assignment:
Students work in VA hospitals at various health-related assignments.

Duration:
Summer.

Eligibility:
Second or third year college students who are enrolled in programs in such health care and related fields as nursing, social work, psychology, biology, dietetics, dentistry, medicine, engineering, physical therapy, occupational therapy, and pharmacy.

Number of Awards:
Limited number.

Financial Data:
Students are paid salaries based on an annual rate of approximately $6,200 - $8,900; specific amount depends on the level of schooling completed.

Stipulations:
Some VA hospitals may not be able to offer Summer employment.

Application Deadline:
Applications should be submitted as soon as possible but no later than approximately April 15.

Request Application from:
Applicants should contact the VA hospital where they desire employment; hospitals are listed in local telephone directories under United States Government - Veterans Administration.

U.S. VETERANS ADMINISTRATION [368]

Program Title:
Work-Study Program

Purpose:
To offer a program where veterans may work in VA-related jobs and by so doing supplement their regular VA education benefits.

Nature of Assignment:
Students perform various services including VA outreach; preparation and processing of VA paperwork; VA domiciliary and medical treatment services; and any other VA activity which is approved by the Administrator.

Duration:
Maximum of 250 hours per contract.

Eligibility:
Applicants must be veterans enrolled as full time VA students with preference given to service-connected disabled veterans rated 30 percent or more.

Financial Data:
Students receive $2.50 per hour up to a maximum of $625 per agreement; payment for the first 100 hours of work is made in advance.

Application Deadline:
Applications are accepted at any time during a veteran's full-time enrollment.

Request Application from:
Applicants should contact the nearest VA Regional Office. Additional information can also be obtained from:
Education and Rehabilitation Service
Department of Veterans Benefits
Veterans Administration
Washington, D.C. 20420

UTAH COUNTY, UTAH [369]

Program Title:
Student Internship Program

Purpose:
To give students work experience and to utilize professional skills at a low cost to the County.

Nature of Assignment:
Students are assigned various tasks in County departments and agencies.

Duration:
12 months, part time; or 4 months, full time.

Eligibility:
Interested students who are matriculated in an accredited college or university. Certain assignments require specialized skills.

Number of Awards:
Approximately 5 per year.

Financial Data:
Students are paid an average of $3.00 an hour.

Application Deadline:
Applications are accepted at any time.

Request Application from:
Student Internship Program
105 County Building
Provo, Utah 84601

V

VENTURA COUNTY MENTAL HEALTH SERVICES [370]

Program Title:
Clinical Psychology Predoctoral Internship

Purpose:
To train psychologists to function as clinical consultants in community mental health services.

Nature of Assignment:
Interns are given rotating work assignments in crisis intervention services, day treatment, inpatient care, community services, outpatient clinics, and children's services.

Duration:
12 months; full time.

Eligibility:
Doctoral candidates in clinical psychology who would benefit from training experience in a community mental health setting. Bilingual (English/Spanish) candidates are encouraged to apply.

Number of Awards:
2 per year.

Financial Data:
Interns receive $8,000 for the year of work.

Application Deadline:
Application inquiries are accepted at any time.

Request Application from:
Training Officer
Ventura County Mental Health Services
300 Hillmont Avenue
Ventura, California 93003

VIRGINIA MUSEUM [371]

Program Title:
Professional Fellowship

Purpose:
To promote work in the arts including painting, sculpture, graphics, crafts, photography, filmmaking, design, architecture, interior design, museum methods, art history, acting, theatre design and other such professions.

Nature of Assignment:
Support is provided for additional experience in the arts or for work on a specified project which will benefit the people of Virginia.

Eligibility:
Virginians who were born in the state or who have lived in Virginia for at least 5 years and who are professional artists involved in one or more of the fields listed above. Those in music or dance are not eligible.

Financial Data:
$2,400 usually paid over a 10 - 12 month period.

Stipulations:
Applicants must be available for personal interview at the Museum.

Application Deadline:
April 1 for awards announced the following month.

Request Application from:
Education in the Arts Committee
Virginia Museum
Boulevard and Grove Avenue
Richmond, Virginia 23221

VOLUNTARY ACTION CENTER OF NORTHWEST GEORGIA, INC. [372]

Program Title:
Volunteer On-the-Job Training

Purpose:
To address needs of the community and recruit volunteers to fit those needs.

Nature of Assignment:
Volunteers are assigned various tasks. Highly supervised on-the-job training is provided but with much opportunity for innovation.

1st SUPPLEMENT

Directory of Internships, Work Experience Programs, and On-the-Job Training Opportunities

Duration:
At least 3 months.

Eligibility:
Individuals who have appropriate interests; some assignments might require special skills.

Financial Data:
Volunteer only.

Application Deadline:
Applications are accepted at any time.

Request Application from:
V.A.C.
102 West Waugh Street
Dalton, Georgia 30720

VOLUNTARY ACTION CENTER OF TOLEDO [373]

Program Title:
Internship/Work Experience/On-the-Job Training

Purpose:
To aid and encourage the best possible volunteer solutions to community needs.

Nature of Assignment:
Participants are involved in varied and numerous activities with training offered in all areas according to job requirements. Possible assignments cover a tri-county area.

Duration:
Varies; short-term to ongoing.

Eligibility:
Individuals who have appropriate interests with specific skill requirements depending on type of placement involved.

Financial Data:
Volunteer only.

Application Deadline:
Applications are accepted at any time.

Request Application from:
Voluntary Action Center
One Stranahan Square
Toledo, Ohio 43604

VOLUNTEER JACKSONVILLE, INC. [374]

Program Title:
Internship Program

Purpose:
To organize and coordinate volunteer activities, to provide staff/volunteer training and placement of volunteers, and to develop volunteer programs.

Nature of Assignment:
Interns serve as volunteer coordinators, helping to develop and maintain student volunteer programs and learning how to recruit, interview and refer volunteers, how to develop positions for volunteers and how to provide training for staff.

Duration:
To be worked out with Interns.

Eligibility:
Interested individuals who have the ability to work with others, ability to communicate, interest in community involvement, intelligence and sensitivity.

Number of Awards:
2 - 3 per year.

1st SUPPLEMENT

Directory of Internships, Work Experience Programs, and On-the-Job Training Opportunities

Financial Data:
Volunteer only.

Application Deadline:
Applications are accepted at any time.

Request Application from:
Volunteer Jacksonville, Inc.
626 May Street
Jacksonville, Florida 32204

W

WAAB [375]

Program Title:
Summer Internship Program

Purpose:
To give broadcast or journalism students actual experience in radio news.

Nature of Assignment:
Interns attend press conferences and government meetings, cover other events, write news copy, voice some stories, and participate in interview programs.

Duration:
10 weeks during the Summer.

Eligibility:
Broadcast or journalism majors who are attending recognized institutions of higher learning.

Financial Data:
Volunteer only.

Application Deadline:
May 1 of each year.

Request Application from:
WAAB
Box 2148
Mobile, Alabama 36601

WAVE RADIO [376]

Program Title:
Broadcast News Internship

Purpose:
To provide top college students with on-the-job training in all the duties performed in a broadcast news operation.

Nature of Assignment:
Interns are assigned to the various jobs required in a broadcast news gathering organization, such as research, street reporting, photography and stand-up reporting.

Duration:
10 - 12 weeks during the Summer; full time.

Eligibility:
College students affiliated with accredited journalism/radio-TV departments who will be returning to school as juniors or seniors in the Fall following an Internship. Applicants must come from or have parents living in the WAVE coverage area (southeastern Indiana or north central Kentucky) and must have career goals definitely set in broadcast journalism.

Number of Awards:
1 or 2 each year.

Financial Data:
Interns receive salaries of $110 per week.

Application Deadline:
Approximately March 15 of each year.

Request Application from:
WAVE
Box 32970
Louisville, Kentucky 40220

WAVE-TV [377]

Program Title:
TV Production Internship

Purpose:
To provide top college students with on-the-job training as production assistants (floor directors) in a television production department.

Nature of Assignment:
Interns perform duties in all jobs required of a production assistant, such as operation of character generator and teleprompter crawl, floor directing, prop set up and maintenance, and lighting.

Duration:
10 - 12 weeks during the Summer; full time.

Eligibility:
College students affiliated with accredited radio-TV departments who will be returning to school as juniors or seniors in the Fall following an Internship. Applicants must come from or have parents living in the WAVE coverage area (southeastern Indiana or north central Kentucky) and must have career goals definitely set in TV production.

Number of Awards:
1 or 2 each year.

Financial Data:
Interns receive salaries of $110 per week.

Application Deadline:
Approximately March 15 of each year.

Request Application from:
WAVE-TV Internship
Box 32970
Louisville, Kentucky 40220

WCAO RADIO [378]

Program Title:
News Program

Purpose:
To train students in news gathering procedures.

Nature of Assignment:
Participants conduct telephone interviews, handle news writing assignments and are involved in other related work.

1st SUPPLEMENT

Directory of Internships, Work Experience Programs, and On-the-Job Training Opportunities

Duration:
2 - 4 months.

Eligibility:
Journalism students who have interests and abilities appropriate to the work.

Number of Awards:
2 - 3 per year.

Financial Data:
Volunteer only.

Application Deadline:
Applications are accepted at any time.

Request Application from:
WCAO Radio
8001 Park Heights Avenue
Pikesville, Maryland 21208

WCAS RADIO [379]

Program Title:
Music Internship

Purpose:
To provide students with experience in assisting a musical director.

Nature of Assignment:
Interns review news releases and perform other tasks by mutual agreement.

Duration:
Varies.

Eligibility:
Individuals who have interests and abilities appropriate to working with the musical director.

Number of Awards:
1 each year.

Financial Data:
Volunteer only.

Application Deadline:
Application inquiries are accepted at any time; deadlines are rotating.

Request Application from:
WCAS Radio
380 Green Street
Cambridge, Massachusetts 02139

WCAS RADIO [380]

Program Title:
News Department Internships

Purpose:
To provide students wtih experience in assisting a professional staff report news, produce features and maintain files.

Nature of Assignment:
Intern assignments include preparation of public service announcements, rewriting copy, coverage of news events, production of news drop-ins and programs, and other duties as abilities indicate. Basically, Interns gain experience in all facets of news programming, except anchoring.

Duration:
Minimum 15 hours per week commitment for flexible periods of time.

Eligibility:
College students with demonstrated writing abilities who have a willingness to learn and high level of personal motivation. Previous radio experience is desirable.

1st SUPPLEMENT

Directory of Internships, Work Experience Programs, and On-the-Job Training Opportunities

Number of Awards:
3 - 4 per year, depending on anticipated need.

Financial Data:
Volunteer only.

Special Features:
Interns can possibly arrange to receive academic credit for their work.

Application Deadline:
Application inquiries are accepted at any time; deadlines are rotating.

Request Application from:
WCAS Radio
380 Green Street
Cambridge, Massachusetts 02139

WDNR RADIO [381]

Program Title:
Work Experience

Purpose:
To provide interested newcomers with marketable broadcasting experience on an FM educational radio station.

Nature of Assignment:
Participants gain broadcasting experience within a progressive non-commercial musical format and are involved in such other station functions as production and news programming.

Duration:
Part-time work for varying lengths of time.

Eligibility:
Responsible and interested people who have skills appropriate to the work. Applicants must have a third-class Radio Operator's License or better in order to do broadcasting.

Number of Awards:
Varies from year to year.

Financial Data:
Volunteer only.

Application Deadline:
Applications are accepted at any time.

Request Application from:
WDNR
Box 1000
Widener College
Chester, Pennsylvania 19013

WEBR NEWSRADIO [382]

Program Title:
News Internship

Purpose:
To give beginning broadcast journalists experience in professional radio in order to let them know what broadcast journalism is really like.

Nature of Assignment:
Interns begin with assignments at the most basic level and are allowed to progress as far as their talents and initiative will take them.

Duration:
Varies, depending on individual Interns; generally full time.

Eligibility:
Interested individuals who are at least 18 years old and want a career in radio or television news. Applications from people wanting to be disc jockeys are not accepted.

Number of Awards:
Approximately 5 per year.

Financial Data:
Volunteer only.

Stipulations:
An interview must be conducted before an Internship is awarded.

Application Deadline:
Applications are accepted at any time.

Request Application from:
News Director
WEBR Newsradio
23 North Street
Buffalo, New York 14221

WEEK-TV [383]

Program Title:
WEEK-TV News Internship

Purpose:
To teach the skills of television news gathering necessary to function in a television newsroom.

Nature of Assignment:
Interns are given on-the-job training as reporters or camerapeople. Reporters learn to write newscopy, interview, shoot and edit 16mm film and videotapes, and produce newscasts. Photographers learn to shoot and edit 16mm film and videotapes.

Duration:
1 academic term.

Eligibility:
College seniors in broadcasting sequences who have serious interest in broadcast journalism.

Number of Awards:
Varies; as many as 12 per year.

Financial Data:
Volunteer; some work-related expenses (travel, some meals) are reimbursed.

Application Deadline:
Applications are accepted at any time.

Request Application from:
News Manager
WEEK-TV
2907 Springfield Road
East Peoria, Illinois 61611

WEHT-TV [384]

Program Title:
WEHT-TV Training Program

Purpose:
To develop competent individuals in the area of broadcasting and to assist people in becoming familiar with television.

Nature of Assignment:
Trainees are offered varied assignments in the technical, production and news aspects of broadcasting.

Duration:
13 weeks during the Fall or Spring.

Eligibility:
High school graduates who have interests and skills appropriate to the work; preference is given to minorities.

Number of Awards:
2 per year.

Financial Data:
Participants receive the minimum wage.

Application Deadline:
January 1 for training during the Spring and June 1 for training in the Fall.

Request Application from:
General Manager
WEHT-TV
Box 395
Evansville, Indiana 47703

WFIF [385]

Program Title:
WFIF Internship Program

Purpose:
To encourage prospective broadcasters to enter news related fields in radio and to provide practical, relevant experience.

Nature of Assignment:
Interns work with the professional news staff; their assignments include observing staff activities, accompanying personnel to meetings, and writing and producing features. Critiques and evaluations are furnished Interns as a form of constructive teaching.

Duration:
Open to negotiation.

Eligibility:
Individuals who have interests and skills appropriate to the work. Applicants are screened for character, attitude and ability.

Number of Awards:
Open.

Financial Data:
Intern positions are volunteer, with expenses paid; as Interns develop, remuneration may be arranged.

Stipulations:
Interviews are required of all applicants.

Application Deadline:
Applications are accepted at any time.

Request Application from:
WFIF
90 Jay Avenue
Milford, Connecticut 06460

WGBY-TV [386]

Program Title:
WGBY Production Internship

Purpose:
To provide hands-on production experience on studio and remote television programs with broadcast quality equipment.

Nature of Assignment:
Interns are assigned as regular crewmembers on local and contract productions where they receive on-the-job training in each phase of broadcast operations and exposure to the broad range of skills required. As part of their training,

Interns may serve as camera operators, technical directors (switchers), floor managers, audio assistants and lighting assistants; work in content procedures; and be involved in the legal, ethical and practical considerations related to educational and public affairs broadcasting.

Duration:
Full-time commitment for 6 months or more is preferred.

Eligibility:
Individuals who are interested in the training and have had previous work experience in any job situation. Preference is given to applicants with some education/experience in television production. Although not required, a second class truck driver's license would be helpful.

Number of Awards:
5 per year.

Financial Data:
Nothing firmly established. Students can arrange to fit the Internship into College Work-Study Programs. There is also the possibility of a $2,000 Intern stipend.

Application Deadline:
Applications are accepted at any time.

Request Application from:
WGBY-TV
1 Armory Square
Springfield, Maine 01105

WGLF FM RADIO [387]

Program Title:
WGLF Internship Program

Purpose:
To train students in the many tasks of radio, and to show them how to go about conducting a radio station.

Nature of Assignment:
Students are trained in all aspects of radio work, from news to programming. Assignments are given in the areas of news reporting, traffic, sales, air work and production.

Duration:
3 months.

Eligibility:
College or university students who are mass communcation majors.

Number of Awards:
4 per year.

Financial Data:
Volunteer only.

Application Deadline:
1 month before the beginning of the academic term for which an Internship is desired.

Request Application from:
WGLF Radio
P.O. Box 1815
Tallahassee, Florida 32302

WGPR, INC. [388]

Program Title:
Work Experience/On-the-Job Training

Purpose:
To train possible future personnel for the broadcast media.

1st SUPPLEMENT
Directory of Internships, Work Experience Programs, and On-the-Job Training Opportunities

Nature of Assignment:
Participants are given varied assignments in radio or TV with specific duties depending on each person's interests and background and the needs of the station.

Duration:
Varies.

Eligibility:
Persons who are interested in broadcast media training with specific educational or skills requirements depending on the particular area of broadcasting in which the individual would like to work.

Financial Data:
Some participants are paid in part or whole by government funds; others are volunteer only.

Special Features:
Participants may arrange to receive college credit for their work.

Application Deadline:
Application inquiries are accepted at any time; deadlines vary.

Request Application from:
Controller
WGPR, Inc.
3146 East Jefferson
Detroit, Michigan 48207

WMAZ RADIO AND TELEVISION [389]

Program Title:
Broadcast News Internship

Purpose:
To provide practical experience for black college students interested in seeking a career in broadcast news.

Nature of Assignment:
The Intern is involved in news writing, audio recording, film photography, film editing, and other related facets of radio and television news reporting.

Duration:
Summer only; full time.

Eligibility:
Black college students who have one or more years of school remaining, good grammar and vocabulary, typing ability, and trainable voices.

Number of Awards:
1 per year.

Financial Data:
Minimum wage for 40 hours per week.

Application Deadline:
April 15 of each year.

Request Application from:
WMAZ Radio and Television
P.O. Box 5008
Macon, Georgia 31208

WMCA RADIO [390]

Program Title:
Internship Program

Purpose:
To provide training in news programming and production.

1st SUPPLEMENT
Directory of Internships, Work Experience Programs, and On-the-Job Training Opportunities

Nature of Assignment:
Interns are given on-the-job training through news and programming assignments.

Duration:
Varies; full or part time acceptable.

Eligibility:
Individuals who have interests and skills appropriate to the work.

Number of Awards:
Open.

Financial Data:
Volunteer; authorized expenses are paid.

Stipulations:
Applicants must be available for interview.

Application Deadline:
Applications are accepted at any time.

Request Application from:
WMCA
888 7th Avenue
New York, New York 10019

WNCR/WAAF RADIO STATIONS [391]

Program Title:
Broadcast News and Programming-Production Internships

Purpose:
To initiate Interns into the broadcast operations of modern radio, including news operations, broadcast automation equipment, music, and announcing style; and to deliver enough experience to let them make career decisions.

Nature of Assignment:
Interns are assigned news gathering, editing and writing duties; given an overview of automation equipment and music selection; provided hands-on experience with broadcast equipment in the studio; and involved in commercial voice delivery and production.

Duration:
Semester or Summer.

Eligibility:
Preference is given to applicants who have communications, theatre or speech backgrounds, or demonstrated interest in broadcasting as a career.

Number of Awards:
Up to 3 per Internship period (Semester or Summer).

Financial Data:
Volunteer only; Stations will also aid in placing Interns in residences.

Special Features:
WNCR and WAAF both provide Interns with excellent references and will cooperate in arranging academic credit for participation in the work experience.

Application Deadline:
Applications are accepted at any time.

Request Application from:
Program Director
WNCR/WAAF Radio Stations
34 Mechanic Street
Worcester, Massachusetts 01608

WPLW-AM [392]

Program Title:
Work Experience

1st SUPPLEMENT
Directory of Internships, Work Experience Programs, and On-the-Job Training Opportunities

Purpose:
To train people in broadcast arts, sales and all facets of Christian radio programming.

Nature of Assignment:
Participants are given experience in on-the-air activities, production and sales. Specific assignments are worked out to meet the needs of individual trainees.

Duration:
Flexible working hours and length of training.

Eligibility:
Individuals who have a broadcast endorsed F.C.C. license and an interest in Christian broadcasting.

Number of Awards:
5 - 10 per year.

Financial Data:
Remuneration is negotiable; there is the possibility for qualified trainees to obtain permanent positions with station expansion.

Application Deadline:
Applications are accepted at any time.

Request Application from:
Hickling Broadcast Company
201 Ewing Road
Pittsburgh, Pennsylvania 15205

WPOP NEWSRADIO-14 [393]

Program Title:
Internship Program

Purpose:
To provide hands-on experience in the WPOP newsroom.

Nature of Assignment:
Interns are given various newsroom assignments, such as carting network feeds and making police checks.

Duration:
Summer only; 6 a.m. - 2 p.m.

Eligibility:
College or university students who have backgrounds in either journalism or college radio.

Financial Data:
Volunteer only; no expenses paid.

Application Deadline:
Applications should be submitted by May preceding a desired Summer Internship.

Request Application from:
Operations Manager
WPOP Newsradio-14
P.O. Box 11-1410
Newington Branch
Hartford, Connecticut 06111

WRJZ RADIO [394]

Program Title:
Work Experience

Purpose:
To provide the opportunity to learn the inside workings of a radio station in general and to gain work experience in the specific areas of music, research, and/or news.

Nature of Assignment:
Participants are given experience in music/research (tally requests, in-store interviews, phone-out surveying) and news activities.

1st SUPPLEMENT

Directory of Internships, Work Experience Programs, and On-the-Job Training Opportunities

Duration:
Flexible.

Eligibility:
People who have a sincere interest to learn.

Financial Data:
Volunteer only at present.

Application Deadline:
Applications are accepted at any time.

Request Application from:
WRJZ Radio
Box 3367
Knoxville, Tennessee 37917

WRTV 6 [395]

Program Title:
Call For Help Volunteer Program

Purpose:
To aid the general public in solving their problems through the Call For Help referral service.

Nature of Assignment:
Participants handle telephone calls, make referrals, keep extensive records (incoming calls and where referred) do followup work and sometimes help solve problems.

Duration:
Varies.

Eligibility:
Interested individuals who have excellent telephone rapport, can talk to all levels of the general and professional public, are quick thinkers, and like to find solutions or answers. Applicants must be able to cope with all kinds of problems from all types of people. College students majoring in sociology are desirable.

Financial Data:
Volunteer.

Special Features:
Students may arrange to receive academic credit for their work.

Application Deadline:
Applications are accepted at any time.

Request Application from:
WRTV 6
1330 North Meridian Street
Indianapolis, Indiana 46206

WSKG [396]

Program Title:
WSKG Internship

Purpose:
To open new opportunities for experience in public TV and FM.

Nature of Assignment:
Interns work as production assistants as well as in news and graphics.

Duration:
Flexible.

Eligibility:
Individuals who are interested in TV or FM work.

Financial Data:
Volunteer only.

Application Deadline:
Applications are accepted at any time.

1st SUPPLEMENT

Directory of Internships, Work Experience Programs, and On-the-Job Training Opportunities

Request Application from:
General Manager
WSKG
Box 97
Endwell, New York 13760

WTTW/CHANNEL 11 [397]

Program Title:
News Division Internship

Purpose:
To provide on-the-job experience for students in TV news.

Nature of Assignment:
Interns assist producers in nightly production of news broadcasts; are given exposure to assignment desk, studio and field productions, and the editing process; screen tapes; and do some research, mostly telephone.

Duration:
12 weeks; 40 hours per week.

Eligibility:
College students with some journalism background who will be seniors and are majoring in television production. Applicants must arrange to receive college credit for the Internship work.

Financial Data:
Volunteer.

Application Deadline:
Applications are accepted at any time.

Request Application from:
WTTW/Channel 11
233 North Michigan - Suite 1911
Chicago, Illinois 60601

WVII-TV [398]

Program Title:
Work Experience

Purpose:
To provide students with an opportunity to acquire commercial broadcast skills.

Nature of Assignment:
Participants gain experience in all phases of TV: news, production and sales.

Duration:
13 weeks or longer.

Eligibility:
College students who have interests and skills appropriate to the work.

Financial Data:
Volunteer only; work-related expenses are paid.

Application Deadline:
Applications are accepted at any time.

Request Application from:
Manager
WVII-TV
41 Farm Road
Bangor, Maine 04401

WASHINGTON. COUNCIL FOR POSTSECONDARY EDUCATION [399]

Program Title:
State Work/Study Program

Purpose:
To provide employment opportunities for needy students.

Nature of Assignment:
Wherever possible, students are given job assignments related to their academic pursuits.

Eligibility:
Undergraduate, graduate or professional students who are attending public or private postsecondary institutions in the State of Washington. Applicants must qualify for financial aid through their schools. Preference is given to Washington residents.

Financial Data:
Students are paid varying salaries depending upon their qualifications and the employing organization.

Application Deadline:
Application to the Program is automatic upon application to school financial aid offices.

Request Application from:
Students interested in the Program should contact the Financial Aid Officer at their institutions.

WASHINGTON CENTER FOR THE STUDY OF SERVICES [400]

Program Title:
Internship Program

Purpose:
To give experience in investigative consumer research techniques and data gathering as well as general office procedures.

Nature of Assignment:
Interns are assigned to determine, test and use research techniques to rate services in the metropolitan Washington, D.C., area. They then analyze the data and communicate the results in a form easily comprehensible to the general population.

Eligibility:
Individuals interested in the Program with preference given to applicants who have social science/statistical/journalism backgrounds.

Number of Awards:
2 per year.

Financial Data:
Volunteer only.

Application Deadline:
Applications are accepted at any time.

Request Application from:
Washington Center for the Study of Services
1910 K Street, N.W. - Suite 201
Washington, D.C. 20006

WASHINGTON, D.C. CITY COUNCIL [401]

Program Title:
D.C. Council Internship Program

Purpose:
To provide training for students at various educational levels, and to contribute significantly to the preparation of a cadre of competent and commited administrators for service in the public sector.

Nature of Assignment:
Students are given work assignments which augment their academic programs with job descriptions prepared in consultation with Interns. Duties assigned include drafting of legislation, various writing activities, and research tasks.

Duration:
1 Semester.

Eligibility:
College students from any relevant field who are interested in the Program. Students must have the written approval of their department chairperson to participate as an Intern. Applicants must submit writing samples.

Number of Awards:
4 or 5 each year.

Financial Data:
Volunteer only.

Application Deadline:
Applications are accepted at any time.

Request Application from:
D.C. Council Internship Program
14 and E Streets, N.W.
Washington, D.C. 20004

WASHINGTON PEACE CENTER [402]

Program Title:
Counter-Recruiting Action Program

Purpose:
To assist in offering students in the D.C. public school system the information they need in order to make a well-balanced decision about enlisting in the military.

Nature of Assignment:
Participants assist Center staff members arrange meetings among school counselors, teachers, students and program community workers; help distribute literature; and attend meetings and conventions of educators.

Duration:
1 - 6 months.

Eligibility:
Interested individuals who have communication skills (in writing, in person and by phone), organization acumen, and motivation to be involved in issues of militarism.

Number of Awards:
6 per year.

Financial Data:
No salary; expenses are paid and assistance is offered in finding housing.

Application Deadline:
Applications are accepted at any time.

Request Application from:
Washington Peace Center
2111 Florida Avenue, N.W.
Washington, D.C. 20008

WASHINGTON PEACE CENTER [403]

Program Title:
Peace Action Community Organizing Program

Purpose:
To effectively coordinate related peace action activities among groups and individuals in the Washington, D.C., area.

Nature of Assignment:
Participants assist Center staff (i.e., organizing meetings, speakers, and public actions) and undertake occasional research projects into issues, such as voting behavior.

1st SUPPLEMENT — Directory of Internships, Work Experience Programs, and On-the-Job Training Opportunities

Duration:
1 - 6 months.

Eligibility:
Interested individuals who have communication skills (in writing, in person and by phone), organizational acumen, and motivation to be involved in issues of militarism.

Number of Awards:
6 per year.

Financial Data:
No salary; expenses are paid and assistance is offered in finding housing.

Application Deadline:
Applications are accepted at any time.

Request Application from:
Washington Peace Center
2111 Florida Avenue, N.W.
Washington, D.C. 20008

WENATCHEE WORLD [404]

Program Title:
Internship Program

Purpose:
To give practical newspaper experience to journalism students.

Nature of Assignment:
Interns are involved in all aspects of newspaper reporting. They work under close supervision and are given frequent analysis of their job performance.

Duration:
3 months (i.e., each academic term).

Eligibility:
College and university journalism majors who are preferably juniors or seniors.

Number of Awards:
1 position each academic term.

Financial Data:
Interns receive $450 a month plus a free, furnished apartment.

Application Deadline:
Applications should be submitted approximately 3 months before the academic term for which an Internship is desired.

Request Application from:
Managing Editor
Wenatchee World
P.O. Box 1511
Wenatchee, Washington 98801

WEST VIRGINIA. LEGISLATIVE SERVICES [405]

Program Title:
Legislative Graduate Student Internship Program

Purpose:
To raise the quality of professional and technical staff services to the Legislature; to develop academic interest in state government with emphasis on the legislative branch; and to develop a pool of professional people who are qualified to become employees of the Legislature and its various agencies.

1st SUPPLEMENT

Directory of Internships, Work Experience Programs, and On-the-Job Training Opportunities

Nature of Assignment:
During legislative sessions, Interns may be assigned duties in the Senate and House of Delegates, attend some sessions, and serve in various other capacities (such as drafting bills and working with the Judiciary, Finance or other Committees). Upon adjournment of the session, Interns return to Legislative Services where they are assigned to conduct research and other related duties.

Duration:
4 months, starting in January.

Eligibility:
Graduate students in cooperating institutions who are interested in government affairs. Each student must be recommended to the Director of Legislative Services by the academic supervisor of the program in his/her department.

Financial Data:
Stipend of $660 per month.

Special Features:
Interns receive 6 semester hours of credit toward a graduate degree.

Application Deadline:
Late Fall of each year.

Request Application from:
Legislative Services
E-132 State Capitol
Charleston, West Virginia 25305

WESTERN MARYLAND MANPOWER CONSORTIUM [406]

Program Title:
Garrett County Youth Employment Training

Purpose:
To provide work experience, vocational training, continued education and counseling to economically disadvantaged youth in order to improve their chances for employment in the job market.

Nature of Assignment:
Participants are given the opportunity to learn vocational and educational skills and techniques through work experience, counseling, enrollment in appropriate courses, and seminar sessions that are designed to improve future employability.

Eligibility:
Residents of Garrett County, Maryland, who are 16 or 17 years old, unemployed, school drop-outs and from economically disadvantaged families.

Financial Data:
Participants are paid the minimum wage and are reimbursed for training related expenses.

Application Deadline:
Applications are accepted at any time.

Request Application from:
Garrett County Youth Employment Training
Garrett Community College - Oakland Center
104 East Center Street
Oakland, Maryland 21550

THE WINE MUSEUM OF SAN FRANCISCO [407]

Program Title:
Docent Council of Volunteers

Purpose:
To provide exposure to a specialized museum.

Nature of Assignment:
Participants do some museum work but primarily lead guided tours through The Christian Brothers Collection of wine-in-the-arts. Volunteers must attend a training program which, although primarily devoted to art and history, includes a wine seminar.

Duration:
Training involves 1 afternoon a week for 3 months; volunteer work varies.

Eligibility:
Individuals who are interested in the work and able to attend the training course, which is usually held from October through December.

Financial Data:
Volunteer only.

Application Deadline:
September 25 of each year.

Request Application from:
The Wine Museum of San Francisco
633 Beach Street
San Francisco, California 94109

WISCONSIN. STATE BUREAU OF PERSONNEL [408]

Program Title:
Summer Minority Intern Program

Purpose:
To give college students a work-related experience during the Summer months.

Nature of Assignment:
Students are placed in State departments and agencies where they are given on-the-job work experience in areas related to their academic majors.

Duration:
Full time during the Summer; possibly part time during the school year.

Eligibility:
College and university juniors, seniors or graduate students who are minority members or women and who qualify for employment by the State.

Number of Awards:
Varies year to year.

Financial Data:
Students are paid varying salaries depending on their qualifications and the employing agency or department involved.

Special Features:
Successful completion of the Intern Program qualifies Interns for permanent positions with the State.

Application Deadline:
Approximately May 15 of each year.

Request Application from:
State Affirmative Action Officer
1 West Wilson Street - Room 239
Madison, Wisconsin 53702

WOMANART GALLERY [409]

Program Title:
Intern Program

1st SUPPLEMENT

Directory of Internships, Work Experience Programs, and On-the-Job Training Opportunities

Purpose:
To cultivate, foster, sponsor, and develop understanding, appreciation and interest in the female artist and her creative product.

Nature of Assignment:
Interns are given experience in setting up exhibitions, cataloging, and promotional PR, and are involved in creative exhibition programs, gallery talks, growth seminars and counseling, and workshops.

Duration:
Varies.

Eligibility:
Women artists who can meet jury specifications. Applicants should be generally interested in the arts, including public relations and lecturing aspects.

Financial Data:
Interns are paid for their work with free exhibition space.

Application Deadline:
Applications are accepted at any time.

Request Application from:
Director
Womanart Gallery
41 West 57th Street
New York, New York 10019

WOMAN'S CENTER [410]

Program Title:
Rape Awareness Program

Purpose:
To provide advocacy referral and/or counseling to sexual assault victims and to give public education presentations to community groups, schools and businesses.

Nature of Assignment:
Participants are assigned a variety of tasks from counseling victims to public relations, community organization, fund raising, grant writing, public speaking, gathering and analysis of data, and making audio-visual programs. In-service training is provided, under the supervision of experienced professionals.

Duration:
Open; can be full time; part time and/or Summer.

Eligibility:
People who have a willingness to work for (or with) sexual assault victims in a feminist environment.

Financial Data:
Volunteer only; travel expenses are paid.

Application Deadline:
Applications are accepted at any time.

Request Application from:
Woman's Center
107 West Lawrence
Helena, Montana 59601

WOMEN'S EQUITY ACTION LEAGUE EDUCATIONAL AND LEGAL DEFENSE FUND [411]

Program Title:
WEAL FUND Intern Program

243

Purpose:
To work with the Fund in its attempt to secure legal and economic rights for women by carrying out educational and research projects in the area of sex discrimination, monitoring the implementation and enforcement of civil rights and other laws, and initiating and supporting law suits in the field of equal rights.

Nature of Assignment:
Interns work on Fund projects, gaining organizational and administrative training by so doing. Possible project areas include analyzing women's access to fellowships and training opportunities, developing a sports clearinghouse, monitoring the status and role of women in the military, and cooperating with other groups monitoring administrative policy development, especially in education and employment. Within these broad areas, Interns select specific projects that are of interest to them and of importance to the Fund.

Duration:
Minimum overall commitment of 120 hours; part or full time. Scheduling is flexible, according to Intern needs.

Eligibility:
Individuals who desire short-term work experience in areas of interest to the Fund. High school, college or graduate students are welcome to apply, as are persons seeking an avenue of reentry into the job market and retirees who would like to continue using their skills.

Financial Data:
Majority of Internships are volunteer, with Interns receiving small daily expense allowances. There is one paid Internship reserved for a law student and one Limited Resources Internship per quarter for individuals with unique financial needs.

Special Features:
Interns may arrange to receive academic credit for their work.

Application Deadline:
Applications are accepted at any time.

Request Application from:
WEAL FUND Intern Program
733 15th Street, N.W. - Suite 200
Washington, D.C. 20005

WOODROW WILSON INTERNATIONAL CENTER FOR SCHOLARS [412]

Program Title:
Guest Scholar Program

Purpose:
To provide limited facilities for short-term use by arrangement with the Director of the Center.

Nature of Assignment:
Participants work on scholarly projects utilizing Center facilities.

Duration:
Generally not beyond 2 months.

Eligibility:
Scholars who have appropriate projects. Particularly favored are projects related to the research supported through the Center's Fellowship Program with such work falling into 3 areas: social and political studies; historical and cultural studies; and resources, environment and interdependence.

Financial Data:
No financial support is provided.

Stipulations:
Since it is frequently difficult to predict the availability of space at the Center, applicants may not receive definite confirmation of their appointments until a relatively short time before the desired beginning date.

Application Deadline:
Applications are accepted at any time.

Request Application from:
Woodrow Wilson International Center for Scholars
Smithsonian Institution Building
Washington, D.C. 20560

WOODROW WILSON NATIONAL FELLOWSHIP FOUNDATION [413]

Program Title:
Administrative Internship Program

Purpose:
To help meet the need for well-trained administrative management at historically black colleges, Appalachian mountain schools, and certain other "developing" colleges, such as Native American institutions.

Nature of Assignment:
Interns are assigned to participating schools where they serve as assistants to presidents and business managers, or as directors of research, planning and development. In the past, Interns have also been active in such areas as budgeting, investment analysis, operations analysis and research, student personnel administration, public relations, community projects, classroom teaching, and working at hospitals associated with participating colleges.

Duration:
Minimum of 1 year; full time.

Eligibility:
Interested individuals who, by June of the Internship year, will hold M.B.A., M.P.A., Ed.D., Ph.D. or J.D. degrees. The Program is open to any qualified candidate who wishes to apply his/her professional training to the administrative needs of educational institutions.

Number of Awards:
5 - 15 per year.

Financial Data:
Interns are full-time employees of participating institutions and salary negotiations are strictly between Interns and institutions; past salaries have averaged approximately $15,000.

Application Deadline:
February 1 of each year.

Request Application from:
Administrative Internship Program
P.O. Box 642
Princeton, New Jersey 08540

WORCESTER FOUNDATION FOR EXPERIMENTAL BIOLOGY, INC. [414]

Program Title:
Summer Junior Research Fellowship in Experimental Biology

1st SUPPLEMENT

Directory of Internships, Work Experience Programs, and On-the-Job Training Opportunities

Purpose:
To introduce students to current biomedical research problems and to certain techniques used in basic research, and to provide a challenging training setting for the development of first-rate scientific personnel.

Nature of Assignment:
Fellows work in the Foundation laboratory under the direct supervision of a scientist. The research training includes actual use of many types of laboratory equipment.

Duration:
10 weeks during the Summer, from early June to mid-August.

Eligibility:
College and university science majors who have completed 2 years of academic work with an overall grade point average of at least 3.0 and the same GPA for science courses.

Number of Awards:
Approximately 20 per year.

Financial Data:
Fellows receive stipends of approximately $500 which they may augment with work-study funds from their schools.

Application Deadline:
March 1 of each year.

Request Application from:
Director
Summer Training Program
Worcester Foundation for Experimental Biology
222 Maple Avenue
Shrewsbury, Massachusetts 01545

WORLD PRESS INSTITUTE [415]

Program Title:
Foreign Journalist Fellowships

Purpose:
To provide foreign journalists with a firsthand understanding of the United States.

Nature of Assignment:
Participants are involved in essentially an experiential program, although they do attend some academic and other seminars or lectures for background information. Fellows go out on frequent interviews and may lead some cross-cultural activities or assist with newsletters.

Duration:
Mid-September - mid-May; full time.

Eligibility:
Foreign journalists who are interested in learning about the United States. Applicants can come from various backgrounds, but their ability to handle interpersonal relations is extremely important.

Number of Awards:
12 per year.

Financial Data:
Expenses are paid.

Application Deadline:
Applications can be submitted at any time during the academic year.

Request Application from:
The Executive Director
World Press Institute
Macalester College
St. Paul, Minnesota 55105

y

YORK COUNTY 4-H CLUBS [416]

Program Title:
Volunteer 4-H Leader

Purpose:
To help young people become creative and productive citizens.

Nature of Assignment:
Participants organize Clubs or teach projects and act as resource people for special programs, such as leadership training.

Duration:
Varies; 6 - 8 weeks if involved in teaching projects.

Eligibility:
Applicants must be interested in working with young people 8 - 19 years old.

Number of Awards:
No limit.

Financial Data:
Volunteer only.

Application Deadline:
Applications are accepted at any time.

Request Application from:
York County Extension Service
21 East Market Street
Court House
York, Pennsylvania 17401

YOUNG CONCERT ARTISTS, INC. [417]

Program Title:
Artist Management Services Training

Purpose:
To provide an opportunity to learn about the varied facets of management services and materials.

Nature of Assignment:
Trainees prepare follow-up materials for concert engagements, handle telephone calls, keep mailing lists, take on some office duties, and perform follow-up work connected with the presentation of New York concerts.

Duration:
Summer only, June through September.

Eligibility:
Individuals who have knowledge of classical music, interest in working for musicians or with the presentation of concerts, and good typing skills.

Number of Awards:
1 each Summer.

Financial Data:
No financial remuneration is offered; carfare and similar expenses within the city are reimbursed and complimentary tickets to concerts are provided.

Special Features:
Trainees have the possibility of future regular employment.

Application Deadline:
April 1 for training experience during the Summer of that year.

Request Application from:
Young Concert Artists, Inc.
75 East 55th Street
New York, New York 10022

YOUNG MEN'S CHRISTIAN ASSOCIATION. DOVER, DELAWARE [418]

Program Title:
Juvenile Justice Diversion

Purpose:
To work with young boys and girls referred from police, courts, probation or school as young people with problems.

Nature of Assignment:
Participants work in relationship building assignments, serving as youth advocates, counselors or friends.

Duration:
Part time during any time of the year, although Summer would be best.

Eligibility:
Individuals who like young people and want to work with them.

Number of Awards:
2 or 3 per year.

Financial Data:
Volunteer only.

Application Deadline:
Applications are accepted at any time.

Request Application from:
YMCA of Dover and Kent County
1137 South State Street
Dover, Delaware 19901

YOUNG MEN'S CHRISTIAN ASSOCIATION. LEXINGTON, KENTUCKY [419]

Program Title:
Field Placements/Internships

Purpose:
To provide a better understanding of the YMCA and to develop participants both personally and professionally.

Nature of Assignment:
Participants are assigned tasks in recreation and physical education and are given general experience in the necessary job skills for employment with the YMCA.

Duration:
Minimum of 6 weeks, maximum of 1 year; full or part time.

Eligibility:
College students or graduates who are interested in the YMCA and in working in a very strong Christian atmosphere. Some experience with children or group work would be helpful.

Number of Awards:
8 - 15 per year.

Financial Data:
Most positions are volunteer, although some payment is possible for part-time work.

Application Deadline:
Applications are accepted all year; however, submission in May, August or December is preferred.

Request Application from:
Membership Director
YMCA of Greater Lexington
239 East High Street
Lexington, Kentucky 40507

YOUNG MEN'S CHRISTIAN ASSOCIATION. NATIONAL BOARD. INTERNATIONAL DIVISION [420]

Program Title:
International Nongovernmental Internship Program

Purpose:
To provide outstanding college students with experience working in international nongovernmental and intergovernmental agencies.

Nature of Assignment:
Interns are assigned to cooperating agencies (United Nations, National Council of Churches, Bread for the World, YMCA and others) where their work tends to focus on social activism, such as involvement with international economic and trade issues and with cross-serving organizations. Occasional travel may be necessary and relevant training is offered.

Duration:
Flexible, although periods of 3 - 6 months are preferred.

Eligibility:
Outstanding college seniors who have the maturity and ability to assume responsibility. Honors students or those highly recommended by their department chairmen receive first priority. Research and language skills are helpful but not essential. Strong interests in social justice and/or world trade issues are also desirable.

Number of Awards:
Varies; about 25 per academic term.

Financial Data:
Volunteer only; necessary travel expenses are normally covered.

Special Features:
Interns can arrange to receive academic credit for participation in the Program.

Application Deadline:
January 15, April 15, July 15 and October 15.

Request Application from:
Special Projects Director
International Division
National Board of YMCA's
291 Broadway
New York, New York 10007

YOUNG RADIO, INC. [421]

Program Title:
Training Program

Purpose:
To provide an opportunity for broadcast training.

Nature of Assignment:
Trainees are given experience in news, production, and engineering.

Duration:
No fixed length.

Eligibility:
Individuals who have interests and skills appropriate to the work.

Financial Data:
Volunteer.

Application Deadline:
Applications are accepted at any time.

Request Application from:
Young Radio Inc.
P.O. Box 2250
Napa, California 94558

YOUTH INDUSTRIES, INC. [422]

Program Title:
Training Program

Purpose:
To provide skills training, work adjustment counseling and direct job placement for young adults from low socio-economic backgrounds.

Nature of Assignment:
Participants receive training in upholstery, woodworking and cashier sales coupled with counseling and other supportive services.

Duration:
October 1 - September 30.

Eligibility:
Young adults 16 - 21 years of age who are unemployed or underemployed and are socially or economically disadvantaged.

Financial Data:
Varies.

Application Deadline:
Applications are accepted at any time.

Request Application from:
Youth Industries, Inc.
6534 Northwest 7th Avenue
Miami, Florida 33150

YOUTH OPPORTUNITIES UPHELD, INC. [423]

Program Title:
Program Internship/Clinical Internship

Purpose:
To assist in providing a multifaceted intensive probation program for court-referred adolescents.

Nature of Assignment:
Interns participate in such daily activities as tutoring, arts and crafts, and recreation. Clinical Interns work in cooperation with individual staff members and are involved in family and individual therapy as well as advocacy with court and schools. Program Interns receive weekly supervision.

Duration:
At least 1 school semester.

Eligibility:
Any person who is interested in and relates well to adolescents.

Financial Data:
Volunteer; work-study arrangements are possible.

Stipulations:
Applicants must be available for personal interview and be able to spend a day in the program before an Internship will be awarded.

Application Deadline:
Applications are accepted at any time.

Request Application from:
Director of Volunteers
Youth Opportunities Upheld, Inc.
5 Pleasant Place
Worcester, Massachusetts 01608

APPENDICES

1st SUPPLEMENT

Directory of Internships, Work Experience Programs, and On-the-Job Training Opportunities

APPENDIX A

Job Corps Centers

The following is a list of vocational courses offered at 60 Job Corps centers located in 31 States and Puerto Rico.

Authorized by title IV of the Comprehensive Employment and Training Act, Job Corps provides intensive programs of education, vocational training, work experience, and counseling on a residential or nonresidential basis. These facilities and programs, and the vocational courses listed in the following pages, are available for training youth and adults who are out of work or school and who need additional skills to secure and hold meaningful employment.

Job Corps currently operates three types of centers:

Civilian Conservation Centers (CCC's) — residential centers for about 200 enrollees located in national parks and other public lands owned by the U.S. Department of Agriculture (Forest Service) or the U.S. Department of the Interior and managed by these agencies for the U.S. Department of Labor.

Contract Centers — training centers for 200 to 2,200 trainees operated under contracts with State or local government agencies, private nonprofit organizations, or profitmaking organizations selected through competition.

Extension Centers — centers offering advanced training. The two extension centers are Santa Rosa, operated by the Marine Cooks and Stewards Union, providing advanced food service training, and the BRAC Minneapolis Center, operated by the Brotherhood of Railway and Airline Clerks.

Centers approved for coeducational training programs are identified by an asterisk (*). In the *capacity* item (R) indicates residential and (NR), nonresidential.

ARIZONA

Phoenix*

No. 400 — Job Corps Center

Capacity — 165 women (R) (NR); 185 men (R) (NR)

Operator — Teledyne Economic Development Co.

Courses — Automotive trades, bricklaying, business and clerical skills, carpentry, cement masonry, commercial art, computer programming, cosmetology, diesel mechanics, electronics assembly, food service, health occupations (licensed practical nurse, nurse assistant), keypunch operator, painting, plastering, radio-TV repair, welding

Address — 518 South Third Street, Phoenix, Arizona 85004

Telephone — (602) 254-5921

ARKANSAS

Cass

No. 009 — Civilian Conservation Center

1st SUPPLEMENT

Directory of Internships, Work Experience Programs, and On-the-Job Training Opportunities

Capacity — 168 men (R)

Operator — Forest Service, U.S. Department of Agriculture

Courses — Automotive trades, building maintenance, carpentry, cement masonry, cooking, heavy equipment, painting, welding

Address — Ozark, Arkansas 72949

Telephone — (501) 667-3686

Travel directions: Drive 18 miles north of Ozark on State Highway No. 23, in the Ozark National Forest

Ouachita

No. 098 — Civilian Conservation Center

Capacity — 176 men (R)

Operator — Forest Service, U.S. Department of Agriculture

Courses — Automotive trades, brick and stone masonry, building maintenance, carpentry, cooking, painting, plastering, welding

Address — Royal, Arkansas 71968

Telephone — (501) 767-2707

Travel directions: Drive 12 miles west of Hot Springs on U.S. Highway No. 270

CALIFORNIA

Los Angeles*

No. 702 — Job Corps Center

Capacity — 445 women (R) (NR); 50 men (R) (NR)

Operator — Los Angeles YWCA

Courses — Auto body and fender repair, barbering, black and white TV repair, broadcasting, business and clerical skills, child development, computer operator, computer repair, corrections, cosmetology, drafting, electronics, fashion design, floral design, food service, health occupations, industrial welding, library assistant, office machine repair, offset printing, painting/paperhanging, pipefitting, police science, railway clerk, real estate, recreational assistant, technical illustration, truck driving (light), veterinary assistant

Address — 1106 South Broadway, Los Angeles, California 90015

Telephone — (213) 748-2784

San Jose*

No. 440 — Job Corps Center

Capacity — 180 men (R); 60 women (R)

Operator — Singer/Graflex

Courses — Appliance repair, automotive trades, building maintenance, clerical skills, cooking, drafting, electronics assembly, electronics technician, health occupations, machinist apprentice, offset press printing, veterinary assistant, welding

Address — 201 South 11th Street, San Jose, California 95112

Telephone — (408) 998-1120

COLORADO

Collbran

No. 243 — Civilian Conservation Center

Capacity — 190 men (R)

Operator — Bureau of Reclamation, U.S. Department of the Interior

Courses — Brick and stone masonry, building and custodial maintenance, carpentry, cement masonry, cooking, heavy equipment, painting, welding

1st SUPPLEMENT

Directory of Internships, Work Experience Programs, and On-the-Job Training Opportunities

Address — P.O. Box 307, Collbran, Colorado 81624

Telephone — (303) 487-3576

Travel directions: Drive from Grand Junction to one-half mile west of the town of Collbran

GEORGIA

Atlanta*

No. 850 — Job Corps Center

Capacity — 250 women (R); 150 women (NR)

Operator — Thiokol Chemical Corp.

Courses — Clerical skills, cosmetology, day care, food services, health occupations (licensed practical nurse, medical office assistant, nurse assistant), offset printing, photography

Address — 239 West Lake Drive, NE, Atlanta, Georgia 30314

Telephone — (404) 794-9512

HAWAII

Hawaii*

No. 806 — Job Corps Center

Capacity — 200 men (R); 50 women (R)

Operator — State of Hawaii, Department of Labor and Industrial Relations

Courses — Air conditioning, auto body repair, auto mechanics, auto parts (clerk), building maintenance, business occupations, carpentry, cement masonry, cooking, office machine repair, painting, plumbing, warehousing (stock clerk), welding

Address — P.O. Box 7638, Honolulu, Hawaii 96821

Telephone — (808) 395-2361

IDAHO

Marsing

No. 251 — Civilian Conservation Center

Capacity — 168 men (R)

Operator — Bureau of Reclamation, U.S. Department of the Interior

Courses — Automotive trades, bricklaying/stone masonry, building maintenance, carpentry, cement masonry, cooking, painting, welding

Address — Route 1, Marsing, Idaho 83639

Telephone — (208) 896-4127

Travel directions: Drive 20 miles west of Boise on U.S. Highway No. 30 to Nampa; then follow State Highway No. 72 to Marsing

ILLINOIS

Golconda

No. 109 — Civilian Conservation Center

Capacity — 224 men (R)

Operator — Forest Service, U.S. Department of Agriculture

Courses — Automotive trades, brick and stone masonry, building maintenance, carpentry, cooking, emergency medical technician, heavy equipment, painting, welding

Address — Route 4, Golconda, Illinois 62938

1st SUPPLEMENT

Directory of Internships, Work Experience Programs, and On-the-Job Training Opportunities

Telephone — (618) 285-6601

Travel directions: Drive 30 miles south of Harrisburg, and 10 miles east of Golconda, on the north bank of the Ohio River, in the Shawnee National Forest

INDIANA

Atterbury*

No. 905 — Job Corps Center

Capacity — 900 men (R); 350 women (R)

Operator — AVCO Corp.

Courses — Auto body repair, auto mechanics, auto service, baking, building maintenance, clerical, cooking, health occupations (medical records clerk, nursing assistant, ward clerk), welding

Address — Box 217, Edinburg, Indiana 46124

Telephone — (812) 526-5581

Travel directions: Drive 30 miles south of Indianapolis on U.S. Highway No. 31

KENTUCKY

Breckinridge*

No. 906 — Job Corps Center

Capacity — 1,850 men (R); 450 women (R)

Operator — Singer/Graflex

Courses — Automotive trades, bricklaying, building and grounds maintenance, business and clerical skills, carpentry, cooking, drafting, electrical trades, engine and power training, health occupations (nursing assistant), heavy equipment operation/repairing, household appliance repair, offset operator, painting, plumbing, sheet metal worker, welding

Address — Morganfield, Kentucky 42437

Telephone — (502) 389-2419

Travel directions: Drive 38 miles southwest of Evansville, Indiana, on U.S. Highway No. 41 to Henderson, then follow U.S. Highway No. 60

Great Onyx

No. 258 — Civilian Conservation Center

Capacity — 214 men (R)

Operator — National Park Service, U.S. Department of the Interior

Courses — Automotive trades, bricklaying/stone masonry, building maintenance, carpentry, cement masonry, cooking, painting, plastering

Address — Mammoth Cave, Kentucky 42259

Telephone — (502) 758-2214

Travel directions: Drive 40 miles northeast of Bowling Green on State Highway No. 70, in Mammoth Cave National Park, to 4 miles from entrance to the Cave

Pine Knot

No. 031 — Civilian Conservation Center

Capacity — 224 men (R)

Operator — Forest Service, U.S. Department of Agriculture

Courses — Automotive trades, bricklaying/stone masonry, building maintenance, carpentry, cement masonry, construction labor, cooking, painting, welding

Address — Pine Knot, Kentucky 42635

Telephone — (606) 354-2176

1st SUPPLEMENT
Directory of Internships, Work Experience Programs, and On-the-Job Training Opportunities

Travel directions: Drive 90 miles north of Knoxville, Tennessee, or 124 miles south of Lexington on U.S. Highway No. 27

Whitney M. Young, Jr.

No. 835 — Job Corps Center

Capacity — 193 men (R)

Operator — Res-Care, Inc.

Courses — Air conditioning and refrigeration, automotive trades, bricklaying/stone masonry, building maintenance, carpentry, cooking, welding

Address — P.O. Box 366, Simpsonville, Kentucky 40067

Telephone — (502) 722-8862

Travel directions: Drive 13 miles east of Louisville on Interstate Route 64 to Veechdale Road exit, left to U.S. Route 60, left to Center

MARYLAND

Maryland

No. 830 — Job Corps Center

Capacity — 250 men (R)

Operator — RCA Service Co. (Division of RCA)

Courses — Automotive trades, bricklaying, building maintenance, carpentry, cement masonry, cooking, electrical skills, painting, plastering, plumbing, welding

Address — Woodstock, Maryland 21163

Telephone — (301) 461-1100

Travel directions: From Baltimore – Drive 8 miles northwest on Liberty Road (Route 26) to Old Court Road (Route 125), turn left, 6 miles to Center

MICHIGAN

Detroit*

No. 430 — Job Corps Center

Capacity — 150 men (R); 125 women (NR)

Operator — Singer/Graflex

Courses — Automotive mechanics, building maintenance, clerical skills, health occupations (medical transcription, nursing aid, ward clerk), welding

Address — 10401 East Jefferson Avenue, Detroit, Michigan 48214

Telephone — (313) 821-7000

MISSOURI

Excelsior Springs*

No. 706 — Job Corps Center

Capacity — 285 women (R); 120 men (R)

Operator — Singer/Graflex

Courses — Building maintenance, business and clerical skills, food service, health occupations, railway clerical skills, welding

Address — Box 338, Excelsior Springs, Missouri 64024

Telephone — (816) 637-5501

Travel directions: Drive 30 miles northeast of Kansas City, Missouri, on U.S. Highway No. 69

Mingo

No. 270 — Civilian Conservation Center

Capacity — 168 men (R)

Operator — Fish and Wildlife Service, U.S. Department of the Interior

1st SUPPLEMENT

Directory of Internships, Work Experience Programs, and On-the-Job Training Opportunities

Courses — Bricklaying/stone masonry, building maintenance, carpentry, cooking, heavy equipment, painting, welding

Address — Box F, Puxico, Missouri 63960

Telephone — (314) 222-3537

Travel directions: Drive 13 miles east of Poplar Bluff on U.S. Highway No. 60, 10 miles north on State Route 51, and then 2 miles west on County Route T, in Mingo National Wildlife Refuge

MONTANA

Anaconda

No. 172 — Civilian Conservation Center

Capacity — 216 men (R)

Operator — Forest Service, U.S. Department of Agriculture

Courses — Automotive trades, building maintenance, carpentry, cooking, heavy equipment, painting, truckdriving, warehousing, welding

Address — Anaconda, Montana 59711

Telephone — (406) 563-3476

Travel directions: Drive 8 miles west of Anaconda on State Highway No. 10A and 2 miles north on forest access road, in Deer Lodge National Forest

Kicking Horse*

No. 274 — Job Corps Center

Capacity — 150 men (R); 50 women (R)

Operator — Tribal Council of the Confederated Salish and Kootenai Tribes of the Flathead Indian Reservation

Courses — Automotive trades, business and clerical skills, carpentry, counselor aide, food service, forestry, heavy equipment operation/repairing, truckdriving, warehousing

Address — Ronan, Montana 59864

Telephone — (406) 644-2217

Travel directions: Drive 57 miles north of Missoula on State Highway No. 93

Trapper Creek

No. 046 — Civilian Conservation Center

Capacity — 216 men (R)

Operator — Forest Service, U.S. Department of Agriculture

Courses — Automotive trades, building maintenance, carpentry, cooking, painting, welding

Address — Darby, Montana 59827

Telephone — (406) 821-3286

Travel directions: Drive 12 miles southwest of Darby on U.S. Highway No. 93, in the Bitterroot National Forest

NEBRASKA

Pine Ridge

No. 051 — Civilian Conservation Center

Capacity — 168 men (R)

Operator — Forest Service, U.S. Department of Agriculture

Courses — Automotive trades, building maintenance, carpentry, cement masonry, cooking/culinary arts, painting, plastering, warehousing, welding

Address — Star Route 1, Box 39-F, Chadron, Nebraska 69337

Telephone — (308) 432-3316

Travel directions: Drive 11 miles south of Chadron on U.S. Highway No. 385, in the Nebraska National Forest

NEW JERSEY

New Jersey

No. 800 — Job Corps Center

Capacity — 300 men (R)

Operator — New Jersey State Department of Education

Courses — Automotive trades, cooking, heating and ventilating, industrial maintenance, painting, warehousing, welding

Address — Plainfield Avenue, Edison, New Jersey 08817

Telephone — (201) 985-1939

Travel directions: Drive south of Newark – or north of New Brunswick – on U.S. Highway No. 1

NEW MEXICO

Albuquerque*

No. 709 — Job Corps Center

Capacity — 311 women (R); 84 men (R) (NR)

Operator — Teledyne Economic Development Co.

Courses — Clerical skills, cosmetology, electronics assembly, health occupations (dental assistant, nursing aide), key punching, retail sales (clerical), stenography, teaching (teacher aide)

Address — 1500 Indian School Road, NW, P.O. Box 1246, Albuquerque, New Mexico 87107

Telephone — (505) 842-6500

NEW YORK

Glenmont*

No. 820 — Job Corps Center

Capacity — 175 men (R); 100 women (R)

Operator — Singer/Graflex

Courses — Air conditioning, automotive trades, building maintenance, clerical skills, cooking, electronic/electrical trades, health occupations

Address — P.O. Box 188, Glenmont, New York 12077

Telephone — (518) 767-9391

Travel directions: Drive 4 miles south of Albany on Route 144

NORTH CAROLINA

Lyndon B. Johnson

No. 058 — Civilian Conservation Center

Capacity — 168 men (R)

Operator — Forest Service, U.S. Department of Agriculture

Courses — Automotive trades, bricklaying/stone masonry, building maintenance, carpentry, concrete finishing, cooking, painting, welding

Address — Route 1, Box 477, Franklin, North Carolina 28734

Telephone — (704) 524-4446

1st SUPPLEMENT

Directory of Internships, Work Experience Programs, and On-the-Job Training Opportunities

Travel directions: Drive 8 miles west of Franklin on State Highway No. 64, or 78 miles from Asheville on State Highway No. 23

Oconaluftee

No. 300 — Civilian Conservation Center

Capacity — 180 men (R)

Operator — National Park Service, U.S. Department of the Interior

Courses — Automotive trades, bricklaying, building maintenance, carpentry, cement masonry, cooking, painting, plastering, welding

Address — P.O. Box 306, Cherokee, North Carolina 28719

Telephone — (704) 497-5411

Travel directions: Drive 2 miles northwest of Cherokee on State Highway No. 441, in the Great Smoky Mountains National Park

Schenck

No. 059 — Civilian Conservation Center

Capacity — 204 men (R)

Operator — Forest Service, U.S. Department of Agriculture

Courses — Automotive trades, brick and stone masonry, building maintenance, carpentry, cooking, painting, warehousing, welding

Address — P.O. Box 98, Pisgah Forest, North Carolina 28768

Telephone — (704) 877-3291

Travel directions: Drive 4 miles north of Brevard on State Highway No. 276, or 32 miles south of Asheville

OHIO

Cincinnati*

No. 815 — Job Corps Center

Capacity — 150 men (R); 50 women (NR)

Operator — AVCO Corp.

Courses — Automotive trades, business skills, custodial maintenance, dry wall application, food service, heating and cooling, welding

Address — 1409 Western Avenue, Cincinnati, Ohio 45214

Telephone — (513) 651-2000

Cleveland*

No. 701 — Job Corps Center

Capacity — 340 women (R) (NR); 100 men (NR)

Operator — Alpha Kappa Alpha Sorority, Inc.

Courses — Business and clerical skills, health occupations, keypunch, library assistant, teacher aide, veterinary assistant, welding

Address — 10660 Carnegie Avenue, Cleveland, Ohio 44106

Telephone — (216) 795-8700

OKLAHOMA

Guthrie*

No. 715 — Job Corps Center

Capacity — 480 women (R); 120 men (R)

Operator — Teledyne Economic Development Co.

Courses — Automotive trades, building maintenance, business and clerical skills, cosmetology, dietetics, drafting, electronics assembly, health occupations, lithography, welding

Address — P.O. Box 978, Guthrie, Oklahoma 73552

Telephone — (405) 282-9930

Treasure Lake

No. 305 — Civilian Conservation Center

Capacity — 168 men (R)

Operator — Fish and Wildlife Service, U.S. Department of the Interior

Courses — Automotive trades, bricklaying/stone masonry, carpentry, cement masonry, cooking, painting, plastering, welding

Address — Indiahoma, Oklahoma 73552

Telephone — (405) 246-3203

Travel directions: Drive 12 miles north of Indiahoma on State Highway No. 48, in the Wichita Mountains Wildlife Refuge, or 30 miles west of Lawton on Highway No. 64

Tulsa

No. 855 — Job Corps Center

Capacity — 104 women (R); 40 women (NR)

Operator — RCA Service Co. (Division of RCA)

Courses — Automotive trades, business and clerical skills, cosmetology, food service, health occupations, horticulture, machine shop, video operator, welding

Address — 116 West Fifth Street, Tulsa, Oklahoma 74103

Telephone — (918) 585-9111

OREGON

Angell*

No. 144 — Civilian Conservation Center

Capacity — 152 men (R); 32 women (R)

Operator — Forest Service, U.S. Department of Agriculture

Courses — Automotive trades, carpentry, construction worker, cooking, forestry, maintenance painting, welding

Address — Star Route North, Box 900, Yachats, Oregon 97394

Telephone — (503) 547-3137

Travel directions: Drive 5 miles south of Waldport on U.S. Highway No. 101

Portland*

No. 410 — Job Corps Center

Capacity — 153 women (R) (NR); 122 men (R) (NR)

Operator — Portland Public Schools, School District No. 1, Multnomah County

Courses — Agribusiness, auto body repair, business occupations, cosmetology, food service, health occupations (nursing assistant), small engine repair, welding

Address — 1022 S.W. Salmon Street, Portland, Oregon 97205

Telephone — (503) 224-0190

Timber Lake

No. 064 — Civilian Conservation Center

Capacity — 224 men (R)

Operator — Forest Service, U.S. Department of Agriculture

Courses — Automotive trades, building maintenance, carpentry, cement masonry, cooking, painting, plastering, warehousing

1st SUPPLEMENT

Directory of Internships, Work Experience Programs, and On-the-Job Training Opportunities

Address — Star Route, Box 109, Estacada, Oregon 97023

Telephone — (503) 834-2291

Travel directions: Drive 60 miles southeast of Portland on State Highway No. 224, or 25 miles southeast of Estacada

Tongue Point*

No. 717 — Job Corps Center

Capacity — 335 women (R); 83 men (R)

Operator — RCA Service Co. (Division of RCA)

Courses — Business and clerical skills, cosmetology, food service, health occupations (dental assistant, nursing assistant), maintenance technology, railway clerk, telephone communications, welding

Address — Astoria, Oregon 97103

Telephone — (503) 325-2131

Travel directions: Drive 3 miles east of Astoria on U.S. Highway No. 30

Wolf Creek

No. 145 — Civilian Conservation Center

Capacity — 224 men (R)

Operator — Forest Service, U.S. Department of Agriculture

Courses — Automotive trades, building maintenance, carpentry, cement masonry, construction worker, cooking, forestry, painting, plastering, warehousing, welding

Address — Little River Route, Glide, Oregon 97443

Telephone — (503) 496-3507

Travel directions: Drive 28 miles east of Roseburg on State Route 138, in the Umpqua National Forest

PENNSYLVANIA

Keystone*

No. 716 — Job Corps Center

Capacity — 450 women (R); 50 men (R)

Operator — RCA Service Co. (Division of RCA)

Courses — Automotive mechanics, bricklaying, business and clerical skills, cement masonry, day care, dietetics, food service, forklift operation, health occupations, key punching, painting, plastering, telephone operator, welding

Address — P.O. Box 37, Drums, Pennsylvania 18222

Telephone — (717) 788-1164

Travel directions: Drive south of Wilkes-Barre on U.S. Highway No. 81

Pittsburgh

No. 825 — Job Corps Center

Capacity — 200 men (R)

Operator — Teledyne Economic Development Co./AFL-CIO Appalachian Council

Courses — Automotive trades, sheet metal work, small engine repairing, telephone lineperson, welding

Address — 3113 Forbes Avenue, Pittsburgh, Pennsylvania 15213

Telephone — (412) 683-8350

PUERTO RICO

Arecibo

No. 605 — Job Corps Center

Capacity — 175 men (R)

Operator — The Commonwealth Department of Education

Courses — Auto body repairing, auto mechanics, carpentry, electrical skills, upholstering

Address — Arecibo, Puerto Rico 00612

Telephone — (809) 767-2274

Travel directions: Take rental car or bus from San Juan to Center

Rio Grande

No. 608 — Job Corps Center

Capacity — 135 men (R)

Operator — The Commonwealth Department of Education

Courses — Auto body repairing, auto mechanics, carpentry, cement masonry, electrical skills, plumbing

Address — Rio Grande, Puerto Rico 00745

Telephone — (809) 767-2274

Travel directions: Take rental car or bus from San Juan to Center

SOUTH DAKOTA

Boxelder

No. 088 — Civilian Conservation Center

Capacity — 208 men (R)

Operator — Forest Service, U.S. Department of Agriculture

Courses — Automotive trades, building maintenance, carpentry, cement masonry, cooking, painting, welding

Address — P.O. Box 47, Nemo, South Dakota 57759

Telephone — (605) 578-2371

Travel directions: Drive 25 miles from Rapid City to Nemo, then 3 miles west on unnumbered county road

TENNESSEE

Jacobs Creek

No. 070 — Civilian Conservation Center

Capacity — 200 men (R)

Operator — Forest Service, U.S. Department of Agriculture

Courses — Automotive trades, brick and stone masonry, building maintenance, carpentry, cooking, heavy equipment, painting, welding

Address — Drawer W, Bristol, Tennessee 37620

Telephone — (615) 968-3117

Travel directions: Drive 18 miles east of Bristol, Virginia, on State Highway No. 421, on the Tennessee side of Cherokee National Forest

TEXAS

El Paso*

No. 810 — Job Corps Center

Capacity — 210 men (R) (NR); 40 women (NR)

Operator — Texas Educational Foundation, Inc.

Courses — Automotive trades, building maintenance, food service, health occupations (nursing assistant), small engine repairing, welding

Address — P.O. Box 119, El Paso, Texas 79941

Telephone — (915) 542-1663

Gary*

No. 903 — Job Corps Center

Capacity — 1,624 men (R); 576 women (R)

Operator — Texas Educational Foundation, Inc.

Courses — Air conditioning, automotive trades, bricklaying/stone masonry, building trades, business and clerical skills, carpentry, diesel mechanics, electrical/electronics, food services, forklift operator, gas engine repair, health occupations (nursing assistant), heavy equipment, machine tool, offset duplicating machine operator, painting, petrochemical handling, plastering, sheet metal work, upholstering, warehousing, welding

Address — San Marcos, Texas 78666

Telephone — (512) 396-6652

Travel directions: Drive 4 miles southeast of San Marcos on U.S. Highway No. 35

McKinney

No. 710 — Job Corps Center

Capacity — 620 women (R)

Operator — Texas Educational Foundation, Inc.

Courses — Business and clerical skills, food service, health occupations (nursing assistant, ward clerk), retail sales warehousing, welding

Address — Box 750, McKinney, Texas 75069

Telephone — (214) 542-2623

Travel directions: Drive north from Dallas on U.S. Highway No. 75

UTAH

Clearfield

No. 910 — Job Corps Center

Capacity — 1,100 men (R)

Operator — Thiokol Chemical Corp.

Courses — Automotive trades, building maintenance, food service, machine shop, printing, teacher aide, social service aide, welding

Address — Freeport Center Station, Clearfield, Utah 84106

Telephone — (801) 773-1433

Travel directions: Drive 12 miles from Ogden to Clearfield

Weber Basin

No. 323 — Civilian Conservation Center

Capacity — 224 men (R)

Operator — Bureau of Reclamation, U.S. Department of the Interior

Courses — Bricklaying/stone masonry, building and custodial maintenance, carpentry, cement masonry, construction, cooking, heavy equipment, painting, welding

Address — P.O. Box 389, Ogden, Utah 84401

Telephone — (801) 399-9806

Travel directions: Drive south on U.S. Highway 89, 7 miles from Ogden

VIRGINIA

Blue Ridge

No. 552 — Job Corps Center

1st SUPPLEMENT

Directory of Internships, Work Experience Programs, and On-the-Job Training Opportunities

Capacity — 180 women (R)

Operator — RCA Service Co. (Division of RCA)

Courses — Clerical skills, community college program, dietetics, health occupations, retail sales

Address — 245 West Main Street, Marion, Virginia 24354

Telephone — (703) 783-7221

Travel directions: Drive south from Roanoke to Marion on Interstate 81

Flatwoods

No. 161 — Civilian Conservation Center

Capacity — 168 men (R)

Operator — Forest Service, U.S. Department of Agriculture

Courses — Automotive trades, bricklaying/stone masonry, carpentry, cement masonry, construction worker, cooking, painting, plastering, welding

Address — P.O. Box 82, Coeburn, Virginia 24230

Telephone — (703) 395-3384

Travel directions: Drive from Bristol to Coeburn

WASHINGTON

Columbia Basin

No. 343 — Civilian Conservation Center

Capacity — 200 men (R)

Operator — Bureau of Reclamation, U.S. Department of the Interior

Courses — Automotive trades, bricklaying/stone masonry, building maintenance, carpentry, cement masonry, cooking, floor covering, painting, plastering, warehousing, welding

Address — Building 2402 — 24th Street, Moses Lake, Washington 98837

Telephone — (509) 762-5581

Travel directions: Drive 15 miles southeast to Ephrata on U.S. Highway No. 17

Curlew

No. 078 — Civilian Conservation Center

Capacity — 180 men (R)

Operator — Forest Service, U.S. Department of Agriculture

Courses — Automotive trades, building maintenance, carpentry, construction worker, cooking, forestry, painting, warehousing, welding

Address — Star Route, Curlew, Washington 99118

Telephone — (509) 779-2611

Travel directions: Drive northwest from Spokane on U.S. Highway No. 395 and State Routes 30 and 21, or drive west 12 miles from Curlew

Fort Simcoe

No. 340 — Civilian Conservation Center

Capacity — 200 men (R)

Operator — Bureau of Indian Affairs, U.S. Department of the Interior

Courses — Automotive trades, bricklaying/stone masonry, building maintenance, carpentry, cement masonry, cooking, heavy equipment, painting, plastering, warehousing, welding

Address — P.O. Box 137, White Swan, Washington 98952

Telephone — (509) 874-2244

Travel directions: Drive 20 miles west of Toppenish on State Highway No. 220, on the Yakima Indian Reservation

WEST VIRGINIA

Charleston*

No. 703 — Job Corps Center

Capacity — 320 women (R); 15 women (NR); 15 men (NR)

Operator — Thiokol Chemical Corp.

Courses — Barbering, business and clerical skills, commercial art, composer operation, cosmetology, food service, health occupations (licensed practical nurse, medical assistant, nursing assistant), offset press printing, public service (police officer), railway clerical skills

Address — Virginia and Summers Streets, Charleston, West Virginia 25301

Telephone — (304) 344-4041

Harpers Ferry

No. 350 — Civilian Conservation Center

Capacity — 200 men (R)

Operator — National Park Service, U.S. Department of the Interior

Courses — Automotive trades, bricklaying/ stone masonry, building maintenance, carpentry, cement masonry, cooking, graphic arts, painting, plastering, welding

Address — Harpers Ferry, West Virginia 25425

Telephone — (304) 725-2011

Travel directions: Drive west from Baltimore, Maryland, on U.S. Highways No. 70-N and No. 340

WISCONSIN

Blackwell

No. 082 — Civilian Conservation Center

Capacity — 200 men (R)

Operator — Forest Service, U.S. Department of Agriculture

Courses — Automotive trades, bricklaying/ stone masonry, maintenance, carpentry, cooking, heavy equipment, painting, welding

Address — Route 1, Laona, Wisconsin 54541

Telephone — (715) 674-2311

Travel directions: Drive 5 miles southeast of Laona or 45 miles east of Rhinelander

1st SUPPLEMENT — *Directory of Internships, Work Experience Programs, and On-the-Job Training Opportunities*

APPENDIX B

Civil Service Commission Area Offices

The following is a list of Civil Service Commission Offices where individuals can obtain information about possible job opportunities with the Federal Government. In addition, these offices can supply the names of places within each state where Federal Summer Employment Examinations are held.

ALABAMA
HUNTSVILLE AREA OFFICE
Southerland Bldg.
806 Governors Dr., SW, 35801

ALASKA
ANCHORAGE AREA OFFICE
617 G St., 99501

ARIZONA
PHOENIX AREA OFFICE
522 N. Central Ave., 85004

All of Arizona, except the Navajo-Hopi Indian Reservations

ARKANSAS
LITTLE ROCK AREA OFFICE
700 West Capitol Ave., 72201

All of Arkansas (except Crittenden and Miller Counties)

CALIFORNIA
LOS ANGELES AREA OFFICE
851 South Broadway, 90014

Kern; Los Angeles; Orange; San Luis Obispo; Santa Barbara; Ventura; Riverside; and San Bernardino Counties

SAN DIEGO AREA OFFICE
Federal Bldg.
880 Front St., 92188

San Diego and Imperial Counties

SAN FRANCISCO AREA OFFICE
450 Golden Gate Ave., 94102

Alameda, Contra Costa, Marin, Monterey, Napa, San Benito, San Francisco, San Mateo, Santa Clara, Santa Cruz, Solano, and Sonoma Counties

SACRAMENTO AREA OFFICE
650 Capitol Mall, 95814

All other California Counties, except Lassen County

COLORADO
DENVER AREA OFFICE
1845 Sherman St., 80203

All of Colorado
States of Montana, North Dakota, South Dakota, Utah and Wyoming
Clay County, Minnesota

CONNECTICUT
HARTFORD AREA OFFICE
Federal Bldg.
450 Main St., 06103

All of Connecticut
Berkshire, Franklin, Hampden, and Hampshire Counties in Western Massachusetts

1st SUPPLEMENT

Directory of Internships, Work Experience Programs, and On-the-Job Training Opportunities

DELAWARE
WILMINGTON AREA OFFICE
Federal Office Bldg.
844 King St., 19801

DISTRICT OF COLUMBIA
WASHINGTON, D.C. AREA OFFICE
U.S. Civil Service Commission
1900 E. St. NW, 20415

District of Columbia; Charles, Montgomery, and Prince Georges Counties, Maryland; Arlington, Fairfax, Loudoun, Prince William, King George and Stafford Counties, and cities of Alexandria, Fairfax and Falls Church, Virginia

FLORIDA
ORLANDO AREA OFFICE
Federal Bldg. &
U.S. Courthouse
80 N. Hughey Ave., 32801

GEORGIA
ATLANTA AREA OFFICE
Federal Office Bldg.
275 Peachtree St. NE., 30303

HAWAII
HONOLULU AREA OFFICE
1000 Bishop St., 96813

IDAHO
BOISE AREA OFFICE
Federal Bldg.
550 W. Fort St., 83702

ILLINOIS
CHICAGO AREA OFFICE
219 South Dearborn St., 60604

All of Illinois (except Madison and St. Clair Counties)

INDIANA
INDIANAPOLIS AREA OFFICE
46 E. Ohio St., 46204

All of Indiana (except Clark, Dearborn, and Floyd Counties)
Henderson County, Kentucky

IOWA
ST. LOUIS AREA OFFICE
1520 Market St.
St. Louis, Missouri 63103

All of Iowa (except Scott and Pottawattamie Counties)

KANSAS
WICHITA AREA OFFICE
120 S. Market St., 67202

All of Kansas (except Johnson, Leavenworth, and Wyandotte Counties)

KENTUCKY
LOUISVILLE AREA OFFICE
600 Federal Place, 40202

All of Kentucky (except Boone, Boyd, Campbell, Henderson, and Kenton Counties)
Clark and Floyd Counties, Indiana

LOUISIANA
NEW ORLEANS AREA OFFICE
Federal Bldg.
610 South St., 70130

1st SUPPLEMENT

Directory of Internships, Work Experience Programs, and On-the-Job Training Opportunities

MAINE

AUGUSTA AREA OFFICE
Federal Bldg., 04330

MARYLAND

BALTIMORE AREA OFFICE
Garmatz Federal Bldg.
101 W. Lombard St., 21201

All of Maryland (except Montgomery, Prince Georges and Charles Counties)

(See District of Columbia)

MASSACHUSETTS

BOSTON AREA OFFICE
3 Center Plaza, 02108

Boston area (County of Essex; Norfolk; Middlesex; Plymouth; Suffolk and Worcester)

MICHIGAN

DETROIT AREA OFFICE
477 Michigan Ave., 48226

MINNESOTA

TWIN CITIES AREA OFFICE
Federal Bldg., Rm. 196
Fort Snelling
Twin Cities, 55111

All of Minnesota (except Clay County)
Douglas County, Wisonsin

MISSISSIPPI

JACKSON AREA OFFICE
802 North State St., 39201

MISSOURI

KANSAS CITY AREA OFFICE
601 East 12th St., 64106

Western Missouri
Johnson, Leavenworth, and Wyandotte Counties, Kansas

ST. LOUIS AREA OFFICE
1520 Market St., 63103

Eastern Missouri
Madison and St. Clair Counties, Illinois

MONTANA

DENVER AREA OFFICE
1845 Sherman St.
Denver, Colorado 80203

NEBRASKA

ST. LOUIS AREA OFFICE
1520 Market St.
St. Louis, Missouri 63103

All of Nebraska
Pottawattamie County, Iowa

NEVADA

RENO AREA OFFICE
50 S. Virginia St., 89505

All of Nevada
Lassen County, California

NEW HAMPSHIRE

PORTSMOUTH AREA OFFICE
Federal Bldg., 03801

All of New Hampshire (except Hanover and Lebanon, New Hampshire areas)

1st SUPPLEMENT
Directory of Internships, Work Experience Programs, and On-the-Job Training Opportunities

NEW JERSEY
NEWARK AREA OFFICE
970 Broad St., 07102

All of New Jersey (except Camden County)

NEW MEXICO
ALBUQUERQUE AREA OFFICE
421 Gold Ave. S.W., 87102

All of New Mexico (except Dona Ana and Otero Counties)

NEW YORK
NEW YORK CITY AREA OFFICE
26 Federal Plaza, 10007

New York City, Long Island and Rockland; Westchester; Orange; Duchess; and Putnan Counties

SYRACUSE AREA OFFICE
100 S. Clinton St., Rm. 843, 13202

Northern New York State

NORTH CAROLINA
RALEIGH AREA OFFICE
310 New Bern Ave., 27601

NORTH DAKOTA
DENVER AREA OFFICE
1845 Sherman St.
Denver, Colorado 80203

State of North Dakota
Clay County, Minnesota

OHIO
DAYTON AREA OFFICE
200 W. 2nd St., Rm. 507, 45402

OKLAHOMA
OKLAHOMA CITY AREA OFFICE
210 NW 6th St., 73102

OREGON
PORTLAND AREA OFFICE
1220 SW 3rd., 97205

State of Oregon
Clark County, Washington

PENNSYLVANIA
PITTSBURGH AREA OFFICE
Federal Bldg.,
1000 Liberty Ave., 15222

Central and Western Pennsylvania

PHILADELPHIA AREA OFFICE
W.J. Green Jr. Fed. Bldg.
600 Arch St., 19106

Eastern Pennsylvania
Camden City, New Jersey

PUERTO RICO
PUERTO RICO AREA OFFICE
Carlos E. Chardon St., Rm. 12
Hato Rey, Puerto Rico 00918

All of Puerto Rico and Virgin Islands

RHODE ISLAND
PROVIDENCE AREA OFFICE
Federal-P.O. Bldg.
Kennedy Plaza, 02903

All of Rhode Island
Barnstable, Bristol, Duke, and Nantucket Counties, Massachusetts

SOUTH CAROLINA
CHARLESTON AREA OFFICE
Federal Office Bldg.
334 Meeting St., 29403

1st SUPPLEMENT

Directory of Internships, Work Experience Programs, and On-the-Job Training Opportunities

SOUTH DAKOTA

DENVER AREA OFFICE
1845 Sherman St.
Denver, Colorado 80203

TENNESSEE

MEMPHIS AREA OFFICE
100 N. Main St., Suite 1312, 38103

All of Tennessee
Crittenden County, Arkansas
Walker County, Georgia

TEXAS

DALLAS AREA OFFICE
1100 Commerce St., 75242

Northern Texas
Miller County, Arkansas

EL PASO AREA OFFICE
411 North Stanton, 79901

El Paso County, Texas
Dona Ana and Otero Counties, New Mexico

HOUSTON AREA OFFICE
702 Caroline St., 77002

Southeastern Texas

SAN ANTONIO AREA OFFICE
643 E. Durango St., 78205

Southwestern Texas

UTAH

DENVER AREA OFFICE
1845 Sherman St.
Denver, Colorado 80203

VERMONT

BURLINGTON AREA OFFICE
Federal Bldg., 05401

All of Vermont
Hanover and Lebanon, New Hampshire areas

VIRGINIA

NORFOLK AREA OFFICE
415 St. Paul Blvd., 23510

All of Virginia (except Arlington, Fairfax, Loudoun, Stafford, Prince William, and King George Counties)
(See District of Columbia)

WASHINGTON

SEATTLE AREA OFFICE
Federal Bldg.
915 Second Ave., 98174

All of Washington (except Clark County)

WEST VIRGINIA

CHARLESTON AREA OFFICE
Federal Bldg.
500 Quarrier St., 25301

All of West Virginia
Belmont, Jefferson, and Lawrence Counties, Ohio
Boyd County, Kentucky

WISCONSIN

MILWAUKEE AREA OFFICE
161 West Wisconsin Ave., 53203

All of Wisconsin (except Douglas County)

WYOMING

DENVER AREA OFFICE
1845 Sherman St.,
Denver, Colorado 80203

INDEXES

Program Title Index

References in Program Title Index refer to entry numbers

1st SUPPLEMENT

Directory of Internships, Work Experience Programs, and On-the-Job Training Opportunities

a

AAR/NEA Mid-Career Fellowships, 7

AAR/NEH Fellowships, 8

ABC/Washington Task Force on African Affairs Volunteer and Internship Program, 2

ACE Cooperative Personnel Exchange, 17

ADA Youth Caucus January Internship Program, 30

AIA/RC Intern Program, 21

APA-AAAS Congressional Science Fellow Program, 27

Academic/Merit Internships, 337

Administrative Internship Program, 413

Aleutian-Bering Sea Expedition Internships, 20

Announcer Trainee, 216

Apprenticeship in Archives and Manuscript Collections, 76

Apprenticeship in Editing of Historical Books and Magazines, 77

Apprenticeship in Interpretation and Administration of Historical Sites, 75

Architectural Intern Program, 33

Archives Program, 44

Artist Management Services Training, 417

Arts and Crafts Training Program, 307

Assembly Faculty Fellow, 244

b

BIPAC Intern Program, 50

BRADD Internship Program, 41

Bear Valley Winter Experience, 105

Bi-Partisan Intern Program, 334

Bonior Internship Program, 331

Broadcast News and Programming-Production Internships, 391

Broadcast News Internships
    WAVE Radio, 376
    WMAZ Radio and Television, 389

Business Management Fellowship Program, 351

Business Management Internships, 115

c

C.D.C. Student Practicum Internship, 269

CETA Training
    Albuquerque, New Mexico, 4
    Architects' Community Team, 33

1st SUPPLEMENT

Directory of Internships, Work Experience Programs, and On-the-Job Training Opportunities

Arkansas. Arts and Humanities Office, 35

Cage Teen Center, 52

Girls Club of Albany, Georgia, Inc., 128

Larimer County, Colorado, 183

Tuscaloosa, Alabama. Regional Alcoholism Council, 323

CFA Internship Program, 83

Call for Help Volunteer Program, 395

City of Bowie Internship Program, 43

Civic Orchestra of Chicago, 67

Clinical Internship for Master's Level Psychologists and Social Workers, 275

Clinical Psychology Predoctoral Internships

    Community Mental Health Center of Scott County, 79

    Ventura County Mental Health Services, 370

College Intern Program, 295

College Internship Program, 130

College Internships, 208

College-Level Internship Program, 211

College Student Summer Employment: Artist Position, 141

College Student Summer Employment: Information Position, 142

College Work-Study/Graduate Assistantships/Internships, 242

College Work Study Program, 283

Community Development Internship Program, 147

Community Organization Outreach Internship, 263

Community Organizer Internship Program, 38

Congressional Internship Programs, U.S. Congress

    Rep. David E. Bonior, 331

    Rep. John Conyers, Jr., 332

    Rep. Philip M. Crane, 333

    Rep. Bob Eckhardt, 334

    Rep. Mickey Edwards, 335

    Rep. Harold Ford, 336

    Rep. Lamar Gudger, 337

    Rep. Richard Kelly, 338

    Rep. Edward I. Koch, 339

    Rep. Jim Leach, 340

    Rep. Matthew F. McHugh, 341

    Rep. Ron Marlenee, 342

    Rep. Ned Pattison, 343

    Rep. Richardson Preyer, 344

    Rep. Fortney H. Stark, Jr., 345

    Rep. Don Young, 346

    Sen. Mike Gravel, 347

    Sen. Orrin G. Hatch, 348

    Sen. George McGovern, 349

    Sen. William Proxmire, 350

Coop and Internship Program, 150

Corporate Relations Intern Program, 111

Counter-Recruiting Action Program, 402

d

D.C. Council Internship Program, 401

Docent Council of Volunteers, 407

1st SUPPLEMENT
Directory of Internships, Work Experience Programs, and On-the-Job Training Opportunities

e

Editing Internship Program, 247

Editorial Internship Program, 86

Editorial Internships, 114

Education Department Internship, 45

Education Internship Program, 18

Educational Visiting Scientist, 190

Environmental Education Internships

    Audubon Center in Greenwich, 222

    Aullwood Audubon Center, 223

    Aullwood Audubon Farm, 224

    Richardson Bay Wildlife Sanctuary, 225

    Sharon Audubon Center, 226

    Whittell Education, Center, 225

Executive Staff Internship Program, 134

f

FASST Internships

    Business Management Internships, 115

    FASST Internship Program, 116

    Journalism Internships, 117

    Marketing Internships, 118

    Research Internships, 119

Family Life Education Program Trainee, 80

Federal Summer Employment Program for Youth: Summer Aids, 327

Federal Summer Intern Program, 328

Fellowship Award for the Study of Chinese Painting, 25

Fellowships

    Dumbarton Oaks Center for Studies in the History of Landscape Architecture, 97

    East-West Center, 99

    The Edmund Niles Huyck Preserve, Inc., 106

    Lunar Science Institute, 191

    National Urban Fellows, Inc., 238

    Smithsonian Institution, 297

Field Placements/Internships, 419

Field Training Program for Occupational Therapy Students, 201

Foreign Journalist Fellowships, 415

g

Garrett County Youth Employment Training, 406

German Studies (MAT) Summer Program, 120

Governmental Affairs Office Internship Program, 220

Governor's Intern Program, 304

Governor's Internship Program, 303

1st SUPPLEMENT

Directory of Internships, Work Experience Programs, and On-the-Job Training Opportunities

Governor's Summer Internship Program, 199

Graduate and Undergraduate Placements, 64

Graduate Intern in Counseling, 264

Graduate Internships, 215

Graduate Student Intern Program, 157

Graduate Student Summer Employment Program, 364

Grants for Summer Study in Numismatics, 24

Guest Scholar Program, 412

h

HUD Work Study Program, 178

High School Internship Program, 214

High School or College Internship Program, 332

Hochschulferienkurs, 121

House Democratic Caucus Intern Program, 148

House Internship Program, 210

i

IAESTE Trainee Program, 158

Illinois Private Sector Legislative Internship Program, 144

In-School Work Experience/Adult Work Experience/On-the-Job Training, 266

Independent Interns, 46

Industrial Postdoctoral Fellowship Program, 232

Information and Referral Volunteer, 31

Information Visits, 122

Inpatient/Outpatient Services, 96

Institute in Intercultural Human Relations, 187

Institutional Development Interns, 166

Intern and Page Program, 305

International Nongovernmental Internship Program, 420

Internship/Associate-Volunteer Staff, 218

Internship in Arts Management, 29

Internship in Child Care Administration, 296

Internship in Community Mental Health, 184

Internship in Congressional Office, 345

Internship in Residential Treatment, 281

Internship in Social Work, Psychology and Occupational Therapy, 81

Internship in Vocational Evaluation, 273

Internship on Southern Africa, 15

Internships

    Alliance for Arts Education, 6

    American Association of University Women. Educational Center, 11

    American Cancer Society. Minnesota Division, 12

    American Council of the Blind, 16

    Andromeda, Inc., 32

    Arkansas Democrat, 36

1st SUPPLEMENT

Directory of Internships, Work Experience Programs, and On-the-Job Training Opportunities

Bureau of Rehabilitation of the National Capital Area, 49

California. Office of the Lieutenant Governor, 53

Call for Action, Inc., 56

Centre County Youth Service Bureau, 65

Children's Museum, Inc., 69

Coastal Telecommunications Corporation, 73

Community Health Education Council, Inc., 78

Concert Artists Guild, 82

Cooper-Hewitt Museum, 85

Creative Arts Therapy Institute, 87

DC Public Interest Research Group, 89

District of Columbia. Superior Court, 94

District of Columbia Lung Association, 95

East Tennessee Community Design Center, 98

The Experiment in International Living, 108

Fine Arts Museum of San Francisco, 112

Girls Club of Albany, Georgia, Inc., 128

Harrisburg Area Rape Crisis Center, 133

High Point Museum, 136

Hungarian Cultural Foundation, 143

Inner City Cultural Center, 151

International Program for Human Resource Development, Inc., 160

Iowa. House of Representatives, 162

Jackson County, Oregon, 163

The Junction, Youth Resource Center, 169

KCSJ/KDJQ Radio, 170

Kentucky. Department for Local Government, 179

Locust Grove Historic Home, 188

Lynn Historical Society, 196

Maryland. Legislative Study Group, 202

Massachusetts. Internship Office, 203

Missouri Volunteer Office, 212

National Association of Accountants for the Public Interest, 221

National Council for a World Peace Tax Fund, 229

National Historical Publications and Records Commission, 230

National Moratorium on Prison Construction, 231

National Urban Coalition, 237

Oaklawn Community Mental Health Center, 251

Offender Aid and Restoration of the U.S., Inc., 253

Oregon. Legislative Assembly, 257

The Population Institute. Education Division, 268

Rensselaer County Historical Society and Museum, 276

Resource Center for Nonviolence, 278

St. Cloud Daily Times, 287

San Juan, Puerto Rico. Washington Office, 291

The Solomon R. Guggenheim Museum, 302

South County Community Mental Health Center, 306

U.S. Congress. House. Office of Matthew F. McHugh, 341

U.S. Congress. House. Office of Richardson Preyer, 344

U.S. Congress. Senate. Office of Mike Gravel, 347

United Nations. International League for Human Rights, 324

United Nations Association, USA, 325

Volunteer Action Center of Toledo, 373

Volunteer Jacksonville, Inc., 374

WMCA Radio, 390

WPOP Newsradio-14, 393

Washington Center for the Study of Services, 400

Wenatchee World, 404

Womanart Gallery, 409

j

Joint Doctoral Research Intern Awards, 100

Joint Legislative Internship Program, 161

Journalism Fund, 282

Journalism Internships

    The Advertiser-Tribune, 1

    Forum for the Advancement of Students in Science and Technolgy (FASST), 117

    Star-News, 312

Juvenile Division Internship/Paraprofessional Program, 322

Juvenile Justice Diversion, 418

k

KIVA-TV Internship Program, 173

KIXY Internship Program, 174

KSO/KGGO News Internship, 316

KWKI Internship Program, 175

l

LBJ Internships

    U.S. Congress. House. Office of John Conyers, Jr., 332

    U.S. Congress. House. Office of Lamar Gudger, 337

    U.S. Congress. House. Office of Edward I. Koch, 339

    U.S. Congress. House. Office of Jim Leach, 340

1st SUPPLEMENT

Directory of Internships, Work Experience Programs, and On-the-Job Training Opportunities

LEARN and VIPS, 72

Legal Clerkships, 308

Legal Internship, 314

Legal Internships, 309

Legislative Council Internship Program, 254

Legislative Graduate Student Internship Program, 405

Legislative Internship Programs

    American Civil Liberties Union of the National Capital Area, 13

    Arizona. State Legislature, 34

    Center for Governmental Services, 60

    Tennessee. General Assembly, 318

Library Interns, 47

Louise Wallace Hackney Fellowship for the Study of Chinese Art, 26

Lyndon B. Johnson Congressional Intern Program, 339

Lyndon Baines Johnson Intern Program and Senior Citizen Volunteers, 340

m

MPA Internship, 177

Management Associate Program, 363

Margaret Mead Internship in Policy Related Science, 292

Marketing Internships, 118

Mayor's Summer Intern Program, 149

Merchandising Co-Op, 182

Mid-Career Fellowships in Architecture and Design, 9

Minority Access to Research Careers (MARC), 358

Minority Program, 209

Minority Summer Internship Program, 315

Museum (Art) Internship, 301

Museum Associate Internship, 189

Museum Education Internship Program, 68

Museum Study Program, 298

Music Internship, 379

n

National Consumer Affairs Internship Program, 228

National Neighborhood Institute, 227

National Research Service Awards (NRSA), 359

National Suggestion Box Internship Program, 233

Naturalist Training Program

    Audubon Center in Greenwich, 222

    Aullwood Audubon Center, 223

1st SUPPLEMENT
Directory of Internships, Work Experience Programs, and On-the-Job Training Opportunities

Aullwood Audubon Farm, 224
Richardson Bay Wildlife Sanctuary, 225
Sharon Audubon Center, 226
Whittell Education Center, 225

Neighborhood Community Center, 288
Neighborhood Studies Internship Program, 239
Newark Justice Program, 19
News/Advertising Internship, 91
News/Community Affairs Internship Program, 172
News Department Internships, 380
News Division Internship, 397
News Internship, 382
News Internship Program, 171
News Program, 378
Newspaper Internship, 14
Newsroom Internship Program, 107
North Central Youth Service Bureau Training Program, 249

o

OAS Student Intern Program, 258
O.B.C. Air Personality Internship, 259
O.B.C. News Internship, 260
Office Internship, 342
On-Job Training/Apprenticeship, 365

p

PIE-F Internship, 271
PMC Radio Training Program, 265
Parks and Recreation Internship Program, 310
Peace Action Community Organizing Program, 403
Postdoctoral Fellowship in Child Clinical Psychology, 319
Postdoctoral Internship in Clinical/Community Psychology, 54
Pre-Apprenticeship Training in Painting and Carpentry, 52
Predoctoral Internship in Community/Clinical Psychology, 55
Presidential Management Intern Program, 329
The President's Stay-in-School Program, 330
Press-Public Relations Program, 51
Professional Associate Awards, 101
Professional Fellowship, 371
Professional Intern Awards, 102
Program Development Internships, 146
Program Internship/Clinical Internship, 423
Project Interns, 270
Psychology Internship, 313
Psychology Internship Program, 261
Public Affairs Interns, 167

1st SUPPLEMENT
Directory of Internships, Work Experience Programs, and On-the-Job Training Opportunities

Public Service Intern Program, 240

Public Service Internship Program, 62

q

Quaker U.N. Interns Program, 272

r

Radio Internship, 206

Radio Sales Trainee, 217

Rape Awareness Program, 410

Recreational Program Trainee, 250

Reporting and Editing Internships, 311

Reporting Internship Program, 248

Research Assistantships, 22

Research Career Development Awards (RCDA), 360

Research Intern Awards, 103

Research Interns, 168

Research Internships, 119

Research Scientist, 192

Research Training Programs in Aging and Adulthood, 63

Resocialization Program, 88

Resource Development Internship Project, 62

Rome Prize Fellowships, 10

s

Scientists and Engineers in Economic Development (SEED) Program, 362

Sea Semester, 293

Senior or Graduate Interns, 48

Short-Term Resident Fellowships for Individual Research, 245

Short Term Study and Research, 123

Short-Term Visits, 299

Social Work Graduate Student Trainees, 366

Social Work Intern Program, 39

Social Work with the Handicapped, 180

Special Internships, 131

1st SUPPLEMENT

Directory of Internships, Work Experience Programs, and On-the-Job Training Opportunities

Special Projects Intern, 338

Special Student Trainee Program, 284

Specialized Recreation Program, 181

State Government Intern Program, 243

State Work/Study Program, 399

Student Field Work Program, 241

Student Intern Programs

    Institute of Society, Ethics and the Life Sciences, 156

    Rhode Island Historical Society, 279

    Utah County, Utah, 369

Student Trainee Program, 285

Student Volunteers, 262

Study and Research Appointments, 300

Study and Research Program, 124

Study Visits, 125

Summer Aids and Technicians, 355

Summer and Winter Senate Interns, 348

Summer College Intern Program, 357

Summer Employment/Internships

    Albuquerque Journal, 3

    The Augusta Chronicle, 40

    Cathedral Church of St. John the Divine, 59

    The Daily News, 90

    Federal Home Loan Bank Board, 110

    The Historical Society of Delaware, 130

    INROADS/Milwaukee, Inc., 152

    National Trust for Historic Preservation, 234

    The News Journal, 246

    Pine Bluff Commercial, 267

    Sacramento County, California, 286

    San Antonio, Texas, 289

    Seaside Post News-Sentinel, 294

    U.S. Bureau of the Census, 326

    U.S. Congress. House. Office of Don Young, 346

    U.S. Congress. Senate. Office of George McGovern, 349

    U.S. Department of Commerce, 352

    U.S. Department of State, 353

    U.S. Fish and Wildlife Service, 354

    U.S. Geological Survey, 356

    U.S. Veterans Administration, 367

    WAAB, 375

Summer Employment: Park Rangers/Technicians/Aids, 361

Summer Hiring Program, 255

Summer Intern Program in State Government, 155

Summer Journalism Internships for Minorities, 37

Summer Junior Research Fellowship in Experimental Biology, 414

Summer Language Courses at Goethe Institutes, 126

Summer Law Clerk Program, 207

Summer Minority Intern Program, 408

Summer News Department Interns, 280

Summer News Intern Program, 113

Summer Newsroom Intern Program, 92

Summer Technician Program, 321

1st SUPPLEMENT

Directory of Internships, Work Experience Programs, and On-the-Job Training Opportunities

t

TV Production Internship, 377

Tobias Landau Fellowships in Marine Biology, 135

Traditional and New Special Projects, 57

Traineeships in Agriculture, 127

Training in Community Organizing, 213

Training in Human Services, 205

Training Programs

    American Red Cross. South Eddy County Chapter, 28

    Cook County Legal Assistance Foundation, Inc., 84

    Immigration History Research Center, 145

    John Woodman Higgins Armory Museum, 165

    Lexignton Planned Parenthood Center, Inc., 186

    McKinley Area Services for the Handicapped, Inc., 197

    Macon Chronicle-Herald, 198

    Offender Aid and Restoration of North Carolina, 252

    Pico-Union Neighborhood Council, 266

    U.S. Veterans Administration, 365

    Voluntary Action Center of Toledo, 373

    WGPR, Inc., 388

    Young Radio, Inc., 421

    Youth Industries, 422

u

United Services Volunteer Program, 277

Urban Corps

    Albuquerque, New Mexico, 5

    Cincinnati, Ohio, 70

    Dayton, Ohio, 93

    Grand Rapids, Michigan, 129

Urban Management Internships, 71

v

Visiting Graduate Fellow, 193

Visiting Research Associate Awards, 104

Visiting Scientist Program, 194

Visiting Undergraduate Intern, 195

Volunteer Action Service Teams (VAST), 138

Volunteer 4-H Leader, 416

Volunteer Management Training, 290

1st SUPPLEMENT

Directory of Internships, Work Experience Programs, and On-the-Job Training Opportunities

Volunteer on Southern Africa, 15

Volunteer On-the-Job Training, 372

Volunteer Programs

    American Labor History Series, Inc., 23

    Arkansas. Arts and Humanities Office, 35

    Center for Inquiry and Discovery, 61

    District of Columbia. Superior Court, 94

    Farnham Youth Development Center, 109

    Girls Club of Albany, Georgia, Inc., 128

    Hope Community Center, 185

    Institute of Contemporary Art, 154

    International Institute of Buffalo, 159

    Leadership Training Institute, 185

    Manchester Historic Association, 200

    National Historical Publications and Records Commission, 230

    Radio Free Georgia Broadcasting Foundation, Inc., 274

    Support Center, 317

    Tuscaloosa, Alabama. Regional Alcoholism Council, 323

    U.S. Congress. House. Office of Mickey Edwards, 335

W

WEAL FUND Intern Program, 411

WEEK-TV News Internship, 383

WEHT-TV Training Program, 384

WFIF Internship Program, 385

WGBY Production Internship, 386

WGLF Internship Program, 387

WSKG Internship, 396

West Indies Workcamp Program, 256

Williamsburg Seminar on Historical Administration, 235

Woodlawn Conference on Historic Site Administration, 236

Work Experience Programs

    Big Brothers of the National Capital Area, 42

    Capitol Broadcasting Company, 58

    Cerrell Associates, Inc., 66

    The College of Insurance, 74

    Dayton, Ohio, 93

    East Tennessee Community Design Center, 98

    Immigration History Research Center, 145

    Jackson County, Oregon, 164

    Kansas. Department of Health and Environment, 176

    McKinley Area Services for the Handicapped, Inc., 197

    Manchester Historic Association, 200

    Museum of Cartoon Art, 219

    National Association of Accountants for the Public Interest, 221

    New England Gerontology Center, 242

    Pico-Union Neighborhood Council, 266

    The Solomon R. Guggenheim Museum, 302

1st SUPPLEMENT

Directory of Internships, Work Experience Programs, and On-the-Job Training Opportunities

Theater Workshop Boston, 320

U.S. Congress. Senate. Office of William Proxmire, 350

U.S. Veterans Administration, 368

Voluntary Action Center of Toledo, 373

WDNR Radio, 381

WGPR, Inc., 388

WPLW-AM, 392

WRJZ Radio, 394

WVII-TV, 398

Work-Study Internship for Undergraduate Potters, 132

Work-Study on Southern Africa, 15

y

Youth and Community Development Program, 140

Youth Guidance and Campus Life Internship Program, 137

Geographic Index

References in Geographic Index refer to entry numbers

1st SUPPLEMENT

Directory of Internships, Work Experience Programs, and On-the-Job Training Opportunities

a

Alabama
See: Gadsen, Alabama; Mobile, Alabama; Tuscaloosa, Alabama

Alaska
See also: Anchorage, Alaska
U.S. Forest Service, 355

Albany, Georgia
See also: Georgia
Girls Club of Albany, Georgia, 128

Albany, New York
See also: New York
New York. Assembly, 244

Albuquerque, New Mexico
See also: New Mexico
Albuquerque Journal, 3
Albuquerque, New Mexico, 4, 5
U.S. Fish and Wildlife Service, 354
U.S. Forest Service, 355

Anchorage, Alaska
See also: Alaska
KANC Radio, 216, 217
Mt. Susitna Broadcasting Corporation, 216, 217

Annapolis, Maryland
See also: Maryland
Maryland. Legislative Study Group, 202

Arizona
See also: Scottsdale, Arizona; Tucson, Arizona
Arizona. State Legislature, 34

Arkansas
See also: Hampton, Arkansas; Little Rock, Arkansas; Pine Bluff, Arkansas
Arkansas. Arts and Humanities Office, 35

Asheville, North Carolina
See also: North Carolina
U.S. Congress. House. Office of Lamar Gudger, 337
U.S. Forest Service, 355

Asia
See also: Foreign countries
East-West Center, 99-104

Athens, Georgia
See also: Georgia
Athens Community Council on Aging, Inc., 39

Atlanta, Georgia
See also: Georgia
National Moratorium on Prison Construction, 231
Radio Free Georgia Broadcasting Foundation, Inc., 274
U.S. Fish and Wildlife Service, 354
U.S. Forest Service, 355
U.S. National Park Service, 361
WRFG, 274

Augusta, Georgia
See also: Georgia
The Augusta Chronicle, 40

Augusta, Maine
Maine. Office of the Governor, 199

b

Baltimore, Maryland
See also: Maryland
Camp Fire Girls, Inc., 57

1st SUPPLEMENT

Directory of Internships, Work Experience Programs, and On-the-Job Training Opportunities

Coastal Telecommunications Corporation, 73
North Central Federation, Inc., 249
People for Community Action. Youth Services Bureau, 263, 264

Bangor, Maine
See also: Maine
WVII-TV, 398

Bernalillo County, New Mexico
See also: New Mexico
Albuquerque, New Mexico, 4

Bethesda, Maryland
See also: Maryland
International Program for Human Resource Development, Inc., 160
National Institutes of Health, 358-360

Big Rapids, Michigan
See also: Michigan
Mecosta County, Michigan. Commission on Aging, 205

Bloomington, Illinois
See also: Illinois
State Farm Insurance Companies, 314, 315

Bloomington, Indiana
See also: Indiana
Center for Public Affairs Service — Learning, 62
Indiana University, 62

Boston, Massachusetts
C. Paul Luongo Company, 51
Children's Museum, 68
Dr. Solomon Carter Fuller Mental Health Center, 96
Institute of Contemporary Art, 154
Massachusetts. Internship Office, 203
Massachusetts Arts and Humanities Foundation, 204
Theater Workshop Boston, 320
U.S. Fish and Wildlife Service, 354
U.S. National Park Service, 361

Bowie, Maryland
See also: Maryland
Bowie, Maryland, 43

Bowling Green, Kentucky
See also: Kentucky
Barren River Area Development District, 41

Brentwood, Maryland
See also: Maryland
Neighborhoods Uniting Project, Inc., 239

Bronx, New York
See also: New York
The Bronx County Historical Society, 44

Brooklyn, New York
See also: New York
The Brooklyn Museum, 45

Buffalo, New York
See also: New York
Buffalo and Erie County Historical Society, 46-48
International Institute of Buffalo, 159
WEBR Newsradio, 382

C

California
See also: Freemont, California; Gilroy, California; Los Angeles, California; Napa, California; Pasadena, California; Riverside, California; Sacramento, California; San Francisco, California; Santa Barbara, California; Santa Cruz, California; Seaside, California; Tiburon, California; Ventura, California

1st SUPPLEMENT

Directory of Internships, Work Experience Programs, and On-the-Job Training Opportunities

California. Office of the Lieutenant Governor, 53
California Community Services Centers, Inc., 54, 55
German Academic Exchange Service (DAAD), 120
U.S. Forest Service, 355
U.S. National Park Service, 361

Cambridge, Massachusetts
See also: Massachusetts
WCAS Radio, 379, 380

Canada
See also: Foreign countries
The American Numismatic Society, 24
National Research Council of Canada, 232

Carlsbad, New Mexico
See also: New Mexico
American Red Cross. South Eddy Chapter, 28

Carson City, Nevada
Nevada. Mental Hygiene and Mental Retardation Division, 240

Chapel Hill, North Carolina
See also: North Carolina
Institute of Government, 155
North Carolina. University, 155

Charleston, West Virginia
West Virginia. Legislative Services, 405

Charlottesville, Virginia
See also: Virginia
Offender Aid and Restoration of the U.S., 253

Chester, Pennsylvania
See also: Pennsylvania
WDNR, 381
Widener College, 381

Chicago, Illinois
See also: Illinois
American Dental Hygienists' Association, 18
American Judicature Society, 22
Chicago Symphony Orchestra, 67
Civic Orchestra of Chicago, 67
Cook County Legal Assistance Foundation, 84
The Newberry Library, 245
Ravenswood Hospital Community Mental Health Center, 275
WTTW/Channel 11, 397

Cincinnati, Ohio
Cincinnati, Ohio. Citizens' Committee on Youth, 70

Cleveland Heights, Ohio
Cleveland Heights, Ohio, 71

Clinton County, Ohio
Clinton County Volunteer Action Center, 72

Colorado
See also: Denver, Colorado; Fort Collins, Colorado; Grand Junction, Colorado; Lakewood, Colorado; Pueblo, Colorado
U.S. Forest Service, 355
U.S. National Park Service, 361

Columbia, Maryland
See also: Maryland
International Association for the Exchange of Students for Technical Experience/United States (IAESTE/US), 158

Columbia, South Carolina
South Carolina. Arts Commission, 303
South Carolina. Division of Administration, 304
South Carolina. State Senate and Office of the Lieutenant Governor, 305

Connecticut
See: Greenwich, Connecticut; Hartford, Connecticut; Milford, Connecticut; New Haven, Connecticut; Sharon, Connecticut

Cook County, Illinois
See also: Illinois

1st SUPPLEMENT

Directory of Internships, Work Experience Programs, and On-the-Job Training Opportunities

Cook County Legal Assistance Foundation, Inc., 84

d

Dallas, Texas
See also: Texas
The Dallas News, 92
Hope Community Center, 185
Leadership Training Institute, 185

Dalton, Georgia
See also: Georgia
Voluntary Action Center of Northwest Georgia, 372

Danvers, Massachusetts
See also: Massachusetts
Hawthorne Girl Scouts Council, Inc., 134

Davenport, Iowa
See also: Iowa
Community Mental Health Center of Scott County, 79

Dayton, Ohio
Dayton, Ohio, 93
Inland Division, General Motors Corporation, 150
National Audubon Society. Aullwood Audubon Center, 223
National Audubon Society. Aullwood Audubon Farm, 224

Dearborn, Michigan
See also: Michigan
Greenfield Village, 131, 132

Henry Ford Museum, 131, 132

Decator, Georgia
See also: Georgia
Central DeKalb Mental Health and Mental Retardation Center, 64

Deer Lodge Tennessee
See also: Tennessee
Morgan-Scott Project for Cooperative Christian Concerns, 215

Delaware
See: Dover, Delaware; Wilmington, Delaware

Denver, Colorado
See also: Colorado
Children's Museum, Inc., 69
Creative Arts Therapy Institute, 87
U.S. National Park Service, 361

Des Moines, Iowa
Iowa. General Assembly, 161
Iowa. House of Representatives, 162
KSO/KGGO, 316
Stoner Broadcasting, 316

Detroit, Michigan
See also: Michigan
WGPR, Inc., 388

Dexter, Missouri
See also: Missouri
Daily Statesman, 91

District of Columbia
See: Washington, D.C.

Dover, Delaware
YMCA of Dover and Kent County, 418

Durham, New Hampshire
New England Gerontology Center, 242

Durham, North Carolina
See also: North Carolina
Center for the Study of Aging and Human Development, 63
Duke University Medical Center, 63

1st SUPPLEMENT

Directory of Internships, Work Experience Programs, and On-the-Job Training Opportunities

e

East Peoria, Illinois
See also: Illinois
WEEK-TV, 383

Elkhart, Indiana
See also: Indiana
Oaklawn Community Mental Health Center, 251

Elyria, Ohio
Elyria Chronicle-Telegram, 107

Endwell, New York
See also: New York
WSKG, 396

Erie County, New York
See also: New York
Buffalo and Erie County Historical Society, 46-48

Erie, Pennsylvania
See also: Pennsylvania
Holy Trinity Community Center, 140

Etowah County, Alabama
Anchor, Inc., 31

Eugene, Oregon
See also: Oregon
KEED, 171

Evansville, Indiana
See also: Indiana
WEHT-TV, 384

f

Farmington, New Mexico
See also: New Mexico
KIVA-TV, 173

Florida
See also: Jacksonville, Florida; Miami, Florida; Orlando, Florida; Tallahassee, Florida; West Palm Beach, Florida
Florida Publishing Company, 113

Foreign countries
See also: Names of specific countries
East-West Center, 99-104
Institute in Intercultural Human Relations, 187
Inter-American Foundation, 157
International Association for the Exchange of Students for Technical Experience/United States (IAESTE/US), 158
International League for Human Rights, 324
International Program for Human Resource Development, Inc., 160
The Lisle Fellowship, Inc., 187
Operations Crossroads Africa, 256
Organization of American States, 258
Quaker United Nations Office, 272
U.S. National Science Foundation, 362
United Nations, 324
World Peace Institute, 415

Fort Collins, Colorado
See also: Colorado
Larimer County, Colorado, 183
U.S. Forest Service, 355

Fort Worth, Texas
Fort Worth Star-Telegram, 114

Frankfurt, Kentucky
See also: Kentucky
Kentucky. Department for Local Government, 178, 179

Freehold, New Jersey
Monmouth County, New Jersey. Board of Freeholders, 214

Fremont, California
See also: California
Eco Tour, 105

g

Gadsen, Alabama
Anchor, Inc., 31

Gallup, New Mexico
See also: New Mexico
McKinley Area Services for the Handicapped, Inc. (MASH), 197

Galveston, Texas
See also: Texas
St. Vincent's House, 288
Texas. University. Medical Branch. Division of Child and Adolescent Psychiatry, 319

Garden City, Kansas
Kansas. Department of Health and Environment, 176

Garrett County, Maryland
See also: Maryland
Garrett Community College — Oakland Center, 406
Garrett County Youth Employment Training, 406
Western Maryland Manpower Consortium, 406

Georgia
See also: Albany, Georgia; Athens, Georgia; Atlanta, Georgia; Augusta, Georgia; Decator, Georgia; Macon, Georgia; Stone Mountain, Georgia
U.S. Fish and Wildlife Service, 354
U.S. Forest Service, 355
U.S. National Park Service, 361
Voluntary Action Center of Northwest Georgia, Inc., 372

Germany
See also: Foreign countries
German Academic Exchange Service (DAAD), 120-127

Gilroy, California
See also: California
South County Community Mental Health Center, 306

Grand Junction, Colorado
See also: Colorado
Community Services, Inc., 80

Grand Rapids, Michigan
See also: Michigan
Grand Rapids, Michigan, 129
Mecosta County, Michigan. Commission on Aging, 205

Greensboro, North Carolina
See also: North Carolina
Center for Creative Leadership, 238
National Urban Fellows, Inc., 238

Greenwich, Connecticut
Museum of Cartoon Art, 219
National Audubon Society. Audubon Center in Greenwich, 222

h

Hampton, Arkansas
See also: Arkansas
Independent Community Consultants, Inc., 147

Harrisburg, Pennsylvania
Harrisburg Area Rape Crisis Center, 133
Pennsylvania. House of Representatives, 262

1st SUPPLEMENT
Directory of Internships, Work Experience Programs, and On-the-Job Training Opportunities

Hartford, Connecticut
   WPOP Newsradio-14, 393

Hastings-on-Hudson, New York
   See also: New York
   The Hastings Center, 156
   Institute of Society, Ethics and the Life Sciences, 156

Hawaii
   See: Honolulu, Hawaii

Hayesville, North Carolina
   See also: North Carolina
   Hinton Rural Life Center, 138

Helena, Montana
   See also: Montana
   Woman's Center, 410

High Point, North Carolina
   See also: North Carolina
   High Point Museum, 136
   High Point Youth for Christ, Inc., 137

Honolulu, Hawaii
   East-West Center, 99-104
   Honolulu, Hawaii. Mayor's Office of Information and Complaint, 141, 142

Houston, Texas
   See also: Texas
   Johnson Space Center, 191-195
   Lunar Science Institute, 190-195

i

Illinois
   See also: Bloomington, Illinois; Chicago, Illinois; East Peoria, Illinois; Springfield, Illinois; Wheaton, Illinois
   Illinois Legislative Studies Center, 144

Indiana
   See also: Elkhart, Indiana; Evansville, Indiana; Indianapolis, Indiana; Terre Haute, Indiana
   Center for Public Affairs Service — Learning, 62
   Indiana University, 62
   WAVE Radio, 376
   WAVE-TV, 377

Indianapolis, Indiana
   See also: Indiana
   Indiana. House of Representatives, 148
   Indianapolis, Indiana, 149
   WRTV 6, 395

Iowa
   See also: Davenport, Iowa; Des Moines, Iowa
   Iowa. General Assembly, 161
   Iowa. House of Representatives, 162

Israel
   See also: Foreign countries
   Hebrew University of Jerusalem, 135

Italy
   See also: Foreign countries
   American Academy in Rome, 7-10

j

Jackson County, Oregon
   See also: Oregon
   Jackson County, Oregon, 163, 164

Jackson, Mississippi
   Capitol Broadcasting Company, 58

Jacksonville, Florida
   Florida Publishing Company, 113
   Volunteer Jacksonville, Inc., 374

1st SUPPLEMENT

Directory of Internships, Work Experience Programs, and On-the-Job Training Opportunities

Jefferson City, Missouri
    Missouri. House of Representatives, 211
    Missouri Volunteer Office, 212

Juneau, Alaska
    U.S. Forest Service, 355

k

Kalamazoo, Michigan
    See also: Michigan
    American Institute for Exploration, 20

Kansas
    See also: Topeka, Kansas
    Kansas. Department of Health and Environment, 176

Kansas City, Missouri
    See also: Missouri
    Architects' Community Team, 33
    KWKI-FM, 175
    Kansas City, Missouri, 177

Kent County, Delaware
    YMCA of Dover and Kent County, 418

Kentucky
    See also: Lexington, Kentucky; Louisville, Kentucky; Owensboro, Kentucky
    Barren River Area Development District, 41
    Kentucky. Department for Local Government, 178, 179
    WAVE Radio, 376
    WAVE-TV, 377

King County, Washington
    See also: Washington
    King County Association for Retarded Citizens, 180, 181

Knoxville, Tennessee
    See also: Tennessee
    East Tennessee Community Design Center, 98
    WRJZ Radio, 394

l

Lakewood, Colorado
    See also: Colorado
    U.S. Forest Service, 355

Lancaster, Massachusetts
    See also: Massachusetts
    Robert F. Kennedy Children's Center, 281

Landsdale, Pennsylvania
    See also: Pennsylvania
    North Penn Valley Boys' Club, 250

Lansing, Michigan
    See also: Michigan
    Oldsmobile Division, General Motors, 255

Larimer County, Colorado
    See also: Colorado
    Larimer County, Colorado, 183

Las Vegas, Nevada
    See also: Nevada
    Las Vegas Mental Health Center, 184

Latin America
    See also: Foreign countries
    Inter-American Foundation, 157
    Organization of American States, 158

Lexington, Kentucky
    See also: Kentucky
    Lexington Planned Parenthood Center, Inc., 186
    YMCA of Greater Lexington, 419

1st SUPPLEMENT

Directory of Internships, Work Experience Programs, and On-the-Job Training Opportunities

Little Rock, Arkansas
   See also: Arkansas
   Arkansas Democrat, 36
   Association of Community Organizations for Reform Now (ACORN), 38

Los Angeles, California
   See also: California
   California Community Services Centers, Inc., 54, 55
   Cerrell Associates, Inc., 66
   Inner City Cultural Center, 151
   Los Angeles County Museum of Art, 189
   National Urban Fellows, Inc., 238
   Pico-Union Neighborhood Council, 266

Louisiana
   U.S. Forest Service, 355

Louisville, Kentucky
   See also: Kentucky
   Locust Grove Historic Home, 188
   WAVE Radio, 376
   WAVE-TV, 377

Lynn, Massachusetts
   See also: Massachusetts
   Lynn Historical Society, 196

m

Macon, Georgia
   See also: Georgia
   WMAZ Radio and Television, 389

Macon, Missouri
   See also: Missouri
   Macon Chronicle-Herald, 198

Madison, Wisconsin
   Wisconsin. State Bureau of Personnel, 408

Maine
   See also: Bangor, Maine; Springfield, Maine; Woods Hole, Maine
   Maine. Office of the Governor, 199

Manchester, New Hampshire
   Manchester Historic Association, 200

Mansfield, Ohio
   The News Journal, 246

Marion County, Indiana
   See also: Indiana
   Indianapolis, Indiana, 149

Maryland
   See also: Annapolis, Maryland; Baltimore, Maryland; Bethesda, Maryland; Bowie, Maryland; Brentwood, Maryland; Columbia, Maryland; Oakland, Maryland; Pikesville, Maryland; Rockville, Maryland
   North Central Federation, Inc., 249
   Western Maryland Manpower Consortium, 406

Massachusetts
   See also: Boston, Massachusetts; Cambridge, Massachusetts; Danvers, Massachusetts; Lancaster, Massachusetts; Lynn, Massachusetts; Shrewsbury, Massachusetts; West Springfield, Massachusetts; Worcester, Massachusetts
   U.S. Fish and Wildlife Service, 354
   U.S. National Park Service, 361

Mecosta County, Michigan
   See also: Michigan
   Mecosta County, Michigan. Commission on Aging, 205

Medford, Oregon
   See also: Oregon
   Jackson County, Oregon, 163, 164

Miami, Florida
   See also: Florida
   Youth Industries, Inc., 422

1st SUPPLEMENT
Directory of Internships, Work Experience Programs, and On-the-Job Training Opportunities

Michigan
　See also: Big Rapids, Michigan; Dearborn, Michigan; Detroit, Michigan; Grand Rapids, Michigan; Kalamazoo, Michigan; Lansing, Michigan; St. Helen, Michigan
　U.S. Congress. House. Office of David E. Bonior, 331

Milford, Connecticut
　WFIF, 385

Milwaukee, Wisconsin
　See also: Wisconsin
　INROADS/Milwaukee, Inc., 152
　U.S. Forest Service, 355

Minneapolis, Minnesota
　See also: Minnesota
　American Cancer Society. Minnesota Division, 12
　Minneapolis Tribune, 208, 209
　U.S. Fish and Wildlife Service, 354

Minnesota
　See also: Minneapolis, Minnesota; St. Cloud, Minnesota; St. Paul, Minnesota
　Minneapolis Tribune, 208
　U.S. Fish and Wildlife Service, 354
　U.S. Forest Service, 355

Mississippi
　See: Jackson, Mississippi; Starkville, Mississippi

Missoula, Montana
　U.S. Forest Service, 355

Missouri
　See also: Dexter, Missouri; Jefferson City, Missouri; Kansas City, Missouri; Macon, Missouri; St. Louis, Missouri
　Missouri. House of Representatives, 211

Mobile, Alabama
　Mobile Community Organization, 213
　WAAB, 375

Monmouth County, New Jersey
　Monmouth County, New Jersey. Board of Freeholders, 214

Montana
　See also: Helena, Montana
　U.S. Forest Service, 355

Mount Vernon, Virginia
　See also: Virginia
　National Trust for Historic Preservation, 236

n

Napa, California
　See also: California
　Young Radio, Inc., 421

Nebraska
　U.S. National Park Service, 361

Nevada
　See also: Las Vegas, Nevada
　Nevada. Mental Hygiene and Mental Retardation Division, 240

New Castle County, Delaware
　New Castle County, Delaware. Department of Parks and Recreation, 241

New Hampshire
　See: Durham, New Hampshire; Manchester, New Hampshire; Portsmouth, New Hampshire

New Haven, Connecticut
　American Oriental Society, 25, 26
　National Urban Fellows, Inc., 238
　Yale University, 25, 26

New Jersey
See: Freehold, New Jersey; Newark, New Jersey; Princeton, New Jersey

New Mexico
See also: Albuquerque, New Mexico; Carlsbad, New Mexico; Farmington, New Mexico; Gallup, New Mexico
New Mexico. State Personnel Office, 243
U.S. Fish and Wildlife Service, 354
U.S. Forest Service, 355
U.S. National Park Service, 361

New Orleans, Louisiana
U.S. Forest Service, 355

New York
See also: Albany, New York; Bronx, New York; Brooklyn, New York; Buffalo, New York; Endwell, New York; Hastings-on-Hudson, New York; New York City, New York; Oswego, New York; Rensselaerville, New York; Troy, New York; White Plains, New York
U.S. Congress. House. Office of Edward I. Koch, 339

New York City, New York
See also: New York
American Academy in Rome, 7-10
American Committee on Africa, 15
American Labor History Series, 23
The American Numismatic Society, 24
Association for Education in Journalism, 37
Cathedral Church of St. John the Divine, 59
The College of Insurance, 74
Concert Artists Guild, 82
Cooper-Hewitt Museum, 85
German Academic Exchange Service (DAAD), 120-127
Institute of Afro-American Affairs, 37
International League for Human Rights, 324
Korvettes, 182
Operation Crossroads Africa, 256
Quaker United Nations Office, 272

Scientists Institute for Public Information, 292
The Solomon R. Guggenheim Museum, 302
United Nations, 324
WMCA Radio, 390
West Indies Program, 256
Womanart Gallery, 409
Young Concert Artists, Inc., 417
Young Men's Christian Association. National Board, 420

Newark, New Jersey
American Friends Service Committee, 19

North Carolina
See also: Durham, North Carolina; Greensboro, North Carolina; Hayesville, North Carolina; High Point, North Carolina
Institute of Government, 155
North Carolina. University, 155
Offender Aid and Restoration of North Carolina, 252
U.S. Congress. House. Office of Lamar Gudger, 337
U.S. Forest Service, 355

O

Oakland, Maryland
See also: Maryland
Garret Community College — Oakland Center, 406
Garrett County Youth Employment Training, 406
Mt. Top Youth for Christ, 218

Western Maryland Manpower Consortium, 406

Ogden, Utah
U.S. Forest Service, 355

Ohio
See: Cincinnati, Ohio; Cleveland Heights, Ohio; Dayton, Ohio; Elyria, Ohio; Mansfield, Ohio; Tiffin, Ohio; Toledo, Ohio; Wilmington, Ohio

Oklahoma
Oklahoma. State Legislative Council, 254

Oklahoma City, Oklahoma
Oklahoma. State Legislative Council, 254

Olympia, Washington
See also: Washington
Thurston Youth Services Society. The Union Street Center, 322

Omaha, Nebraska
U.S. National Park Service, 361

Oregon
See also: Eugene, Oregon; Medford, Oregon; Portland, Oregon
Oregon. Legislative Assembly, 257
U.S. Fish and Wildlife Service, 354
U.S. Forest Service, 355

Orlando, Florida
See also: Florida
Sentinel Star Company, 295

Oswego, New York
See also: New York
Farnham Youth Development Center, 109

Ottawa, Canada
See also: Foreign countries
National Research Council of Canada, 232

Owensboro, Kentucky
See also: Kentucky
Owensboro Broadcasting, Inc., 259, 260
WOMI/WBKR, 259, 260

p

Palm Beach County, Florida
See also: Florida
Palm Beach County Mental Health Center, 261

Pasadena, California
See also: California
Star-News, 312

Pennsylvania
See also: Chester, Pennsylvania; Erie, Pennsylvania; Harrisburg, Pennsylvania; Landsdale, Pennsylvania; Philadelphia, Pennslvania; Pittsburgh, Pennsylvania; State College, Pennsylvania; York, Pennsylvania
U.S. Forest Service, 355
U.S. National Park Service, 361

Philadelphia, Pennsylvania
Greater Philadelphia Group Newspapers, 130
The Historical Society of Delaware, 139
U.S. National Park Service, 361

Pierce County, Washington
See also: Washington
Comprehensive Mental Health Center of Tacoma-Pierce County, 81

Pikesville, Maryland
See also: Maryland
WCAO Radio, 378

Pine Bluff, Arkansas
See also: Arkansas
Pine Bluff Commercial, 267

1st SUPPLEMENT

Directory of Internships, Work Experience Programs, and On-the-Job Training Opportunities

Pittsburgh, Pennsylvania
  See also: Pennsylvania
  Hickling Broadcast Company, 392
  WPLW-AM, 392

Port Angeles, Washington
  See also: Washington
  The Daily News, 90

Portland, Oregon
  See also: Oregon
  Portland Community Design Center, 269
  U.S. Fish and Wildlife Service, 354
  U.S. Forest Service, 355

Portsmouth, New Hampshire
  The Junction, Youth Resources Center, 169

Prince George's County, Maryland
  See also: Maryland
  Neighborhoods Uniting Project, Inc., 239

Princeton, New Jersey
  The Newspaper Fund, 247, 248
  Woodrow Wilson National Fellowship Foundation, 413

Providence, Rhode Island
  Rhode Island Historical Society, 279

Provo, Utah
  See also: Utah
  Utah County, Utah, 369

Pueblo, Colorado
  See also: Colorado
  KCSJ/KDJQ Radio, 170

r

Racine, Wisconsin
  See also: Wisconsin
  Silver Street Day Care Center, Inc., 296

Raleigh, North Carolina
  See also: North Carolina
  Offender Aid and Restoration of North Carolina, 252

Rensselaer, New York
  See also: New York
  Rensselaer County Historical Society, 276
  Rensselaer County, New York. Mental Health Department, 277

Rensselaerville, New York
  See also: New York
  The Edmund Niles Huyck Preserve, Inc., 106

Reston, Virginia
  See also: Virginia
  U.S. Geological Survey, 356

Rhode Island
  See: Providence, Rhode Island

Richmond, Virginia
  Richmond Times-Dispatch, 280
  Virginia Museum, 371

Riverside, California
  See also: California
  In Records Audio Presentations, 146

Rockville, Maryland
  See also: Maryland
  The Lisle Fellowship, Inc., 187

Rome, Italy
  See also: Foreign countries
  American Academy in Rome, 7-10

Rosslyn, Virginia
  See also: Virginia
  Inter-American Foundation, 157

S

Sacramento, California
See also: California
Sacramento County, California, 283-286
California. Office of the Lieutenant Governor, 53

Sacramento County, California
See also: California
Sacramento County, California, 283-286

St. Cloud, Minnesota
See also: Minnesota
St. Cloud Times, 287

St. Helen, Michigan
See also: Michigan
R.O.O.C. Workshop, 273

St. Louis, Missouri
See also: Missouri
INROADS/St. Louis, Inc., 153

St. Paul, Minnesota
See also: Minnesota
Immigration History Research Center, 145
Macalester College, 415
Minnesota. House of Representatives, 210
Minnesota. University, 145
3M Company, 321
U.S. Forest Service, 355
World Press Institute, 415

Salem, Oregon
See also: Oregon
Oregon. Legislative Assembly, 257

San Angelo, Texas
See also: Texas
The KIXY Stations, 174

San Antonio, Texas
See also: Texas
San Antonio, Texas, 289

San Francisco, California
See also: California
DeYoung Museum Art School, 112
Fine Arts Museum of San Francisco, 112
Haight-Ashbury Community Radio, 265
KFRC Radio, 172
National Association of Accountants for the Public Interest, 221
National Moratorium on Prison Construction, 231
People's Media Collective, 265
San Francisco Volunteer Burearu/Voluntary Action Center, 290
U.S. Forest Service, 355
U.S. National Park Service, 361
The Wine Museum of San Francisco, 407

San Juan, Puerto Rico
San Juan, Puerto Rico. Washington Office, 291

Santa Barbara, California
See also: California
Sabre Foundation, 282

Santa Cruz, California
See also: California
Resource Center for Nonviolence, 278

Sante Fe, New Mexico
See also: New Mexico
New Mexico. State Personnel Office, 243
U.S. National Park Service, 361

Scott County, Iowa
See also: Iowa
Community Mental Health Center of Scott County, 79

1st SUPPLEMENT

Directory of Internships, Work Experience Programs, and On-the-Job Training Opportunities

Scottsdale, Arizona
  See also: Arizona
  Creative Life Services, 88

Seaside, California
  See also: California
  Seaside Post News-Sentinel, 294

Seattle, Washington
  See also: Washington
  King County Association for Retarded Citizens, 180, 181
  U.S. National Park Service, 361

Sharon, Connecticut
  National Audubon Society. Sharon Audubon Center, 226

Shrewsbury, Massachusetts
  See also: Massachusetts
  Worcester Foundation for Experimental Biology, 414

South America
  See also: Foreign countries
  Organization of American States, 258

South Carolina
  South Carolina. Arts Commission, 303
  South Carolina. Division of Administration, 304
  South Carolina. Senate and Office of the Lieutenant Governor, 305

South County, California
  See also: California
  South County Community Mental Health Center, 306

South Dakota
  U.S. Congress. Senate. Office of George McGovern, 349

South Eddy County, New Mexico
  See also: New Mexico
  American Red Cross. South Eddy County Chapter, 28

Spokane, Washington
  See also: Washington
  Spokane Legal Services Center, 308, 309
  Spokane, Washington. Parks and Recreation Department, 310
  The Spokesman Review, 311

Springfield, Illinois
  Illinois Legislative Studies Center, 144
  Sangamon State University, 144

Springfield, Maine
  See also: Maine
  WGBY-TV, 386

Starkville, Mississippi
  Starkville, Mississippi. Regional Mental Health Complex, 313

State College, Pennsylvania
  See also: Pennsylvania
  Centre County Youth Service Bureau, 65

Stone Mountain, Georgia
  See also: Georgia
  Hungarian Cultural Foundation, 143

t

Tacoma, Washington
  See also: Washington
  Comprehensive Mental Health Center of Tacoma-Pierce County, 81

Tallahassee, Florida
  See also: Florida
  WGLF Radio, 387

Tennessee
  See also: Deer Lodge, Tennessee; Knoxville, Tennessee

1st SUPPLEMENT
Directory of Internships, Work Experience Programs, and On-the-Job Training Opportunities

East Tennessee Community Design Center, 98
Tennessee. General Assembly, 318
U.S. Congress. House. Office of Harold Ford, 336

Terre Haute, Indiana
See also: Indiana
Center for Governmental Services, 60
Indiana State University, 60

Texas
See also: Dallas, Texas; Galveston, Texas; Houston, Texas; San Angelo, Texas; San Antonio, Texas
Fort Worth Star-Telegram, 114

Tiburon, California
See also: California
National Audubon Society. Richardson Bay Wildlife Sanctuary and Whittell Education Center, 225

Tiffin, Ohio
The Advertiser-Tribune, 1

Toledo, Ohio
Southwest Youth Development, 307
Voluntary Action Center of Toledo, 373

Topeka, Kansas
See also: Kansas
Midland Broadcasting, 206

Troy, New York
See also: New York
Rensselaer County Historical Society, 276
Rensselaer County, New York. Mental Health Department, 277

Tucson, Arizona
See also: Arizona
National Consumer Affairs Internship Program, 228

Tuscaloosa, Alabama
Tuscaloosa, Alabama. Regional Alcoholism Council, 323

u

United States
See also: Names of specific states, counties and cities
Alliance for Arts Education, 6
American Council on Education, 17
American Institute of Architects Research Corporation, 21
The American Numismatic Society, 24
American Oriental Society, 25, 26
Association of Community Organizations for Reform Now (ACORN), 38
Call for Action, Inc., 56
Center for Public Affairs Service — Learning, 62
The College of Insurance, 74
The Experiment in International Living, 108
Hinton Rural Life Center, 138
International Association for the Exchange of Students for Technical Experience/ United States (IAESTE/US), 158
Korvettes, 182
The Lisle Fellowship, Inc., 187
Migrant Legal Action Program, Inc., 207
National Association of Accountants for the Public Interest, 221
National Consumer Affairs Internship Program, 228
National Moratorium on Prison Construction, 231
National Trust for Historic Preservation, 234
National Urban Fellows, Inc., 238
The Newspaper Fund, 247, 248
Offender Aid and Restoration of the U.S., Inc., 253

1st SUPPLEMENT
Directory of Internships, Work Experience Programs, and On-the-Job Training Opportunities

Sabre Foundation, 282
Scientists Institute for Public Information, 292
U.S. Civil Service Commission, 327-330
U.S. Department of Commerce. Office of Minority Business Enterprise (OMBE), 351
U.S. Fish and Wildlife Service, 354
U.S. Forest Service, 355
U.S. Geological Survey, 356
U.S. National Institutes of Health, 358-360
U.S. National Park Service, 361
U.S. Postal Service, 363
U.S. Veterans Administration, 364-368
Woodrow Wilson National Fellowship Foundation, 413
World Press Institute, 415
Young Men's Christian Association. National Board. International Division, 420

Upper Darby, Pennsylvania
See also: Pennsylvania
U.S. Forest Service, 355

Utah
See also: Provo, Utah
U.S. Forest Service, 355

Utah County, Utah
See also: Utah
Utah County, Utah, 369

V

Ventura, California
See also: California
Ventura County Mental Health Services, 370

Ventura County, California
See also: California

Ventura County Mental Health Services, 370

Virginia
See also: Charlottesville, Virginia; Mount Vernon, Virginia; Reston, Virginia; Richmond, Virginia; Rosslyn, Virginia; Williamsburg, Virginia
Virginia Museum, 371

W

Washington
See also: Olympia, Washington; Port Angeles, Washington; Seattle, Washington; Spokane, Washington; Tacoma, Washington; Wenatchee, Washington
The Daily News, 90
U.S. National Park Service, 361
Washington. Council for Postsecondary Education, 399

Washington, D.C.
African Bibliographic Center, 2
Alliance for Arts Education, 6
American Association of University Women, 11
American Civil Liberties Union of the National Capital Area, 13, 14
American Council of the Blind, 16
American Council on Education, 17
American Institute of Architects Research Corporation, 21
American Psychological Association, 27
American Theatre Association, 29

1st SUPPLEMENT

Directory of Internships, Work Experience Programs, and On-the-Job Training Opportunities

Americans for Democratic Action. Youth Caucus, 30
Andromeda, Inc., 32
Association of American Colleges, 270
Big Brothers of the National Capital Area, 42
Bureau of Rehabilitation of the National Capital Area, 49
Business-Industry Political Action Committee, 50
Call for Action, Inc., 56
Center for Inquiry and Discovery, 61
Consumer Federation of America, 83
Council for Advancement and Support of Education, 86
DC Public Interest Research Group, 89
District of Columbia. Superior Court, 94
District of Columbia Lung Association, 95
Dumbarton Oaks Center for Studies in the History of Landscape Architecture, 97
The Experiment in International Living, 108
Federal Home Loan Bank Board, 110
Federal National Mortgage Association (Fannie Mae), 111
Forum for the Advancement of Students in Science and Technology (FASST), 115-119
Hebrew University of Jerusalem, 135
Joint Center for Political Studies, 166-168
Kennedy Center, 6
The Lisle Fellowship, Inc., 187
Migrant Legal Action Program, Inc., 207
National Archives, 230
National Association for Retarded Citizens, 220
The National Center for Urban Ethnic Affairs, 227
National Collection of Fine Arts, 301
National Council for a World Peace Tax Fund, 229
National Historical Publications and Records Commission, 230
National Moratorium on Prison Construction, 231

National Neighborhood Institute, 227
National Suggestion Box, 233
National Trust for Historic Preservation, 234-236
National Urban Coalition, 237
Organization of American States, 258
The Population Institute. Education Division, 268
Project on the Status and Education of Women, 270
Public Interest Economics Foundation, 271
San Juan, Puerto Rico. Washington Office, 291
Smithsonian Institution, 297-301, 412
Support Center, 317
United Nations Association, USA, 325
U.S. Bureau of the Census, 326
U.S. Civil Service Commission, 327-330
U.S. Congress. House, 331-346
U.S. Congress. Senate, 347-350
U.S. Department of Commerce, 326, 351, 352
U.S. Department of State, 353
U.S. Fish and Wildlife Service, 354
U.S. Forest Service, 355
U.S. Information Agency (USIA), 357
U.S. National Park Service, 361
U.S. National Science Foundation, 362
U.S. Postal Service, 363
U.S. Veterans Administration, 364-368
Washington Center for the Study of Services, 400
Washington, D.C. City Council, 401
Washington Peace Center, 402, 403
Women's Equity Action League Educational and Legal Defense Fund, 411
Woodrow Wilson International Center for Scholars, 412

Wausau, Wisconsin
 See also: Wisconsin
Marathon Health Care Center, 201

1st SUPPLEMENT
Directory of Internships, Work Experience Programs, and On-the-Job Training Opportunities

Wenatchee, Washington
See also: Washington
Wenatchee World, 404

West Indies
See also: Foreign countries
Inter-American Foundation, 157
Operation Crossroads Africa, 256
San Juan, Puerto Rico. Washington Office, 291

West Palm Beach, Florida
See also: Florida
Palm Beach County Mental Health Center, 261

West Springfield, Massachusetts
See also: Massachusetts
Community Health Education Council, Inc., 78

West Virginia
West Virginia. Legislative Services, 405

Westchester County, New York
See also: New York
Cage Teen Center, 52

Wheaton, Illinois
See also: Illinois
Youth For Christ, Inc., 137

White Plains, New York
See also: New York
Cage Teen Center, 52

Williamsburg, Virginia
See also: Virginia
College of William and Mary, 75-77
Colonial Williamsburg Foundation, 75, 76
Earl Gregg Swem Library, 76
Institute of Early American History and Culture, 77
National Trust for Historic Preservation, 235

Wilmington, Delaware
The Historical Society of Delaware, 139

New Castle County, Delaware. Department of Parks and Recreation, 241

Wilmington, Ohio
Clinton County Volunteer Action Center, 72

Wisconsin
See also: Milwaukee, Wisconsin; Racine, Wisconsin; Wausau, Wisconsin
Wisconsin. State Bureau of Personnel, 408

Woods Hole, Maine
See also: Maine
Sea Education Association, 293

Worcester, Massachusetts
See also: Massachusetts
John Woodman Higgins Armory Museum, 165
WNCR/WAAF Radio Stations, 391
Youth Opportunities Upheld, Inc., 423

y

York County, Pennsylvania
See also: Pennsylvania
York County 4-H Clubs, 416
York County Extension Service, 416

York, Pennsylvania
See also: Pennsylvania
York County 4-H Clubs, 416

Subject Index

References in Subject Index refer to entry numbers

1st SUPPLEMENT

Directory of Internships, Work Experience Programs, and On-the-Job Training Opportunities

a

Academic credit: 12, 16, 21, 37, 38, 45, 49, 50, 53, 58, 71, 78, 96, 105, 111, 115-120, 128, 131, 132, 144, 155, 160, 161, 172, 196, 203, 211, 220, 257, 258, 268, 292, 293, 298, 312, 318, 323, 339, 380, 388, 391, 395, 397, 405, 411, 420

Accounting: 71, 110, 115, 242, 317. See also Business and finance

Administration. See Management

Administration, Personnel. See Personnel management

Advertising: 37, 91, 167, 174, 175, 198, 206, 217, 320, 387, 392, 398. See also Business and finance; Public relations

Advocacy: 95, 169, 184, 263, 264, 288, 296, 410, 418

Aerospace sciences: 191-195, 328. See also Engineering; Lunar sciences; Sciences

African affairs: 2, 15. See also International affairs

Aged and aging: 39, 59, 63, 88, 168, 201, 205, 242, 251

Agriculture and agricultural sciences: 127, 158, 224

Alcoholism: 201, 251, 306, 323. See also Drugs and drug abuse

American history. See History, American

American studies: 188, 258, 279. See also History, American

Announcing. See Broadcast media; Radio broadcasting; Television broadcasting

Antimilitarism: 229, 402, 403

Apprenticeship training: 52, 75-77, 365. See also On-the-job training

Archaeology: 10, 24, 75. See also History

Architecture: 7, 9, 10, 21, 33, 75, 98, 158, 163, 234, 269, 371. See also Arts and artists; Building and construction; Landscape architecture; Urban and regional planning

Archives and archival work: 44, 75, 76, 145, 154, 219, 230. See also Museums

Area studies. See American studies; Chinese studies; German studies; Hungarian studies; Italian studies; Latin American studies; South American studies

Art: 188, 189, 196, 302. See also Arts and artists; Crafts; Fine arts

Art, Classical: 8, 10

Art, Oriental: 25, 26

Art Education: 6, 112, 135, 189. See also Art; Education

Art galleries. See Museums

Art history: 8, 10, 24, 85, 97, 154, 189, 234, 276, 279, 301, 371, 407. See also Art; Arts and artists; Fine arts; History

Art museums. See Museums

Arts and artists: 6, 35, 75, 112, 151, 203, 204, 297-300, 307, 353, 371, 409, 423. See also Art; Crafts; Fine arts; Humanities; Specific arts by name

Arts management: 29, 35, 83, 136, 154, 165, 204, 235, 236, 303, 417. See also Arts and artists; Management; Museums

317

1st SUPPLEMENT
Directory of Internships, Work Experience Programs, and On-the-Job Training Opportunities

Arts therapy: 32, 87

Asian studies. *See* Chinese studies

Associations: 18, 134, 144, 228, 317, 325. *See also* Educational organizations

Astronomy: 190. *See also* Aerospace sciences; Planetary sciences; Sciences

Automobile industry: 150, 255. *See also* Engineering

b

Banks and banking. *See* Business and finance

Behavrioral sciences: 359, 360. *See also* Psychology; Social sciences; Sociology

Bilingualists: 32, 176, 370. *See also* Languages

Biochemistry: 63. *See also* Biological sciences; Chemistry

Biological sciences: 63, 292, 328, 354, 355, 362, 364, 367, 414. *See also* Biomedical sciences; Chemistry; Life sciences; Medical sciences and research; Sciences

Biomedical sciences: 359, 360, 414. *See also* Biological sciences; Medical sciences and research

Blueprinting: 33. *See also* Architecture

Broadcast media: 37, 58, 167, 174, 316, 375-377, 382, 383, 387-389. *See also* Communications; Radio broadcasting; Television broadcasting

Budgeting. *See* Business and finance

Building and construction: 98, 231, 256. *See also* Architecture; Engineering; Housing

Business administration: 5, 50, 74, 101, 110, 115, 152, 166, 182, 203, 315, 351, 352, 363, 413. *See also* Advertising; Business and finance; Industry; Insurance; Management; Manufacturing; Marketing; Personnel management; Retail selling; Trade

Business and finance: 62, 71, 83, 99, 110, 111, 155, 302, 329, 351, 352, 413. *See also* Accounting; Economics; Management

c

CETA programs: 4, 33, 35, 52, 128, 183, 323

Camps and camping: 20, 57, 59. *See also* Day camps; Recreation

Cancer: 12. *See also* Medical sciences and research

Carpentry: 52, 422

Cataloging: 44, 47, 48, 61, 76, 139, 145, 154, 189, 200, 219, 276, 302. *See also* Libraries and librarianship; Museums

Chemistry: 321. *See also* Physical sciences; Sciences

Child care centers: 57, 296

Children. *See* Youth services and programs

Chinese studies: 24-26

1st SUPPLEMENT

Directory of Internships, Work Experience Programs, and On-the-Job Training Opportunities

Church history: 8. *See also* History

Church-related programs: 59, 138, 140, 215, 288. *See also* Religious programs

City and regional planning. *See* Community development; Urban and regional planning

City government. *See* Government, Local

Civil engineering. *See* Engineering

Civil law. *See* Law

Civil rights: 13, 14, 89, 270, 282, 324, 411, 420. *See also* Political science

Classical studies: 8, 10, 24. *See also* History

Clerical skills. *See* Secretarial science

Clinical training: 32, 54, 55, 57, 79, 80, 169, 184, 261, 275, 313, 319, 370, 423. *See also* Community mental health centers

Colleges and universities. *See* Education, Higher

Commerce. *See* Business administration

Commercial law. *See* Law

Communications: 19, 37, 56, 101, 108, 109, 203, 233, 353, 357, 391, 402, 403. *See also* Broadcast media; Information sciences; Journalism; Publishing and publications; Radio broadcasting; Television broadcasting; Writers and writing

Community development: 33, 62, 140, 147, 168, 178, 215. *See also* Environmental issues and research; Urban and regional planning

Community education: 12, 89, 95, 133, 185, 215, 235, 251, 278, 313, 323, 410. *See also* Education

Community mental health centers: 32, 64, 79, 81, 96, 184, 201, 251, 261, 275, 306, 313, 370. *See also* Community services; Mental and emotional health; Public health

Community organizing: 38, 140, 213, 227, 239, 253, 263, 402, 403, 410. *See also* Social work

Community services: 28, 54, 55, 71, 78, 79, 80, 98, 185, 215, 288, 290, 372, 374, 402. *See also* Community mental health centers; Social services

Computer sciences: 242, 292, 326, 328, 331, 342, 352. *See also* Information sciences; Mathematics; Operations research

Conferences. *See* Seminars and conferences

Congressional programs. *See* Government, Federal; Legislative research, Federal

Conservation, Art objects: 131, 165, 189, 235, 276, 302. *See also* Museums

Construction. *See* Building and construction

Consumer affairs: 38, 62, 83, 89, 228, 400. *See also* Business and finance

Counseling and guidance: 42, 49, 65, 78, 79, 94, 105, 109, 133, 137, 153, 180, 184, 186, 218, 249, 261, 263, 264, 275, 277, 289, 306, 319, 322, 323, 406, 409, 410. *See also* Education; Family counseling; Mental and emotional health; Psychology; Social work

County government. *See* Government, County

Crafts: 35, 131, 160, 196, 256, 307, 371, 423. *See also* Arts and artists; Photography; Potters and pottery

Creative writing: 10. *See also* Writers and writing

Crime prevention: 65. *See also* Juvenile delinquency

Criminal justice: 49, 94, 231, 252-254, 292. *See also* Incarceration; Justice, Administration of

Criminal law. *See* Law

Crisis intervention: 64, 109, 133, 251, 261, 263, 306, 323, 370. *See also* Counseling and guidance

Cross-cultural relations. *See* Intercultural relations

Curatorial work: 45, 46, 48, 85, 131, 165, 189, 276, 302. *See also* Museums

d

Dance: 246

Data processing: 326, 400, 410. *See also* Computer sciences; Information sciences

Day camps: 59, 138. *See also* Youth services and programs

Day care services. *See* Child care centers

Democratic Party: 66. *See also* Political parties; Political science

Demography. *See* Population studies

Dentistry: 359, 364, 367. *See also* Medical sciences and research

Design: 7, 9, 10, 21, 33, 85, 97, 98, 196, 269, 371. *See also* Architecture

Dietetics: 364, 367. *See also* Health care; Medical sciences and research

Disabled. *See* Handicapped

Dissertation research: 26, 55, 97, 100, 123, 124, 245

Draftsmanship: 33, 163, 269. *See also* Architecture

Drugs and drug abuse: 78, 168, 201, 251, 263, 306

e

Earth sciences: 190, 362. *See also* Planetary sciences; Sciences

Ecology. *See* Environmental issues and research

Economic development: 62. *See also* Economics

Economics: 8, 24, 63, 71, 83, 110, 168, 178, 234, 258, 271, 318, 326, 352, 420. *See also* Business and finance; Management; Social sciences

Editing: 1, 3, 14, 36, 77, 86, 90, 92, 107, 113, 114, 130, 160, 167, 173, 208, 209, 247, 267, 279, 280, 287, 295, 311, 316, 328. *See also* Journalism; Publishing and publications

Education: 53, 61, 72, 85, 99, 101, 102, 112, 128, 155, 159, 168, 169, 186, 196, 203, 222-226, 249, 258, 268. *See also* Art education; Counseling and guidance; Tutoring

Education, Administration of. *See* Management

1st SUPPLEMENT

Directory of Internships, Work Experience Programs, and On-the-Job Training Opportunities

Education, Art. *See* Art education

Education, Elementary and secondary: 120. *See also* Students, High school

Education, Higher: 17, 24, 27, 120, 122, 125, 190, 243, 270, 353, 358, 362, 413

Education, International: 108, 362. *See also* Educational exchange

Education, Special: 281. *See also* Rehabilitation

Educational exchange: 108, 120-127, 353

Educational organizations: 11, 17, 268

Elections. *See* Political campaigns

Electronic data processing. *See* Data processing

Electronics. *See* Engineering

Elementary education. *See* Education, Elementary and secondary

Emotional health. *See* Mental and emotional health

Energy resources and research: 21, 89, 292, 334. *See also* Engineering

Engineering: 71, 150, 152, 155, 158, 232, 255, 321, 352, 355, 356, 359, 362, 364, 367. *See also* Aerospace sciences; Technology; Sciences

Environmental issues and education: 21, 62, 105, 203, 222-226, 334, 412. *See also* Forests and forestry; Natural resources; Wildlife conservation and sanctuaries

Equal rights. *See* Civil rights

Exchange programs: 17, 158, 353

Exhibitions and exhibits: 45, 69, 75, 112, 136, 189, 200, 219, 222, 224, 276, 302, 409. *See also* Museums

Expeditioning: 20

f

Faculty. *See* Education, Higher

Family counseling: 54, 55, 80, 184, 263, 264, 306, 319, 366. *See also* Counseling and guidance

Family planning: 186. *See also* Population studies; Social sciences; Social welfare

Farm management. *See* Agriculture and agricultural sciences

Federal government. *See* Government, Federal

Fellowships: 7-10, 25-27, 97, 99, 106, 135, 191, 193, 232, 238, 244, 245, 297, 319, 351, 371, 414, 415

Fieldwork: 99-104, 120, 137, 158, 187, 201, 222-226, 241, 256, 356, 419

Film making: 371, 383, 389. *See also* Television broadcasting

Finance. *See* Business and finance

Fine arts: 10, 112, 301. *See also* Arts and artists; Specific fine arts by name

Fire sciences: 352, 355

Fish and fisheries: 354. *See also* Marine sciences; oceanography

Floor staff: 61, 68, 69, 200, 407. *See also* Museums

Food science and industry: 83. *See also* Agriculture and agricultural sciences; economics

Foreign affairs. *See* International affairs

Foreign languages. *See* Languages

Foreign relations. *See* International relations

Forests and forestry: 155, 355. *See also* Environmental issues and research

Freedom: 15

Fund raising: 69, 87, 109, 115, 219, 265, 317, 410

g

Gardens: 97, 266. *See also* Horticulture; Landscape architecture

Geography: 168, 196, 326. *See also* Social sciences; Sciences

Geology: 356. *See also* Earth sciences; Sciences

German studies: 120-127

Gerontology. *See* Aged and aging

Government: 99, 101, 148, 155, 220, 233, 282, 291, 347, 353, 401. *See also* Laws and legislation; Political science; Public administration

Government, City. *See* Government, Local

Government, County: 183, 214, 238, 283-286, 369. *See also* Public administration

Government, Federal: 2, 13, 16, 17, 27, 30, 50, 83, 111, 220, 228, 229, 238, 291, 325-357, 361, 363. *See also* Legislative research; Public administration

Government, Local: 4, 41, 43, 71, 93, 129, 149, 177-179, 238, 289, 291. *See also* Public administration

Government, State: 34, 53, 60, 144, 148, 155, 161, 162, 178, 179, 199, 202, 210-212, 238, 240, 243, 244, 254, 257, 262, 304, 305, 318, 399, 405, 408. *See also* Legislative research; Public administration

Government, Municipal. *See* Government, Local

Graphic arts: 14, 61, 141, 196, 219, 371, 396. *See also* Arts and artists; Fine arts

h

Handicapped: 16, 87, 180, 197, 201, 220, 284. *See also* Education, Special; Occupational therapy; Physical therapy; Rehabilitation; Visual disorders

Health and safety: 83. *See also* Health care

Health care: 38, 71, 89, 95, 176, 186, 205, 266, 364, 366, 367. *See also* Community mental health centers; Health professions; Medical sciences and research; Mental and emotional health; Public health

Health professions: 18, 176, 358-360, 364, 367. *See also* Individual professional fields

High school. *See* Education, Elementary and secondary; Students, High school

Higher education. *See* Education, Higher

Historical publications: 77, 230, 279. *See also* History; Publishing and publications

1st SUPPLEMENT

Directory of Internships, Work Experience Programs, and On-the-Job Training Opportunities

Historical sites: 75, 188, 234-236, 279. *See also* Preservation, Historical sites and resources

Historical societies: 44, 46-48, 139, 196, 200, 276, 279

History: 8, 10, 24, 46, 77, 168, 188, 196, 234, 276, 318, 412. *See also* Archaeology; Art history; Historical sites; Historical societies; Area studies by name

History, American: 23, 75-77, 139, 200, 230. *See also* American studies; Historical sites

History, Art. *See* Art history

Horticulture: 75, 97, 234. *See also* Gardens; Landscape architecture

Hospitals: 251, 275, 319, 413. *See also* Community mental health centers; Health care

Housing: 71, 89, 98, 168, 266. *See also* Building and construction; Urban and regional planning

Human rights. *See* Civil rights

Human services: 65, 87, 187, 203, 205. *See also* Social services

Humanities: 8, 10, 112, 204, 234, 297-300. *See also* Specific humanities by name

Hungarian studies: 143

i

Immunology: 63. *See also* Biomedical sciences; Medical sciences and research

Incarceration: 19, 49, 231, 252, 253. *See also* Justice, Administration of; Penal reform

Indexing: 2, 44, 47

Industrial design: 10, 321. *See also* Engineering

Industry: 150, 232, 255, 321. *See also* Business administration

Information and referral services: 31, 56, 88, 109, 205, 263, 323, 395. *See also* Community services; Social services

Information sciences: 2, 317. *See also* Communications; Computer sciences; Data processing; Libraries and librarianship

Information storage and retrieval. *See* Information sciences

Inner city: 151. *See also* Urban affairs; Urban Corps

Insurance: 74, 83, 315. *See also* Business administration

Intercultural relations: 101, 108, 159, 187, 197, 256, 353, 412, 415. *See also* International affairs; International relations

Interior design: 371. *See also* Design

International affairs: 2, 11, 160, 272, 282, 324, 353, 420. *See also* African affairs; Intercultural relations; Political science; United Nations

International education. *See* Education, International; Educational exchange

International exchange. *See* Exchange programs

International relations: 11, 272, 324, 353. *See also* International affairs

Internships: 1-3, 6, 11-16, 18, 20, 21, 29, 30, 32-34, 36-41, 43, 45-50, 53-56, 58, 59, 60, 62, 65, 68, 69, 71, 73, 78, 79, 81-83, 85-87,

89-95, 97, 100, 102, 103, 107, 108, 111-119, 128, 130-134, 136, 139, 144, 146-152, 155-157, 160-163, 166-175, 177, 179, 184, 188, 189, 196, 199, 202, 203, 206, 208-212, 214, 215, 218, 220, 221-226, 228-231, 233, 234, 237-240, 242, 243, 246-248, 251, 253, 254, 257-261, 263, 264, 267-273, 275, 276, 278-282, 287, 291, 292, 294-296, 301-306, 309-316, 318, 322, 324, 325, 328, 329, 331-334, 336-349, 353, 357, 369, 370, 373-377, 379, 380, 382, 383, 385-387, 389-391, 393, 396, 397, 400, 401, 404, 405, 408, 409, 411, 413, 419, 420, 423

Italian studies: 8, 10

j

Journalism: 1-3, 14, 36, 37, 40, 53, 69, 83, 86, 90-92, 107, 111, 113, 114, 117, 130, 142, 166, 167, 198, 208, 209, 233, 234, 246-248, 267, 280, 282, 287, 294, 295, 311, 312, 318, 353, 375, 376, 378, 382, 383, 387, 393, 397, 400, 404, 415. *See also* Advertising; Broadcast media; Communications; Editing; News reporting; Newspapers; Photography; Public relations; Publishing and publications; Public relations; Radio broadcasting; Television broadcasting; Writers and writing

Justice, Administration of: 19, 22, 420. *See also* Criminal justice

Juvenile delinquency: 65, 78, 137, 140, 169, 231, 249, 263, 322, 418. *See also* Criminal justice

l

Labor. *See* Business and finance; Economics; Management

Land surveying: 163, 355

Landscape architecture: 10, 97, 234

Languages: 108, 145, 158, 189, 302, 324, 353

Languages, Asian: 100

Languages, Chinese: 25, 26

Languages, French: 2, 157, 258

Languages, German: 120-127

Languages, Hungarian: 143, 145

Languages, Italian: 7-10

Languages, Portuguese: 157, 258

Languages, Spanish: 32, 157, 176, 258, 370

Latin American studies: 24, 157, 258

Law and legal services: 71, 83, 84, 110, 155, 156, 168, 203, 207, 234, 308, 309, 314, 318, 324, 328, 352, 361, 411, 413. *See also* Justice, Administration of; Juvenile delinquency; Laws and legislation; Legal research; Legislative research

Laws and legislation: 13, 16, 34, 60, 83, 161, 202, 211, 220, 254, 339, 401, 405. *See also* Government; Law and legal services; Legal research; Legislative research

Leadership training: 20, 185, 416

Legal research: 22, 83, 156, 157, 308, 314. *See also* Law and legal services; Legislative research

Legislative research, Federal: 2, 13, 16, 119, 220, 291, 325, 332, 333, 335, 336, 338-342, 344, 346-350

1st SUPPLEMENT

Directory of Internships, Work Experience Programs, and On-the-Job Training Opportunities

Legislative research, State: 34, 53, 60, 144, 148, 161, 202, 210, 211, 254, 257, 262, 305, 318, 405

Libraries and librarianship: 47, 76, 85, 139, 143, 145, 154, 164, 200, 234, 242, 279, 364. *See also* Information sciences; Museums

Life sciences: 156. *See also* Sciences

Literature, History of: 8, 10

Lobbying: 95, 229. *See also* Laws and legislation; Political science

Local government. *See* Government, Local

Lunar sciences: 190-195. *See also* Aerospace sciences; Sciences

m

Magazines and journals: 2, 37, 86, 282. *See also* Historical publications; Publishing and publications

Mangement: 46, 62, 71, 87, 96, 102, 115, 134, 151, 154, 155, 160, 225, 226, 241, 242, 252, 258, 289, 290, 302, 317, 318, 329, 351, 353, 363, 413, 417. *See also* Business administration; Business and finance; Economics; Personnel management

Management, Personnel. *See* Personnel management

Manufacturing: 150, 255, 321

Marine biology: 135. *See also* Biological sciences; Marine sciences

Marine sciences: 293. *See also* Fish and fisheries; Oceanography; Sciences

Marketing: 83, 115, 118, 160, 166, 352. *See also* Advertising; Business and finance; Public relations; Retail selling

Mass media. *See* Broadcast media; Communications; Journalism; Radio broadcasting; Television broadcasting

Mathematics: 71, 158, 326. *See also* Computer sciences; Sciences; Statistics

Mechanical engineering. *See* Engineering

Medical science and research: 155, 156, 359, 364, 367. *See also* Chemistry; Areas of medicine and medical professions by name

Medieval studies: 8, 24. *See also* History

Mental and emotional health: 32, 54, 55, 64, 78, 79, 81, 96, 201, 240, 251, 277, 281, 306, 313, 319. *See also* Community mental health centers; Psychiatry; Psychology

Mental health centers. *See* Community mental health centers

Mental retardation: 52, 64, 180, 181, 220, 240, 313. *See also* Mental and emotional health; Handicapped

Microbiology. *See* Biological sciences

Migrants: 176, 207

Militarism. *See* Antimilitarism

Minorities and minority groups: 12, 37, 152, 153, 166-168, 170, 189, 209, 216, 217, 238, 259, 260, 265, 315, 351, 358, 384, 389, 408, 413

Municipal government. *See* Government, Local

Museums: 45-48, 61, 68, 69, 75, 85, 112, 134-136, 154, 165, 188, 189, 196, 200, 219, 234, 236, 276, 279, 297, 301, 302, 371, 407

Music: 8, 10, 35, 67, 82, 256, 379, 381, 394, 417

n

Narcotics. *See* Drugs and drug abuse

National government. *See* Government, Federal

Natural resources: 412. *See also* Environmental issues and research; Fish and fisheries; Forest and forestry; Resource development

Natural sciences: 106, 222. *See also* Physical sciences; Sciences

Nature study and naturalists: 105, 106, 222-226. *See also* Wildlife conservation and sanctuaries

Neighborhoods: 33, 38, 98, 140, 213, 227, 239, 266, 280. *See also* Community development; Community organizing

Neuroendocrinology: 63. *See also* Biological sciences; Medical sciences and research

News reporting: 1-3, 14, 36, 40, 90-92, 107, 113, 114, 130, 170-174, 198, 206, 208, 209, 246, 248, 260, 267, 280, 287, 294, 295, 311, 312, 316, 375, 376, 378, 380, 383-385, 387, 389-391, 393, 394, 396-398, 404, 421. *See also* Journalism

Newspapers: 1, 3, 14, 36, 37, 40, 90-92, 107, 111, 113, 114, 130, 198, 208, 209, 246-248, 267, 280, 287, 294, 295, 311, 312, 404

Nonprofit organizations. *See* Associations

Nonviolence: 278

Numismatics: 24

Nursery schools. *See* Child care centers

Nurses and nursing: 71, 96, 176, 186, 359, 364, 367. *See also* Health care; Medical sciences and research

o

Occupational therapy: 32, 81, 201, 364, 367. *See also* Handicapped; Rehabilitation

Oceanography: 293. *See also* Earth sciences; Marine sciences; Physical sciences; Sciences

Office skills. *See* Secretarial science

On-the-job training: 4, 6, 32, 37, 45, 52, 69, 84, 93, 97, 110, 111, 129, 134, 136, 145, 146, 158, 163, 182, 183, 186, 197, 198, 205, 206, 213, 216, 217, 222-226, 234, 249, 250, 252, 255, 259, 260, 265, 266, 274, 287, 290, 296, 306, 307, 310, 312, 316, 319-321, 365, 366, 373, 376-378, 384, 386-388, 390, 421, 422. *See also* Apprenticeship training; Research training; Work experience

Operations research: 326, 413

Oriental studies. *See* Chinese studies

Outpatient services: 96, 184, 251, 277, 313, 370

Outreach services: 88, 109, 185, 205, 263, 277, 288, 368. *See also* Community services; Social services

1st SUPPLEMENT

Directory of Internships, Work Experience Programs, and On-the-Job Training Opportunities

p

Parks and recreational areas: 241, 310, 328, 355, 361. See also Environmental issues and research; Forests and forestry; Historic sites; Recreation; Urban and regional planning

Painting: 10, 25, 26, 371. See also Arts and artists; Fine arts

Peace: 229, 272, 402, 403

Penal reform: 19, 231. See also Justice, Administration of

Performing arts. See Dance; Music; Theatre

Personnel management: 5, 62, 115, 328, 329, 413. See also Management

Pharmacology: 63, 364, 367. See also Medical sciences and research

Photography: 20, 33, 36, 90, 107, 130, 173, 287, 312, 371, 376. See also Fine arts; Journalism

Physical education: 250, 353, 411, 419. See also Education

Physical sciences: 355, 362. See also Chemistry; Natural sciences; Physics; Sciences

Physical therapy: 364, 367. See also Handicapped; Rehabilitation

Physics: 321, 356. See also Mathematics; Physical sciences; Sciences

Planetology: 190-195. See also Aerospace sciences; Sciences

Planning. See Urban and regional planning

Political campaigns: 50, 66, 168. See also Political science

Political parties: 30. See also Political science

Political philosophy: 278. See also Political science

Political science: 8, 30, 60, 63, 71, 83, 155, 168, 178, 203, 254, 291, 318, 347, 412. See also Government; International affairs; International relations; Law and legal services; Laws and legislation; Public administration; Social sciences

Policy sciences: 63. See also Political science; Public administration

Population studies: 268, 326. See also Family planning; Social sciences; Sociology

Postdoctoral programs: 8, 26, 27, 54, 63, 97, 99, 123-125, 135, 189, 191, 192, 232, 244, 245, 319, 358-360, 362, 413

Potters and pottery: 132. See also Crafts

Preschool education and care. See Child care centers

Preservation, Historical sites and resources: 139, 234-236, 279. See also Historical sites

Press. See Journalism; Newspapers

Printing: 302. See also Graphic arts; Publishing and publications

Prisons and prisoners. See Incarceration

Probation and parole: 5, 49, 94. See also Criminal justice; Incarceration; Justice, Administration of

Psychiatry: 32, 63, 96. See also Mental and emotional health; Psychology

1st SUPPLEMENT
Directory of Internships, Work Experience Programs, and On-the-Job Training Opportunities

Psychology: 27, 32, 54, 55, 63, 78, 79, 81, 96, 184, 186, 232, 261, 263, 275, 277, 306, 313, 319, 328, 364, 367, 370. *See also* Clinical training; Counseling and guidance; Family counseling; Mental and emotional health; Psychotherapy; Psychiatry; Social sciences; Therapy

Psychotherapy: 54, 55, 79, 184, 261, 306. *See also* Psychology; Therapy

Public administration: 27, 30, 71, 163, 167, 168, 177, 178, 203, 214, 221, 238, 271, 329, 353, 401, 403. *See also* Government; Political science

Public assistance. *See* Social welfare

Public education. *See* Community education

Public health: 64, 176, 186, 319. *See also* Community mental health centers; Health care; Medical sciences and research

Public policy. *See* Public administration

Public relations: 29, 37, 51, 60, 71, 75, 82, 87, 108, 109, 131, 134, 142, 151, 160, 167, 219, 229, 253, 265, 274, 317, 322, 409, 410, 413

Public schools. *See* Education; Education, Elementary and secondary

Public service: 62, 155, 240, 258. *See also* Public administration; Social services

Public welfare. *See* Social welfare

Public works: 71. *See also* Public administration

Publishing and publications: 2, 11, 19, 37, 75, 87, 111, 117, 143, 151, 317. *See also* Historical publications; Magazines and journals; Newspapers

r

Radio broadcasting: 146, 170-172, 175, 206, 216, 217, 259, 260, 265, 274, 375, 376, 378-382, 385, 287, 388-394, 396, 421. *See also* Broadcast media

Recreation: 43, 88, 96, 105, 128, 138, 169, 181, 203, 250, 355, 419, 423. *See also* Parks and recreational areas

Regional planning. *See* Urban and regional planning

Rehabilitation: 181, 197, 273, 364. *See also* Education, Special; Handicapped; Occupational therapy

Religious programs: 137, 215, 218, 392, 419. *See also* Church-related programs

Reporting. *See* News reporting

Research: 2, 13, 15, 21, 23, 25, 26, 41, 43, 46, 47, 50, 56, 62, 83, 89, 95, 97, 99, 102, 104, 106, 119, 123-125, 133, 135, 155-157, 168, 179, 191, 192, 194, 203, 225, 228, 229, 232, 233, 237, 239, 245, 258, 272, 289, 292, 296, 302, 322, 323, 325, 353, 362, 412. *See also* Legislative research; Research training

Research training: 20, 63, 94, 100, 103, 127, 169, 193, 195, 272, 297, 300, 358-360, 414. *See also* Research

Resource development. *See* Economic development; Natural resources

328

1st SUPPLEMENT

Directory of Internships, Work Experience Programs, and On-the-Job Training Opportunities

Retail selling: 160, 182, 422. *See also* Marketing

Retardation. *See* Mental retardation

Rural areas: 65, 197, 313

S

Sanctuaries, Wildlife. *See* Wildlife conservation and sanctuaries

Schools. *See* Education

Sciences: 20, 115-119, 158, 232, 258, 292, 297-300, 321, 355, 358-360, 362, 414. *See also* Specific sciences by name

Sculpture: 10, 371. *See also* Arts and artists; Fine arts

Secondary education. *See* Education, Elementary and secondary; Students, High school

Secretarial sciences: 16, 61, 84, 160, 176, 266

Seminars and conferences: 24, 235, 236

Social development: 147, 258

Social problems: 27, 156, 420. *See also* Alcoholism; Drugs and drug abuse; Juvenile delinquency

Social sciences: 22, 99-104, 157, 185, 297-300, 362, 400, 412. *See also* Specific social sciences by name

Social services: 71, 212. *See also* Aged and aging; Community mental health centers; Community services; Human services; Outreach services; Social work

Social welfare: 28, 180. *See also* Social services; Social work

Social work: 32, 39, 96, 180, 212, 215, 239, 250, 263, 275, 277, 306, 318, 364, 366, 367. *See also* Counseling and guidance; Social services; Social welfare

Sociology: 5, 21, 63, 78, 81, 168, 242, 250, 318, 326, 395. *See also* Social sciences

South American studies: 258

Space sciences. *See* Aerospace sciences

Special education. *See* Education, Special

Speech: 391. *See also* Communications

Sports. *See* Physical education

State government. *See* Government, State

Statistics: 168, 326, 328, 352, 400. *See also* Mathematics

Students, College and university: 1, 3-5, 11, 12, 14, 16, 18, 21, 22, 24-26, 29, 30, 32, 34, 36, 37, 39-41, 43, 45-48, 50, 51, 53, 55, 56, 58-60, 62, 64, 65, 70, 71, 73-79, 81, 86, 90-94, 96-98, 105-108, 110, 111, 113-124, 126, 127, 129-134, 136, 138, 139, 141-144, 147-150, 153, 155-158, 161-164, 166-173, 175, 177-182, 184, 186-189, 193, 195, 196, 198-203, 205-212, 220, 221, 223, 225, 228, 230, 234, 235, 237, 239-243, 247-251, 254-258, 261-264, 267-269, 271, 272, 275, 279, 280, 283, 285, 287, 289-293, 295-305, 308-316, 318, 321, 323, 325, 326, 328-330, 332, 333, 336-339, 341-343, 345, 347-358, 361, 364, 366-370, 375-378, 380, 383, 386, 387, 389, 393, 395, 397-399, 401, 404, 405, 408, 411, 414, 419, 420

Students, High school: 59, 69, 108, 152, 153, 169, 203, 206, 214, 219, 256, 266, 267, 284, 286, 327, 330, 332, 351, 411, 422

329

Summer opportunities: 3, 4, 6, 16, 21, 22, 24, 36, 37, 40, 45, 49, 53, 59, 62, 67-70, 73, 82, 83, 86, 90, 92, 96, 106, 107, 110, 113, 114, 120, 121, 126, 127, 132, 138-143, 147, 149, 150, 152, 155, 156, 158, 176, 178, 179, 187, 188, 195, 198, 199, 203, 205, 207, 212, 228, 234, 235, 238, 241, 243, 246-249, 255, 256, 258-260, 263, 264, 267, 268, 271, 275, 279, 280, 281, 286-289, 294-297, 301-304, 310, 311, 314-316, 320, 321, 325-328, 331, 334, 336, 339-341, 343, 344, 346, 349-357, 361, 364, 367, 375-377, 389, 391, 393, 408, 410, 414, 417, 418

Surveying. *See* Land surveying

Systems sciences. *See* Computer sciences; Mathematics

t

Taxation: 115, 229

Teachers and teaching. *See* Education

Technical assistance: 41, 203, 252, 253

Technology: 115-119, 150, 158, 292, 321. *See also* Engineering

Telecommunications. *See* Television broadcasting

Television broadcasting: 23, 73, 173, 377, 382-384, 386, 388, 389, 396-398. *See also* Broadcast media

Theatre: 6, 35, 320, 371, 391. *See also* Arts and artists

Therapy, Individual and group: 32, 54, 55, 81, 184, 275, 306, 313, 319, 423. *See also* Arts therapy; Counseling and guidance; Family counseling; Psychology; Psychotherapy

Tourism: 352

Trade: 420. *See also* Business and finance; International relations

Transportation and traffic engineering. *See* Automobile industry

Travel: 7-10, 25, 26, 99-104, 120-127, 158, 362. *See also* Educational exchange; Exchange programs

Tutoring: 72, 128, 159, 249, 256, 423. *See also* Education

u

United Nations: 272, 324, 325, 420

Universities. *See* Education, Higher

Urban affairs: 37, 71, 168, 237-239, 291. *See also* Community development; Community services; Inner city; Urban Corps; Urban studies

Urban and regional planning: 7, 10, 33, 41, 71, 98, 163, 168, 178, 203, 234

Urban Corps: 5, 70, 93, 129

Urban development. *See* Community Development

Urban government. *See* Government, Local

Urban studies: 196. *See also* Urban affairs

1st SUPPLEMENT

Directory of Internships, Work Experience Programs, and On-the-Job Training Opportunities

V

Veterinary sciences: 359

Visual arts: 35. *See also* Arts and artists

Visual disorders: 6, 364. *See also* Handicapped

Vocational education: 94, 249 250, 336, 406. *See also* Education

Vocational rehabilitation. *See* Rehabilitation

Volunteerism: 212, 290, 372-374

W

Welfare. *See* Social welfare

Wildlife conservation and sanctuaries: 222-226, 354, 355. *See also* Fish and fisheries; Forest and forestry; Natural resources; Nature study and naturalists

Women: 270, 409-411. *See also* Minorities and minority groups

Work experience: 1, 3, 5, 11, 17, 18, 33, 36, 40, 42, 43, 58, 66, 67, 70, 73, 74, 90-92, 97, 107, 113, 114, 127, 130, 141, 142, 145, 152, 164, 170-176, 183, 197, 206, 219, 228, 230, 238, 246-248, 266, 269, 273, 280, 283-286, 294, 295, 302, 306, 308, 309, 311, 320, 326-330, 350-357, 361, 363, 364, 367-369, 372, 373, 375, 379-383, 385, 386, 388, 389, 391-394, 396-400, 404, 408, 416. *See also* On-the-job training

Work-study: 5, 6, 12, 15, 21, 81, 93, 115-119, 128, 129, 132, 164-168, 178, 200, 203, 221, 242, 249, 283, 289, 302, 309, 368, 386, 399, 414, 423. *See also* Academic credit

Workshops: 101

Writers and writing: 1-3, 11, 19, 36, 51, 86, 111, 130, 133, 142, 160, 167, 222, 229, 233, 282, 316, 328. *See also* Journalism; News reporting; Newspapers; Public relations; Publishing and publications

Y

Youth services and programs: 42, 57, 59, 65, 68, 69, 128, 134, 137, 138, 140, 169, 185, 218, 249, 250, 263, 264, 281, 306, 307, 319, 322, 406, 416, 418, 419, 422, 423. *See also* Child care centers; Juvenile delinquency

Combined Sponsor Index

References in Combined Sponsor Index refer to entry numbers

1st SUPPLEMENT

Directory of Internships, Work Experience Programs, and On-the-Job Training Opportunities

*References in **bold italic type** refer to entries in the first edition of the Directory.*

a

ACTION, *1, 2*

The Advertiser-Tribune, 1

The Advocate, *3*

African Bibliographic Center, 2

Agency for International Development (AID), *375*

Agnes Scott College, *4*

Alabama. University, *5*

Albuquerque Journal, 3

Albuquerque, New Mexico, 4, 5

Albuquerque, New Mexico. Public Schools, 6

All News Radio 14, *7*

Alliance for Arts Education, 6

Alternative, 282

American Academy in Rome, 7-10

American Association for Higher Education, *8*

American Association for the Advancement of Science, *9, 10,* 27

American Association of University Women. Educational Center, 11

American Cancer Society. Minnesota Division, 12

American Chemical Society. Division of Analytical Chemistry, *11*

American Civil Liberties Union of the National Capital Area, 13, 14

American Committee on Africa, 15

American Council of Learned Societies, *12*

American Council of the Blind, 16

American Council on Education, *13,* 17

American Dental Hygienists' Association, 18

American Enterprise Institute for Public Policy, *14*

American Federation of Labor-Congress of Industrial Organizations (AFL-CIO), *15*

American Friends Service Committee, *16, 17,* 19

American Hospital Association, 19

American Institute for Exploration, 20

American Institute of Architects, *18, 19*

American Institute of Architects Research Corporation, 21

American Institute of Indian Studies, *20*

American Judicature Society, 22

American Labor History Series, Inc., 23

American Library Association. Association of College and Research Libraries, *21*

335

1st SUPPLEMENT

Directory of Internships, Work Experience Programs, and On-the-Job Training Opportunities

The American Numismatic Society, 24

American Oriental Society, 25, 26

The American Philosophical Society, 139

American Political Science Association, **22, 231**

American Psychological Association, 27

American Red Cross. South Eddy County Chapter, 28

American Society of Magazine Editors, **23**

American Theatre Association, 29

American Theatre Festival, 6

American Youth Hostels, Inc., **24**

American Zionist Youth Foundation, **25-34**

Americans for Democratic Action, **35**

Americans for Democratic Action. Youth Caucus, 30

Americans for Indian Opportunity, Inc., **36**

Ames Research Center, **434-436**

Anchor, Inc., 31

The Anderson Herald, **37**

Andromeda, Inc., 32

Architects' Community Team, 33

Argonne National Laboratory, **38-46**

Arizona. State Legislature, 34

Arkansas. Arts and Humanities Office, 35

Arkansas Democrat, 36

Association for Education in Journalism, 37

Association for World Education, **47**

Association of American Colleges, 270

Association of College and Research Libraries, **21**

Association of Community Organizations for Reform Now (ACORN), 38

The Association of Motion Picture and Television Producers, **123**

Association of University Programs in Health Administration, **48**

Athens Community Council on Aging, Inc., 39

Atlanta University Center, **49, 50**

Atomic Energy Commission (AEC), **381**

Audubon Center in Greenwich, 222

Audubon Society, **208,** 222-226

The Augusta Chronicle, 40

Aullwood Audubon Center, 223

Aullwood Audubon Farm, 224

b

The Baltimore Museum of Art, **51**

Barren River Area Development District, 41

Beatrice Daily Sun, **52**

Big Brothers of the National Capital Area, 42

Bowie, Maryland, 43

Bridgeport, Connecticut, **53**

The Bronx County Historical Society, 44

Brookhaven National Laboratory, **54**

1st SUPPLEMENT

Directory of Internships, Work Experience Programs, and On-the-Job Training Opportunities

The Brooklyn Museum, 45

Buffalo and Erie County Historical Society, 46-48

Bureau of Rehabilitation of the National Capital Area, *55,* 49

Burlington Standard Press, *515*

The Bush Foundation, *56*

Business-Industry Political Action Committee (BIPAC), 50

C

C. Paul Luongo Company, 51

Cage Teen Center, 52

California. Department of Alcoholic Beverage Control, *57*

California. Department of Conservation, *58*

California. Department of Health, *59*

California. Department of Industrial Relations, *60*

California. Department of Rehabilitation, *61-63*

California. Governor's Office, *64*

California. Legislature. Assembly Rules Committee, *65*

California. Legislature. Senate, *66, 67*

California. Office of the Lieutenant Governor, 53

California. Public Utilities Commission, *68*

California. State Personnel Board, *69, 70*

California Community Services Centers, Inc., 54, 55

Call for Action, Inc., 56

Camp Fire Girls, Inc., 57

Capitol Broadcasting Company, 58

Carolina Broadcasting Company, *71*

Cathedral Church of St. John the Divine, 59

Catholic University Law School, *74*

Cecilwood Theatre, *72*

Center for Coordination of Research on Social Indicators, *339*

Center for Defense Information, *73*

Center for Governmental Services, 60

Center for Inquiry and Discovery, 61

Center for National Policy Review, *74*

Center for National Security Studies, *75*

Center for Public Affairs Service-Learning, 62

Center for Science in the Public Interest, *76*

Center for Studies in Landscape Architecture, 97

Center for the History of the American Indian, *271-273*

Center for the Study of Aging and Human Development, 63

Central DeKalb Mental Health and Mental Retardation Center, 64

Centre County Youth Service Bureau, 65

Cerrell Associates, Inc., 66

1st SUPPLEMENT

Directory of Internships, Work Experience Programs, and On-the-Job Training Opportunities

The Charles Edison Memorial Youth Fund, **77**

Chesapeake Bay Center for Environmental Studies, **338**

Chicago. University, **20**

Chicago Sun Times/Daily News, **78**

Chicago Symphony Orchestra, 67

Children's Museum, 68

Children's Museum, Inc., 69

Chrysler Corporation, **79**

The Cincinnati Enquirer, **80**

Cincinnati, Ohio. Citizens' Committee on Youth, 70

Citizens Conference on State Legislatures, **81**

Citizens Crime Commission of Philadelphia, **82**

Cleveland Heights, Ohio, 71

Clinton County Volunteer Action Center, 72

Coalition of Independent College and University Students (COPUS), **83**

Coastal Telecommunications Corporation, 73

The College of Insurance, 74

College of William and Mary, 75-77

College Republican National Committee, **84**

Colonial Williamsburg Foundation, 75, 76

The Columbus Ledger/The Columbus Enquirer, **85**

Commission on White House Fellows, **470**

Common Cause, **86**

Community for Creative Non-Violence, **87**

Community Health Education Council, Inc., 78

Community Mental Health Center of Scott County, 79

Community Services, Inc., 80

Comprehensive Mental Health Center of Tacoma-Pierce County, 81

Compton, California, **88**

Concert Artists Guild, 82

Connecticut. Commission on Arts, **89**

Connecticut. Department of Children and Youth Services, **90**

Connecticut. Department of Mental Health, **91-93**

Connecticut. General Assembly. Joint Committee on Legislative Management, **94**

Connecticut Public Television, **95**

The Conservation Foundation, **96**

Consumer Federation of America, 83

Cook County Legal Assistance Foundation, Inc., 84

Cooper-Hewitt Museum, 85

Corcoran Gallery of Art, **97**

Coro Foundation, **98**

Corporation for Public Broadcasting, **99, 100**

Council for Advancement and Support of Education (CASE), 86

Council for the Advancement of Science Writing, Inc. (CASW), **101**

Council on Library Resources, **102**

Council on National Priorities and Resources, **103**

The Courier-Journal, **104**

Creative Arts Therapy Institute, 87

Creative Life Services, 88

1st SUPPLEMENT

Directory of Internships, Work Experience Programs, and On-the-Job Training Opportunities

d

DC Gazette, *105*

DC Public Interest Research Group, 89

The Daily News, 90

The Daily Reporter, *106*

Daily Statesman, 91

The Dallas Morning News, 92

Daughters of the American Revolution. Museum, *107*

Dayton, Ohio, 93

Dayton, Ohio. Office of Voluntarism, *108*

Defenders of Wildlife, *109*

Democratic National Committee, *110*

Des Moines, Iowa. Office of the City Manager, *111, 112*

Des Plaines Publishing Company, *113*

Detroit. Personnel Department, *114*

Detroit Free Press, *115*

The Devereux Foundation, *116-122*

DeYoung Museum Art School, 112

Directors Guild of America, *123*

District of Columbia. Superior Court. Social Service Division, 94

District of Columbia Lung Association, 95

Dr. Solomon Carter Fuller Mental Health Center, 96

Duke University Medical Center, 63

Dumbarton Oaks Center for Studies in the History of Landscape Architecture, 97

Dynamy, Inc., *124*

e

Earl Gregg Swem Library, 76

The Earl Warren Legal Training Program, Inc., *125, 126*

East Coast Migrant Projects, *127*

East Tennessee Community Design Center, 98

East-West Center, 99-104

Eastern Farmworkers Association, *249*

Eco Tour, 105

The Edmund Niles Huyck Preserve, Inc., 106

Elyria Chronicle-Telegram, 107

Encampment for Citizenship, Inc., *128*

Environmental Action Foundation, *129-134*

Epilepsy Foundation of America, *135-137*

The Evening and Sunday Bulletin, *138*

The Evening News, *139*

The Evening Press, *140*

The Experiment in International Living, 108

1st SUPPLEMENT

Directory of Internships, Work Experience Programs, and On-the-Job Training Opportunities

f

Farnham Youth Development Center, 109

Federal Communications Commission (FCC), **407**

Federal Home Loan Bank Board, 110

Federal National Mortgage Association (Fannie Mae), 111

Federal Power Commission, **409**

Fine Arts Museum of San Francisco, 112

Fletcher School of Law and Diplomacy, **362**

Florida. Legislature. House of Representatives, **141**

Florida Publishing Company, 113

Folger Shakespeare Library, **142, 143**

Food and Agricultural Organization (FAO), **370, 371**

Ford Motor Company, **144**

Fort Worth Star-Telegram, 114

Forum for the Advancement of Students in Science and Technology (FASST), 115-119

Friends Committee on National Legislation, **145**

Friends of the Earth, **146**

g

Garrett County Youth Employment Training, 406

The Gazette, **147**

General Conference Mennonite Church, **148**

General Foods Corporation, **149**

General Motors Corporation, 150, 255

George Washington University. Institute for Educational Leadership, **150**

Georgia. Governor's Office, **151**

Georgia State University, **152, 347**

German Academic Exchange Service (DAAD), 120-127

Giant Food, Inc., **153**

Girls Club of Albany, Georgia, Inc., 128

Goddard Space Flight Center, **437-439**

Grand Rapids, Michigan, 129

The Grass Foundation, **154**

Greater Philadelphia Group Newspapers, **155,** 130

Greenfield Village and Henry Ford Museum, 131, 132

The Guide, **156**

1st SUPPLEMENT

Directory of Internships, Work Experience Programs, and On-the-Job Training Opportunities

h

Habitat Institute for the Environment, **157**

Haight-Ashbury Community Radio, 265

Hampton, Virginia. Youth Opportunity Commission, **158**

Harrisburg Area Rape Crisis Center, 133

Hartford, Connecticut. Office of the Mayor, **159**

The Hastings Center, 156

Hawaii. Executive Department, **160**

Hawaii. State Legislature, **161**

Hawaii. University, **160, 161**

Hawthorne Girl Scout Council, Inc., 134

Health Policy Advisory Center (Health/Pac), **162**

Hebrew University of Jerusalem, 135

Heinz Steinitz Marine Biology Laboratory, 135

Henry Ford Museum, 131

Hickling Broadcast Company, 392

Higgins Armory, 165

High Point Museum, 136

High Point Youth for Christ, Inc., 137

Hinton Rural Life Center, 138

Historic Deerfield, Inc., **163**

The Historical Society of Delaware, 139

Holiday Magazine, **164**

Holy Trinity Community Center, 140

Honolulu, Hawaii. Mayor's Office of Information and Complaint, 141, 142

Hope Community Center, 185

Hudson River Museum, **165**

Hughes Aircraft Company, **166**

Hungarian Cultural Foundation, 143

i

Idaho. Governor's Office, **167**

The Idaho Statesman, **168**

Illinois. Legislative Council, **169**

Illinois. Office of the Governor, **170**

Illinois Legislative Studies Center, 144

Immigration History Research Center, 145

In Records Audio Presentations, 146

Independent Community Consultants, Inc., 147

Indiana. House of Representatives, 148

Indiana State University, 60

Indiana University, 62

Indianapolis, Indiana, 149

Inland Division, General Motors Corporation, 150

Inner City Cultural Center, 151

1st SUPPLEMENT

Directory of Internships, Work Experience Programs, and On-the-Job Training Opportunities

INROADS/Milwaukee, Inc., 152

INROADS/St. Louis, Inc., 153

Institute for Educational Leadership, **150**

The Institute for Local Self Reliance, **171**

Institute of Afro-American Affairs, 37

Institute of Contemporary Art, 154

Institute of Early American History and Culture, 77

The Institute of Ecology, **172**

Institute of Government, 155

Institute of Medicine, **231**

Institute of Society, Ethics and the Life Sciences, 156

Institute on Comparative Political and Economic Systems, **77**

Inter-American Foundation, 157

International Agency for Research on Cancer, **521**

International Association for the Exchange of Students for Technical Experience/United States (IAESTE/US), 158

International Association of Students in Economics and Management, **173**

International Institute of Buffalo, 159

International Program for Human Resource Development, Inc., 160

International Research and Exchanges Board, **174, 175**

International Visitors Service Council, **176**

International Voluntary Services, **177**

Iowa. General Assembly, 161

Iowa. House of Representatives, 162

Izaak Walton League of America, **178**

j

Jackson County, Oregon, 163, 164

The Jackson Laboratory, **179-184**

The Jackson Sun, **185**

Jesuit Volunteer Corps, **340**

Jet Propulsion Laboratory, **186, 187**

John Woodman Higgins Armory Museum, 165

Johnson Space Center, **440-442,** 191-195

Joint Center for Political Studies, 166-168

The Journal Times, **188**

The Junction, Youth Resource Center, 169

Junior Achievement, Inc., **189**

k

KANC Radio, 216, 217

KCAV-TV, **190**

KCSJ/KDJQ Radio, 170

KEED, 171

KFRC Radio, 172

KIVA-TV, 173

KIXY Stations, 174

1st SUPPLEMENT

Directory of Internships, Work Experience Programs, and On-the-Job Training Opportunities

KSO/KGGO, 316

KSPS-TV, **191**

KWKI-FM, 175

Kansas. Department of Health and Environment, 176

Kansas City, Missouri, 177

Kentucky. Commission on Women, **192**

Kentucky. Department for Local Government, 178, 179

Kentucky. Department of Personnel, **193**

Kentucky. Legislative Research Commission, **194**

Kentucky River District Health Department, **195**

Kentucky School for the Deaf, **196**

King County Association for Retarded Citizens, 180, 181

Kitt Peak National Observatory, **197**

Korvettes, 182

l

Langley Research Center, **443-446**

Larimer County, Colorado, 183

Las Vegas Mental Health Center, 184

Law Enforcement Assistance Administration (LEAA), **421-423**

Law Students Council, **198**

Leadership Training Institute. Hope Community Center, 185

Lewis Research Center, **447**

Lexington-Fayette Urban County, Kentucky. Human Rights Commission, **199**

Lexington Planned Parenthood Center, Inc., 186

The Library Company of Philadelphia, 139

Licking Valley Community Action Program, Inc., **200**

The Lisle Fellowship, Inc., 187

Locust Grove Historic Home, 188

Los Angeles, California. Office of the Mayor, **201, 202**

Los Angeles County Museum of Art, 189

Los Angeles Free Press, **203**

Los Angeles Urban Corps, Inc., **204**

The Louisville Times, **104**

Lunar Science Institute, 190-195

Lutheran Council in the U.S.A., **205**

Lutheran World Federation, **206**

Lynn Historical Society, 196

m

Macalester College, 415

McKinley Area Services for the Handicapped, Inc. (MASH), 197

Macon Chronicle-Herald, 198

Maine. Office of the Governor, 199

Manchester Historic Association, 200

Marathon Health Care Center, 201

Maryland. Legislative Study Group, 202

Massachusetts. Internship Office, **207,** 203

Massachusetts Arts and Humanities Foundation, 204

Massachusetts Audubon Society, **208**

Mecosta County, Michigan. Commission on Aging, 205

Mennonite Brethren Church of North America, **209**

Mennonite Central Committee, **210**

Mennonite Disaster Service, **211**

Mennonite Voluntary Service, **148**

The Metropolitan Museum of Art, **212-218**

Metropolitan Washington Coalition for Clean Air, 95

Metropolitan Washington Council of Governments, **219**

Michigan. Department of Civil Service, **220**

Michigan. Department of Natural Resources, **221**

Midland Broadcasting, 206

Migrant Legal Action Program, Inc., 207

The Milwaukee Journal, **222**

Minneapolis, Minnesota, **223**

The Minneapolis Institute of Arts, **224**

The Minneapolis Society for the Blind, Inc., **225**

Minneapolis Tribune, 208, 209

Minnesota. House of Representatives, 210

Minnesota. Office of the Governor, **226**

Minnesota. University, 145

Missouri. House of Representatives, 211

Missouri Volunteer Office, 212

Mobile Community Organization, 213

Monmouth County, New Jersey. Board of Freeholders, 214

Morgan-Scott Project for Cooperative Christian Concerns, 215

Mt. Lebanon, Pennsylvania, **227**

Mt. Susitna Broadcasting Corporation, 216, 217

Mt. Top Youth for Christ, 218

Museum of African Art, **228**

Museum of Cartoon Art, 219

Museum of Northern Arizona, **229**

n

National Abortion Rights Action League, **230**

National Academy of Sciences. Institute of Medicine, **231**

National Aeronautics and Space Administration (NASA), **426-448**

National Archives, 230

National Association for Retarded Citizens, 220

1st SUPPLEMENT

Directory of Internships, Work Experience Programs, and On-the-Job Training Opportunities

National Association of Accountants for the Public Interest, 221

National Association of Health Services Executives, **48**

National Association of Schools of Public Affairs and Administration, **232**

National Audubon Society, 222-226

National Board of YMCA's, 420

National Center for Resource Recovery, Inc., **233, 234**

The National Center for Urban Ethnic Affairs, 227

National Center for Voluntary Action, **235**

National Child Day Care Association, **236**

National Citizens Committee for Broadcasting, **237**

National Collection of Fine Arts, 301

National Committee Against Repressive Legislation, **238**

National Committee for an Effective Congress, **239**

National Conference of State Legislatures, **240**

National Consumer Affairs Internship Program, 228

National Consumers Congress, **241**

National Council for a World Peace Tax Fund, 229

National Council of Organizations for Children and Youth, **242**

National Council on Crime and Delinquency, **243**

National Endowment for the Arts, **244,** 7

National Endowment for the Humanities, 8

The National Fellowships Fund, **245**

National Gallery of Art, **246**

The National Health Service Corps, **350**

National Historical Publications and Records Commission, **415,** 230

The National Institute for Lay Training, **247, 248**

National Institute of Law Enforcement and Criminal Justice, **423**

National Labor Federation. Eastern Farmworkers Association, **249**

National Moratorium on Prison Construction, 231

National Municipal League, **250**

National Neighborhood Institute, 227

National Organization for the Reform of Marijuana Laws, **251**

National Recreation and Park Association, **252**

National Research Council, **253, 448, 459**

National Research Council of Canada, **254,** 232

National Science Foundation (NSF), **456-462,** 362

National Student Lobby, **255**

National Suggestion Box, 233

National Trust for Historic Preservation, 234-236

National Urban Coalition, 237

National Urban Fellows, Inc., 238

National Urban League, Inc., Washington Bureau, **256**

National Wildlife Federation, **257**

National Women's Education Fund, **258**

National Women's Political Caucus, **259**

345

1st SUPPLEMENT

Directory of Internships, Work Experience Programs, and On-the-Job Training Opportunities

National Youth Alternatives Project, **260**

Natural Resources Defense Council, Inc., **261**

Neighborhoods Uniting Project, Inc., 239

Nevada. Mental Hygiene and Mental Retardation Division, 240

New Castle County, Delaware. Department of Parks and Recreation, 241

New England Gerontology Center, 242

The New Jersey Shakespeare Festival, **262**

New Mexico. State Personnel Office, 243

New Republic, 282

New York. Assembly, **263-265,** 244

New York. State University, Albany, **266**

New York. State University, Buffalo, **267**

New York City, New York. Office of the Mayor, **268, 269**

The Newberry Library, **270,** 245

The Newberry Library. Center for the History of the American Indian, **271-273**

Newport Historical Society, **274**

The News Journal, 246

News-Times, **275**

The News-Tribune, **276**

The Newspaper Fund, 247, 248

Newsweek, **277**

North Atlantic Treaty Organization (NATO), **278**

North Carolina. Department of Administration, **279**

North Carolina. Internship Office, **280, 281**

North Carolina. University, 155

North Carolina. University. North Carolina Health Manpower Development Program, **282**

North Carolina Public Interest Research Group, **283**

North Central Federation, Inc., 249

North Central Youth Service Bureau, 249

North Dakota. Legislative Council, **284**

North Penn Valley Boys' Club, 250

Northwest College and University Association for Science (NORCUS), **285-288**

O

Oak Ridge Associated Universities, **289-291**

Oaklawn Community Mental Health Center, 251

The Octagon, **18**

Offender Aid and Restoration of North Carolina, 252

Offender Aid and Restoration of the U.S., Inc., 253

Ohio. Department of Administrative Services, **292-294**

Ohio. Legislative Service Commission, **295**

Oklahoma. Legislative Council, 254

Oklahoma State Regents for Higher Education, **296**

1st SUPPLEMENT

Directory of Internships, Work Experience Programs, and On-the-Job Training Opportunities

Oldsmobile Division, General Motors, 255

Onondago County, New York. Executive Department, **297**

Operation Crossroads Africa, 256

Oregon. Legislative Assembly, 257

Organization of American States, 258

Owensboro Broadcasting Company, Inc., 259, 260

p

Palm Beach County Mental Health Center, 261

The Palm Beach Post, **298**

Pennsylvania. Department of Education, **299**

Pennsylvania. Historical and Museum Commission, **300**

Pennsylvania. House of Representatives, 262

People for Community Action. Youth Services Bureau, 263, 264

People's Media Collective, 265

Philadelphia, Pennsylvania. Area Manpower Planning Council, **301**

Philadelphia, Pennsylvania. District Attorney's Office, **302**

Phillips Petroleum Company, **303**

Phoenix, Arizona. Budget and Research Department, **304**

Pico-Union Neighborhood Council, 266

Pine Bluff Commercial, 267

Pittsfield, Massachusetts. Office of the Mayor, **305**

The Plain Dealer, **306**

The Population Institute, **307**

The Population Institute. Education Division, 268

Portland Community Design Center, 269

The Post-Standard, **308**

Pratt & Whitney Aircraft, **309**

President's Commission on White House Fellows, **470**

Project on the Status and Education of Women, 270

The Psychiatric Institute of Washington, D.C., **310**

Public Citizen, **311**

Public Citizen Visitor Center, **312**

Public Interest Economics Foundation, 271

Public Law Education Institute, **313**

q

Quaker United Nations Office, 272

The Quebec-Labrador Mission Foundation, Inc., **314**

r

RFK Children's Center, 281

R.O.O.C. Workshop, 273

Radio Free Georgia Broadcasting Foundation, Inc., 274

Ralph Nader, *311*

Ravenswood Hospital Community Mental Health Center, 275

Reason, 282

Record Newspapers, *315*

Regional Alcoholism Council, 323

Regional Mental Health Complex, 313

Religious Coalition for Abortion Rights, *316*

Rensselaer County Historical Society and Museum, 276

Rensselaer County, New York. Mental Health Department, 277

Resource Center for Nonviolence, 278

Rhode Island. Commission on State Government Internships, *317*

Rhode Island. Division of Youth Development, *318-321*

Rhode Island Historical Society, 279

Richardson Bay Wildlife Sanctuary, 225

Richmond Times-Dispatch, 280

Ripon Society, Inc., *322*

Robert F. Kennedy Children's Center, 281

Robert F. Kennedy Memorial, *323, 324*

The Rockefeller Foundation, *325-327*

Rolling Stone Magazine, *328*

s

Sabre Foundation, 282

Sacramento County, California, 283-286

St. Cloud Daily Times, 287

St. Paul's School, *329*

St. Petersburg Times-Evening Independent, *330*

St. Vincent's House, 288

San Antonio, Texas, 289

San Antonio, Texas. Public Service Careers, *331*

San Diego, California. Civil Service Commission, *332*

San Francisco, California. Human Rights Commission, *333*

San Francisco Volunteer Bureau/Voluntary Action Center, 290

San Juan, Puerto Rico. Washington Office, 291

SANE/A Citizens' Organization for a Sane World, *334*

Sangamon State University, *169,* 144

Scientists Institute for Public Information, 292

1st SUPPLEMENT

Directory of Internships, Work Experience Programs, and On-the-Job Training Opportunities

Sea Education Association (SEA), 293

Sears, Roebuck and Company, **335**

Seaside Post News-Sentinel, 294

Sentinel Star Company, 295

Sharon Audubon Center, 226

Sierra Club International, **336**

Silver Street Day Care Center, Inc., 296

Smithsonian Institution, **337, 338, 519,** 297-301, 412

Social Science Research Council, **12, 339**

Society of Jesus, **340**

The Solomon R. Guggenheim Museum, **341,** 302

South Carolina. Arts Commission, 303

South Carolina. Division of Administration, 304

South Carolina. State Personnel Division, **342**

South Carolina. State Senate and Office of the Lieutenant Governor, 305

South County Community Mental Health Center, 306

South Dakota. Department of Education and Cultural Affairs, **343**

South Dakota. Legislative Research Council, **344**

The Southern Fellowships Fund, **345**

Southern Governmental Monitoring Project, **347**

Southern Regional Council, Inc., **346, 347**

Southern Regional Training Program, **5**

Southwest Youth Development, 307

Spokane Legal Services Center, 308, 309

Spokane, Washington. Parks and Recreation Department, 310

The Spokesman Review, 311

Star-News, 312

Starkville, Mississippi. Regional Mental Health Complex, 313

State Farm Insurance Companies, 314, 315

Stoner Broadcasting, 316

Student American Medical Association, **348-350**

Student Conservation Association, Inc., **351, 352**

Sun Newspapers, **353**

Support Center, 317

Syracuse, New York. Department of Personnel and Labor Relations, **354**

t

Taylor Daily Press, **355**

Teacher Corps Washington, **356**

Technical Information Project, **357**

Tenant Services and Organization Assistance, Inc., **358**

Tennessee. General Assembly, 318

Texas. Office of the Governor, **359**

Texas. University. Medical Branch. Division of Child and Adolescent Psychiatry, 319

1st SUPPLEMENT

Directory of Internships, Work Experience Programs, and On-the-Job Training Opportunities

Texas Historical Commission, **360**

Theater Workshop Boston, 320

3M Company, **361,** 321

Thurston Youth Services Society. The Union Street Center, 322

Tufts University. Fletcher School of Law and Diplomacy, **362**

Tupperware Home Parties, **363**

Tuscaloosa, Alabama. Regional Alcoholism Council, 323

u

The Union Street Center, 322

United Church of Christ, **364-366**

The United Methodist Church. Board of Global Ministries, **367**

United Nations, **368**

United Nations. Development Program, **369**

United Nations. Food and Agriculture Organization, **370, 371**

United Nations. Institute for Training and Research (UNITAR), **372**

United Nations. International League for Human Rights, 324

United Nations. Office of Public Information, **373**

United Nations Association, USA, 325

United Planning Organization, **374**

U.S. Agency for International Development (AID), **375**

U.S. Agricultural Marketing Service, **376**

U.S. Agricultural Research Service, **377**

U.S. Air Force Data Automation Agency, **378**

U.S. Air Force Logistics Command, **379**

U.S. Animal and Plant Health Inspection Service, **380**

U.S. Atomic Energy Commission, **381**

U.S. Attorney's Office, **382**

U.S. Bureau of Land Management, **383**

U.S. Bureau of the Census, 326

U.S. Civil Aeronautics Board, **384**

U.S. Civil Service Commission, **385, 386,** 327-330

U.S. Congress. House. Office of David E. Bonior, 331

U.S. Congress. House. Office of John Conyers, Jr., 332

U.S. Congress. House. Office of Philip M. Crane, 333

U.S. Congress. House. Office of Bob Eckhardt, 334

U.S. Congress. House. Office of Mickey Edwards, 335

U.S. Congress. House. Office of Harold Ford, 336

U.S. Congress. House. Office of Lamar Gudger, 337

U.S. Congress. House. Office of Richard Kelly, 338

U.S. Congress. House. Office of Edward I. Koch, 339

1st SUPPLEMENT

Directory of Internships, Work Experience Programs, and On-the-Job Training Opportunities

U.S. Congress. House. Office of Jim Leach, 340

U.S. Congress. House. Office of Matthew F. McHugh, 341

U.S. Congress. House. Office of Ron Marlenee, 342

U.S. Congress. House. Office of Ned Pattison, 343

U.S. Congress. House. Office of Richardson Preyer, 344

U.S. Congress. House. Office of Fortney H. Stark, Jr., 345

U.S. Congress House. Office of Don Young, 346

U.S. Congress. Senate. Office of Mike Gravel, 347

U.S. Congress. Senate. Office of Orrin G. Hatch, 348

U.S. Congress. Senate. Office of George McGovern, 349

U.S. Congress. Senate. Office of William Proxmire, 350

U.S. Consumer Product Safety Commission, **387**

U.S. Customs Service, **388**

U.S. Defense Communications Agency, **389**

U.S. Defense Supply Agency, **390**

U.S. Department of Agriculture, **391, 469**

U.S. Department of Commerce, 326, 351, 352

U.S. Department of Health, Education and Welfare, **392, 393**

U.S. Department of Housing and Urban Development, **394, 395**

U.S. Department of Justice, **396**

U.S. Department of Labor, **397**

U.S. Department of State, **398,** 353

U.S. Department of the Air Force, **399, 400**

U.S. Department of the Navy, **401, 402**

U.S. Department of the Treasury, **403**

U.S. Department of Transportation, **404**

U.S. Domestic and International Business Adminsitration, **405**

U.S. Environmental Protection Agency, **406**

U.S. Federal Communications Commission, **407**

U.S. Federal Energy Administration, **408**

U.S. Federal Power Commission, **409**

U.S. Fish and Wildlife Service, 354

U.S. Food and Nutrition Service, **410**

U.S. Foreign Agricultural Service, **411**

U.S. Forest Service, **412,** 355

U.S. General Services Administration, **413-415**

U.S. Geological Survey, 356

U.S. Information Agency (USIA), 357

U.S. Internal Revenue Service, **416-418**

U.S. International Trade Commission, **419**

U.S. Judge Advocate General's Corps, **420**

U.S. Law Enforcement Assistance Administration, **421-423**

U.S. Library of Congress, **424**

U.S. Maritime Administration, **425**

U.S. National Aeronautics and Space Administration (NASA), **426-433, 448**

U.S. National Aeronautics and Space Administration. Ames Research Center, **434-436**

1st SUPPLEMENT

Directory of Internships, Work Experience Programs, and On-the-Job Training Opportunities

U.S. National Aeronautics and Space Administration. Goddard Space Flight Center, **437-439**

U.S. National Aeronautics and Space Administration. Johnson Space Center, **440-442**

U.S. National Aeronautics and Space Administration. Langley Research Center, **443-446**

U.S. National Aeronautics and Space Administration. Lewis Research Center, **447**

U.S. National Bureau of Standards, **449**

U.S. National Capitol Planning Commission, **450**

U.S. National Institute of Education, **451**

U.S. National Institutes of Health, 358-360

U.S. National Labor Relations Board, **452**

U.S. National Oceanic and Atmospheric Administration, **453**

U.S. National Park Service, **454, 455,** 361

U.S. National Science Foundation (NSF), **456-462,** 362

U.S. Nuclear Regulatory Commission, **463**

U.S. Office of Education, **464, 465**

U.S. Office of Minority Business Enterprise, 351

U.S. Office of the Secretary of Defense, **466**

U.S. Patent and Trademark Office, **467**

U.S. Pension Benefit Guaranty Corporation, **468**

U.S. Postal Service, 363

U.S. President. Commission on White House Fellowships, **470**

U.S. Public Health Service, **471**

U.S. Securities and Exchange Commission, **472-475**

U.S. Social and Economic Statistics Administration, **476**

U.S. Social and Rehabilitation Service, **477**

U.S. Social Security Administration, **478, 479**

U.S. Supreme Court, **480, 481**

U.S. Veterans Administration, 364-368

U.S. White House, **482**

United States Committee for UNICEF, **483, 484**

The United States National Student Association, **485**

University Council for Educational Administration, **486**

Utah. State Historical Society, **487**

Utah County, Utah, 369

V

Ventura County Mental Health Services, 370

Virginia. Division of Personnel, **488**

Virginia Museum, 371

Visitors' Services Center, **489, 490**

Vocational Foundation, Inc., **491, 492**

Voluntary Action Center of Northwest Georgia, Inc., 372

Voluntary Action Center of Toledo, 373

Volunteer Jacksonville, Inc., 374

1st SUPPLEMENT
Directory of Internships, Work Experience Programs, and On-the-Job Training Opportunities

W

WAAB, 375

WAAF Radio, 391

WAVE Radio, 376

WAVE-TV, 377

WBKR, 259, 260

WCAO Radio, 378

WCAS Radio, 379, 380

WDNR Radio, 381

WEBR Newsradio, 382

WEEK-TV, 383

WEHT-TV, 384

WFIF, 385

WFRV-TV, **493**

WGBY-TV, 386

WGLF FM Radio, 387

WGPR, Inc., 388

WLYH-TV, **494**

WMAZ Radio and Television, 389

WMCA Radio, 390

WNCR/WAAF Radio Stations, 391

WOMI/WBKR, 259, 260

WPLW-AM, 392

WPOP Newsradio-14, 393

WRFG, 274

WRJZ Radio, 394

WRTV 6, 395

WSKG, 396

WSOC-TV, *71*

WSTV-TV9, *495*

WTAR Radio-TV Corporation, *496*

WTTW/Channel 11, 397

WVII-TV, 398

Washington. Council for Postsecondary Education, 399

Washington. Department of Personnel. Interagency Training Division, **497**

Washington Center for Learning Alternatives, **498**

Washington Center for the Study of Services, 400

Washington, D.C. City Council, 401

Washington, D.C. Office of Youth Opportunities Services, **499**

Washington, D.C. Public Schools, **500**

Washington Dismas Project, Inc., **501**

Washington Peace Center, 402, 403

The Washington Post, **502**

Washington Star Station Group, **503**

Waukesha Freeman, **504**

Wenatchee World, 404

West Bend News, **505**

West Toledo Herald, **506**

West Virginia. Department of Welfare, **507**

West Virginia. Legislative Services, 405

Western Interstate Commission for Higher Education (WICHE) **508-510**

Western Maryland Manpower Consortium, 406

Weyerhaeuser Company, **511, 512**

353

Whitney Museum of American Art, **513**

Whittell Education Center, 225

Winant and Clayton Volunteers, Inc., **514**

The Wine Museum of San Francisco, 407

Wisconsin. State Bureau of Personnel, 408

Wisconsin Newspaper Association, **515**

Womanart Gallery, 409

Women's Center, 410

Women's Equity Action League, **516**

Women's Equity Action League Educational and Legal Defense Fund, 411

Women's History Research Center, Inc., **517**

Women's International League for Peace and Freedom, **518**

Woodrow Wilson International Center for Scholars, **519,** 412

Woodrow Wilson National Fellowship Foundation, 413

Worcester Foundation for Experimental Biology, Inc., 414

The World Bank, **520**

World Health Organization. International Agency for Research on Cancer, **521**

World Press Institute, 415

Wyoming. State Archives and Historical Department, **522**

y

YMCA of Dover and Kent County, 418

YMCA of Greater Lexington, 419

York County 4-H Clubs, 416

Young Concert Artists, Inc., 417

Young Men's Christian Association. Dover, Delaware, 418

Young Men's Christian Association. Lexington, Kentucky, 419

Young Men's Christian Association. National Board. International Division, 420

Young Radio, Inc., 421

Youth for Christ, Inc., 137

Youth for Federal Union, **524**

Youth Industries, Inc., 422

Youth Opportunities Upheld, Inc., 423

Ypsilanti Township, Michigan. Park Commission, **523**

z

Zero Population Growth, **525**

2376-6
5-40